POLYNESIA: Readings on a Culture Area

Chandler Publications in ANTHROPOLOGY AND SOCIOLOGY
LEONARD BROOM, General Editor

ANTHROPOLOGY
L. L. LANGNESS, Editor

POLYNESIA

READINGS ON A CULTURE AREA

EDITED BY

ALAN HOWARD

Bernice P. Bishop Museum, Honolulu

CHANDLER PUBLISHING COMPANY

An Intext Publisher • Scranton / London / Toronto

INTERNATIONAL STANDARD BOOK NUMBER 0-8102-0372-3
LIBRARY OF CONGRESS CATALOG CARD NO. 74-111876
PRINTED IN THE UNITED STATES OF AMERICA

Design by Joseph M. Roter
Maps by Joan D. Langness and Joseph M. Roter

This book is dedicated to
all persons of Polynesian ancestry who
love and respect their heritage,
wherever they may be.

CONTENTS

SERIES PREFACE

Oceania, with its immense variety, has been the scene of much anthropological work since before the turn of the century. It has been a training ground for generations of anthropology students and the subject of innumerable university courses. Quite likely it will be the focus of even more attention in the immediate future. Yet, strangely, there is very little by way of text materials for the area. This series of readings is designed to provide such materials. It is hoped the readings together will provide coverage in depth, while individually providing the flexibility required for more particular interests.

NOTES ON CONTRIBUTORS

JEREMY BECKETT is Senior Lecturer in the Department of Anthropology at the University of Sydney. He was educated at London University and received his postgraduate degrees at the Australian National University. His research has been among part-Aborigines, Torres Strait Islanders, and in the Cook Islands. Dr. Beckett is the author of many articles pertaining to Oceania.

MELVIN EMBER received his Ph.D. in 1958 and did postdoctoral research at Yale University. He was a research anthropologist at the National Institute of Mental Health and taught at both Antioch College and Hunter College of the City University of New York, where he is now Chairman of the Department of Anthropology. He has done cross-cultural research on residence patterns, first-cousin marriages, and correlations between archeological and enthnographic data. He has authored a monograph, *The Emergence of Neolocal Residence*, as well as many articles.

RAYMOND FIRTH began his distinguished career at Auckland University College. His Ph.D. work was supervised by Malinowski at the London School of Economics. He has taught students from the London School of Economics, the University of Sydney, the University of Hawaii, the University of British Columbia, and Cornell University. He is Emeritus Professor of Anthropology at the University of London and holds honorary degrees from the Universities of Oslo, Michigan, East Anglia, Chicago and from the Australian National University. He is a past Secretary and President of the Royal Anthropological Institute. He has been awarded the Viking Medal in General Anthropology and the Huxley Memorial Medal. His books include *Elements of Social Organization; Economics of the New Zealand Maori; We, the Tikopia; The Work of the Gods in Tikopia; Social Change in Tikopia;* and *Tikopia Ritual and Belief.* His latest work is *Rank and Religion in Tikopia.*

DEREK FREEMAN is Professorial Fellow in Anthropology at the Research School of Pacific Studies of the Institute of Advanced Studies at the Australian National University. He attended Victoria University College in Wellington, New Zealand, and did his graduate work at the London School of Economics and University College of the University of London and at King's College, Cambridge University. His field research includes much time in Samoa and among the Iban of Borneo. In addition to many articles, he has edited *Anthropology in the South Seas* (with W. L. Geddes) and is bringing out a second edition of his *Report on the Iban.*

F. ALLAN HANSON became interested in French Polynesia when he did field work in Tahiti as part of finishing his undergraduate work at Princeton in 1961. He has also done research on the island of Rapa and in Paris. He completed his Ph.D. at the University of Chicago in 1966. He did postdoctoral studies at the University of Oxford during 1969–1970 while on leave from the University of Kansas, where he is Associate Professor of Anthropology. He is the author of *Rapan Lifeways: Society and History on a Polynesian Island.*

IAN HOGBIN is Professorial Fellow at the new Macquarie University in Sydney, a capstone to his outstanding career. He did his first field work on Rennell Island in 1927. His undergraduate education was completed at the University of Sydney under Radcliffe-Brown. The University of London granted his Ph.D. as a student of Malinowski. He served at the University of Sydney from 1936 until 1969. He is the recipient of many honors, including the Wellcome and Rivers Medals of the Royal Anthropological Institute, the Harbison-Higinbotham Prize of the University of Melbourne in both 1951 and 1959; and he has been chosen Josiah Mason Lecturer at the University of Birmingham and Marett Memorial Lecturer at the University of Oxford. His research has included work in the islands of Ontong-Java, Guadalcanal, Malaita, Wogeo, and Busama. His many publications include *Law and Order in Polynesia; Experiments in Civilization; Transformation Scene; Social Change; Kinship and Marriage in a New Guinea Village; The Kaoka Speakers: A Guadalcanal Society;* and *The Island of Menstruating Men.*

ALAN HOWARD was educated at Stanford University, where he received his Ph.D. in 1962. His research areas include the islands of Rotuma, Fiji, and Oahu in Hawaii. He has taught at Auckland University, the University of Copenhagen, and the University of Hawaii. He is currently on the staff of the Bernice P. Bishop Museum. In addition to numerous articles, he is co-editor of *Polynesian Culture History* and *Namakamaka O Nanakuli: Studies in a Hawaiian Community* and author of *Learning to Be Rotuman.*

PAUL KAY obtained his B.A. at Tulane University and studied in Paris. Harvard University granted his Ph.D. in 1963. His field research includes work in Tahiti and Mexico, and he has held postdoctoral fellowships at Stanford University and at the Center for Advanced Study in the Behavioral Sciences. He has taught at the Massachusetts Institute of Technology and at the University of California at Berkeley, where he is now Associate Professor. He is co-author of *Universality and Evolution of Basic Color Categories* and editor of *Explorations in Mathematical Anthropology.*

ROBERT I. LEVY received his M.D. at New York University and did his residency in psychiatry at Bellevue Hospital. He has been a Senior Specialist in Psychological Anthropology at the East-West Center and a Research Professor at the Social Science Research Institute of the University of Hawaii. He has done field work in Tahiti and has published a number of articles on psychological anthropology. His book, *The Organization of Tahitian Experience,* is about to go to press. Dr. Levy is Professor of Anthropology at the University of California, San Diego.

MARGARET MEAD is presently Curator Emeritus of Ethnology at the American Museum of Natural History and Adjunct Professor of Anthropology at Columbia University. She is also Chairman and Professor in the Social Science Division of the Liberal Arts College, Lincoln Center Campus, Fordham University. Dr. Mead was educated at Barnard College and Columbia University, which granted her Ph.D. in 1929. Her extensive field work has been done in Samoa, Manus, Bali, and New Guinea and with American Indians, beginning in 1925 and continuing to the present. Some of the best-known works from her outstanding bibliography include *Coming of Age in Samoa; New Lives for Old; Growing Up in New Guinea; Male and Female;* and her latest, *Culture and Commitment: A Study of the Generation Gap.* Dr. Mead is a past President of the American Anthropological Association and of the World Federation for Mental Health. She has been Sloan Professor of the Menninger Foundation and holds many honorary degrees.

TORBEN MONBERG is currently Professor of Cultural Sociology at the University of Copenhagen, where he was educated and received his Ph.D. He has done field research in the British Solomon Islands of Rennell and Bellona and in Tikopia. He was Research Fellow and subsequently Research Professor at the University of Copenhagen. He is the author of *From the Two Canoes: Oral Traditions of Rennell and Bellona* (with S. H. Elbert) and *The Religion of Bellona Island.*

RUSIATE R. NAYACAKALOU, born and educated in Fiji, received his M.A. in Social Anthropology from the University of Auckland and his Ph.D. from the London School of Economics in 1963. He was a Senior Scholar at the East-West Center at the University of Hawaii in 1964 and Lecturer in Social Anthropology at the University of Sydney from 1965 to 1968. He left the University of Sydney to become Manager of the Native Land Trust Board at Suva, Fiji, in 1969. He has published on kinship in Fiji, land tenure in

Tonga and Samoa, and is the author of *Fijian Leadership in a Situation of Change.*

JAMES E. RITCHIE received his training under Ernest Beaglehole at Victoria University, where he did graduate work in both anthropology and psychology. He held a Rockefeller postdoctoral fellowship, visiting Harvard and Columbia Universities. He was awarded a Fulbright and a Carnegie visiting-scholar grant. He has taught at the University of California, Santa Cruz, and presently holds the Chair of Psychology at the University of Waikato, New Zealand. He has assisted the Department of Education in the Territory of Papua and New Guinea for the past two years in the development of a high-school curriculum in the social sciences. His many publications include *Basic Personality in Rakau* and *The Making of a Maori.*

MARSHALL D. SAHLINS received his A.B. and A.M. from the University of Michigan. He completed his graduate studies at Columbia University in 1954. He was Lecturer at Columbia University and then joined the faculty of the University of Michigan, where he is now Professor of Anthropology. He was Fellow of the Center for Advanced Study in the Behavioral Sciences and has been a John Simon Guggenheim Memorial Fellow. He is co-author of *Evolution and Culture* and author of *Moala; Culture and Nature on a Fijian Island; Social Stratification in Polynesia;* and *Tribesmen.*

LAURA THOMPSON received her B.A. from Mills College and her Ph.D. from the University of California. Her career has included the Bernice P. Bishop Museum as ethnologist, the University of Hawaii as research associate, and the United States Office of Indian Affairs. She has also been Professor of Sociology and Anthropology at the City University of New York and has taught at the University of North Carolina, North Carolina State College, Southern Illinois University, and San Francisco State College. She was Consultant in Anthropology to the Rockefeller Foundation, the United States Naval Government of Guam, and the National Indian Institute. Her field work has been done in Fiji, Guam, Hawaii, and Iceland and among the Hopi, Papago, Zuñi, Navaho, and Sioux. Some of her publications are *Culture in Crisis; Toward a Science of Mankind;* and, her latest, *The Secret of Culture: Nine Community Studies.*

MALCOLM C. WEBB has an A.B. from the University of Pennsylvania and an M.A. and a Ph.D. from the University of Michigan. Since 1962 he has been teaching at the New Orleans campus of Louisiana State University, where he is now Associate Professor and Chairman of the Department of Anthropology and Geography. He has done archeological research in Michigan and Illinois as well as field work in the Gulf Coast region of Mexico.

POLYNESIA: Readings on a Culture Area

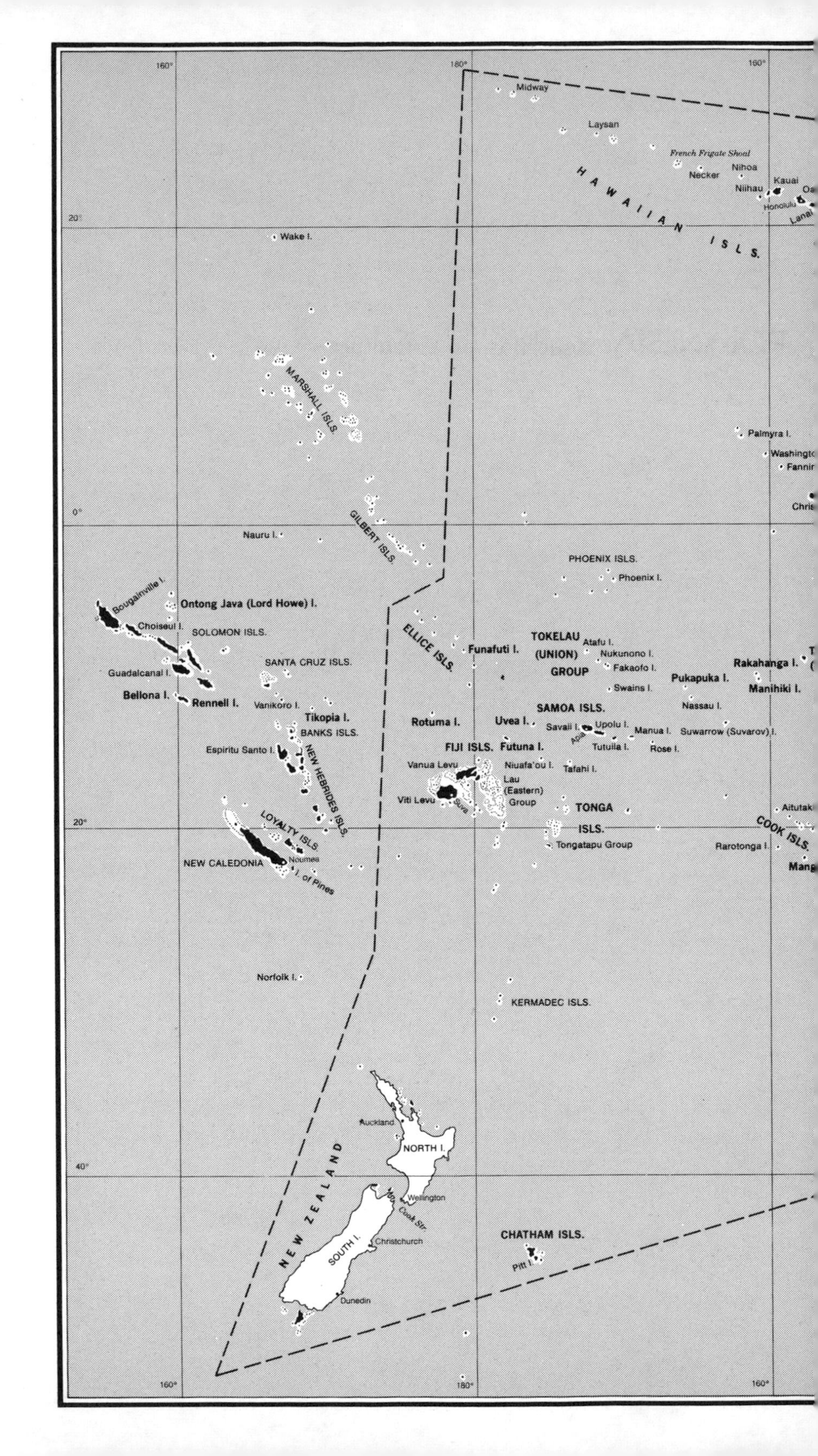

160°
180°
160°
Midway
Laysan
French Frigate Shoal
Necker
Nihoa
Kauai
Niihau
Honolulu
Lanai
HAWAIIAN ISLS.
20°
Wake I.
MARSHALL ISLS.
Palmyra I.
0°
Nauru I.
GILBERT ISLS.
PHOENIX ISLS.
Phoenix I.
Bougainville I.
Ontong Java (Lord Howe) I.
Choiseul I.
SOLOMON ISLS.
ELLICE ISLS.
Funafuti I.
TOKELAU
(UNION)
GROUP
Atafu I.
Nukunono I.
Fakaofo I.
Swains I.
Guadalcanal I.
SANTA CRUZ ISLS.
Pukapuka I.
Rakahanga I.
Manihiki I.
Bellona I.
Rennell I.
Vanikoro I.
SAMOA ISLS.
Nassau I.
Tikopia I.
BANKS ISLS.
Rotuma I.
Uvea I.
Savaii I.
Upolu I.
Apia
Manua I.
Suwarrow (Suvarov) I.
Tutuila I.
Rose I.
Espiritu Santo I.
NEW HEBRIDES ISLS.
FIJI ISLS.
Futuna I.
Vanua Levu
Niuafa'ou I.
Tafahi I.
Lau
(Eastern)
Group
Viti Levu
Suva
TONGA
ISLS.
Aitutaki
20°
LOYALTY ISLS.
COOK ISLS.
NEW CALEDONIA
Noumea
I. of Pines
Tongatapu Group
Rarotonga I.
Norfolk I.
KERMADEC ISLS.
Auckland
NORTH I.
NEW ZEALAND
40°
Wellington
Cook Str.
SOUTH I.
Christchurch
CHATHAM ISLS.
Pitt I.
Dunedin
160°
180°
160°

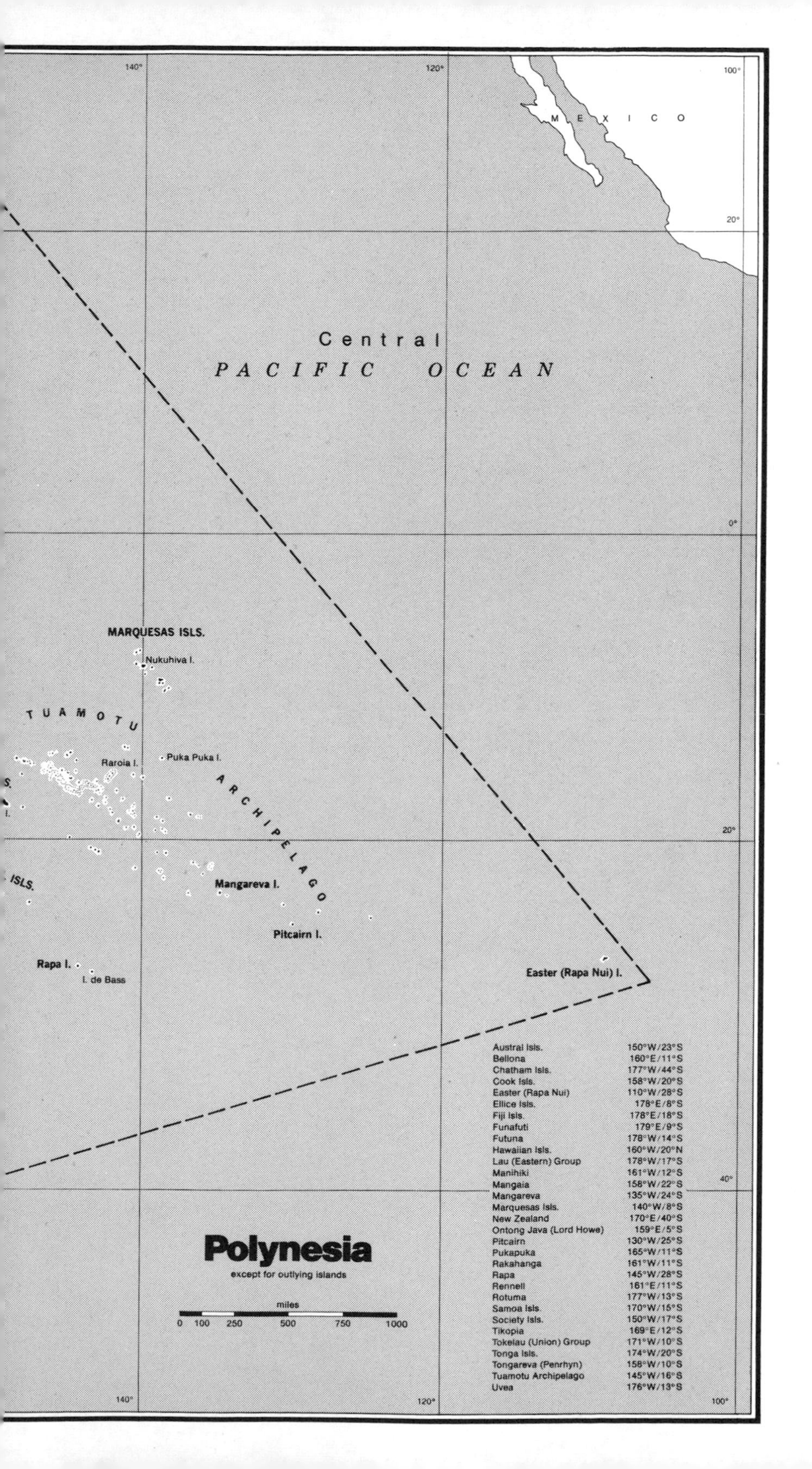

Island	Position
Austral Isls.	150°W/23°S
Bellona	160°E/11°S
Chatham Isls.	177°W/44°S
Cook Isls.	158°W/20°S
Easter (Rapa Nui)	110°W/28°S
Ellice Isls.	178°E/8°S
Fiji Isls.	178°E/18°S
Funafuti	179°E/9°S
Futuna	178°W/14°S
Hawaiian Isls.	160°W/20°N
Lau (Eastern) Group	178°W/17°S
Manihiki	161°W/12°S
Mangaia	158°W/22°S
Mangareva	135°W/24°S
Marquesas Isls.	140°W/8°S
New Zealand	170°E/40°S
Ontong Java (Lord Howe)	159°E/5°S
Pitcairn	130°W/25°S
Pukapuka	165°W/11°S
Rakahanga	161°W/11°S
Rapa	145°W/28°S
Rennell	161°E/11°S
Rotuma	177°W/13°S
Samoa Isls.	170°W/15°S
Society Isls.	150°W/17°S
Tikopia	169°E/12°S
Tokelau (Union) Group	171°W/10°S
Tonga Isls.	174°W/20°S
Tongareva (Penrhyn)	158°W/10°S
Tuamotu Archipelago	145°W/16°S
Uvea	176°W/13°S

INTRODUCTION

The islands of Polynesia have held an enduring fascination for scholars since the time of their "discovery" by European explorers. The major focus of concern has been on the prehistory of the area: Where did the Polynesians come from? How did they get to the islands? How long ago? And by what routes? These questions were stimulated by the incredible dispersion of the Polynesian culture area over a vast expanse of the Pacific Ocean.

The majority of Polynesian islands are contained within a triangular region formed by drawing a line from Hawaii in the north, to Easter Island in the southeast, and to New Zealand in the southwest. By bending the line between Hawaii and New Zealand slightly westward, we can encompass the major Polynesian islands missed by a true triangle; these include Uvea, Futuna, and the Ellice Islands. Although they are somewhat marginal to Polynesia, Fiji and Rotuma could also be brought into the enclosure by straining the western boundary a little farther. For the purposes of this volume they will be included. This would still leave the "outliers," a small group of isolates in Melanesia and Micronesia inhabited by people who speak Polynesian languages.

When one ponders the hardships of traversing the area in outrigger canoes, the distances involved are impressive. The southern baseline from New Zealand to Easter Island is about 4,000 miles long, while from this line to the northern Hawaiian apex is approximately 5,000 miles. Furthermore, some of the islands are remarkably isolated. The Hawaiian chain is more than 2,000 miles from its nearest inhabited neighbor, and Easter Island is more than 1,000 miles away from other land. On the basis of these geographical facts alone, the Polynesians would have to qualify as some of the greatest seafaring people of all time.

When compared with the cultural diversity of Melanesia, Polynesian culture appears remarkably uniform in character. Nevertheless, anthropologists have delineated subcultural differences within the region on the basis of variable culture traits. The basic distinction has been between Western Polynesia, centered in the islands of Samoa and Tonga, and Eastern

Polynesia, epitomized by the cultures of the Society Islands, Hawaii, and —perhaps oddly at first glance—the New Zealand Maori. The reason for placing New Zealand in the eastern division despite its location to the far west of the triangle is justified on cultural grounds; accumulated evidence has made it abundantly clear that the ancestors of the Maori came from the Society and/or Marquesan Islands to the east. Some scholars have preferred to divide the Eastern Polynesian area into two subgroups which they have labeled Central Polynesia (Society Islands, Hawaii, Cook Islands, the Australs, and Tuamotus) and Marginal Polynesia (the Marquesas, Easter Island, Pitcairn, New Zealand, and the Chatham Islands). However, the more we learn from archeological evidence, the less convincing these divisions become, and the more compelling are similarities rather than differences.

As a result of preoccupation with the fascinating problem of settlement, social anthropology in Polynesia has been overshadowed by studies aimed at unraveling the mysteries of prehistory. The majority of ethnographies, for example, most of which were done in the period between the two world wars, have essentially been catalogs of material culture, legends, and social customs, all of which are treated as "culture traits." The object has been to compare and contrast the culture traits of different islands in order to determine historical relationships. Information on social life, as well as on other topics, was obtained from old people who presumably were learned in the ways of the traditional culture.

For many social anthropologists, Polynesian cultures have appeared too disrupted by foreign contact to be of interest in their contemporary forms. Thus Ralph Linton referred to the Marquesan culture of the 1920's as "broken" (1939:137).* Like so many Polynesian islands, the Marquesas had been traumatized by the white man's physical and cultural invasion. Stricken by diseases for which they had little or no immunity, and demoralized by white domination, they underwent a massive depopulation, nearly to the point of extinction. In a rather touching though somewhat questionable passage, Linton remarks:

> When the Marquesans were finally forced to submit to white domination, they adopted the only means of dignified and effective resistance opened to them; they ceased to breed. This was a perfectly deliberate measure, the people preferring extinction to subjection (Linton 1939:137).

Nevertheless, Polynesia has contributed its share of pioneering studies to the fields of social and cultural anthropology. Most of these were carried out on islands that had escaped the full impact of European culture contact, such as peripheral islands in the Samoan and Tongan groups and Polynesian outliers such as Tikopia and Ontong Java. The work of Ernest Beaglehole, Raymond Firth, Ian Hogbin, and Margaret Mead—to mention only some

*For full bibliographical data of works mentioned in the Introduction and in the Further Readings at the end of each part, see the Bibliography at the end of this volume.

of the leading figures—has added important dimensions to the scope of social theory.

Among the trends in anthropological research that gained impetus during the interim between the world wars was the study of culture change. Polynesian islands were a natural laboratory for such research, and a number of impressive studies were carried out in the region by scholars like Beaglehole and Felix Keesing. These studies not only helped to reveal important local and universal processes of culture change, but also shed considerable light on the functioning of the traditional societies. This occurred partly as the result of a developing awareness of a mass of historical literature built up by explorers, missionaries, traders, and other early visitors. Studies of change revealed a remarkable degree of cultural persistence. Despite massive changes in the more visible aspects of culture—changes in technology, religion, and sociopolitical organization—study after study demonstrated that at the more subtle level of values, beliefs, and style of interpersonal relations, even the most traumatized peoples were still remarkably Polynesian in character. This finding led Ernest and Pearl Beaglehole to suggest that the process of socialization may be critical in perpetuating character structure despite rapid social change (1941:140).

Since World War II, the range and scope of anthropological research has broadened considerably. Orientations have ranged from a concern for specific problems to broad-scale ethnographic research, and recent students have brought a diversity of new theoretical and methodological approaches into the field. Among the more noticeable trends is a willingness to accept the current amalgamated cultures of Polynesia in their contemporary ecological contexts instead of focusing on the precontact "uncontaminated" versions. Studies of social structure and social dynamics have been particularly rewarding and have generated considerable interpretive and theoretical debate. Polynesian societies simply do not fit the neat structural models that were so elaborately built on the basis of careful ethnographic work in other geographical areas.

The study of culture change has also diversified. In addition to further work on change from traditional to amalgamated Polynesian cultures, recent studies have focused on the processes of modernization and urbanization. Robert Levy has summarized these processes thus:

> They consist of successive shifts from partial subsistence economies to market and, finally, wage economies; of progressive urbanization of centrally located island towns with the creation of hinterlands and of peasant conditions; of the development of an active labor market and the creation of a town proletariat; and of the development of widespread, low-cost communication networks, on the one hand bringing in masses of tourists, and on the other allowing opportunities for the islanders to seek work in various "developed" countries (Levy 1969:7-8).

Still another major development is taking place in the area of psychological anthropology. This is not an entirely new field of research in Polynesia.

Even during the heyday of historicalism, two of the foremost pioneers in culture and personality studies, Ernest Beaglehole and Margaret Mead, were using Polynesia as a psychological laboratory. The most striking aspect of recent research, however, is the entry of individuals trained in psychology and psychiatry into the field situation. Their studies promise to add new dimensions of understanding to the persistence of Polynesian character and to the dynamics of Polynesian social organization.

It is on the basis of these studies, past and present, that a comparative sociology is now emerging in Polynesia, but we still have a long way to go before it can be said that the social anthropology of the region is well understood. For this reason I hope student readers will treat the papers included in this volume less as a report of indisputable fact than as the work of scholars struggling to understand a way of life.

The volume has been organized in four parts, each of which is preceded by a brief introduction and followed by a guide to further reading. Like all divisions of material not explicitly written for a preconceived framework, the one I have chosen is somewhat arbitrary and perhaps a bit strained. It is roughly based on what I believe is the most usual sequence of topics followed in area anthropology courses; but each part, as an introduction to the literature on Polynesian ethnography, is sufficiently self-contained so that it can be read independently of the other parts.

In selecting articles, I have followed several guiding principles. Most salient has been an attempt to provide a reasonably well-balanced picture of the Polynesian life style. Articles that present case material have therefore been given priority over papers which were of a more formalistic or theoretical nature. Only in the part on social structure is high priority given to theoretical issues, the reason being that the debate is so central to an understanding of Polynesian society that it cannot be ignored. Consideration has also been given to geographical representation. I tried to include something from each of the major island groups and from atolls as well as high islands. Nevertheless, there are some major imbalances. Samoa, for instance, is overrepresented, while there is nothing on Tonga. This disparity reflects the fact that Samoa has been more extensively studied than have most of the other island groups and that Samoa has been the subject of considerable interpretive debate. Tonga, on the other hand, has been virtually neglected by social anthropologists, and I was unable to find pieces sufficiently focused for inclusion in this volume. Two items dealing with Fiji have been included, and one concerning the island of Rotuma, which is politically though not culturally a part of Fiji. The inclusion of these papers in an anthology on Polynesia might be subject to debate, inasmuch as Fiji and Rotuma are marginal to the culture area. However, they are also marginal to other Oceanic culture areas, and since recent interpretations favor Fiji as the birthplace of Polynesian culture, it was deemed more appropriate to include them in this volume than in the companion volumes on Melanesia and Micronesia. Still another principle of selection was accessibility. Some of the articles were originally published in journals that are available only in well-stocked, established libraries. They were chosen over items which are more readily accessible.

PART I ECOLOGY AND ECONOMICS

Culture does not exist in a vacuum. It is shaped to a considerable extent by the physical environment in which its bearers live. Some of the ecological niches into which our species has found its way have provided an abundance of natural resources and the basis for cultural elaboration; others have been sparse and restrictive. The islands of Polynesia offer a wide range of environments, but essentially they are of four types: (1) continental islands such as Viti Levu in Fiji and the islands that constitute New Zealand, (2) volcanic islands like Hawaii and Tahiti, (3) raised coral islands like Makatea in the Tuamotus, and (4) coral atolls. The continental and weathered volcanic islands provided their human settlers with a means for sustaining large populations. In contrast, the coral atolls, smaller in size and containing poorer soils, were frequently marginal in their capacity to support human life. On nearly all islands, even those with substantial endowment, the threat of starvation was ever present. A lengthy drought or a severe hurricane could destroy the subsistence base at any time. Anything that seriously disturbed the rather delicate ecological balance, whether an act of nature or an act of man (such as overpopulation), was a threat to existence. For this reason, Polynesians had to pay a good deal of attention to maintaining harmony within their ecosystems, and many of their customs are best understood in the light of this requirement.

The opening selection in this part, by Laura Thompson, describes in functional terms the ecological balance worked out among men, animals, and plants over the centuries on the islands of southern Lau in Fiji. Thompson shows how the traditional social system and cultural patterns contributed to an efficient and stable balance between man and his natural environment, and documents the dangers of introducing rapid social change without due consideration for their ecological consequences.

In the second article, Ian Hogbin helps to clarify the relationship between cultural practices and the maintenance of a viable way of life. Examining the apparently wasteful custom of ceremonial exchange that characterizes the island cultures, he finds that they play a very useful part in the lives of the people.

Both these papers were written from a functional point of view. Customs and social institutions are perceived as contributing to man's biological adaptation to his environment and to the harmonious functioning of society as a whole. From a historical viewpoint, the paper by Hogbin represents one of the first attempts to apply functional theory to Polynesian societies. Thompson's paper, published nearly twenty years later, adds a time dimension to Hogbin's more synchronic analysis.

The final paper in this part, by Marshall Sahlins, represents a further shift in the direction of concern for diachronic processes. Although still based on functional assumptions, Sahlins' viewpoint is more explicitly evolutionary. He assumes that cultural differences within Polynesia were produced by a process of "adaptive differentiation"—a single cultural genus becoming differentiated into "species" variations as a result of adapting to different ecological niches. His specific concern is with forms of social organization, and he distinguishes two major types of descent group, each associated with distinct high-island ecologies. Modifications of these two types take place on low coral atolls, the islands that present Polynesians with their most limiting ecological niches.

1

THE RELATIONS OF MEN, ANIMALS, AND PLANTS IN AN ISLAND COMMUNITY (FIJI)[1]

Oversimplification; data to fit hypothesis

Laura Thompson

The problem of the ecological base of cultural phenomena is undergoing reconsideration by anthropologists from various points of view.[2] As part of this trend the present paper attempts to relate and interpret, from a total ecological viewpoint,[3] field findings of a geologist, a botanist, a naturalist and an anthropologist on an isolated community in Fiji.[4] Although the available data are limited, particularly as regards the botanical and zoological aspects of the problem, they seem to be sufficient to meet the needs of the present effort, which is designed to test the usefulness of a total ecological approach.

The community selected for study is located at the southern end of the Lau or Eastern Archipelago, a north-south belt of 100 small islands, 30 of which are inhabited. It consists of an isolated group of six inhabited islands and their uninhabited satellites.[5] Three inhabited islands, namely Fulanga, Ongea and Namuka, as well as all of the uninhabited ones, are composed of limestone. The other inhabited islands, namely Mothe, Komo and Kambara, are formed either wholly or in part of volcanic rocks.

No two islands are exactly alike in structure or mode of origin but in general the volcanic islands (e.g., Mothe) are eroded to rounded, reed-covered hills and gentle slopes or low, rocky promontories. They have miniature drainage systems which originate at high points near the central interior and form small streams with dentritic patterns. Their valleys are lined with relatively deep, rich soil which supports a variety of vegetation including yams *(Dioscorea)* and other garden crops.[6]

On the other hand, the limestone islands (e.g., Fulanga) have cliffs and forested low plateaus, which tend to erode into basins whose sharp-crested rims drop steeply to the sea. They have no valleys or streams, all the rainfall sinking underground and reaching the sea by an intricate system of subterranean caverns. Except in Namuka, where the soil is relatively deep, only

Reproduced by permission of the American Anthropological Association and Laura Thompson from the *American Anthropologist,* 51:253-267 (April-June, 1949).

a thin layer of rather poor topsoil occurs in pockets in the interior basins. Such limestone soil supports a distinctive flora. Useful hardwoods, such as the greenheart of India *(Intsia bijuga), mbau (Pittosprum brackenridgei)* and *makota (Dysoxylum richii),* as well as other jungle plants which are absent or scarce on the volcanics, flourish on the limestones of southern Lau. However, yams do not grow well in this type of soil. Apparently these islands had no horticulture before manioc and sweet potato *(Ipomoea batatas)* found their way to Lau in historic times.[7]

In sum, good garden land and food are generally limited on the limestone islands but plentiful on the volcanics, while forest products are scarce on the volcanics but abundant on the limestones. Thus, the resources of the two geological types complement each other, the fifteen islands forming a naturally balanced community or self-sufficient native trade area.

The foundations of this ecological arrangement extend far back in the geological history of the region. On the basis of paleogeological evidence, Ladd and Hoffmeister[8] infer that organic life in the island community under consideration began during the Lower Miocene before the Lau group had emerged above sea level, and it played a major part in the formation of the various islands and in laying the foundations for their present ecological structures. As soon as the islands projected above the level of the sea and the processes of erosion began to develop topsoil, we assume that the fundamental biotics of each island began to develop—limestone biotics on the limestones and volcanic biotics on the volcanics.

While we lack the data to describe these two types of biotics, we do know that their development in Lau has been influenced and limited by the following major factors.[9] First, rocks are of only two types: impervious volcanic and soluble limestones. Second, most of the islands are small, isolated, and closely surrounded by open sea at least 100 fathoms deep. They are separated from the main Fiji group to the northwest by a distance of some 200 miles and from Tonga to the southeast by some 400 miles. Third, located mainly between 17 and 19 degrees[10] south latitude and in the vicinity of 179 degrees west longitude, the Lau group has a tropical climate, the mean annual temperature being estimated at about 73 degrees Fahrenheit, the humidity range from about 70 to 90 per cent. Fourth, the islands lie in the belt of the southeast trade winds which prevail during the cool, dry season from April to November. This condition is strongly reflected in reef and island contours and in rock type distributions. During the remainder of the year, the warm, wet season, the southwest monsoon blows intermittently, especially from January to March when hurricanes may be expected. Fifth, practically all of the annual precipitation, which averages about 80 inches, falls during the wet season, much of it in the form of torrential downpours which erode basins and caverns in the limestone islands, and valleys in the volcanics. Sixth, the basic ecological balances of each island developed in the absence of large land animals, including man.[11]

By the time that the first men arrived in Lau in comparatively recent times, the delicately balanced, natural ecological arrangements, characteristic of southern Lau, had attained their basic patterns. The advent of man meant much more than the intrusion of a single species, namely *Homo sapiens*, as had been the case when many ocean- or air-borne species found their way to these islands. The advent of man meant the intrusion into the group of a whole complex of exotic species of both fauna and flora carried by man during his migration by canoe eastward into the Pacific basin. Culture-historical evidence in southern Lau[12] suggests that these included the pig, the dog, and the fowl, as well as various food plants such as yam, breadfruit and banana. Man brought, furthermore, various stone and shell tools such as adzes, gouges, awls and pounders with which he could somewhat alter the face of nature; various skills, such as fire-making, horticulture, stone-cutting, house-building, basketry and mat-plaiting; and he brought the sailing canoe with which he traveled between the islands and connected their heretofore disparate ecological arrangements.

Not much is known of these first human inhabitants of Lau but, on the basis of internal evidence in the present-day culture and of archeological findings,[13] we infer that they settled on the larger islands and formed small clan-hamlets in the bush. On the limestone islands the aborigines subsisted chiefly on jungle fruits, edible green leaves from the bush, fish, pigs and fowl, while on the volcanics this basic diet was supplemented with such garden produce as yams.

After the first men arrived, a new ecological arrangement seems to have gradually taken form on the basis of the old; and recently introduced species of flora and fauna, including *Homo sapiens*, became a part of the total balance. The culture of the first human inhabitants of Lau indicates that, on the foundations of attitudes and behavior patterns which they had brought with them into Lau, the aborigines developed a culture which integrated the human group with the other species of the natural community in environmental context and which symbolically explained, validated and supported the group's way of life.[14] What the effect of the aborigines was on the environment we do not know. It has been suggested, however, that man's cultivation of the volcanic islands has been responsible to some degree for the fact that much of their flora has degenerated to rank grasslands and other low growth. The limestone localities, on the other hand, apparently were and still are less affected by man's presence. The soil is less fertile and less responsive to cultivation of food plants by means of technology available to the natives, while the low, dense, scrubby forest, its tangle of underbrush, together with the rough, pitted terrain, help to discourage change through human activity.[15]

The next major event in the culture history of the area was the conquest of the aborigines, apparently about fifteen generations ago, by a small band of warriors reputed to have come from northwest Viti Levu in west Fiji.

Marrying aboriginal women who brought them parcels of land, the conquerors settled on the more fertile islands and founded new clans. The newcomers were very different in skills, interests and values from the aborigines. They were a raiding, fishing people who preferred to sail and gather their food from the sea rather than to till the soil. The conquerors, moreover, were fascinated by their genealogies and by the idea of rank based on male primogeniture and they introduced ancestor worship into Lau.[16]

The aborigines and their descendants, however, kept most of the land, their food-producing patterns, and their basic ecological adjustment to the environment. They also kept their nature religion, related to that adjustment, and many of their traditional attitudes and values. In time manioc and sweet potato, exotic food plants which made gardening possible to a limited extent on the limestone islands, found their way into Lau, allowing an increase in food production and population. Gradually, on the basis of ancient structures, the ecological and cultural pattern of the area developed a new balance. Although Tongan and European influences have somewhat altered it in recent years, in that warfare has ceased and most of the Lauan religious practices have been lost due to missionary influences, the basic structure of the ecocultural arrangement apparently persists to the present in southern Lau.

Space would not permit a complete description of Lauan culture from the total ecological viewpoint even if the available data allowed it. It will suffice for our purpose to note certain aspects of the productive and distributive system in ecological context. The food problem looms large in this community on account of many interrelated factors. Among them are the frequency of drought and destructive hurricanes in the area, the scarcity and poor quality of garden land on the limestone islands, the fact that most manioc (staple of the limestones since its introduction) is inedible before it has been processed by a tedious operation to remove the poison, and the difficulty of preserving and storing food in the tropics under native conditions.

Under such circumstances we might expect the diet of the Lauans to be deficient both in quantity and in nutritional balance. No systematic studies of diet have been made in this area, but we note that to be satisfactory from the native viewpoint, a meal or a feast must consist of two parts: 1. steamed "true food" (called *kana ntchina*), namely a staple such as yam, breadfruit, sweet potato, manioc, or Tahitian chestnut *(Inocarpus edulis);* and 2. a boiled relish (called *mboro*) made of fresh green leaves, fish and coconut "cream," seasoned with bird's eye pepper. Pigs and sea turtle are feast foods. This pattern of diet requires little or no fresh water in a community where fresh water is exceedingly scarce, another adaptation to the environment. Moreover, it appears to be well-balanced from the nutritional viewpoint, the "true food" providing the bulk of carbohydrates, some proteins, fats, minerals and vitamins, while the relish furnishes proteins of superior quality and fat (i.e., from ripe coconut "cream"),[17] as well as certain indispensable vitamins and minerals found in fresh green leaves and red peppers. Furthermore, although food does not drop off the trees and rot on the ground (as it does on many Pacific islands—e.g., in Guam before the last war), the Lauan diet appears, under native conditions, to have been relatively adequate in quantity except in time of hurricane or drought.

The traditional diet of the Lauans is the result of a complicated and ingenious structure of attitudes, habits and institutions which function to develop and reinforce the basic ecology of the area according to the needs of its population, and to relate and adjust the community as a whole to the total environment. To gain some insight into this structure, let us begin with the daily menu. The Lauans eat only one main meal a day, at about sundown, and the major activities of both sexes are directed toward procuring and preparing the food for this meal. The men and boys of the household are responsible for the daily supply of "true food" for their own group and this they either raise in the household's garden land or collect from the bush. They then carefully prepare it, wrap it in leaves, place each package of food in the earth-oven pit on stones which have previously been heated, cover the whole with leaves and earth, and allow it to steam for at least an hour. The women and girls of the household, on the other hand, are responsible for the relish. They collect fresh green leaves daily—either edible leaves from the bush or sweet potato leaves from the garden. The women also collect shellfish on the reef or fish with nets in the lagoon and they clean the catch on the beach. Then, at the household kitchen huts, they pick leaves from stems, grate and strain the fatty flesh of ripe coconuts to make coconut "cream," and boil the mixture with fish and pepper in pots for at least an hour over a wood fire.

When both parts of the meal, the "true food" and the relish, are finally ready, they are combined and divided into shares, one for each member of the household according to rank, age and sex. Thus the two parts of the daily meal are always procured and prepared separately. Indeed, no woman is allowed near the earth-oven, which is strictly a male domain located some distance from the kitchen hut. This complementary and balanced sexual division of the rather time-consuming labor of meal-getting functions effectively toward insuring that the daily diet will be reasonably adequate, varied, and sufficient in quantity to fulfill the needs of the group, without placing undue burden on either sex or on any one individual. The method of sharing the feast tends toward a systematic, equitable distribution of food within the household group.

Now it should be noted that, for the self-maintenance of this diet pattern, each household must have access to three types of resources: namely, garden land, bush, and fishing grounds. With this point in mind, let us glance at the system of land use in southern Lau.[18] After the British took over the Fiji Islands in 1874 and peace was established between native factions, the clan-hamlets moved out of the interior of the Lau islands and settled on adjacent lots on the windward[19] shores, forming coastal villages. But they kept their ancient land divisions and proprietary clan rights. Volcanic islands like Mothe were divided into pie-shaped sections bounded by natural ridges which separate the fertile valleys, and each clan had the use of the garden lands, uplands, and fishing grounds of the section wherein its hamlet had formerly been located. On limestone islands like Fulanga where the valley and ridge conformation is absent, land sections were not pie-shaped; but a similar principle of land division nonetheless prevailed. Formerly the bush and fishing grounds in the vicinity of each site occupied by a clan-hamlet, its jungle fruits, garden lands, and other resources belonged to the hamlet. Each household within a clan-hamlet had the use of a piece of the hamlet's garden lands and all the households of the hamlet together had access to the hamlet's bush and fishing grounds.

After the establishment of coast villages, the bush and fishing grounds belonging to the clans of a village were used in common by the whole village group, but the ancient division of garden lands by clans and households persisted. Furthermore, certain clans or villages claim ownership of one or more of the small uninhabited limestone islands in the community. For example, Naivotavota clan of Nggalinggali village on Kambara claims the island of Wangava and its members supplement the crops they raise on their meager garden lands on Kambara with those they raise on Wangava, and also use Wangava's rather extensive forest and lake products. Undu village on Kambara claims ownership of the island of Marambo and uses its resources. Indeed, all the uninhabited islands of the community are claimed and used to supplement the resources of the owning groups. Thus the land use system of Lau is closely related to the basic ecological arrangement of the area and functions to insure a balanced distribution of various types of island resources among the local groups of each island and to render accessible to each household means of obtaining a balanced daily diet.

The traditional diet was further safeguarded by an ingenious and self-regulating system of co-operative production and distribution, which encompassed all the local groups in the community. On each inhabited island an hereditary officer called the *vaka vanua* is custodian of the jungle fruits and crops. The traditional role of the crop custodian was to watch the island's food supply and, as each major food crop (whether wild or cultivated) matured, to place a tabu on it. When the custodian considered the crop under tabu to have ripened sufficiently, his traditional role was to remove the tabu and to arrange for the collection of first fruits by village and clan groups. The first fruits were then placed on the village ceremonial ground *(rara)* and divided by the custodian into two portions, one for the island chief and one for the people. The chief's portion was presented to the chief ceremonially by the custodian or by another officer of the aboriginal class, called the *takala.* The portion of the first fruits reserved for the people was divided by still another officer, called the headman of the ceremonial ground *(tui rara),*[20] a title hereditary in an aboriginal clan. It was the responsibility of this official to divide the food so that each clan received a fair share. When crops were abundant, part of the first fruits were set aside to be fermented and stored against time of scarcity. After the first fruits ceremony the people of the island were free to gather the remainder of the crop, each group from its own lands.

In this island community where food was none too plentiful and famine a constant threat, the institution of the crop custodian functioned, in total context, to conserve and augment the food supply of each island by preventing the crops from being consumed before they had attained their full size and maturity and their highest nutritive value. It thus served as a public health and resources conservation measure of considerable significance to guard against famine, to obtain the optimum size and food value of the crops, to insure a more equitable distribution of the limited food resources of the community as a whole, to build up community health through more adequate nutrition, and to accumulate a surplus in times of plenty for use in times of scarcity. It should be noted that on each island only the major food crops were placed under tabu. These differed from island to island and from season to season, depending on local conditions as judged by crop custodians, and thus the custodian institution had considerable flexibility.

When the British system of indirect rule was established in Lau, however, the office of crop custodian was not incorporated into the administrative set-up. Indeed, its very existence was probably unknown to Europeans. Moreover, the Lauans soon became confused as to which chief should receive the offering of first fruits—the traditional island chief, whose office had not been recognized officially in the new government system, or the local village chief, an officer newly created by British regulation. Consequently the crop custodian, although continuing to function in a limited way on all the inhabited islands of the community (except Namuka where the crops abundantly cover the needs of the population), has lost considerable authority and prestige. The number of fruit and garden crops placed under tabu for first fruits presentation has decreased in number, at least part of each crop being consumed before it has fully matured, especially on the limestone islands. Food is rarely stored against time of famine, and in general the crops are smaller in size than formerly and less valuable from the viewpoint of nutrition.

As part of the production and distribution system mentioned above, each inhabited island also had a master fisherman (called *ndau ni nggoli*), who had charge of all the island's fishing grounds, communal fishing expeditions and turtle hunts. The office of master fisherman is held by a clan belonging to the noble class, except on islands where that class is absent. The traditional role of the *ndau ni nggoli* was to master the fish lore and fishing techniques of the island and to study the habits of various edible species of marine life in relation to the local fishing grounds, the tide and currents, the weather, the lunar cycle, the seasons, and the presence of noxious plants which render edible species poisonous to man. Although men and women caught fish offshore singly or in groups of two or three by means of nets, lines, and spears for their daily household needs without special permission from the master fisherman, they observed his regulation of the fishing grounds and no large, organized fishing expeditions took place without his sanction. Indeed, the master fisherman himself organized and led all communal turtle hunts and most large fishing parties. Women's communal fishing was led by the wife or daughter of the *ndau ni nggoli.*

The institution of the master fisherman functioned to increase the total catch by protecting the local fishing grounds from over-fishing and undue disturbance, and by taking advantage of the various group-fishing techniques in relation to the weather, the seasons, and the habits of various edible species. In a community where fishing provided the major protein constituent in the daily diet and an indispensable part of every feast, this institution operated as a public health measure of prime importance in creating and maintaining a balanced relation between the community and its marine food supply. The traditional functions of this institution and its ecological significance are clarified by the fact that, although the prestige and authority of the master fisherman have not been reinforced by the British and consequently this native official has lost status, he still operates unofficially to a limited extent on every inhabited island in the community. As a result of his lowered status and decreased power, however, informants say that the fishing grounds of the various islands are more disturbed than formerly, that there are fewer organized fishing expeditions, and that the catches are smaller than they used to be.

Another institution which is part of the total system under discussion is the intervillage ceremonial exchange, called *solevu.* Food from the volcanic islands is exchanged for craft goods such as mats, barkcloth, wooden bowls and canoes from the limestone islands, by means of the *solevu,* a complicated pattern of exchange between related villages based on an adaptation of the ancient ceremony used in the presentation of first fruits, mentioned above. Along with the public ceremonial exchange of goods between the two participating villages, there occurs during the four days of the *solevu* a certain amount of private exchange of gifts and barter between related individuals from the two villages. This gives a high degree of flexibility to the arrangement. The *solevu* also provides an occasion for the exchange of feasts, dances, and songs between the two groups and for intervillage games and sports.

The institution of the *solevu* functions not only to provide a pleasant interlude in the daily routine of hard work necessary to group survival in southern Lau, but also as an efficient and self-regulatory "mechanism" to stimulate production of food and craft articles and to expand the system of distribution of each island to include a group of both limestone and volcanic islands whose complementary resources form a natural trade area. We have noted how the institutions of the crop custodian and the master fisherman, in the ecological context of each island, function traditionally to increase in size and nutritive value the local food supply and operate toward its more equitable distribution. We now observe that the *solevu* provides an integrating, logical link in the total productive and distributive system, which unites the various islands of the community into a balanced, interdependent and co-operative whole whereby sectional differences in resources are transformed into assets and each group, regardless of its resources, is enabled to obtain what it needs for a balanced diet and economy.

The importance of the *solevu* in the total economy of southern Lau is brought into relief by the effect of its prohibition by the Colonial Government. Some years ago British officials outlawed large ceremonial exchanges in Fiji, because, it was said, they thought such a prohibition would prevent waste of needed energy and resources. Doubtless, in other parts of Fiji, where food is more plentiful, there was a wastage of resources in connection with the *solevu.* The effect of the regulation in the community under consideration, however, was not to abolish the *solevu* but rather to reduce the number of *solevus* held in the area. This in turn tended to reduce the output of craft goods, especially mats and barkcloth, the main *solevu* craft goods. According to the local division of labor, mats and barkcloth are made by the women, who also tend the babies, care for the houses, and, as noted above, procure and prepare part of the food. The men, on the other hand, besides their food producing and cooking functions already noted, hunt and fish with spears, care for the pigs, build and sail large sea-going canoes, trade between islands, and produce wooden bowls and sennit. This nice balance of labor between the sexes in Lau has been disturbed by the diminution in the production of women's crafts, due mainly to the government's prohibition of the *solevu,* the women being left with a considerable amount of time on their hands which they formerly used in creative activity. The men, on the other hand, tend to labor more than ever, trying to compensate for the diminished food supply. But since garden lands are insufficient in quantity and quality on most islands to cover the needs of the population without importing food, regardless of the amount of energy expended in gardening by native methods, food is scarcer than ever. It should be added that, although the supply of hardwoods, found only on the limestones, is limited, there seems to be little danger that the forests will be depleted by the small amount of timber cut for canoes and craft goods by means of native technology. Thus, instead of operating to prevent wastage of energy and resources, the prohibition of the *solevu* actually operates toward throwing out of line the nicely adjusted system of food production and distribution and the balanced sexual division of labor in the community, reducing the work and creativity of the women, increasing the work of the men, and engendering a food shortage on many of the islands.

The entire system of production and distribution described above, it should be noted, is basically accommodative and co-operative, and it is effected with a minimum of coercion, since rewards in the form of group prestige go automatically to the group (and incidentally also to the individual) who willingly gives or contributes most to the whole. Stinginess means loss of prestige. Within the system, however, rivalry between groups functions as a creative stimulus toward the goal of increased production of high quality products and more equitable distribution of these to the whole community. Apparently it is an indispensable ingredient contributing toward the self-maintenance and self-regulation of the system. Moreover, institutionalized, competitive group-giving prevents the development of an economic monopoly which might otherwise emerge in an area where the distribution of local resources is irregular and where rank and status are highly developed. Under it not even the chiefs may keep their tribute but rather, under penalty of losing face, must redistribute it to their followers. Thus, traditionally, the system prevents the accumulation of wealth in the hands of any one group or individual, and it insures that community resources will remain available to the whole group for immediate use according to need.

Before concluding we should note one more point which is vital to an understanding of the Lauan system of production and distribution described above. Despite its fine adjustment to the ecological setting and its basically self-perpetuating nature, this system could not operate effectively unless it were counterbalanced by a psychocultural arrangement which functioned to regulate and limit the size of the human population in relation to the resources of the community made available by the indigeneous technology. Analyzing Lauan culture from this viewpoint, we find a complementary set of institutions which do actually tend to function toward just this end.

For example, after the birth of a child the father moves out of the family dwelling and sleeps in the men's house of the clan. He is not allowed to have sexual intercourse with his wife until the baby is weaned, a period of from nine months to two years. The strict observance of this custom is attested by the fact that siblings in Lau are almost without exception at least eighteen months apart. Thus the men's house complex, correlated with certain tabus, functions as a means of birth spacing and population control and of protecting maternal and infant health. Ritual continence was practiced in Lau on many occasions. Several methods of abortion were used, mainly by unmarried mothers. In Fulanga old people who had outlived their usefulness, according to native standards, were formerly abandoned on a small island in the lagoon. Where chieftainship was highly developed, those who broke tabus concerning the nobility were clubbed to death. Raiding between villages, in the course of which men, women and children were killed, was not infrequent in the group and those who were captured, regardless of age or sex, were consumed by the victors at cannibalistic feasts. These are some of the Lauan practices which, together with accidents, hurricanes, disease, and a rate of infant and maternal mortality which was probably rather high, tended to limit the size of the population in relation to the available resources within the natural and cultural setting. Although in historic times Fijian population totals were greatly reduced, especially by the ravages of white man's diseases, the low point was reached at about 1911. Thereafter the trend has been slowly upward. The population of southern Lau gained 155 per 1,000 between 1921 and 1935.[21] At the time of the present field work, the population of the community was about 1,500.

Certain significant generalizations which grow out of the foregoing analysis may now be formulated.

We noted that in our island community a unique and balanced biotic system developed in isolation over a very long period of time and in the absence of large land animals. The advent of man, which occurred relatively late in the ecological developmental sequence, introduced not only a new species, namely *Homo sapiens,* into this natural community but also other fauna and flora, as well as the artifacts carried by man as part of his cultural equipment. Still more important, perhaps, it added human cultural processes to the fundamental ecological processes already operating in the area. In a relatively short time, from the eco-historical viewpoint, there emerged, on the basis of the ancient biotics, a new eco-cultural structure which involved plants, animals and human groups in a mutually interdependent and balanced web of life. And whereas formerly each island had formed an independent natural community, the new eco-cultural arrangement, including man, extended over several islands, and related a number of heretofore disparate communities.

Certain ecologically significant structures of the human culture which developed in this extended island community were analyzed, namely the system of production and distribution in relation to population controls. Its foundation in the self-selected, balanced diet of the human group was noted. The findings suggest that, although certain of its activities may be harmful to the whole arrangement, the human group has tended to organize and integrate its habits of feeling, thought, and behavior systematically with the world of nature in such a way as to play a basically *positive* and *logical* role in the multi-dimensional process of attaining and maintaining a balanced, healthy adjustment of the whole community. The findings also suggest that its major economic institutions are basically accommodative and co-operative, with competitive attitudes and arrangements serving as an essential dynamic toward its self-maintenance and toward the development of a high standard of production and a high degree of creativity.

It is well known that isolated natural communities tend in time, by processes of symbiosis, accommodation and competition, to develop a delicately balanced, ecological organization wherein the various species of flora and fauna attain a mutually advantageous adjustment within the total environment. Ordinarily we think of the process mainly in terms of plants and animals in relation to the geological structure, climate, soil, water supply and other features of the physical environment. However, a broad-gauged analysis of the available data from this remote, relatively isolated community (where geological and ecological processes have proceeded for millennia relatively undisturbed and where cultural processes have operated for centuries with little interference from without) suggests that all of life is involved in a self-regulating web of relationships, human groups as well as so-called lower animals and plants. Seen as a whole, a natural community actually consists of its total population—plants, animals and human beings—in a complex, mutually interdependent relationship in environmental context.

The analysis indicates, however, that the dynamic, total ecological structure of a community emerges only if processes whose time-span is relatively long are taken into account. But such long-phase processes tend to escape the attention of scientists for many reasons, including the limitations of most frames of reference currently in vogue; the habit of observing only short-phase processes; the habit of concentrating on one dimension of the nature or culture process and even on one limited aspect of that one dimension; and the habit of working independently rather than as part of a multiple-discipline, co-operative group.

Our data suggest further that, once firmly established and embodied in the symbol system, the attitudes and the habits of a human community, a balanced, functional, eco-cultural structure tends to endure if the human community is not wiped out or severed from its natural setting. The data also suggest that such an eco-cultural community structure is the living core of relationships which the human group, either consciously or unconsciously, tries in multiple ways to perpetuate. An understanding of this core may be expected to throw light on the problem of so-called "cultural resistance," or a people's acceptance or rejection of certain extraneous patterns of belief, thought and behavior. For example, in Lau the community has tended to reject foreign patterns of feeling, thought and behavior which interfere with, or break down, its basic eco-cultural structure, regardless of the regulations or the penalties involved. It would seem that to the extent the Lauans have been unsuccessful in their resistance to harmful interference with their group life processes, the intentional or forced introduction of nonfunctional patterns or the prohibition of functional ones has tended to throw off balance the community's whole eco-cultural structure and has operated directly against its well-being. The implications that these findings have for the problem of prediction in social science are manifold.

Finally, the findings point up the practical significance of the eco-cultural approach and suggest that an understanding of a community's long-time, dynamic pattern of relationships is basic to the formulation of adequate norms or standards for the advancement of community welfare and for the development of community-oriented government administration.[22] Accordingly, the significant problem regarding community welfare and the conservation of resources does not emerge simply as the question of how human health and institutions may be improved, or of how topsoil may be saved, or watersheds, and forest land protected, or organic species preserved from extinction, important though each of these aspects may be. The significant problem of community welfare emerges as a matter of using and adapting local beliefs, attitudes, habits and institutions, supplemented where necessary by appropriate new ones, to the end that human groups, through natural eco-cultural processes, may foster the development and maintenance of a balanced, healthy *total* community—plants and animals, as well as human groups.

NOTES

1. I take this opportunity to thank Edwin H. Bryan, Jr., John Collier, Harry S. Ladd, Emma Reh, Ward Shepard, Albert C. Smith and Margaret Titcomb for help or comments on the manuscript.

2. See, for example, Gayton, 1946; Hallowell, 1949.

3. The term "total ecological viewpoint" is used to include the relations of organic species, including man, to one another in environmental context.

4. The field projects on which this paper is based were unrelated and none of the researchers collected or analyzed their material systematically within a total ecological frame of reference. Edwin H. Bryan, Jr., naturalist, made a survey of the Lau group in 1924. Dr. Albert C. Smith, taxonomist, collected plants in 1934. Dr. Harry S. Ladd, geologist, studied the geology of Lau in 1934; and I investigated a culture-historical and culture contact problem in 1933-1934. Unless otherwise specified, conditions and institutions are described as of 1933-1934.

5. The inhabited islands are Mothe, Komo, Namuka, Kambara, Fulanga and Ongea. The uninhabited islands are Karoni, Tavunasithi, Wangava, Marambo, Yangasa Levu, Navutu-i-loma, Navutu-i-ra, Yuvutha and Ongea Ndriki.

6. Bryan (MSS.) states: "The dominant plant over much of the volcanic islands is a plume grass, *Eulalia japonica,* called *ngasau* by the natives. There are also several species of wiry ferns, including the "staghorn"; a low scrub, made up of about a half a dozen widespread species of shrubs and stunted trees; and scattered *Pandanus* and *Casuarina.* The dominant littoral species are: *ndilo (Calophyllum inophyllum), vutu (Barringtonia speciosa), evu (Tournefortia argentea), evueve (Hernandia peltata), nawanawa (Cordia subcordata), tatang-ngia (Acacia lauriflora), vevendu (Scaevola koenigii), tavola (Terminalia littoralis), ndrala (Erythrina indica),* etc. Besides these there are the usual *Pandanus,* numerous vines and groves of coconut palms."

7. According to Bryan (MSS.): "All the limestone islands . . . support one type of forest. It is made up throughout the group of the same fifty or so species of trees and tall shrubs, with an undergrowth of *Piper (wangawa),* bird's eye pepper *(rokete),* ferns, herbs and several vines. The luxuriance alone depends upon the size and elevation of the island. There is an interesting, rapid and progressive increase in the number of species and the height of growth, from the nearly bare rocks, such as Latei Viti and Bacon Island with but two or three species of prostrate herbs, to the splendid forests of Kambara, Mango, etc. First to appear after the herbs and vines are low, stunted trees of such widespread species as *Hernandia peltata, Tournefortia argentea,* and a *Ficus* with orange fruit commonly eaten by pigeons. A few of the small islands have native palms in considerable numbers. *Pandanus* and *Casuarina* appear early in the scale."

8. Ladd and Hoffmeister, 1945; Ladd, 1934.

9. Ladd and Hoffmeister, 1945; Bryan, 1948; Thompson, 1940a, 1940b.

10. Vatoa and Ono-i-Lau lie farther to the south, and accordingly have a slightly cooler climate.

11. According to Bryan (MSS.): "Except for birds and insects there is a poverty of native animal life in Lau. The only mammal noted was the rat. About a dozen species of water birds and over 28 species of land birds were encountered throughout the group. Two species of land snakes and one banded water snake were caught. Lizards of various species were abundant. The largest was the green *vokai.* Various sizes of geckos and skinks were more abundant. Land crabs, including the large 'coconut' crab and hermit crabs, were present in quantity."

12. Thompson, 1938.

13. Thompson, 1938, 1940b.

14. In time apparently the migration of their ancestors from the west was forgotten and the aborigines of Lau came to believe that they originated locally in some natural phenomenon, such as a tree or an animal. The people of each island also had a species of bird and a species of fish which was sacred to them, and they believed in a local abode of the dead. Their deity was apparently a great, pervasive, spiritual power believed to be the source of all *mana* and was worshiped at sacred places such as caves, trees or stones.

15. Bryan, 1948.

16. They set their clans up over those of the aborigines as a noble class, each clan having three species sacred to it, namely a tree, a fish and a bird. They required that their first-born males be regarded as sacred chiefs and be rendered tribute by the people in the form of first fruits. They developed a system of worshiping their warrior forefathers by means of hereditary priests in small temples.

17. The proximate composition of "coconut cream" is: protein, 3.55%; fat, 33.15%; carbohydrate, 8.62%; calories per 100 grams, 347. (Concepcion, 1947). On this point, Emma Reh, nutrition officer, Food and Agriculture Organization of the United Nations, writes, "The protein content of 'coconut cream' is fairly high considering this is a liquid product. The protein is of good quality, like proteins of pulses, oily seeds and nuts, and superior to those of cereals, starchy roots and other vegetable foods. It is rich in most of the amino acids essential in nutrition. The fat content of the 'coconut cream' is also high, but the fat is low in the unsaturated fatty acids needed by the body. The requirements are however small, and probably met by fats contained in other foods."(Reh, 1948).

18. For details *see* Thompson, 1940a, 1940b.

19. Except Tokalau and Lomatchi located on Kambara's leeward shore near the anchorage.

20. The *tui rara's* functions were performed on Fulanga by the *tui naro,* an aboriginal clan title.

21. For details *see* Thompson, 1940a, p. 137.

22. See Thompson, 1949.

BIBLIOGRAPHY

BRYAN, EDWIN H., JR., MSS. *Preliminary Report on the Lau Group, Fiji, 1924,* Bishop Museum, Honolulu.

———, 1948, Personal Correspondence.

CONCEPCION, ISABELO, 1947, *Composition and Nutritive Values of Philippine Food Materials,* Manila.

GAYTON, A. H., 1946, "Culture-Environment Integration: External References in Yokuts Life," *Southwestern Journal of Anthropology,* Vol. 2, pp. 252-268.

HALLOWELL, A. I., 1949, "The Size of Algonkian Hunting Territories: A Function of Ecological Adjustment," *American Anthropologist,* Vol. 51, pp. 35-45.

LADD, HARRY S., 1934, "Geology of Vitilevu, Fiji," *Bishop Museum Bull.* 119, Honolulu.

LADD, HARRY S. AND HOFFMEISTER, J. EDWARD, 1945, "Geology of Lau, Fiji," *Bishop Museum Bull.* 181, Honolulu.

REH, EMMA, 1948, Personal Correspondence.

THOMPSON, LAURA, 1938, "The Culture History of the Lau Islands, Fiji," *American Anthropologist,* Vol. 40, pp. 181-197.

———, 1940a, *Fijian Frontier,* Introduction by B. Malinowski, New York.

———, 1940b, "Southern Lau, Fiji. An Ethnography," *Bishop Museum Bull.* 162, Honolulu.

———, 1949, "The Basic Conservation Problem," *Scientific Monthly,* Vol. 68, pp. 129-131.

2

POLYNESIAN CEREMONIAL GIFT EXCHANGES[1]

Ian Hogbin

In the literature dealing with the natives of Polynesia mention has often been made of the ceremonial exchanges of gifts which take place at various times. From the purely economic point of view frequently these exchanges are quite meaningless, since neither party derives real material benefit from them. Indeed, at times the gifts exchanged are of precisely the same kind. Thus a ball of sennit ceremonially presented may be returned by a similar ball of exactly the same size, presented with exactly the same ceremony. Or again, a parcel of food may be returned by another parcel of the same kind of food cooked according to the same recipe. The gifts in most of these exchanges are often of great bulk and, in the eyes of the native, of highest value, frequently months being required to prepare them. The missionary Turner, for example, in describing the marriage ceremony of ancient Samoa, says that one, two, or even three months were required for the collection of the property which was on these occasions always exchanged by the relatives of the bride and the groom. "All the family and relatives of the bride," he says, "are called upon to assist, and thus they raise a great quantity of *tonga,* which includes all kinds of fine mats and native cloth, manufactured by the women. This is invariably the dowery, which is presented to the bridegroom and his friends on the celebration of the nuptials. He and his friends, on the other hand, collect in a similar manner for the family of the bride *oloa,* which includes canoes, pigs, and foreign property of all kinds, such as cloth, garments, etc."[2]

Turner goes on to say that for people of high rank the presentations were made publicly on the *marae.* Here the whole population of the village assembled, or the population of their two villages if the bride and bridegroom belonged to different districts. The bride, accompanied by a few of her friends, paraded down the whole length of the *marae* with her *tonga* or "dowery" so that all had an opportunity to see it. The presentation of the return gift or *oloa* followed later, but with the same publicity. "The

Reproduced by permission of the publishers and Ian Hogbin from *Oceania,* 3:13-39 (1932).

father . . . of the bridegroom had the disposal of the *tonga* which formed the dowery; and . . . the father . . . of the bride had the disposal of the property which was given by the bridegroom."[3] The marriage of common people was celebrated with much less ceremony, but usually a similar gift exchange was made.

The missionary Brown also gives a description of the exchanges made at a marriage. "Preparations," he says, "often extended over several months, as the prospective bridegroom and his immediate relations had to go on begging expeditions to all who were connected with them and collect from them large quantities of property, which in the earlier days consisted of food, canoes, houses, and other native property called *oloa.*" The family of the bride "also collected from all her relatives beautiful fine mats and native cloth, which were designated by the name *tonga.*"[4] At the actual marriage ceremony the *oloa* and *tonga* were exchanged. Dr. Margaret Mead also speaks of these goods and their presentation.[5]

A similar exchange of property took place in Samoa on the birth of a child. Turner describes how again *oloa* goods were collected from the relatives of the husband and *tonga* goods from the relatives of the wife, and how the two were exchanged. "The whole affair was so managed that the friends were the benefited parties chiefly, and the husband and wife left no richer than they were. Still, they had the satisfaction of having seen what they considered a great honour, viz., heaps of property collected on the occasion of the birth of their child."[6] Dr. Mead also says that the *tonga-oloa* exchange was carried out at births as at marriages, but that the biggest exchange was for the first-born.[7]

Exchanges also had a place in the regular funeral ritual, though Dr. Mead says that they did not quite follow the ordinary lines, and that many gifts were returned.[8]

Gifford's account of the marriage ceremony in Tonga reveals that here too the relatives of the bride and of the groom made reciprocal gifts. When a couple decided to marry, he says, the parents made a collection of goods from their relatives. The parents of the bride collected *koloa,* which consisted of fine mats and *tapa* cloth, while the parents of the groom collected *ngaue,* that is, food and *kava* root. The parents did not themselves contribute unless a small quantity of goods only was forthcoming. On the day of the marriage the *koloa* and *ngaue* were exchanged. A portion was set aside for the couple, but the biggest part was distributed among the persons who originally gave. The parents gave them presents also, so that each one received about twice as much in value as he gave. The parents thus had to supply a very considerable amount of property, and it would seem that the more they supplied, the greater was their prestige.[9] Gifford saw a mat twelve feet wide by forty feet long presented. Such a mat could have had no practical use, and must have been kept solely for occasions of this kind.

From Tahiti also we have a description of the exchange which regularly accompanied marriage. The missionary Orsmond writes, "On the eve of the wedding ceremonies, all the relatives and friends of each party assembled at the respective homes of the young people . . . On the morrow representatives of the household of the bridegroom . . . came to escort the bride . . . to his home for the first of the wedding ceremonies . . . With them they brought appropriate presents called the *o*.

"Then the bride's party . . . set out in a grand parade by land if not far to walk, and in new canoes made for the occasion if they had a long way to go, no old canoes being used for weddings. Following them in canoes were their presents, or *o* . . . which consisted of everything that had been prepared for the wedding, in two equal divisions, one from the side of the father and the other from the side of the mother. On arriving at the bridegroom's home, they were welcomed by a great party assembled in the same order as their own and the food and livestock they had brought were presented and received in due form by the family." A great feast prepared by the bridegroom's relatives was then consumed. Later on these people visited the bride's relatives carrying with them presents equivalent in value to what they had received. They too were entertained with a feast.[10]

Orsmond mentions that at births people brought presents, and at deaths the visitors carried with them cloth and mats "for the people generally."[11]

Again in eastern Polynesia elaborate exchanges were made. Thus in the Marquesas on the occasion of a wedding so much property changed hands that cross cousin marriage was the custom among the common people, the object being to prevent the goods from going to strangers.[12] In the upper classes, however, marriage with a person of another tribe was considered desirable, so that in times of war the assistance of this tribe could be depended upon, relatives by marriage being always under the obligation to assist one another. The presentations took the form of feasts, the relatives of each of the contracting parties entertaining one another in turn. In each case the guests had the right to seize and carry away any property they desired, including utensils and weapons. A chief might even take canoes.[13] It is to be presumed that the hosts derived honour from the lavishness of the feasts and the amount of goods of which they were plundered.

We are informed that in the Marquesas when a child was born it was customary for the relatives to come to see it, bringing presents with them. Unfortunately no mention is made of what became of these presents, but presumably they were re-distributed, for they could be of little use to one of such a tender age.

Amongst the Maori of New Zealand Dr. Firth has shown that certain gift exchanges were a substitute for trade. The natural resources of several areas permitted the tribes occupying them to devote their energies to special activities. The tribes of the region in the South Island where nephrite is found, for example, specialized in the manufacture of adzes of this material. For their food they relied very largely on the gifts of those who desired adzes in return. Similarly, other tribes devoted themselves to making cloaks, which they presented to persons who required them, receiving in return garden produce, fish, and birds.[14] The exchanges of central and eastern Polynesia so far mentioned are not to be considered as in any way comparable to these New Zealand exchanges, for always the recipients were able to give away precisely the same kind of goods as they had received. Thus in Samoa if a family had a daughter and a son, from the economic point of view it would have made little difference which married first, despite the fact that in the one case *tonga* would have had to have been provided and in the other *oloa.*[15]

It is not my intention in this paper to deal with what we may call trade gift exchanges, though these took place in central Polynesia as well as in New Zealand. I shall devote my attention only to noneconomic ceremonial gift exchanges.[16] The purpose of the paper is to demonstrate the various ways in which benefits were derived from these exchanges; that is, to show that their uselessness was more apparent than real. There are so many similarities in the social organization throughout the Polynesian area that it seems sufficient to select one society for detailed investigation. The underlying sociological principles can then be thoroughly examined, and afterwards, with certain reservations, the conclusions applied to the rest of central Polynesia. I have selected for detailed treatment Ontong Java, a Polynesian community in the Solomon Islands, because I can speak of it at first hand.[17]

I have already given a brief sketch of the social organization of Ontong Java, so that it will be necessary here to do no more than make a summary. Ontong Java is a coral atoll made up of about one hundred small islands. These are divided between two tribes, each of which has a main village, the one on Luangiua island, and the other on Pelau island. The organization is on the basis of the usual Polynesian patrilineal family group, which I refer to as a joint family. The eldest man of this group acts as headman. Some joint families own outlying islands, and are therefore wealthy, while others of the poorer class own only land within the main village. Coconuts are grown on this land. Garden land, used for growing taro, is owned exclusively by women. Each joint family may be considered as being made up of a number of smaller family groups consisting of brothers and their children. These I have called co-operating groups since the members, owning fishing tackle as they do in common, usually co-operate in fishing expeditions.

Elaborate exchanges of foodstuffs take place in Ontong Java on various occasions. It will be convenient to deal first with the series connected specifically with the ceremonies of betrothal, marriage, pregnancy, birth and death. These always take place when the people concerned are actually living in one or other of the main villages, and not on outlying islands.

Marriage is in this community almost always preceded by betrothal, though the actual arrangements may be made either by the pair themselves or by their parents. In any case, once it has been decided that a boy and girl have been set aside as future mates their parents make an exchange almost at once. If the two families involved belong to wealthy social groups then many other persons will also take part. First the father of the girl goes to the chief man of his co-operating group, or else to the headman of his joint family, and informs him of the betrothal. If the chief man of the co-operating group only has been informed he will tell the headman. This man then gives orders to the women of the joint family to collect taro. At the same time the mother's brother of the girl also tells the headman of his joint family, and the women of this group are likewise ordered to collect taro. On a day agreed upon all the tubers are carried in baskets to the house of the girl's mother. Often several hundredweight are collected. Very early in the morning the women all assemble at the house and proceed to scrape the taro. Frequently they are helped by the wives of the men of their joint families. Unfortunately I neglected to inquire whether these women actually contribute towards the stock of taro, but I am rather of the opinion that they do not. I also failed to find out whether they are definitely expected to help in the preparation of the food for the oven, or whether any assistance they give is merely optional.

While the women are scraping the taro the father of the girl and her mother's brother see to it that several dozen coconuts are carried around to the house. However, on no account do the girl's brothers, or any persons classified with them, take part in these operations.[18] The father usually also takes one or two of his brothers, or men classed with them, to assist the women if they require any help in the preparation of ovens for cooking the taro. As a matter of fact, men rarely have anything to do with the preparation of food, provided women are available, and consequently the assistance of these men is seldom required. Any extra stones for the oven will have been collected during the previous day by the girl and her sisters.

While the taro is being scraped and grated the younger women and the girls of the party set to work to grate the flesh of the coconuts which have been brought. The grated flesh is later made into coconut cream, which is then mixed with the taro mash.[19] This mixture is stirred and kneaded well in wooden bowls. In the meantime two or more ovens have been prepared, and are now hot ready. The mixture, wrapped in taro leaves, is placed inside, and they are sealed up. The actual cooking takes several hours, and as a rule the pudding is not ready till nightfall.

Word is always sent to the parents of the boy informing them of what has been going on. Again I regret to say that I do not know the exact form of the message; that is, whether a formal announcement is made by one particular person, or whether just anyone is told to take word to them. The parents inform all the womenfolk of their respective joint families, together with the wives of the men of these groups. As the time for opening the ovens draws near these same women assemble outside the house where they are, each with a bundle of taro leaves. The ovens are opened by the mother of the girl, but when the puddings are taken out they are handed over, though not necessarily with any ceremony, to the mother of the boy, or to one of his senior female relatives. This woman then proceeds to distribute the puddings among the assembled women. The wives of the headmen of the two joint families concerned, and of any other important personages, always receive a larger share than anyone else. Each woman wraps up her portion in the leaves with which she has provided herself and takes it home. Generally the actual mother of the boy does not get more than anyone else, and she may even keep less.

A return gift of taro puddings is before long made by the parents of the boy. The father asks for the assistance of the headman of his joint family, and he as a rule at once gives orders that all the men in the group are to repair to their island property. Usually the headman asks the husbands of the women of the group to come also. For several days this party proceeds to catch fish and to collect coconuts. As the fish are brought home they are cooked over and over again by the women until at last they are quite dry and hard. When an adequate number of coconuts and fish has been accumulated the party returns to the main village, bringing the food in their canoes. In the meantime the mother's brother of the boy has also been busy, and he too, with the assistance of his kinsmen, has gathered from the property of his joint family a large number of coconuts, though as a rule rather less than the boy's own people.

News of the arrival is now sent to the girl's father. He instructs his kinsfolk, together with the kinsfolk of his wife, to carry the presentation of coconuts and fish to his house. Here a distribution is made, each man receiving a number of coconuts and a number of fish.

From the above description it is clear that when a youth and a girl of important joint families are betrothed a large number of their relatives are involved in the subsequent exchange of gifts. Actually, although the parents of the two young people are the agents, the presentation really comes on the one side from the joint family of the girl and of her mother, and on the other from the joint family of the boy and of his mother. A striking feature is that the presentation from the girl's side is of food grown and prepared by women only, while that from the boy's side is of food caught or gathered only by men. Looked at from one point of view this actually means that the exchange is not entirely reciprocal, for in the one case the women do the work, and in the other the men do, while in both the food is consumed by men and women. However, since the natives regard the gifts as actually coming from the two sets of parents, the fact that they are assisted by different relatives is immaterial.

When persons of poor and insignificant joint families are betrothed naturally the exchanges are not nearly so elaborate. Generally only the members of the actual families, and not the joint families, of the parents participate. Thus the sisters of the father and the mother of the girl will give taro for pudding, and the brothers of the father and of the mother of the boy will give coconuts and fish. The food is distributed also among the members of these four families alone.

Usually when a pair are betrothed they do afterwards marry, but not always, for either the boy or the girl may decide that some other partner will be more suitable. One way for the girl to break the contract is to allow herself to be seen in compromising circumstances with another youth. As a rule the boy to whom she has been formally betrothed then renounces her. However, the affair does not finish here, for her father may be angry and punish her severely. In any case, the father of the youth with whom she has compromised herself may be unwilling to have his son marry her. In this event he refuses to accept any gifts from her father, or to make any himself to him. The good name of the girl is then lost, at least for a time.

While I was living in Luangiua village a girl named Kukanga was betrothed to the son of the headman of one of the wealthiest joint families. This engagement was celebrated with a huge gift exchange. A short time afterwards the girl's mother died, and no sooner had the funeral taken place than she declared that she would not marry this man. He was, as a matter of fact, already considerably above the ordinary age for marriage, while Kukanga was herself about sixteen, which meant that another two years would probably elapse before she would be permitted to marry. From village gossip I gathered that the betrothal had been arranged primarily by the man's father and the girl's mother, a woman of particularly strong character. This woman had insisted upon her daughter's acceptance of the proposal, much against her will. No longer under her mother's dominion, Kukanga therefore absolutely refused to go on with the arrangement. Her father, always a weak and rather ineffective individual, and now preoccupied with grief at the loss of his wife, argued with her, but all to no purpose, for she announced that she was going to marry someone else. The villagers' comment was that she ought to have had a good beating. The father actually appealed for help to the king, but he was informed that this was not a matter of public business, and that he ought to settle his family disputes without assistance from outside. Finally he had to let the girl have her own way. Her betrothed took no active part in the discussion—indeed, a betrothed couple take pains to avoid each other—and there was no open breach between her joint family and his. The affair ended by Kukanga being found asleep one morning in the arms of a man who had just returned to his home after working for a couple of years for Europeans. The pair were discovered actually within this man's house. Fortunately his parents were prepared to accept her as a daughter-in-law, and, despite her age, a hasty marriage was arranged. Nevertheless, the gossips were by no means appeased, and months afterwards whenever she passed by they would loudly compare her morals to those of a dog.[20]

I have never heard of a couple living together after their parents had refused to sanction their union and make the necessary exchanges, but if this has occurred they were certainly ostracized, and any subsequent children were treated as illegitimate.

In the event of a youth wishing to break the betrothal tie he has to risk the anger of his parents. There may also be friction between his joint family and that of the girl. In the old days fights sometimes occurred on this account. Nowadays, of course, fighting is prohibited by the government, and betrothal vows are probably more liable to be broken.

A gift exchange similar to that carried out at betrothal forms also a part of the marriage ceremony. This time, however, the groom's family makes the first gift. His father makes a formal request for assistance to the headman of his joint family, and several men are told to help him to collect coconuts. To these are added others collected by the groom's mother brother, with the assistance of a few of his kinsmen. With these coconuts the father buys from the trading station a bolt of calico or canvas, which he presents to the bride's father, who cuts it up and distributes it among the members of his own and his wife's (his daughter's mother's brother's) joint families. The women of these two groups in return collect taro and make a pudding, which is presented to the groom's father, who distributes it to his own and his wife's (his son's mother's brother's) joint families. Formerly, before trading stations were established, the coconuts were presented by the groom's parents, with the addition of a few woven mats.[21] If, however, the marriage is between members of poor joint families, then, as with the betrothal exchange, only the individual families, and not the joint families, of the parents will be involved.

Every event of importance in the life of a married couple is celebrated with an exchange similar to those already described. Thus, for example, when the wife first realizes that she is pregnant, again her husband's parents present her parents with coconuts. They return the gift with taro puddings of proportionate size. There is also an exchange when the child is born. Contrary to the custom at other times, for pregnancy and birth exchanges the coconuts must be green, that is, unripe. It is when they are in this condition that the fluid is most appreciated as a drink. At other times both green and ripe nuts are presented. After the birth of the first child the mother remains in seclusion for a period of several months. On her emergence from this seclusion again there are presentations. Finally, when the wife dies there is another exchange. An exchange takes place on a man's death only if he is survived by a widow, and on a woman's death only if she is survived by her husband. By this time, of course, the parents are usually also dead. In that case the exchange is made on their behalf by the headmen of the joint families concerned.

If traditions are to be believed, then in the days before Europeans settled in the Solomon Islands Ontong Java was subject to occasional famines. Nevertheless, it seems probable that generally there was sufficient food even for the poorest, and the wealthy had far more than they could in normal circumstances eat. Today, of course, owing to depopulation caused by contact with our civilization, there is far more than enough food to go around. The surplus is largely disposed of to a trading station, and such luxuries as sailing cutters, tweed coats, fancy cotton goods, kerosene lamps and iron bedsteads purchased. Formerly the surplus went entirely in gift exchanges. If these exchanges had not taken place it seems inevitable that most of the coconuts, at least, would have been left lying on the ground. Instead, they were gathered from time to time, and the rare thefts by poorer members of the community were generally punished by death. When a food presentation takes place the recipients always eat to the limit of their capacity and hand on anything not required to relatives who belong to less fortunate joint families. At the same time there is a certain amount of waste, though nothing like that recorded from other parts of Polynesia.

It goes without saying that in a small isolated community where kinship ties extend far more widely than they do with ourselves, and where friendly visits between islands are frequently made, the resources of each joint family are accurately known to everyone. This means that the whole community is aware just exactly how much any group can readily spare for a gift exchange. In the same way when an exchange is made the whole village knows the number of coconuts given and the exact size of the puddings. It would perhaps not be strictly correct to say that the presentations are made publicly, for the food is not piled up in the open for some days so that everyone may see it, nor does each family, as it hands over its gift, make a formal speech which may be listened to by the assembled village. However, everyone has an opportunity to see what is going on. The baskets of taro are carried through the village, and usually so many people assist in grating the tubers that some of them have to sit outside. Passersby generally pause and may even take a peep at which is going on inside the house. In this way the size of the puddings becomes common property. Similarly, the coconuts are also carried through the village streets and are left out of doors in heaps until the husks have been removed. Usually the donors do this before making a gift, but occasionally the recipients have to do it for themselves.

The fact that the whole village knows all the details of every food exchange leads to an interesting result, namely, that with certain reservations the givers acquire prestige from their generosity. When I say that persons acquire prestige I mean that they become important in the eyes of their fellows. They have influence in the village, are generally looked up to, and may even be envied. I do not, of course, wish to imply that eminence is secured only by being generous in exchanges, but simply that this is one of the ways of enhancing a person's reputation. Piaka, one of the leading men of Luangiua village, is said to be generous, but his prestige in the community does not rest on this alone. He is also renowned for his levelheadedness and general common sense. As a result he is always listened to with respect when he speaks, and if he joins a group of people the subject under discussion is always carefully explained to him. The prestige enjoyed by a man named Mamakau, however, does very largely depend upon the reputation he has for giving food away freely. He is comparatively young, but is the headman of a very wealthy joint family. Usually he is referred to as "one of the good men,"[22] and, although he is by no means old enough to be considered as a repository of worldly wisdom, he is usually listened to carefully when he expresses an opinion, even if his advice is not taken. One has the feeling that he is popular, and that people are content to defer to him. I once heard a girl who was affianced to a member of his joint family described as fortunate on that account.

I said that with certain reservations the givers in a food exchange acquired prestige through their generosity. Nevertheless, really only the givers of coconuts, that is, the man's relatives, are able to acquire a reputation by this means. Prestige is never acquired by giving taro puddings. In every exchange except that associated with betrothal the coconuts are given before the puddings, and all that is expected from the woman's relatives is that an adequate return should be made. Prestige would be lost if the puddings were of small size, but this gift is never sufficiently spectacular to stir popular imagination. This is perhaps partly due to the fact that a small number of taro is regarded as the equivalent of quite a large number of coconuts, the reason being that taro has to be cultivated, and considerable labour is required to produce it, whereas coconuts require but little attention. A large taro pudding is thus equivalent in value to several hundred coconuts. It must also be remembered that the cultivation of taro is left exclusively to women, and that garden land, on which the taro is grown, is also owned and inherited by women exclusively. Usually sisters and their daughters own garden land in common. This means that the tubers for any one exchange do not come from properties owned by one closely-knit body, such as a joint family, but from a number of gardens each owned by a small group of women. Thus, although from one point of view the women who contribute are all members of one or other of two joint families, from another point of view they do not form a group strongly differentiated from the rest of the community. Finally, although women in Ontong Java enjoy a high social position, and although descent is occasionally matrilineal, the society is definitely patriarchal. It is therefore unthinkable that a man could derive prestige in the exchanges he makes on behalf of his daughter from work performed entirely by women. It is also equally unthinkable to have an institution through which women could regularly derive prestige. Some women, it is true, have far more influence in the community than others, but this is due to their force of character or ability, and not to their generosity.

The point now requiring our consideration is just exactly who acquires prestige from a presentation of coconuts. Two joint families are involved, that of the man on whose behalf the presentation is being made, and that of his mother's brother. The actual amount contributed is fixed by each headman, and it is these two men, together with the father and the mother's brother, who acquire prestige. Mamakau enjoys his reputation because for every presentation in which members of his group have been involved he has allowed a large number of coconuts to be gathered. The prestige of the father and mother's brother is rather a reflection of that of the headmen of their respective groups. However, if for any reason a headman is displeased with one of his subordinates he is able to discipline him by injuring his reputation. This he does by permitting only a bare minimum of coconuts to be gathered for any exchange in which the subordinate is involved.

It may appear that the kinsmen who help a man to collect coconuts when some event of importance has occurred in the married life of his son are given no reward for their services. Later on I shall show that they are, in fact, recompensed.

Despite all that I have been saying, very definite limits are always placed on a person's generosity, and, although a man is talked about if he is mean, he is apt to become a laughingstock if he is over-lavish. At the betrothal ceremony of the girl Kukanga the father of the man presented her parents with ten large baskets of dried fish, 10,000 ripe coconuts, and 6000 green coconuts for drinking. This was in return for a gift of two taro puddings each about four feet square by six inches thick.[23] As I have mentioned, the man belonged to a very wealthy joint family, and his father, who happened to be the headman, was accorded considerable respect on account of his gift. On the evening that it was made I listened to fireside conversations in several different houses. In every case the father, whose name was Hakuma'o, was praised for his action, and one heard him described as a good and generous man, and compared to his credit with other headmen. At no time did I ever hear the present made by the girl's father even mentioned. A few weeks later when a headman, quite as wealthy as Hakuma'o, gave 17,000 coconuts as a betrothal present on behalf of his son, the whole village made him an object of ridicule. He was described as a boaster, for it was felt that by giving 1000 more nuts than Hakuma'o he was being vulgarly ostentatious.[24]

It is not easy to tell just where the line making a gift worthy of praise or blame will be drawn. The above case makes it clear that it is felt that a man should not give a large amount merely to go one better than his fellows. A good deal also depends on the actual wealth at a man's disposal. It is always felt that sufficient coconuts should be left after any presentation to enable any other men of the joint family shortly to be involved similarly to make as fine a showing—of course, provided they deserve to do so. Some consideration has also to be made for the general feelings of the villagers towards the man making the presentation. I have little doubt that if, for instance, Piaka or Paeke, two individuals looked up to and respected by everybody, had given 17,000 coconuts they would have been praised. Nevertheless, it is probable that they would have had, shall we say, sufficient good taste not to have done this so soon after the gesture of Hakuma'o. They are both in a position to do so, for Piaka is almost as wealthy, and Paeke rather more so. Naturally the biggest reputations are acquired only by the richest men,[25] but the poorer classes are in any case of little social importance. Generally a poor man is satisfied to present hundreds of coconuts where a rich man will present thousands.

The most spectacular exchanges take place at betrothal and marriage, though when a child is born the quantity of goods is very little less. For a pregnancy exchange even the wealthiest people are content with a couple of hundred nuts and a small pudding, and at a funeral never more than 1500 nuts change hands—1000 ripe and 500 green—and a pudding of proportionate size.

* * * *

Professor Boas has shown that amongst the Kwakiutl Indians of British Columbia prestige is acquired by making feasts, in which huge quantities of oil and other products are destroyed, and by purchasing sheets of copper at prices which are absurdly above their value as useful objects. In the Trobriand Islands Professor Malinowski has demonstrated that the natives enhance their reputation by accumulating far more garden produce than they actually require, and at the same time giving quantities of it away to certain relatives. Codrington, again, showed that in the Banks Islands the Sukwe graded society provides an opportunity for social advancement. In order to enter each successive grade of the society increasing quantities of wealth have to be paid to the men who are already members. It would be possible to give examples from other societies of definite recognized methods by which prestige may be secured without actually endangering the normal constitution and harmony of the peoples concerned. The gift exchange of Ontong Java thus has its parallel elsewhere. It provides the individual with an opportunity for the satisfaction of his vanity and pride without physical injury to his fellows.

Vanity and pride are universal traits, and, just as the gift exchange of Ontong Java, by providing an opportunity for the display of generosity, is not the only means of acquiring prestige, so also it is not the only means of giving expression to self regarding sentiments. I have mentioned elsewhere how in the dance, although the movements are carried out in unison, each performer tries to surpass his companions in skill and grace.[27] The spectators applaud a specially good performance, and even clamour for a repetition. So too individual merit always gets its reward after a fishing expedition. The crew of a canoe pool their haul, but this is always displayed before it is divided, and the onlookers congratulate the person who has had most success. Again, wrestling matches and races of various kinds are sometimes held, and invariably the winners are publicly praised. Though the Ontong Javanese are usually modest, it is quite apparent that applause and praise are very much appreciated. Often the person concerned actually puffs out his chest and struts, after the fashion of some Europeans. Nevertheless, it is regarded as wrong for him to boast or be too ostentatious. He may perfume himself and wear ornaments, but not too many of them. The reaction of the community in general is well brought out by a race which is held every year. The men assemble, and at a given signal they all run off along the shore to a spot that has previously been decided upon. The man who arrives first returns direct to the village, but the rest proceed to gather green coconuts, which they bring back with them. The winner of the race, who naturally arrives at the village first, has the right to claim a certain number of nuts from each man. Actually no limit is set, but if he takes too many, or even any at all from old men, the applause with which the women have been showering him for having won the race is at once turned to reproof for his greed. I noticed that if a race had been held, and I came along afterwards and inquired who had won, the winner usually lowered his head and left his companions to tell me of his achievement. This, I learnt, was regarded as the proper thing to do.

It seems clear that if vanity and pride were undisciplined, or given no socially approved outlet, then the community would be bound to suffer, for individuals would seek to express themselves at the expense of their fellows. Quarrels would be the result, and the regular routine of the community would be upset. It is thus probable that every society has institutions and customs comparable to the gift exchange, the dance, the display of the catch of fish, and the races and wrestling matches of Ontong Java. Generally one of these institutions is strongly emphasized, so that the whole society appears to revolve around it. This is what has occurred with regard to the purchase of copper plates and the destruction of property among the Kwakiutl, and with regard to the Sukwe of the Banks Islands. The gift exchange then, by opening up a way to the peaceful satisfaction of self regarding sentiments, is to be regarded as working in the main for law and order. At the same time it acts as a pleasant contrast to the monotonous round of everyday tasks.

The description will also have made it evident that gift exchanges are a spur to industry, for, as I pointed out, if they did not take place many of the coconuts would formerly have been left lying on the ground. The area under taro cultivation would even have been reduced. Too often one finds that European governments of aboriginal communities, and missionaries also, have the impression that the natives are lazy, when, in fact, they have themselves destroyed all the ambition of the natives by stamping out the very institutions around which their industry was previously concentrated.[28] Of course, the native is lazy at plantation work because it is not only monotonous, but without any interest to him in itself, and, since he fails to comprehend most of the implications of our economic system, the monetary reward is an insufficient inducement for him to exert all his energies and to do his best.

In addition to serving as a useful outlet for vanity and as a spur to industry, gift exchanges also help to bind together the two groups concerned. Joint families united by a marriage have a host of obligations towards each other, the chief of which is to give any assistance required in time of misfortune or trouble. Thus if a large number of the coconuts of one group are destroyed perhaps by a severe storm, then the members will be assisted by their relatives by marriage. Similarly, if for some reason a group decides to attack another, as may occur, for example, if one of its members has been injured unlawfully by a person of that group, then again the relatives by marriage will also lend aid. The fact that wealth in the form of food gifts is continually being exchanged actually brings their responsibilities concretely before the eyes of the two groups of people, for they receive presents from the individuals whom they are bound to help, and also hand over presents to them. Gift exchanges thus serve to remind those who participate of their mutual obligations. Receiving a gift also generates goodwill towards the donors in the minds of the recipients, and hence makes them the more willing to carry out those obligations. This is perhaps even more particularly the case when the gifts consist of food, for few activities create more pleasant feelings than eating.

The successful binding together of the relatives of the husband and wife is very important from the point of view of their child, for he is in many ways completely dependent upon them both. As we have seen, both actually contribute towards the presentations his father will make at his betrothal and marriage.

In making a presentation of coconuts on behalf of his son a man has to have the help of several of his relatives, for by himself he cannot collect enough to make much of a showing. This help is given by the direction of the headman of his joint family. The men themselves are willing to obey his orders in the matter because they know that when they have to make a presentation they will then in turn be sure of the co-operation of the man they are helping. Loyalty to kindred, of course, also tempers their obedience. The gift exchange therefore leads to reciprocal ties between members of the joint family. These ties in turn help to increase the cohesion of the group, so that other communal activities can be carried out harmoniously, and any troubles faced by the members with a united front. Some coconuts are also contributed by the mother's brother of the person on whose behalf the presentation is being made. This man is also assisted by his relatives, so reciprocal ties unite the members of his joint family also. This contribution is again a concrete reminder of the strong bonds which join a person to the relatives of his mother and her brother. These relatives are, as a matter of fact, only slightly less important than the relatives of his father, that is, his own joint family. Nevertheless, he is not under any obligation to assist them when they make a collection of coconuts for a formal gift, though he does assist them at other times.

The presentation of taro puddings on a woman's behalf leads to similar results to those already described, only here the women of the joint family are involved instead of the men. They, however, are of more importance to her in everyday matters.[29]

By this time it is I think abundantly clear that ceremonial gift exchanges play a very useful part in the lives of the natives of Ontong Java. The marriage exchange has an additional part to play.

In Africa it is the custom for a gift, known as the bride price or bride wealth, to be presented by the bridegroom's relatives only. This, it has been shown, serves as an indemnity to the bride's family group for the loss of an economic worker, and also stabilizes the union, for if the marriage is dissolved and the man is to blame he loses his wealth as well as his wife, while if the woman is to blame the wealth has to be refunded. Naturally the husband is unwilling to risk so serious a loss, and the relatives of the wife try to bring her up well so that no faults will be found by her husband on closer acquaintance. In Ontong Java there is no indemnity, unless perhaps we regard the exchange as a double indemnity. However, the fact that the relatives of both the contracting parties make a presentation means that the marriage is thereby stabilized, for if divorce takes place both sides lose their goods.[30] The exchange also serves to legalize the union and legitimize any subsequent children. It might perhaps be more correct to say that this is done by the marriage ceremony as a whole, but the exchange is actually by far the most important part of this ceremony. As we saw, if a couple should live together without the requisite exchanges being carried out they would be regarded as social outcasts.

Another point requiring comment is the fact that an exchange is not a part of the funeral ritual on a man's death unless he is survived by a widow. This funeral exchange helps to remind the joint family of the dead man that an obligation rests on them to help the woman to whom one of their number was married, for the widow is provided for by contributions of food from the dead man's relatives as well as from her own relatives. If she is already dead, naturally there is no need for this reminder.

In the early part of the paper I mentioned various ceremonial gift exchanges of central Polynesia. From Samoa there is ample evidence to show that exchanges took place on occasions similar to those of Ontong Java—namely, betrothal, marriage, birth, and death. In Samoa also the persons making a gift were assisted by their relatives, and prestige was derived from giving generously. From the other central Polynesian communities the evidence is not so clear, but it is more than probable that conditions were in broad outline much the same, though probably there would be differences of detail. It is therefore legitimate to conclude that ceremonial exchanges played much the same part throughout this Polynesian area, serving as a useful outlet for vanity and pride, providing a spur to industry, cementing the bonds uniting groups, and helping to bind relatives firmly together.

Hitherto the exchanges considered have been associated with transition rites. In Ontong Java during the annual festival exchanges of a slightly different type were carried out.[31] It will be of interest to examine these, because they played a different part in the social life.

The festival, known as *sanga*, lasted about a month, on every day of which a different ceremony was carried out. For the occasion the people always assembled at one of the main villages. However, while the first of the ceremonies were being performed many of the people were as a rule still on the outlying islands. It was always the custom for a man on arrival at the main village to take a small present of coconuts to the sisters of his wife. They in return presented him with small taro puddings. In the main village marriage is matrilocal, and several families share the one dwelling. This means that during the festival a man will live in the same house as his wife's sisters and their families. The customary exchange of presents therefore had the effect of generating a feeling of goodwill towards one another in the minds of the individuals who would have to live together. The gifts from the men made their sisters-in-law kindly disposed towards them, and those from the women made their brothers-in-law kindly disposed in their turn. Friendly feelings of this type were naturally of value, for they prevented quarrels, thus enabling household affairs to be carried on without unpleasant interruptions. Nevertheless, no special prestige was derived from giving liberally, and no co-operation of members of the joint family was necessary to produce the goods for presentation in the first place.

Later on in the festival there were two other exchanges which differed from those relating to transition rites. In order to understand the following description of these exchanges it is necessary to understand that each main village had four club houses, membership of which was hereditary. There was no rule that a man might marry only a woman whose father belonged to a club house different from his own, but this did often occur. In preparation for both of the exchanges the married men went out fishing and the married women dug taro and cooked puddings. When all was ready the headmen of the joint families retired to the club houses. For the first exchange at a given signal from an official known as the *ka'ala*[32] the men carried their strings of fish from their canoes and presented them to the headmen of their respective joint families. The fish were piled in a heap outside each of the club houses. Meantime the women also brought their puddings, which they presented, not to the headmen of their joint families, but to the headmen of the joint families of their respective husbands. The puddings also were piled outside each of the club houses. First setting aside portions for the priests, the headmen, and himself, the *ka'ala* now distributed the food. Each man received pudding from the heap outside the club house of the headman of his own joint family, while each woman received fish from the heap outside the club house of the headman of her husband's joint family. Thus each man gave fish to his headman and received pudding from him in return, while each woman gave pudding to the headman of her husband and received back fish. In the other exchange the men presented their fish to the headmen of the joint families of their respective wives, while the women presented puddings to the headmen of their own joint families. In return the men were presented with pudding and the women with fish.

The presentations were made publicly, and if a person gave less than a certain amount his reputation inevitably suffered. If, however, he gave too much he made himself equally noticeable as a braggart. The upper limit was usually about half as much again as the lower.

The food a person received was not eaten by himself alone, but taken back home to form part of the usual evening meal. Looked at from the purely utilitarian point of view these exchanges were therefore also quite useless, for each household in the end got back very nearly as much as its individual members had given away. Nevertheless, the community does again seem to have derived benefit from the transactions. The presentation of a gift to the headman of the joint family served as a reminder of a person's obligations and duties towards his kindred, while the presentation to the headman of the joint family of the consort served equally as a reminder of the obligations and duties towards the members of that group. The fact that a gift was made in return demonstrated in a very pleasant way there were also reciprocal obligations, of which, of course, the headmen were at the same time reminded. These exchanges, in other words, served to place emphasis on the bonds created by blood and marriage ties, and also helped to cement them.

It would be possible to go on and describe even more ceremonial gift exchanges, but this seems scarcely necessary, for we have completed the task we set before ourselves and demonstrated fully that their uselessness is indeed more apparent than real. There is no information from central Polynesia, it is true, relating to exchanges of the type discussed in the last couple of pages, but, as I have indicated, there are so many similarities in culture throughout the area that such exchanges may have taken place, and in that case they would have been of the same importance and value. It is to be feared that in the past exchanges were often suppressed by Europeans who misunderstandingly considered them extravagant, unnecessary, and wasteful, when, in fact, they were to a large extent the very reverse.

NOTES

1. This paper was read before a meeting of Section F at the Australian and New Zealand Science Congress held in Sydney in August, 1932.
2. G. Turner, *Nineteen Years in Polynesia,* 187.
3. *Ibid.*, 188.
4. G. Brown, *Melanesians and Polynesians,* 120 *sq*.
5. M. Mead, *Social Organization of Manua* (Bishop Museum Bulletin 76), 96.
6. Turner, *op. cit.*, 178.
7. Mead, *op. cit.*, 89.
8. *Ibid.*, 100. Information relating to gift exchanges in Samoa will be found also in J. B. Stair, *Old Samoa,* 175 and 180, and in A. Krämer, *die Samoa-Inseln,* II, 52 *sqq*. and 105.
9. E. W. Gifford, *Tongan Society* (Bishop Museum Bulletin 6I), 192.
10. T. Henry, *Ancient Tahiti* (Bishop Museum Bulletin 48), 282 *sqq.*
11. *Ibid.*, 187 and 292.
12. Cross cousin marriage was occasionally practised in Tonga, but in the other communities marriage was permitted only with distant relatives, or persons who were not related.
13. E. S. C. Handy, *Native Culture in the Marquesas* (Bishop Museum Bulletin 9), 212.
14. R. Firth, *Primitive Economics of the New Zealand Maori,* Chap. XII.
15. However, since *tonga* was manufactured by women, and *oloa* by men, a family in which one sex predominated was apt to be somewhat handicapped.
16. I shall not deal with non-economic gift exchanges amongst the Maori because the subject has been discussed at length by Dr. Firth in his *Primitive Economics of the New Zealand Maori.* Dr. Firth also treats fully the feast, with which exchanges in many parts of Polynesia are allied. The feasts of central Polynesia are discussed in the paper of F. L. S. Bell, The Place of Food in the Social Life of Central Polynesia, *Oceania,* II, 117.
17. Details concerning conditions of work, time spent in the field etc., will be found in my Social Organization of Ontong Java, *Oceania,* I, 399.
18. Brother and sister avoidance is the rule in Ontong Java, and men consequently never have anything whatever to do with the marriage arrangements of their sisters.
19. I regret to state that I have apparently lost the notes containing the actual recipe for this taro pudding. There are, of course, several different recipes in use, but puddings intended for presentation on occasions of this kind are always made according to one particular recipe. Strangely enough, this is not the one regarded by the natives as the most delicious. In this latter the coconut cream is not mixed with the tubers until they have first been cooked and pounded to a stiff paste. A few very hot stones are put into the paste, and the cream added. The heat of the stones serves to clarify the cream, and afterwards they are removed.
20. *Vide* also my Sexual Life of the Natives of Ontong Java, *Journal of the Polynesian Society,* XL, 25 *sq.*
21. Made on looms from hibiscus fibre by the men.
22. *Kama laue.*
23. Although the present of the man's father appears to be much greater than that of the girl's father, it must not be considered as in any way a bride price. Actually the two gifts were of approximately equivalent value.
24. When he realized how unpopular his action was he retired to his island property and remained there for some months. It was therefore impossible to observe his demeanour in the face of public disapproval.
25. This does not mean, naturally, that a man's reputation is in direct proportion to his wealth. Provided he is rich, however, and other circumstances are favourable, then his reputation will probably be in direct proportion to his generosity.
26. [In omitted text.]
27. Tribal Ceremonies at Ontong Java, *Journal of the Royal Anthropological Institute,* LXI, 1931, 53.
28. Thus the destruction of property and the purchase of copper plates has been forbidden among the Kwakiutl Indians, as has feasting, an institution of similar function, amongst many Melanesian tribes.
29. This does not mean that she is completely independent of her male relatives, but there is a rigid division of labour between the sexes, and most communal tasks are carried out separately. Women are, nevertheless, dependent upon men for certain foods and for protection.

On the other hand, men are in many ways dependent upon their female relatives.

30. In the case of divorce neither the goods nor their equivalent are returned.

31. I have described this festival in a paper entitled Tribal Ceremonies at Ontong Java, *op. cit.* Very few of the ceremonies originally performed in connection with the festival are carried out today.

32. The *ka'ala* was the executive officer of the principal priest (*maakua*), to whom he stood in the relationship of sister's son.

3

DIFFERENTIATION BY ADAPTATION IN POLYNESIAN SOCIETIES[1]

Marshall D. Sahlins

This paper takes as fact the genetic relationship between Polynesian cultures. All Polynesian cultures spring from a common source; all are members of a single cultural genus. In the course of time, these cultures have become differentiated so that they now appear as species variations within the genus. My thesis is that Polynesian cultural differentiation was produced by process of adaptation under varying technological and environmental conditions. A single culture has filled in and adapted to a variety of ecological niches. By clear, strong and close analogy to organic evolution, this process is designated "adaptive differentiation."

My paper is specifically concerned with forms of social organization differentiated by adaptation in Polynesia, most frequently with the structure of descent units and the manner of their combination in socio-political entities.

Two types of descent unit are found on the Polynesian volcanic islands. I shall call them "ramage" and "truncated descent line." Ramages occur in Hawaii, Tonga, Tahiti, Mangaia, Mangareva, Marquesas, New Zealand, Tikopia, Easter Island, and in other less well known islands. Truncated descent lines are found in Samoa, Uvea and Futuna. The ecologies of these two sets of islands will be shown to differ with some consistency.

A ramage is a common descent group internally ranked by a principle of genealogical seniority. Succession to important positions in ramages is by rule of primogeniture. As a corollary, in a ramage a senior line of first sons is distinguished from a number of junior lines, the latter tracing descent to collaterals of the main line. Every line is ranked according to the respective birth order of ancestral figures, and every individual in a ramage holds a different rank—one precisely proportionate to his distance from the senior line. This is the outstanding indicative feature of ramages.

A ramage is an indefinitely expandable, segmentary descent group. It can

Reproduced by permission of Marshall D. Sahlins from the *Journal of the Polynesian Society,* 66:291-300 (1957).

disperse over a section of a large island, a whole island or even a group of islands without changing character as a single descent unit. The entire autonomous polity, such as a Marquesan so-called "tribe" or a Hawaiian island, may be simply a maximal range. At the same time, natal members of a small group of households would be a minimal ramage. Between the minimal and maximal ramages may be others of intermediate order, formed through combination of ramage segments. Ramage expandability is achieved by the maintenance of unity between segmenting branches. Two fissioning units usually remain linked in a ramage of higher order. No new principles of organization are introduced to achieve recombination. One segmenting group becomes the junior line of the other; it will be led by a person whose ancestor stands as younger brother to the ancestor of the chief of the senior line. Segmentation at any order of size will produce the same results until environmental, economic or other factors decree a limit on expansion.

With their characteristics of expandability and internal ranking, ramages are ideally suited to act as political units. One or a few large size ramages may serve as the primary elements of an independent polity. High chieftainship in the polity corresponds to leadership of these ramages. Lower offices fall to heads of segments of the maximal ramage. Chiefly positions are usually linked with territorial as well as kinship integrity, for as a ramage expands, it tends to disperse exclusively over a given locale.[2]

A truncated descent line is a small localized common descent group. It differs from a ramage by absence of internal ranking according to genealogical principles. Although descent lines supply chiefs in territorial units, succession is determined primarily by leadership qualifications, not by rule of primogeniture. Correspondingly, distinction of senior and junior line is not made.

Truncated descent lines do not exclusively disperse over a large domain. Rather, they combine with like but unrelated groups in nucleated village communities. For example, Samoan villages are composed of five to twenty-five descent lines of ten to fifty persons each. These are not mutually related by common descent. Truncated descent lines are not indefinitely expandable. When one divides into two groups which remain in the same community, the common descent ties between them weaken and eventually dissolve. Firth has labelled this type of fission "definitive segmentation" or "gemmation."[3]

A descent line in one village, however, can be affiliated with like groups in other villages by bonds of common ancestry. A multi-local unit of this type occurs in Samoa, where it is called *sa*, although it is absent in Uvea and Futuna, other islands with truncated local descent lines. The descent lines of the Samoan *sa* are not ranked by genealogical priority, in fact the genealogical relations between them may be variously phrased. Unlike a maximal ramage, a *sa* is not a political unit; it is but a part of the village and district organization which includes many *sa*. The extension of a *sa* in different villages of an area probably enhances the district's solidarity. But a *sa* does not act as a collectivity in any way, and may be distinguished from a maximal ramage as a kin category as opposed to a kin group.

The political organization of truncated descent lines is thus different from ramages. The fundamental political units are village aggregations of unrelated (excluding affinal ties) groups. Each village is ruled by a council of titled men, the titles being held by leaders of the descent lines. The standing of a local line depends on which title in the village hierarchy it has captured, and its success in raising the prestige of that title. The status of the title, however, varies quite independently of the genealogical position of the holder's ancestors. The villages are grouped in districts ruled by councils formed by the same principles.

Neither exogamy nor endogamy are indicative features of ramages and truncated descent lines. Both are agamous. Recent discussions of non-unilineal kin groups in Oceania[4] make a brief aside on this question necessary. In most cases of ramages and descent lines, patrilineal descent is the norm. In some instances, however, affiliation is gained by tracing descent through females, this frequently being preceded by a form of post-marital residence other than the usual patrilocality. Where residence is permitted to qualify membership, the descent groups may become *de facto* non-unilineal. In the present discussion internal ranking and segmentary features of descent groups are at issue and "ramage" and "truncated descent lines" are discriminated principally by these criteria. Ramages and truncated descent lines as here understood may be unilineal or non-unilineal. Characteristics of lineality, however, are not features with which we are directly concerned at the moment.[5]

Ramages and truncated descent lines are consistently associated with distinct ecologies and hence have probably differentiated by adaptation. Ramages are usually found with intensive exploitation of dispersed resources—i.e., where from coast line fishing to inland taro or yam cultivation, a number of different zones of production are encountered. The spread of environmental opportunities is so great, and the techniques for dealing with them so developed, that a domestic group cannot cope with the entire range of production. Instead, households tend to specialize in food and goods production according to the relative accessibility of resources. Correspondingly, dispersed hamlet occupation rather than nucleated village settlement is usually indicated. Diversified, scattered zones of production can be documented for ramage-organized Hawaii, Tonga, Marquesas, Mangaia, Tahiti, Mangareva and New Zealand, all but the last also having dispersed settlement.[6] In Hawaii, for example, great variations in altitude, rainfall, soil type, water supply and temperature produce a multitude of ecological niches, to exploit which the Hawaiians selected from an impressive crop range.[7] Specialization in some types of food production existed at the household level, and gift exchanges of different foods, between coastal and inland members of the same ramage, occurred.[8] Evidence of comparable exchange practices may be had for Easter Island, Mangareva, Tahiti, the Marquesas and Tonga.[9]

Ramages are well constituted for exploitation of different, scattered resources. The ties maintained between segmented groups facilitates the distribution of regionally diversified products. This distribution may take the form of gift exchange, as mentioned. It is also achieved by periodic accumulation and redistribution of surpluses by a central agency, namely the head of the ramage concerned. Redistribution is organized through ramage genealogical hierarchies. Lesser chiefs collect goods from lower order ramages and pass them on to the higher chiefs of major and maximal segments. The same hierarchy is used in reverse for redistribution. Widespread redistribution occurs as a safeguard against famine, and in conjunction with religious occasions and communal labour. The net effect of the process is equalization of consumption among kinsmen. Such economic interdependence is grounded on corporate land holding practices. Title to all land used by a high order ramage is vested in its paramount chief, while lesser chiefs hold title of the land of their ramage segments. This system of overlapping titles and accompanying administrative rights descends to the head of the domestic group. The internal ranking of ramages can be understood as an organizational mechanism instituting advantageous forms of distribution and land administration.

Truncated descent lines, by contrast, are associated with an ecology wherein resource zones are not widely separated, but are clustered such that all domestic groups can engage in the entire range of production activities. Truncated descent lines typically occur on islands where narrow concentric zones of exploitation concentrate near the coast. All resources being accessible, small groups tend to be self-sufficient and population nucleates in village form, usually in fertile valley mouths. For example, in Futuna, the descent lines are settled side by side, each at the head of an inland-extending land strip which it claims. Cultivation was largely confined to the area near the shore and each descent line holding contained a cross section of all resource zones.[10] A similar situation can be noted in Samoa, where steep mountain gradients limit effective inland production.[11] As in Futuna, Samoan domestic groups are largely self-sufficient.

Production in clustered resource zones is related to structural features of truncated descent lines. Segmenting lines are apt to move into similar ecological areas and become self-sufficient. Economic ties between fissioning units would not be frequently activated, hence kinship bonds would tend to dissolve and descent groups remain small and discrete. Correspondingly each descent line is a distinct corporate proprietary unit, title being vested in the leader. There is no level of economic incorporation beyond the localized descent line except that of the village, and this only in the weaker sense that the local aggregate of descent lines will collectively defend the village land. Redistribution of surplus goods occurs, but it differs in character and organization from ramage redistribution. Often the accumulation is undertaken mainly by a single descent line, the goods being then widely dispersed in the community. Redistribution of its surplus is in fact the major means by which a descent line raises its title in the village. Succession to titles on the basis of organizing ability (rather than primogeniture) is related to this process. Guaranteed effective leadership is not only necessary in order to maintain the group's self-sufficiency, but also in order to accumulate surplus and thereby compete successfully politically.

There are three possible exceptions to the hypothesis that ramage and truncated descent line structures have differentiated by adaptation to dispersed and concentrated resource exploitation, respectively. These are: Tikopia, Uvea, and Easter Island. In these three the ecological situation is not clearly one of concentrated nor scattered production, but appears intermediate. The selective pressures are minimal or indifferent. Under indifferent selective pressures, either truncated descent line or ramage organization can be expected, depending on the cultural tradition previous to occupation. This explanation would account for Easter Island ramages, the culture having been derived from ramage-organized central Polynesia.[12] Tikopia and Uvea may also be so understood but their history is too little known. At present, they are an unexplained residue.

The kin and socio-political systems in the low coral atolls of Polynesia frequently differ markedly from high island organizations. Yet it can be stated with some assurance that most if not all Polynesian atolls were settled from high islands, often in the not distant past. It appears that atoll organizations have been differentiated by adaptation to atoll environments.

Low island ecologies consistently differ from high island ecologies. In contrast to the volcanic groups, atolls usually have: very limited arable land, small and sporadic surplus production, chronic scarcity periods, and peculiarities of resource distribution. Given these selective factors a specific direction of modification of atoll social organization can be posited. In general terms, a highly adaptive organization in areas of extreme land limitation and food scarcity would place a premium on personnel organization which exploits each resource to its full, and facilitates rapid and equitable goods distribution. Ideally this implies particular alignments of people controlling and working particular resources. With small surpluses, these alignments, however, could not specialize in production of one food and exchange it for others. But if the recruitment of membership in such groups were based on different qualifications, such as descent, age class and residence, then each person could be a member of all groups and automatically share in all economic activities. Thus, an ideally adapted atoll social system is one of a multiplicity of socio-economic groups formed on different principles and connected with production and distribution of different goods or on different scales.

There is a further selective factor in atolls. Being small and exposed, low islands are subject to great devastation from tropical cyclones and tidal waves. Population, material culture and food supply can be decimated overnight. Moreover, almost as if tradition were literally swept away as well, curiously rapid culture changes have been known to follow such cyclonic disasters. In some documented cases, these changes can be construed adaptive. For example, after the 1903 hurricane in Raroia in the Tuamotus, the culture quickly adjusted to intruding European economic conditions.[13] The Raroians largely abandoned subsistence production in favour of selling copra and buying food in trading stores. Coupled with the loss of old time political and religious leaders in the cyclone, profound cultural changes ensued. Danielsson writes: "The cyclone of 1903 constitutes therefore on Raroia, as on many other atolls, a serious break with the old culture. From now on the islanders lived, at least materially, in a western world."[14] Without insisting on the analogy, the process slightly resembles small population effect in producing rapid shifts in gene frequencies in organic populations, and may be similarly designated.

Small population effect has implications for aboriginal organization in the low islands. The atolls were originally equipped with social groups, such as ramages and descent lines, developed in high island ecological contexts. Presumably these organizations, backed by tradition, might only gradually be changed or abandoned to suit the new conditions. But decimation of the atoll—including perhaps death of persons of authority in the old structure—permits complete rearrangment of the organization. From elements of the original system, the society may be restructured in the direction of finer adaptation to low island selective pressures.

Generalizing from this discussion, the following hypotheses are introduced to explain differentiation of kin and political systems in the atolls: (1) In proportion to which the ecological conditions of low productivity, land scarcity and chronic shortages occur, one would expect typical high island organization, as ramage or descent line systems, to be modified; (2) Other factors being equal, the longer the period of settlement, the more likely this effect; (3) The same result is expectable if the atoll has been subject to devastation or small population effect; (4) The tendency in modification would be toward formation of intricate social systems combining different types of groups, each associated with specific economic activities.

Consideration of the several Polynesian low islands ethnographically studied seems to corroborate these expectations, although the evidence is not sufficient to warrant a verdict of "definitely proved." Among the atolls of Tongareva, Manihiki-Rakahanga, Tokelau, Ontong Java and Pukapuka, the last two appear to have been longest inhabited, according to linguistic and genealogical evidence, and show the greatest divergence from high island social systems.[15] In Pukapuka, besides domestic household units, there are matrilineages, patrilineages, age grades, and distinct village and island territorial groupings. Every individual belongs to each type of group; each type of group acts as a unit in property control, production and/or distribution. For example, the patrilineages control and work land strips mostly devoted to coconut cultivation, the matrilineages control excavated taro pits, the villages administer reserve lands of taro, coconuts and wild foods, and the old and young men's age classes organize deep sea fishing and island-wide distribution of fish taken.[16] No features of Pukapukan organization are entirely unique; all have analogues in other low or high islands. In Pukapuka, old elements of Polynesian organization have been recombined into a social structure finely attuned to the exigencies of atoll life. Significantly, Pukapukan traditions record a catastrophic seismic wave about 350 years ago which reduced the population to fifteen men, two women and the remnants of their families and reduced the resources to next to nothing.[17] Many changes in social organization and land tenure are said to have followed the disaster. It is likely that the tidal wave was instrumental in creating the divergent Pukapukan organization. Other long inhabited low islands, such as Ontong Java[18] and the Gilberts[19] (to move slightly out of our area), show a similar trend toward the formation of a complex system of interlocking social groups.

Tongareva, Manihiki and Tokelau, all populated in the main one to three hundred years later than Pukapuka, by genealogical reckoning, are structurally closer to the high islands. None of these appear to have been subject to small population effect. Tongareva has a full-fledged ramage system, only slightly modified from the high island prototype. Notably, ecological conditions on Tongareva more nearly than on all other atolls approximate those associated with high island ramage systems. Total land area is large for an atoll (over five square miles) and land shortage is not a pressing problem.[20] Moreover, the important crop, coconuts, and rich sea food areas are dispersed over the islets, dictating a scattered settlement pattern precisely like that usually found with ramages.

The smaller atolls of Tokelau and Manihiki-Rakahanga show greater modification of volcanic island social structure. In my estimate of the evidence, the organizations of these two islands are very similar. If so, this is a case of convergence, since Tokelau traditions point to descent line Samoa as the original homeland of the major part of the population, while Manihiki was settled from ramage-organized Rarotonga. But it should be cautioned that the ethnographic accounts of social organization in both cases are unclear and entangled with contradictory statements.[21] To some extent, our knowledge must rest on interpretation of the evidence. In this brief space it is unfortunately impossible to do more than advance my notion of the social system and state its adaptive features.

In both Manihiki and Tokelau, small size descent groups are united in village settlements. In Tokelau (at least in the Fakaofu atoll of the group) the descent groups appear to be truncated, in Manihiki they appear to be sections of larger, segmentary units. In both instances, the descent groups have a marked bilateral ingredient produced through frequent uxorilocal residence and subsequent incorporation of uterine relatives in the localized groups. Goodenough has classified the Tokelau descent unit as non-unilinear of his *bwoti* type,[22] i.e., a group composed of all those using a particular land tract by right of descent, through males or females, from the original holder. By my reading of the evidence, the Tokelau unit, and that of Manihiki as well, would belong in Goodenough's *kainga* type, all those *residing* on the land of their ancestor. The *kainga* is not simply an internally unstructural non-unilinear group. It has a singular constitution deriving from the fact that succession to leadership of the group is patrilineal. Since membership must be qualified by residence, this implies that the senior segment of the group continually resides patrilocally. The result is what might be called a "stem lineage." A stem lineage has a core of patrilineal relatives supplying the lineage head—in Tokelau and Manihiki evidently through primogeniture. To this patrilineal stem are attached cognates of various description, affiliated with full and equal rights save that of succession. The lineage holds land corporately, but administration is vested in and monopolized by the core line.

In Manihiki and Tokelau, the stem lineage is usually formed and maintained by mechanisms permitting patrilocal residence for oldest sons despite widespread practice of uxorilocal residence. In Manihiki the rule is simply that oldest sons live patrilocally after marriage, while younger sons have a uxorilocal option. In Tokelau the rules are more complicated as it sometimes happens that the father of a would-be lineage head is living with his wife's family. In that case, the oldest son either builds a house by choice on his father's natal group's land, or is adopted by his father's sister and later brings his wife to reside there. (This, incidentally, is a rare if not unique case of a type of amitalocal residence.) Another alternative is that the male head of the group lives uxorilocally and only nominally controls his natal unit's land, while effective leadership is vested in a female, his sister or father's sister.[23] Whatever path is chosen, the net result is a stem lineage.

Stem lineages incorporate features of high island organization. For example, segmentary stem lineages of the Manihiki type would closely resemble non-unilinear ramages in constitution, differing from these only in the extent of ranking by genealogical seniority and perhaps the extent of non-unilineality. Conceivably, stem lineages were formed from high island ramages or descent lines in the more limited economic opportunities of Tokelau and Manihiki. Differential familial growth makes it difficult to maintain a kin group of definite character in an area of extreme land limitation. On the other hand, a centralized authority structure regulating production and controlling land appears favoured by these conditions—especially considering that the major cultivated food, coconut, is a permanent crop. The stem lineage is a compromise. The patrilineal core regulates land use, while freedom is given to those distant from the main line to affiliate wherever there is available arable land. An equitable land-population ratio results without sacrifice of kin-group stability or of the organizational requirements for production and land control in a scarcity situation.

I shall now briefly summarize my major conclusions. On the Polynesian high island, two characteristic forms of kin group occur, ramage and truncated descent line, which consistently integrate in political aggregates of different form . These types are usually found in different ecological conditions; ramages with intensively exploited scattered resources, descent lines with nucleated resources. The two types, it is concluded, have differentiated by adaptation from a single proto-Polynesian source. The Polynesian atoll social systems derive from the high islands and typically show divergence through adaptation to the unfavourable atoll opportunities. This divergence becomes more marked in proportion to the length of time of occupation, and is occasionally facilitated by small population effect. The direction of extreme modification of low island organization is toward an intricate system of interlocking social groups, each group tending to be exclusively associated with control of different resources and specific forms of production and distribution.

NOTES

1. The description and interpretation of Polynesian social systems contained in this paper modifies, in places extends, and generally develops materials embodied in the latter half of my monograph, *Social Stratification in Polynesia* (1957, . . .), which was originally submitted as a Ph. D. dissertation at Columbia University in 1954. More complete ethnographic documentation than can be given here will be found in that monograph.

2. In various Polynesian islands there are significant deviations from the typical pattern of ramage territorial integrity. Ramage organization also varies in the extent to which incorporation of uterine relatives in the group is permitted. Another differential is the degree to which chiefly positions in the society are monopolized by members of a single minimal ramage, thus producing superstratified ramages. More comprehensive treatment of these differences will be found in Sahlins 1957. cf. Burrows 1939, and Firth 1957.

3. Firth 1957:7.

4. Goodenough 1955; Firth 1957.

5. I am thus departing from Firth's recent redefinition of "ramage" as a non-unilineal kin group—in contrast to "lineage," a strictly unilineal group (Firth 1957). My use of "ramage" corresponds closely to Firth's original usage (Firth 1936:367–372).

6. Sahlins 1957: *passim.*

7. Handy 1940.

8. Handy 1950:178.

9. Routledge 1919:218; Buck 1938:36, 166, 199; Handy 1932:69; Ellis 1853 vol. 1:138; Smith 1813:32; Handy 1923:168; Gifford 1929:146, 177.

10. Burrows 1936:81.

11. Coulter 1941:19, 26, 29; Keesing 1934:265.

12. Sahlins 1955.

13. Danielsson 1955:102.

14. ibid.

15. Pukapukan traditional history and genealogies—admittedly not very reliable sources for dating—would date the settlement at the beginning of the fourteenth century (E. and P.

Beaglehole 1938:378). This appears to be the longest period of uninterrupted occupation among atolls within the Polynesian triangle. The dates of settlement of other atolls are noted by Sahlins 1957.

16. E. and P. Beaglehole 1938.
17. ibid.:386.
18. Hogbin 1930–1931.
19. Goodenough 1955.
20. As witnessed by wide swaths of uncultivated lands used to demarcate boundaries (Buck 1932a).
21. Buck 1932b; MacGregor 1937.
22. Goodenough 1955:76–77.
23. MacGregor 1937:43, 46–47.

BIBLIOGRAPHY

BEAGLEHOLE, ERNEST AND PEARL, 1938. *Ethnology of Pukapuka.* Bernice P. Bishop Museum Bulletin 150, Honolulu.

BUCK, SIR PETER H. (Te Rangi Hiroa), 1932a. *Ethnology of Tongareva.* Bernice P. Bishop Museum Bulletin 92, Honolulu.

———1932b. *Ethnology of Manihiki and Rakahanga.* Bernice P. Bishop Museum Bulletin 99, Honolulu.

———1938. *Ethnology of Mangareva.* Bernice P. Bishop Museum Bulletin 157, Honolulu.

BURROWS, EDWIN G., 1936. *Ethnology of Futuna.* Bernice P. Bishop Museum Bulletin 138, Honolulu.

———1939. "Breed and Border in Polynesia." *American Anthropologist,* 41:1–21, Menasha.

COULTER, JOHN W., 1941. *Land Utilization in American Samoa.* Bernice P. Bishop Museum Bulletin 170, Honolulu.

DANIELSSON, BENGT, 1955. *Work and Life on Raroia.* Stockholm.

ELLIS, WILLIAM, 1853. *Polynesian Researches.* London.

FIRTH, RAYMOND, 1936. *We The Tikopia.* London.

———1957. "A Note on Descent Groups in Polynesia." *Man,* vol. 57, no. 2:4–8. London.

GIFFORD, EDWARD W., 1929. *Tongan Society.* Bernice P. Bishop Museum Bulletin 61, Honolulu.

GOODENOUGH, WARD H., 1955. "A Problem in Malayo-Polynesian Social Organization." *American Anthropologist,* 57:71–83, Menasha.

HANDY, E. S. CRAIGHILL, 1923. *The Native Culture in the Marquesas.* Bernice P. Bishop Museum Bulletin 9, Honolulu.

———1932. *Houses, Boats, and Fishing in the Society Islands.* Bernice P. Bishop Museum Bulletin 90, Honolulu.

———1940. *The Hawaiian Planter.* Bernice P. Bishop Museum Bulletin 161, Honolulu.

———1950. "The Hawaiian Family System." *Journal of the Polynesian Society,* 59:170–179, Wellington.

HOGBIN, H. IAN, 1930–31. "The Social Organization of Ontong Java." *Oceania,* 1:399–425, Melbourne.

KEESING, FELIX M., 1934. *Modern Samoa.* Stanford.

MACGREGOR, GORDON, 1937. *Ethnology of Tokelau Islands.* Bernice P. Bishop Museum Bulletin 146, Honolulu.

ROUTLEDGE, MRS. SCORESBY, 1919. *The Mystery of Easter Island.* London.

SAHLINS, MARSHALL D., 1955. "Esoteric Efflorescence in Easter Island." *American Anthropologist,* 57:1045-1052, Menasha.

———1957. . . . *Social Stratification in Polynesia.* American Ethnological Society Monograph, Seattle.

SMITH, WILLIAM, 1813. *Journal of a Voyage in the Missionary Ship "Duff."* New York.

FURTHER READINGS

Among the sources to be consulted on ecology and economics are geographical accounts, studies by ecologists, and anthropological reports. Historical sources, particularly the accounts of early explorers and naturalists, also provide a wealth of material. For general guidance, Taylor's *A Pacific Bibliography* should be consulted.

For a general geographical orientation to the area, the papers by Freeman, Bryan, and Bowman in *Geography of the Pacific*, edited by Freeman, can be consulted. An excellent starting point for getting into the ecological literature is *Man's Place in the Island Ecosystem*, edited by Fosberg. Wiens' *Atoll Environment and Ecology* and the issues of the *Atoll Research Bulletin* will provide further background on atoll ecology. Barrau's *Subsistence Agriculture in Polynesia and Micronesia* is a useful general guide to agricultural practices in the area, while more intensive studies are provided by Best's *Maori Agriculture*, Handy's *The Hawaiian Planter*, and the volume edited by Fox and Cumberland, *Western Samoa*. Nordhoff's "Notes on the Off-Shore Fishing of the Society Islands" presents an excellent description of the exploitation of marine life. An interesting early functional account of "The Place of Food in the Social Life of Central Polynesia" is provided by Bell. For detailed studies of Polynesian economic practices, the reader is directed to Firth's *Primitive Economics of the New Zealand Maori* and *Primitive Polynesian Economy* and to Danielsson's *Work and Life on Raroia*. Those desiring a more elaborate exposition of Sahlins' approach should consult his monograph *Social Stratification in Polynesia*.

PART II SOCIAL STRUCTURE

Polynesian social structure was thrust into the limelight of anthropological theory in the late 1950's. The issue which stirred debate was an attempt to interpret Polynesian social systems in terms of descent-group structure. Descent-group theory had reached its most elegant elaboration in the work of social anthropologists who had done field work in Africa. But, unlike most African societies, which contain mutually exclusive patrilineal or matrilineal kinship groups, Polynesian kin-group membership is generally ambiguous. Instead of being assigned at birth to a lineage or clan on the basis of genealogical descent, Polynesians have some option with regard to kin-group affiliation. Thus kin groups usually contain some individuals whose membership is based on paternal ties and others whose ties are maternal. As a result, Polynesian descent-group structure has been variously labeled as "bilateral," "cognatic," or "optative," but many social theorists have refused to consider corporate groups in which choice is possible as descent groups. They would restrict the concept to corporations which are mutually exclusive on genealogical grounds alone. Nevertheless, the majority of anthropologists who have worked in Polynesia (and elsewhere in Oceania where similar theoretical problems exist) feel that there is something to be gained by analyzing social systems in the region in terms of descent-group structure. Most of the papers in this part represent attempts to make sense out of the vagaries of Polynesian kin-group formation.

In the opening selection, Raymond Firth outlines the dimensions of bilateral descent groups. He attempts to move beyond the formal theoretical criteria that have been used by "orthodox" descent-group theorists toward an operational set of criteria. After presenting relevant considerations, he analyzes the social structure of the New Zealand Maori. Maori descent groups, or *hapu,* have long been a topic of theoretical discussion, and Firth's analysis represents a marked advance toward understanding the way in which they function.

The major features of Samoan social structure have also been the focus of considerable controversy. At one pole is Melvin Ember who, in the next two articles, presents a case for classifying Samoa as a nonunilinear society composed of three types of descent groups. The constitution of kin groups, he argues, militated against the development of a centralized political authority. Ember's position is disputed by Derek Freeman in the following paper. Freeman also takes issue with Sahlins' contention that Samoa did not have a ramified descent structure. He presents documentary evidence to support the view that Samoa did indeed have a ramified structure extending beyond the local level and that political integration in ancient Samoa embraced more than single communities. The issue has not yet been resolved.

In applying descent-group theory to the island of Rapa, Allan Hanson suggests that bilateral descent structures be classified along a continuum ranging from "exclusive" to "nonexclusive." He places Rapa toward the nonexclusive pole and demonstrates how, despite the problems inherent in the system, overlapping descent groups can function effectively in important areas like property distribution.

The final paper, by Rusiate Nayacakalou, presents an analysis of the Fijian social system, which, although not without its complexities, is somewhat more clear-cut than those previously described. If Fiji was indeed the immediate homeland of the Polynesians, as most prehistorians now believe, it may well be that the structure described by Nayacakalou represents a basic groundplan from which other Polynesian systems evolved.

4

BILATERAL DESCENT GROUPS: AN OPERATIONAL VIEWPOINT[1]

Raymond Firth

The study of descent groups of the kind commonly called 'bilateral' is still one of the least systematic aspects in the theoretical development of comparative kinship. Definition is much more difficult than with unilineal groups—hence the cautious, noncommittal appellation of 'non-unilineal'. Each of the major terms of the concept is still a matter for argument. In nearly every type of bilateral descent group the bilaterality is not complete. The notion of descent varies from a broad genealogical connexion[2] to the narrower politico-jural aspects of genealogical relations, or even to the unilineal transmission of rights in this field. In the criteria by which a group is recognized, the emphasis varies from a structural conceptualization with little concrete manifestation, to an operational viewpoint, looking at multiple interrelationships in corporate action. In the absence of clear agreement, every student has tended to impose his own illusion of order upon the material.

In recent years contributions, e.g. by Goodenough 1955; Davenport 1959; Fortes 1959; Murdock 1960; Pouwer 1958, 1960; Mabuchi 1960; Freeman 1961; Oosterwal 1961; Scheffler 1961, 1962; Ann Chowning 1962; Paula Brown 1962, have clarified the issues and provided new materials. In amplification of my own earlier work (Firth 1929, 1936, 1957), I give here an analysis of what I regard as significant factors in the operational definition of bilateral descent groups. I indicate also their relevance for consideration of the Maori *hapu,* and the bearing of this on the concept of descent.

For this analysis, in addition to terms defined earlier (e.g. Firth 1957), I use the following:

Universe of kin—all whom a person reckons as kin, an ego-oriented set of people in consanguineous and affinal relation to him. This set of people

Reproduced by permission of the Royal Anthropological Institute of Great Britain and Ireland and Raymond Firth from I. Schapera (ed.), *Studies in Kinship and Marriage* (Royal Anthropological Institute Occasional Paper No. 16, 1963, pp. 22–37). The notes have been numbered to run in sequence throughout the article.

might be termed his personal kin were it not for liability to confusion with the kindred, or personal kindred, as recently redefined. (I see no reason to restrict the term 'kin' to consanguines alone, so that it becomes a synonym for the latter.)

Personal kindred—all a person's cognates, an ego-oriented set of consanguine kin, patrilaterally and matrilaterally reckoned, i.e. by ascending and descending relationships (Freeman 1961; cf. Leach 1950, pp. 61, 72; Firth 1936, pp. 226–9).

Cognatic stock—the descendants of a married pair reckoned through both male and female offspring. This is a theoretical category, not necessarily a group. (See Radcliffe-Brown 1951, p. 22; Freeman 1961, p. 199.)

Cognatic descent group—those descendants of a married pair reckoned through both male and female offspring and operationally defined, so that they share common aims and actions in a corporate manner. This term is equivalent to bilateral descent group.

Descent—in general biological and social terms this means relationship by genealogical tie to an ancestor. In social anthropology descent as a process applies to the transmission of kin group membership, the content of which is socially defined in terms of rights, privileges and obligations corporately held. Leach (1962) has usefully referred to the 'assets' of such a group, and the concept of the descent principle as being essentially juridical has run through the literature from the little-known work of Starcke (1889, pp. 14, 127) to Fortes (1959, p. 207). But for purposes of discussion in this paper I reject the limitation of the notion of descent to unilineal groups alone.

CRITERIA IN DESCENT GROUP FORMATION

In discussing bilateral descent groups, it is necessary first to consider the nature of bilateral groups of the 'personal kindred' or 'ego-oriented' category, since some of the criteria used in the classification of descent groups in general do not clearly and completely demarcate them. (For example, corporateness may vary in degree—Firth 1959, pp. 215–6.) The difference between personal kindred (in whatever terms of 'conceptualization', 'configuration', 'network', it be described) and descent group, early indicated by Seebohm (1895, pp. 101–2), has often since been elaborated. But the degree of separation between these in practice may be partly a matter of the dimension of the kin universe. The structural components of a personal kindred in a small-scale society, such as an Australian tribe or an Oceanic island community, may not be very different from those in a moiety, marriage-section or lineage field. There is a different point of focus—the orientation is towards a single human ego at the centre of a social performance. There may be a different administrative head for the proceedings. Different operations take place—personal-focus operations of initiation or marriage, as against group-focus operations of, say, an aggressive kind in defending a land title. But many of the personnel may be the same, and some of the basic procedures may be the same. In exchange of goods, for instance, it may be difficult to distinguish between men in their personal capacity or as representatives of their descent groups.

In distinguishing between personal kindred and a corporate descent group it is sometimes implied that the personal kindred is a loose untidy collection of individuals from mother's mother's, mother's father's, father's mother's and father's father's descent groups, whereas a lineage is a tidy systematic set of people. It is often assumed for analytical purposes that in a lineage activity everyone present is a member of the lineage in question, and all members are assembled. Yet rarely are all the members of a corporate descent group actually gathered together in one place. They are often simply represented by some of their number; moreover, these are commonly diluted by the presence of wives and other affinal kin coming to help with the jobs at hand. In anthropological analysis the corporate descent group is an ideational concept; it is an abstract unit in relation to units of the same type. For the people themselves it has a unitary abstract character as a component in calculating marriage-exchanges, etc. Empirically it is a smaller unit, representative and operationally selective. But while jurally the whole descent group may act as a unit, in economic and political affairs it may not do so.

'Personal kindred', a selection from a theoretically bilateral universe of kin, is in action also an organizational regrouping, not just all persons of all lineages. We can say that, in such case, structural descent group units are organized within another frame of reference to constitute a man's personal kindred. It may be that an assembly of personal kindred is characterized by the people themselves as having as its components a set of lineages. But commonly a personal kindred, so selectively organized, is enlarged in action by affines from the more general universe of kin. We can distinguish personal kin in situations where some other type of kin unit is strongly structured, e.g. Tikopia, from that in situations where other types of kin units are weakly structured, e.g. the patrinominal 'family' in Britain. (By strongly and weakly structured is meant relatively many or few corporate functions and sanctions, and relatively great or little continuity.)

In societies with strongly structured descent groups it is usually clear from careful examination how far a body of people is operating as a collectivity of descent groups, and how far as a set of ego-oriented kin with the personal aspect of kin relations uppermost. In societies with weakly structured descent groups, e.g. large-scale industrial societies, however, this may not be at all easy to ascertain—hence the question how far descent groups as such really exist in a Western society such as Britain.

My major problem here may be phrased thus. Kinship is bilateral. Out of a bilaterally descended set of kin or cognatic stock abstractly viewed, how are viable descent groups formed in practice? From one point of view descent groups of any kind may be regarded as being formed out of a bilateral set of kin by the use of a few simple fundamental criteria. These may be termed restrictive criteria or criteria of limitation in descent group formation. I prefer to call them operational criteria, since this suggests *mobilization* of some members of the bilateral kin universe for activity rather than the *elimination* of other members. Rarely does any one criterion operate alone. Major criteria normally involved in the demarcation of descent groups, whether unilineal or not, are as follows:

1. Name

The use of a common name transmitted by regular genealogical procedure from one generation to another by members of the descent group is one of the most general phenomena in unilineal systems. In non-unilineal systems also the use of a common name may be one of the most significant defining and relating symbols. Territorially and in many other ceremonial and ordinary social contexts groups of people are distinguished by the names of the units. In the ordinary European system of patrinominal families the use of the patronymic in successive generations as a surname does allow of the recognition of a kin group (not necessarily *descent* group) of members of two or more generations. A European patrinominal kin group is not exclusive, that is, kin bearing other patronyms frequently combine as working members within the same social entity. But the continuity of common name gives a fairly ready means of identification. In the Malay/Arab system on the other hand, where an individual uses his immediate patronymic only (in the form B son of A, A son of B, etc.), it is usually impossible to identify other than siblings by name-relationship. Only by personal knowledge or specific genealogical enquiry can a kin group as such be identified.[3]

Modifications of such a system may be produced either by the entry of specific status interests or by the requirements of some general social needs. For example, in Northern Malaya, allegedly as the result of hypogamous marriage, perpetuating name relationships have been established in titles such as Nik, which a man transmits to all his children, the males of whom transmit it in turn. Such a title, indicating higher status than that of ordinary people, though lower than that of people called Raja, serves in effect as a kind of class surname. On the other hand, in modern Malaya the practice occurs among the intelligentsia of using the father's name not as a non-transmissible patronymic but directly attached to one's name as a surname which will be handed down to one's children. Here the advisability of having a quick means of identification and linkage with other members of one's kin in the modern world where personal documents are so significant seems to have been the mainspring for the change. Incipient patrilineal descent groups seem to be developing here. A common kin name does not necessarily indicate the existence of a descent group. But when the name of a group is given as that of a putative ancestor, then the implication is that a descent group is concerned.

2. Situation

For a cognatic stock restriction may be applied by defining the specific situation in which the descent group may be deemed to operate.

(a) This may be in terms of *specific resource.* It is conceivable that all the descendants of a person X are recognized as a group with relation to a certain type of property, e.g. land, but do not operate as a group for any other social purpose, such as the affairs of everyday life, in ways comparable to descent groups of other kinds. For other situations than the one specified, other types of units are composed. Ethnographically it is rare to find a descent group operating only one specific type of resource.[4] But it appears that the Sagada Igorot recognize the existence of bilateral kin units tracing descent over eight to ten generations from a common ancestor and operating common rights in regard to certain woodlands (F. Eggan 1960, pp. 29–30). These groups do not regulate marriage, nor are they associated with the control of rice fields or irrigation. They do conduct some ceremonial activities and, in particular, have rights of ownership and exploitation of certain hillsides and stands of pine trees. What appears to be of particular significance is Eggan's statement that nowadays these major groups make up the political factions and largely control elections, having been given a new lease of life by the political system introduced during the American period.

(b) The situation in which a bilateral descent group operates may be in terms of a *specific occasion* or a specific set of activities. Some modern Scots clans would seem to give an example of this. The practice of having a clan reunion, with the chief of the clan as the presiding leader, may draw together a numerous set of persons, including some from overseas, whose common tie is that they all claim a common consanguineous relationship. There is a theoretical bilateral descent group consisting of all who bear the name of McX plus all who have an ancestor or ancestress who bore that name. The members who actually assemble are an operational descent group, since they must have been interested in recognizing and tracing their connexion with the group, despite their dispersion. This recognition may include communications as well as actual presence at a clan gathering. It can be differentiated from the personal kindred of the McX clan chief as being only the members who trace common descent, though some other members of his personal kindred and of his wider universe of kin, e.g. representatives of his mother's or his wife's clan, may attend by invitation or presumed right.

While bilaterality may be complete for a specific descent group in relation to a certain resource or activity, it would seem to be always incomplete for the resources or activities of society as a whole. In other words, the specific resource or occasion is not paralleled for every possible descent group originator. Not only is there a *specification* of resources but also an *inequality* of resources for possible descent groups in the society which may therefore be asymmetrical as structural elements. Otherwise the problem of overlapping would seem to be insoluble. (There may, of course, be different kinds of resources or occasions among different descent groups.)

3. Generation Depth

A restrictive criterion may be applied by closure in terms of number of ancestors in sequence counted as valid for recognition of group membership.

(a) Closure may be *automatic* for certain purposes, that is, there may be a specified range, say kinsfolk to the fourth degree, beyond which the bilateral descent group does not act, e.g. in the case of certain land rights.[5]

(b) Closure may be more flexible, for example, it may be by fiat of the group head or by agreement between prominent leaders, etc.

(c) Closure may be a combination of generation depth with some other criterion, such as residential size. (An example may be the Iban *bilek* [Freeman 1955, pp. 7 *seq.*], though it is perhaps more proper to describe this as a domestic group rather than a descent group because of its shallow depth.)

4. Lineality

By definition in terms of continuity, a descent group cannot be non-lineal. It may be unilineal, double unilineal, bilineal, ambilineal, multilineal. The last three descriptions may be aggregated under the term non-unilineal, though this suffers from the lack of any precise indication of structure. It must be noted that the concept of unilineal applied to a descent group, while suggesting etymologically 'one line', does not mean necessarily this in anthropological usage. It means one *form* or *type* of line in consistent principle —the matriline or patriline. In a unilineal but non-exogamous system of descent groups the members of any one group may trace *many lines* back to their ultimate ancestor. If the system is patrilineal one line—the primary one—will have only males on it; others will have at least one female. Hence, multilineal is not a congruent term with unilineal in anthropological usage; it does not mean *many types* of principles of tracing descent, but many lines combining two principles. It is characteristic of bilateral descent groups in that they admit both males and females in any line of descent of their members. By analogy with unilineal, the term bilineal should indicate having two lineal principles. (It might mean also joining two lines, but for this the term duolineal might be preferable. Thus, one might describe a dynastic marriage as duolineal if it united two noble families to produce offspring whose genealogy thence combined both lines of descent.) One term which is antithetical to unilineal is ambilineal, meaning the use of descent lines involving both principles, descent through mother and through father. (Descent groups of the English or American multilineal type,[6] with very shallow genealogical depth, might be termed alineal, since they operate so largely through the recognition of lateral ties.)[7]

5. *Point of Attachment*

A distinction should be drawn between the criterion of lineality and the criterion of point of attachment or laterality. This point is the person through whom membership in the descent group is immediately or directly claimed, normally a parent. (Sometimes a parent is ignored and recognition claimed through a grandparent.) The *point of attachment* may differ from the *point of emphasis.* Empirically the person through whom membership is immediately traced is not necessarily the person on whom emphasis is placed in distinguishing the group, or through whom membership is most effectively claimed in order to yield social advantage. The rule regarding the point of attachment may vary, through male parent, female parent, or through either or through both—unilateral, ambilateral, bilateral. If the point of attachment may be either parent alone, but both cannot be involved, then the term utrolateral would seem to be appropriate.[8]

All societies probably allow some modification in the rule for point of attachment. This modification may be of two kinds: (a) quasi-kinship—the simulation of kinship, e.g. through adoption; (b) heterogeneous filiation, where homogeneous filiation (by unilineal principle) operates generally but certain exceptions are allowed. Hence, we get 'emphasis', 'gradation', 'bias towards patrilineality', 'patrilineal tendency' or 'degrees of patriliny'.[9] But such modification in the rule for point of attachment need not contravene in general the rule of lineality. For example, the Tikopia in ordinary terminology operate a strictly patrilineal system of descent groups. It was regarded as necessary for an immigrant founding ancestor to have local clan attachment for his children (Firth 1959, p. 233). An alien clan attachment would have been unworkable because of the isolated nature of Tikopia society if the customary system of exchanges at personal crises of life was to be preserved. Therefore, the wife of the immigrant, i.e. the mother of his children, was admitted as their point of attachment to the clan. But significantly, this does not occur again in the 'history' of the group concerned. Thence onwards the patrilineal prinicple is preserved. This is very different from taking whichever parent offers the best advantage in any generation, as the Maori have done.

In this respect I have drawn a distinction between definitive descent systems and optative descent systems (Firth 1957). Definitive systems include unilineal systems of a conventional type and 'bilateral' systems of the strict type—that is, where a person *must* belong to *both* mother's *and* father's groups, and conversely descent *must* be counted through both male and female children.

Optative systems involve elements of choice or personal selectivity. Both parents are available as points of attachment to descent groups, and either or both may be chosen according to circumstances and the pre-existing character of the system. 'Ambilateral' can be taken to mean that either or both are available; 'utrolateral' that either is available, but not both. (I would regard utrolateral as a sub-type of ambilateral.)

Two points must be noted: (a) *Choice is a two-way process.* A person may choose the group and the group may choose the person. Where the group or a legitimately entitled member of it chooses the person, as in adoption, we should not speak of an optative system. An optative system of descent group membership is one where choice may be legitimately exercised by what may be termed the 'membership candidate'—though members of the group concerned have responsibility for accepting him. (b) However, in such cases certain conditions have to be met by the membership candidate —conditions of communication (he must keep in touch with the group), or accessibility, or land-holding, or economic or jural responsibility for other members of the descent group. In no case does the person have unrestricted choice to claim membership without doing anything to implement his claim.

6. Residence Rule

This is one of the most common and most important criteria for restrictive definition of bilateral descent groups. It is a criterion of an obvious objective kind—a 'concrete' sociological fact. It involves shared general interests and tasks and the exercise of status. But while actual residence is an empirical matter, the recognition of a person as being a resident involves a question of normality. How is absence counted? For census purposes a person may be registered only where he is actually spending the night; but for many other legal purposes he is counted as resident even though he is absent, provided that he regularly has his abode in the place cited. Continued absence, therefore, poses a problem of degree in the reckoning of group membership. As in many such situations, difference of view may arise between the parties concerned.

Temporary absence seems always to be disregarded, but with long-term absence two alternatives are open. One is a system of simple closure, as with the Iban utrolocal membership of the *bilek.* Another system is one of graded recognition, as with the Maori, where traditionally a person could be a member of kinship of a group in which he or she did not live. His or her children also might count membership in this group, but such membership could not continue indefinitely. Continued absence caused the ties to lapse and the rights of membership to fail. This was a long-term application of the principle which the Iban apply in the short term. But existing descriptions of application of the residence rule to kin group membership often leave certain questions unanswered. How rigorously is the rule applied? What constitutes continuity of membership? How long must absence from the residence group be before membership is regarded as lapsed?

7. Marriage Rule

This would appear to be less important as a defining criterion of 'bilateral' than of unilateral or unilineal descent groups.

(a) *Unilineal exogamy:* This results in the well-known exchanges of property and services. It results also in the creation or intensification of social bonds between groups. Unilineal exogamy is a very clear demarcator of descent groups.

(b) *Endogamy:* Marriage to a member of the same descent group results in conservation of property, retention of services and avoidance of the contraction of external social bonds. Endogamy demarcates the group externally and probably strengthens it internally, by multiplying the ties of kinship between group members. But this raises the question—can endogamy operate effectively without some internal differentiation in the groups concerned? Among the Toda, sub-groups are exogamous within the large endogamous groups.

(c) *'Non-exogamy' of unilineal groups:* This means the possibility of choice of marriage partner from either within or outside the group. If the spouse is from within this results in a lack of external exchange, militates against the creation of external bonds, etc. It may provoke unfavourable judgement—as in Tikopia where it is not thought right to marry a member of one's own lineage; one ought to marry out of the lineage and 'let the property circulate'. Strictly this means a double tie of linkage of a member with his lineage through both his father and his mother. This involves also a reduction in the magnitude of the kin universe on whom one can depend for close support—one's mother's brother, for example, comes from within one's own lineage instead of from outside, and there is possible overlap between the roles of classificatory father's brother and mother's brother.

A tentative inference is that endogamy, if complete for bilateral descent groups, intensifies the character of the group into a 'double unilineal' fused descent system. (This probably would be workable only in terms of sub-unit endogamy.) On the other hand, exogamy, if complete for bilateral descent groups, would ultimately break down unless marriages were continually contracted out of the society altogether. It could operate only when some other principle such as residence enters to restrict possible ties of membership in the descent group in each generation. So, in effect, a system of local exogamy is instituted whereby sections or members of the theoretical bilateral field intermarry, being members of different operational descent groups. (For example, the Iban *bilek* is exogamous on a local basis.) Where, more commonly, no prescribed rule of marriage for bilateral descent groups obtains, this raises a point of terminology. Lowie (1948, p. 9) uses the term *agamy*, a word which he states is in use by biologists to denote absence of marriage, to apply to absence of marriage regulations on the part of a social unit.[10] This specification of usage is probably justifiable so long as its etymology is recognized. It seems clear now that exogamy or the lack of it, or indeed any specific marriage prescription, cannot be used as the sole defining character of kin groups, bilateral or otherwise.

To recapitulate—an attempt to create a typology of bilateral descent groups is difficult if it is based only upon a formal set of theoretical criteria without regard to the operational significance of those criteria.

Of the various criteria discussed only four, generation depth, lineality, point of attachment and rule of residence, provide closure to descent group membership. The use of a common name provides an indicator or referent and, like the marriage rule, is an intensifier of group relationships. Specification of resource or activity to which the bilateral descent group is relevant provides closure in a way by restricting participation of group members to a particular sphere of operations alone. It can be seen from what follows how these criteria apply in the case of the Maori *hapu.*

Character of the Maori Hapu

In discussions about the character of bilateral descent groups, the Maori *hapu* came early to attention (Firth 1929, pp. 98–100; 1936, pp. 582–3). But its position is not yet wholly clear, as is evident from recent statements by Fortes (1959, p. 211) and Freeman (1961, p. 200). Some of this lack of clarity is due to the fact that the empirical data for demonstrating how traditional *hapu* membership was determined are very incomplete. Moreover, since the system has undergone significant changes in modern times (see, e.g. Joan Metge 1963), no detailed body of material can now be collected from actual observation by trained social anthropologists to solve the problem in full. Yet there is enough evidence to enable broad conclusions to be reasonably drawn. A brief representation of it may therefore be helpful, and may also stimulate further attempts to collect more data on the present position.

The *hapu* in traditional Maori society was a group of kin tracing their relationship to one another by genealogies with ultimate point of reference to a common ancestor. The members of the *hapu* were categorized by the use of a common name, transmitted from one generation to another. They operated as a group on specific occasions and in regard to specific resources, but occasions and resources were multiple. The generation depth of a *hapu* varied according to the level of segmentation, but recognition of eight to ten generations was common. The *hapu* was not unilineal. Although weight was attached to tracing group membership by descent through males, membership was recognized if a line of descent included several female names. The point of attachment of a person to the *hapu* could be then through a woman, and choice would be exercised by a person as to whether he would claim *hapu* membership through his father or through his mother or through both. In such a choice a person might take as his basis the difference of status between his parents in their own *hapu.* But the criterion which primarily determined his membership—granted consanguineal kinship tie—was residence. Officially, the Maori marriage practice, which tended to favour unions within the *hapu* rather than outside, meant that for many members of the *hapu* differentiation between membership through father and membership through mother was not a relevant issue. These points can now be expanded.

The conditions in which Maori society operated at the time of the advent of Europeans were in many respects similar to those characteristic of the operation of unilineal descent groups in many parts of Africa. In New Zealand, unlike the position of many Pacific islands, the Maori had a very large terrain, with great stretches of fertile land for agriculture and, for the most part, a favourable climate. Although the land was fairly heavily broken up in many areas by mountains, there were ample communication routes through valleys and passes, by rivers and along the coast. Although the terrain was heavily forested in most areas, clearing by stone axes and by fire was feasible, and over the generations had yielded large areas of relatively open secondary growth. At the time of the arrival of Europeans the Maori were organized into large political units, termed tribes, with leaders of varying rank. Loose associations of tribes for ceremonial and political purposes were given by the recognition of linkage through the traditional canoes of the putative great migration of six hundred years or so ago. But the most significant operational units in the political field, for the control and transmission of land rights, for war, and for the avenging of injury, were the *hapu.* As far as ecology goes, it might seem that Maori society could have developed a system of lineage type in conformity with what Sahlins has described as a situation of predatory expansion (Sahlins 1961; cf. also Vayda 1960). But from the evidence the *hapu* is not strictly a unilineal descent group. Why this should be so is not clear. Part of the answer may lie in the functional value to a person of having an alternative point of attachment for the acquisition of land or of status to take advantage of most favourable circumstances.

How is the group operationally defined? Three main questions are involved here. How does a person have membership of a *hapu?* Could a person be a member of more than one *hapu?* What were the mechanisms whereby *hapu* membership was demarcated? (An unpublished study by Scheffler also usefully pursues these questions.)

Membership of a *hapu* could be based only upon consanguineal kinship. Neither affinal relationship nor residence were sufficient to entitle a person to *hapu* membership. Fortes had misinterpreted the situation when he stated, 'It is significant that membership can apparently also be acquired by marriage to a member and taking up residence in the *hapu* territory' (1959, p. 211). In modern Maori society participation, and even leadership in a local group, can be obtained by such means. But such a group is not described as a *hapu*, and in traditional Maori society it seems clear that title to *hapu* membership in the full sense could never have been gained by such means. This is made clear by Biggs (1960, p. 23). 'Though not conforming to any usually recognised anthropological term the *hapuu*[11] could be termed "territorial kin". It held the ownership of an area of land, and even if not normally occupying a single village, the group would draw together in times of war. All members of a *hapuu* are descended from a single ancestor after whom the group is usually named, but because of frequent intermarriages most members have genealogical links of a closer order. Spouses who have married into and who live with the group do *not* become members of it, though the bi-lateral descent system ensures that their children are members.'

The *hapu* was a localized group with one or more settlements distributed over the land to which the members had a collective title. In general, the Maori system of marriage in pre-European days was virilocal, and this meant that over the generations a person's major link with the local *hapu* was patrilineal. Moreover, Maori society was a ranked society, with an emphasis upon the status of men. When questions of relative status were involved, it was preferable for a person to trace his rank through as long and unbroken a male line as possible. A direct line of descent from an ancestor was, in general, esteemed the greater the more male names it contained.

But since the marriage system was not exogamous as regards *hapu* membership, and many *hapu* were of considerable size (several hundred or even several thousand members), it was not uncommon for a man and a woman of the same *hapu* to marry. In this case their children could trace local *hapu* membership through both their mother and their father. In practice, membership through the father would ordinarily be preferred, but if a person's mother's father had been a man of high rank, then he might prefer to use this line of descent for ceremonial or other public purposes.

Where marriage did not take place between members of the same *hapu*, then the problem of choice arose for the children. Ordinarily the choice would be made, in the case of virilocal marriage, for membership of a father's *hapu.*[12] But uxorilocal marriages for various reasons sometimes took place. Here the children might choose to stay as members of the mother's *hapu*, or to leave the mother's *hapu* and join the father's *hapu*, or to keep both sets of claims alive by some movement between the two. In this situation, the rank of the mother as well as of the father might be relevant because, though the status of women in general terms was less than that of a man, the daughter of a man of high rank herself held high status and could communicate some of this status to her children. In ambilateral systems, in which the element of individual choice is built into the system, the existence of such status differentials is likely to be a significant factor in determining affiliation of the individual and the character and size of the descent group. A person may choose (or be allowed to choose) as his descent group of operational importance, the one in which, say, his mother has relatively high social status, even though the society as a whole has a patrilineal emphasis.

I termed this system ambilateral (Firth 1929; 1957) because both parents were available in obtaining one's *hapu* membership. I used the term ambilateral as against bilateral to indicate that use of both parents was not automatic or necessary, as the latter term might seem to imply.[13] The *hapu* then, as a restricted ambilateral kin group, a ramage, is not equivalent to an ever-expanding set of bilateral kin. On the other hand, as a corporate unit of consanguineal kin selectively organized, it is functionally equivalent to a lineage.

The evidence for a Maori being regarded as a member of more than one *hapu* is not ample,[14] but seems definite. A couple of further instances may be cited here. One is the beginning of a memorial inscription which I recorded some years ago in Rotorua:

> *'Whakamaharatanga*
> *Kia*
> *Te Wiremu Matene*
> *He tangata rangatira i roto i ona hapu*
> *maha o te Arawa me Ngati Raukawa.'*

'In memory of Wiremu Matene (i.e. William Martin) a man of rank in his (plural) *hapu*—of the Arawa and Ngati Raukawa'. These are two major tribal divisions in different parts of New Zealand, and the inscription indicates that he belonged to both. Moreover, the inscription later refers to the fact that he traced descent from four of the ancestral canoes.

About thirty years ago I attended the funeral of a Maori man in a village in the Urewera country, and took down his relevant genealogy. He was described to me as a member of the *hapu* of Ngati Manunui and Ngati Tawhaki through his father, and a member of Ngai Teriu and Ngati Kuri through his mother. All these were local *hapu* with their associated villages within a few miles. The deceased's father was from Ngati Manunui and his FF also. Moreover, his FMM was of Ngati Manunui, her MFF having been Manunui himself, the ancestor who founded that *hapu,* and this title to membership was most esteemed of all. The relationship in Ngati Tawhaki was through his FMF. The deceased's mother, described as belonging to both Ngati Kuri and Ngai Teriu, owed the first *hapu* to her F, FF, and FFF, and the latter to her mother and FM. The deceased had married a member of Ngati Kuri, which would reinforce his children's claim to membership of that *hapu.* The deceased was also described as being a member of another *hapu* with its seat some twenty miles away. This link came from his MFFM;

but like some other fairly remote kin connexion, this did not seem to be seriously regarded.

The point here is that the dead man, theoretically a member of several *hapu*, by tracing his descent by a combination of male and female ancestors, was able operationally by continuity of the *hapu* immediately concerned, to be given a title to membership in four of these. But in his mother's group this was the less significant; it was with Ngati Manunui and Ngati Tawhaki intertwined that he was mainly identified in practice, selective bias being given by his patrilateral tie on the one hand and a direct line of descent through females and males to the eponymous ancestor on the other.

What were the factors which gave restriction to *hapu* membership? Primarily the operational criteria were common residence and common exercise of land rights (especially those of cultivation).[15] These assumed common recognition of the significance of certain selected genealogies and the genealogical position of every member of the *hapu* therein. They were reinforced by common socio-economic interests and activities as in marriage; common political activities as in the recognition accorded to specific individuals as leaders; and combination for action in respect of external units of the same kind, as in war. In such matters the *hapu* behaved as a corporate kin group closely analogous in most of its activities to the behaviour of a unilineal kin group. Likewise, the principle of *hapu* formation was that segmentation of *hapu* could be recognized at different levels within the same overall unit. One can say 'recognized' because of the naming system. Every *hapu* had a name, ordinarily that of the ancestor from whom the *hapu* members traced their specific descent, with the prefix *Ngati* (*Ati, Ngai*) meaning, collectively, 'offspring'.

The key to the effective operation of the *hapu* as a corporate group lay in the mechanism for sloughing off potential members. Although a person was entitled to claim membership of a *hapu* through either father or mother, this entitlement was only in the nature of a claim which had to be validated by social action. On the one hand, it required effective acceptance by the body of the members of the *hapu* with whom he or she would have to live, or at least exercise land rights and other rights in common. The most definite mode of social action for validating one's *hapu* claim was, of course, residence. Residence alone without consanguineal kin tie was invalid. Consanguineal kin tie without residence or some other method of implementing the relationship was also in the long run invalid. It was this mechanism which enabled the *hapu* to function as a corporate unit and allowed it to operate in a fashion analogous to that of a unilineal descent group. As I have noted elsewhere, 'In so far as the concept of descent among the Maori is to be distinguished from kinship connexion it is primarily by reference to rights in land. . . .Integral membership of a group is associated with a title to some of its land. This title is kept alive only by some form of occupation, the commonest being residence in the village where the majority of the members of the kinship unit normally live. . . .Among the Maori descent and the formal structure of the kinship grouping can be understood only by reference to residence and land holding' (Firth 1936, pp. 582-3).

One further point must be made. In pre-European times it was because of the relative difficulty of communication, and because of the much greater possibilities of violence towards a stranger, that extra-*hapu* and certainly extra-tribal marriage must have been much less common than to-day. Hence the patrilineal bias in the *hapu* structure. On the other hand, particularly in rugged mountainous country, it would seem that two or more relatively small *hapu* often grew side by side, and their members intermarried so frequently over the generations that for political purposes, except perhaps land holding, they constituted in effect one unit. Hence a person with parentage from both, living in a joint village, could legitimately be said to be a member of both *hapu*. However, in modern conditions, with the very great developments in communication, the external markets for labour and skills and the general attraction of European centres, members of a *hapu* have become very much dispersed. Consequently, the ambilateral character of the *hapu* system, allowing the claiming of *hapu* membership including land rights, at a distance, has been strengthened. Yet nowadays with young people, *hapu* membership as such, as Metge (1963) has shown, has often been lost to mind. In such cases the effective kin are a relatively small group and use kin ties for individual purposes or for local association rather than for membership of corporate descent groups.

In summary then, in traditional Maori society a person might belong to more than one corporate kin group. But this did not entitle his descendants to perpetual membership of all such groups. Choice was permissible. Claims to group membership were determined primarily by residence and this procedure was effective as a closure in demarcating the group. Essentially, any claim to group membership had to be validated by some form of social action, primarily that of living with the other members of the group concerned.

All this has a bearing on the concept of descent. Some writers, following Rivers (Rivers 1924, p. 86; Peranio 1961, p. 93; Leach 1962, p. 131), have argued that descent should apply only to membership of *unilineal* corporate kin groups.[16] But Rivers's position was not unequivocal. He was prepared to regard membership of the simple family in Britain as unilineally determined, with the term descent applying to it. His criterion here was simply that the child takes the name of the father—though he allowed that it is hardly customary to use the term descent in this case. He was also prepared to use the term descent for the process by which a person becomes a member of a class, as with German or Polynesian nobility. He pointed out that in Polynesian society a child of noble parents is always noble, 'though there are often complexities in the case of marriage between noble and commoner' (1924, p. 87). Here Rivers seems to be confusing descent with status succession or inheritance to title, and it would seem that he was willing to allow the term descent to be used for marginal instances, where more than unilineality of kin group membership was involved. His insistence on the importance of unilineality is probably to be linked with his general committal in his later work to the idea of the basic importance of dual exogamous groups in the history of human society. Hence his statement, 'It is however when dealing with the clan or the moiety of the dual organization that descent becomes of pre-eminent importance, and in connexion with these modes of social grouping the term is indispensable' (op. cit.).[17]

But what is meant by the view that descent should apply only to unilineal kin groups is that it should be an automatic not an optional entitlement. This is what Fortes presumably means by his insistence that the *hapu* is not demarcated by a descent boundary. On his view, to be classed as a descent group a social unit should have its membership closed by kinship alone, and an entitlement which depends upon any other criterion as well, such as residence, is not descent.[18]

Moreover, there is the point made by W. E. Armstrong many years ago. In drawing the distinction between group and grouping (1928, pp. 32-40), Armstrong pointed out that a unit such as a clan or a village community was a group in that a person was definitely a member of it or not, and every member shared with every other the same identification in unit terms. But in a social unit such as a family, every member had a different entitlement; the 'family' of a wife was different from that of her husband, the 'family' of a son from that of his grandparents, etc. In fact, the situation is not as clear-cut as this, since in every unit of an exclusive type, be it clan or village, the rights and position of members are not identical. The principle, however, is broadly valid. Now from this point of view the Maori *hapu* would be a grouping, not a group, in so far as the entitlement of all members is not necessarily identical. Some are members through their fathers, others through their mothers, with different allegiances possibly to other *hapu.*

There is force in these arguments. But it seems to me that to reserve 'descent' for cases of unilineality of group entitlement is an unnecessary restriction. In discussing bilateral kin groups there is need to distinguish the ego-oriented 'personal kindred' from groups of a more definitive and persisting character. But if the group under discussion is of a continuative, corporate type, comprising persons organized and united primarily on a consanguineal kin basis, with a collective name transmitted from one generation to another; if it is a significant structural unit of the society, performing multiple social tasks, then there seems no good reason to deny it the character of a descent group. Hence I would say that ambilateral groups of the *hapu* type use residential and land use criteria as demarcating instruments to close their consanguineal kinship status for operational purposes, and so constitute descent units.

In conclusion, I would make two further points. One is that ambilateral descent-group systems may be divided into ranked and non-ranked. In the former, where high status may be held by women as well as by men, there may be definite inducements for children of a hypogamous marriage to elect for membership in their mother's rather than in their father's group. On the other hand, the fact that the political roles of men, in administration of assets and in particular in war, are usually far more important than those of women, gives a patrilineal bias to any ambilateral system. This tends to be the case whether the system is one in which significance is attached to hereditary rank or not. The operational convenience of having a set of men who are siblings tends then also to facilitate an agnatic ideology in an ambilateral system.

The second point is that the concept of membership of a corporate group need not necessarily be that of a full, exclusive and unitary set of rights and obligations. In a corporate descent group which is also a local group, with its members or most of them living in close proximity, the line between 'membership' of the group and operational participation in the affairs of the group may be fairly clearly marked or it may be very faint indeed. Yet, even in the group which is described as patrilineal, the roles of non-agnates, as Paula Brown has shown, may be almost indistinguishable from those of agnates. I think it possible that further empirical investigation may show that in the concept of 'membership' of a descent group there may be a considerable degree of permitted ambiguity. I would even hazard the suggestion that some elements of ambiguity may exist in practice as distinct from theory in the operations of even those types of descent groups which are recognized as being strictly unilineal. More investigation on this point seems necessary, and we should not allow difficulties of definition to make us turn our backs on the complexity of the facts.

NOTES

1. This article was prepared in an earlier form for a Seminar on Non-Unilineal Kinship held in the early months of 1959 under the chairmanship of G. P. Murdock, at the Center for Advanced Studies in the Behavioral Sciences at Palo Alto, California. I am grateful to Ralph Tyler and other members of the staff of the Center for the facilities which I had there as a Fellow in 1958-59 in the preparation of that paper. I am much indebted also for helpful criticism at various stages to my colleagues at the Center, especially G. P. Murdock, F. Eggan and Meyer Fortes, and to my colleagues at an inter-collegiate seminar in the University of London. For particular suggestions I am very grateful to Lorraine Lancaster, Chie Nakane, H. S. Morris and I. Schapera. For assistance in the preparation of this article I am indebted to a personal research grant from the Behavioral Sciences Division of the Ford Foundation.

2. E.g. 'It is a truism to say that in all societies descent is traced through both parents' (Mitchell 1962, p. 29). Cf. 'optional descent' in Puyuma ritual groups (Mabuchi 1960, p. 136).

3. Such a system can be combined with a unilineal descent system, e.g. in Negri Sembilan, where the use of the patronymic by individuals is operated within a system of matrilineal descent groups recognizable by group names, common land rights, etc. Elsewhere in Malaya specific emphasis given to agnatic ties may result in the creation of incipient patrilineal descent groups of shallow depth (Burridge 1956).

4. It would seem that the control of property in certain types of European wills in effect

maintains a bilateral descent group in operation for some generations through the common interest of every one of the members in the administration of the property. (I owe this suggestion to George Homans.)

5. Cf. Seebohm on medieval Welsh mutual responsibility for crime, 1895, pp. 101 *seq*. Note that he anticipates the modern emphasis on the significance of bilateral kin ties for tribal solidarity.

6. Talcott Parsons 1949, pp. 233-50.

7. The term alineal as used by Maybury-Lewis (1960, p. 191), refers to descent traced through both father and mother, and not to the lack of either a line of descent or of a principle. The concept of lineality is different from the concept of lineation (Löffler 1960, pp. 141-2, 149), which Löffler defines as the system of distribution of imaginary lines determined by parental bonds according to the classificatory system, and specifically stated to be not descent lines. Lineation appears then to comprise the transmission of rights and obligations from one generation to another, irrespective of membership of descent or other kin units.

8. As used by Freeman 1955, p. 7; 1956, no. 93.

9. See, e.g. Murdock 1960, p. 7; Pouwer 1960, pp. 365-72; Burridge 1956, p. 61.

10. The basic usage would seem to be not absence of marriage but absence of sexual action, e.g. agamic reproduction of the female without impregnation by the male. Agamous is equivalent to asexual. But agamy appears to have been used as early as 1796 for absence or non-recognition of the marriage relation.

11. Biggs uses the phonetically more correct form *hapuu,* but I prefer to retain the conventional spelling since there is no confusion thereby.

12. Note that in Maori society a person was often treated as a member of his father's *hapu,* and not of his mother's *hapu;* the system had a definite patrilineal bias.

13. But cf. Webster's dictionary, where 'ambilateral' is given as a medical term pertaining to or affecting both sides, and equivalent to bilateral.

14. E.g., Fenton 1879, pp. 66, 105; Best 1925, pp. 27, 216, 222, 290, 293, 301, 302.

15. Cf. Starcke, 'The choice between the two possible lines [of descent] is decided by the economic organization of the community and by the local grouping of individuals' (1889, p. 118).

16. In effect, Fortes (1953, p. 33; 1959, pp. 210–2) has adopted the same position and hence has held that groups such as the Maori *hapu* should not be classified as descent groups. Yet the title of his classic article 'Structure of Unilineal Descent Groups' (1953) and his use of the term 'bilateral descent group' (1959, p. 206) seem to indicate that he conceived alternative usage possible.

17. It is here assumed that this statement expresses Rivers's own views, but it must be borne in mind that his *Social Organization* was the result of drastic editing by W. J. Perry from little more than lecture notes.

18. Freeman 1961, p. 200, makes a similar point when he states that since cognatic stocks overlap, unless some criterion other than and in addition to descent be brought into operation, it is impossible to achieve a division of a society into discrete groupings. But if the criterion is *additional to* descent, then it seems illogical to deny the term 'descent group' to units such as the *hapu.*

BIBLIOGRAPHY

ARMSTRONG, W. E. 1928. *Rossel Island: An Ethnological Study.* Cambridge.

BEST, E. 1925. *Tuhoe, The Children of the Mist.* 2 vols. New Plymouth.

BIGGS, B. 1960. Maori Marriage. *Polynesian Society Maori Monograph No. 1.* Wellington.

BROWN, PAULA 1962. Non-Agnates among the Patrilineal Chimbu. *J. Polynes. Soc.,* 71, pp. 57–69.

BURRIDGE, K. O. L. 1956. The Malay Composition of a Village in Johore. *Journal of the Malayan Branch Royal Asiatic Society,* 29, pp. 60–77.

CHOWNING, ANN 1962. Cognatic Kin Groups among the Molima of Fergusson Island. *Ethnology,* 1, pp. 92–101.

DAVENPORT, W. 1959, Nonunilinear Descent and Descent Groups. *Amer. Anthrop.,* 61, pp. 557–72.

EGGAN, F. 1960. The Sagada Igorots of Northern Luzon. *Social Structure in Southeast Asia,* G. P. Murdock (ed.), pp. 24–50.

FENTON, F. B. 1879. *Important Judgements Delivered in the Compensation Court and Native Land Court. 1866–1879.* Auckland.

FIRTH, R. 1929. *Primitive Economics of the New Zealand Maori.* London.

FIRTH, R. 1936. *We, The Tikopia.* London.

FIRTH, R. 1957. A Note on Descent Groups in Polynesia. MAN 1957, 2.

FIRTH, 1959. *Social Change in Tikopia.* London.

FORTES, M. 1953. Structure of Unilineal Descent Groups. *American Anthropologist,* 55, pp. 17–41.

FORTES, M. 1959. Descent, Filiation and Affinity: A Rejoinder to Dr Leach. MAN 1959, 309, 331.

FREEMAN, J. D. 1955. *Iban Agriculture.* London.

FREEMAN, J. D. 1956. "Utolateral' and 'Utrolocal'. MAN 1956, 93.

FREEMAN, J. D. 1961. On the Concept of the Kindred. J. R. ANTHROP. INST., 91, pp. 192–220.

GOODENOUGH, W. H. 1955. A Problem in Malayo-Polynesian Social Organization. *American Anthropologist,* 57, pp. 71–83.

LEACH, E. R. 1950. *Social Science Research in Sarawak.* London.

LEACH, E. R. 1962. On Certain Unconsidered Aspects of Double Descent Systems. MAN 1962, 214.

LÖFFLER, L. G. 1960. Patrilateral Lineation in Transition. *Ethnos,* pp. 119–50.

LOWIE, R. H. 1948. *Social Organization. New York.*

MABUCHI, TOICHI 1960. The Aboriginal Peoples of Formosa, in Murdock, *infra,* pp. 127–40.

MAYBURY-LEWIS, D. 1960. Parallel Descent and the Apinayé Anomaly. *Southwestern Journal of Anthropology,* pp. 191–216.

METGE, JOAN 1963. *A New Maori Migration.* LSE Monographs, no. 27.

MITCHELL, J. C. 1962. Marriage, Matriliny and Social Structure among the Yao of Southern Nyasaland. *International Journal of Comparative Sociology,* 3, pp. 29–42.

MURDOCK, G. P. 1960. Cognatic Forms of Social Organisation. *Social Structure in South East Asia,* G. P. Murdock (ed.), pp. 1–14. New York.

OOSTERWAL, G. 1961. *People of the Tor.* Assen.

PARSONS, T. 1949. *Essays in Sociological Theory.* Glencoe, Ill.

PERANIO, R. D. 1961. Descent, Descent Line and Descent Group in Cognatic Social Systems, in *American Ethnological Society Proceedings, Annual Spring Meeting,* pp. 93–113.

POUWER, J. 1958. *Socio-Politische Structuur in de Oostelijke Vogelkop,* I (Mim.) v. also *Nieuw-Guinea Studien,* 4, 1960, pp. 215–34.

POUWER, J. 1960. Loosely Structured Societies in Netherlands New Guinea, *Bijdr. Taal-, Land-, en Volkenkunde,* 116, pp. 109–18.

RADCLIFFE-BROWN, A. R. 1951. *African Systems of Kinship and Marriage,* A. R. Radcliffe-Brown & Daryll Forde (eds.). London.

RIVERS, W. H. R. 1924. *Social Organization.* London.

SAHLINS, M. 1961. The Segmentary Lineage: An Organization of Predatory Expansion. *American Anthropologist,* 63, pp. 322–45.

SCHEFFLER, H. W. 1961. The Study of Ambilateral Societies. *Amer. Anthrop. Ass. Paper* (Mim).

SCHEFFLER, H. W. 1962. Kindred and Kin Groups in Simbo Island Social Structure. *Ethnology,* 1, pp. 135–57.

SCHEFFLER, H. W. n.d. Maori Social Structure: A Re-Analysis (unpub.).

SEEBOHM, F. 1895. *The Tribal System in Wales.* London.

STARCKE, C. N. 1889. *The Primitive Family.* London.

VAYDA, A. P. 1960. Maori Warfare. *Polynesian Society Maori Monograph No. 2.* Wellington.

5

THE NONUNILINEAR DESCENT GROUPS OF SAMOA[1]

Melvin Ember

Perhaps as many as one-third of the world's societies lack unilinear descent. Yet, nonunilinear descent groups have received very little attention from anthropological theorists; consequently, as Murdock (1949:57) has observed, ". . . ethnographers rarely notice their presence and almost never report their absence." This is in spite of the fact that we have much evidence, unclassified to be sure, that descent groups are present in many nonunilinear societies.

For example, we know that Samoa lacks unilinear descent groups. But there clearly are other kinds of descent group in Samoa which, owing to our traditional indifference to such groups, have not been clearly identified in the literature. The present paper, which is based upon data I collected in American Samoa during 1955–56,[2] is designed to fill this gap in the literature. In so doing, it seeks to show that the hitherto elusive data on nonunilinear descent groups are as amenable to systematic study as the data on unilinear descent groups.

Traditional classifications of kinship systems cannot help us in identifying the descent groups of Samoa since these classifications have dealt primarily with unilinear kinship structure. If we are to identify the Samoan descent groups so that they might be systematically compared with descent groups elsewhere, we must first have a classification which abstracts the major types of nonunilinear descent group, preferably in a way which permits their comparison with unilinear types.

We are fortunate that a paper by Davenport [*American Anthropologist*, August, 1959] provides us with such a classification. Surveying the ethnographic literature, Davenport finds that nonunilinear descent groups are coordinate in most respects with unilinear descent groups. Accordingly, he suggests or implies the following typology of nonunilinear kinship structure. Corresponding to the unilinear term "sib," the term "sept" is proposed for

Reproduced by permission of the American Anthropological Association and Melvin Ember from the *American Anthropologist*, 61:573–577 (August, 1959).

the nonunilinear descent group whose members acknowledge a bond of common descent but are unable to trace the actual genealogical connections between individuals (see Murdock 1949:47 for the definition of a sib). In the sib, the bond of common descent is said to reside in the paternal or maternal line; but in the sept, the bond of common descent is said to reside in either or both lines. A descent group produced by either unilinear or nonunilinear descent is known as a "lineage" when it includes only persons who can actually trace their common relationship through a specific series of remembered genealogical links in the given line or lines of descent (cf. Murdock 1949:46). Groups intermediate between sibs (or septs) and lineages may be called "sub-sibs" (or "sub-septs"). And lastly, the term "clan" can still be reserved for the localized segment of a sib (or sept), plus their in-marrying spouses and other dependents (cf. Murdock 1949:68). For ease of reference, the correspondences between unilinear and nonunilinear descent groups are listed in Table 1.

TABLE 1. CORRESPONDENCES BETWEEN UNILINEAR AND NONUNILINEAR DESCENT GROUPS.

Unilinear Descent Groups	*Nonunilinear Descent Groups*
Sib	Sept
Sub-Sib	Sub-Sept
Lineage	Lineage
Clan	Clan

Given Davenport's classification of nonunilinear descent groups, we can proceed to the identification of the descent groups which structure traditional Samoan kinship. Our discussion will be concerned with three structural features of each type of descent group: (1) membership (Who belongs to the group?); (2) residential distribution (Where do the members live?); and (3) relationship to land (What are the group's rights to land?).

THE SAMOAN DESCENT GROUPS

There are three types of descent group in Samoa, only two of which have generic names. They are: (1) the sept or *'aiga sa;* (2) the sub-sept or *faletama;* and (3) the clan.

The sept or 'aiga sa includes all those people who acknowledge common descent from the founder of the group. It is exogamous since the incest taboo is extended to all known relatives. Associated with each sept is a totemic fish or fowl and one or more *matai* titles. The sept takes its name from the senior of its matai titles which is named after the founder of the group; for example, a given sept named the *'aiga sa Faoa* may be defined as the maximal group of consanguineal relatives acknowledging descent from the original holder of the title Faoa. There is no regular rule of succession to the senior matai title; anyone who belongs to the sept may be selected by the members of the sept when they assemble to decide on a new title-holder.

Between 10 and 30 septs are found in a given village; that is, the lands, house sites, and titles of all such septs are located in the territory of that village. In a given sept, however, the members also include residents of other villages. Moreover, the village members of a given sept do not all live on the stretch of house-site land which belongs to the sept; in fact, most of the village members of a sept live on house sites and use lands which belong to other septs of the village.

That most of the members of one sept do not live together is due to the fact that membership in the village septs is overlapping. A given person may consider himself a member of up to seven or eight different local septs. In order to claim membership in a given sept, a person traces a lineal but not unilinear consanguineal relationship to the present and/or a previous holder of the matai title which identifies the sept. A person's potential affiliations are reduced by failure to maintain sept obligations (e.g., contributing food for wedding or funeral feasts) and/or by forgetting consanguineal connections.

Traditionally, cultivable lands and house sites are controlled by the sept as a whole, and the authority or *pule* over such properties is vested in the senior title of the group. This authority must not be equated with ownership in the Western sense, since sept property cannot be transferred by the senior matai without the consent of an assembly of the members of the sept. It is for this reason that earlier writers on Samoa spoke of the senior matai as the custodian of sept property.

Although the sept is the kin group which controls cultivable lands and house sites, it is the clan which actually uses them. But before we go into exactly how these properties are divided among the members of the clan, we must first identify the sub-sept.

The sub-sept or faletama includes all those people who acknowledge common descent from a brother, son, sister, or daughter of the founder of the sept. A sept always has at least two sub-septs (cf. Mead 1930:18, 21). One is the "male line" as Mead describes it; this sub-sept is said to descend from the brother or son of the founder of the sept. The second sub-sept always found in a sept is the "female line" in Mead's terms; this sub-sept is said to descend from the sister or daughter of the founder of the sept. A village sept may have three or four sub-septs, but these always include at least one "male line" and at least one "female line." A sub-sept normally possesses its own matai title; when there is such a title, the sub-sept takes its name from it. For example, if the title is *Palaita,* the sub-sept is called the faletama Palaita. But if there is no title associated with the sub-sept, it takes its name from the founding brother, son, sister, or daughter. As in the case of the senior matai title of the sept, there is no regular rule of succession to the matai title of a sub-sept. Anyone who belongs to the sub-sept may be selected by the members of the sub-sept when they assemble to decide on a new title-holder.

In a given sub-sept, the members include residents of other villages in addition to residents of the home village. And, as in the sept, the village members of a sub-sept do not all live on the stretch of house-site land which belongs to the sept. That is, membership in the sub-septs of the village, as in the village septs, is overlapping. In order to claim membership in a given sub-sept, a person traces a lineal but not unilinear consanguineal relationship to the present and/or a previous holder of the matai title which identifies the sub-sept; or, if there is no such title, a person traces his relationship to someone who is acknowledged to belong to that sub-sept.

We come now to the clan. This group includes all those members of the sept who live on the stretch of house-site land which belongs to the sept. Numbering up to 50 persons (Turner 1861:280), the clan normally comprises at least three extended families, all of which are normally headed by matais whose titles belong to the sept. One of these titles is the senior one of the sept, and the other two or more are each associated with a sub-sept of the sept. The nuclear families comprising a given extended family of the clan may be affiliated through the parent-son relationship (or the parent-daughter if there are no sons), or they may all be headed by brothers. In short, the clan comprises a number of households the heads of which claim descent from a common ancestor (cf. the definition of a clan in Webster's dictionary, as quoted in Murdock 1949:68).

The cultivable lands and house sites which belong to the sept are divided among the members of the clan as follows. One or more particular house sites and one or more particular parcels of cultivable land are reserved for the extended family which is headed by the holder of the senior matai title. Similarly, one or more particular house sites and one or more particular parcels of cultivable land are reserved for each of the other extended families of the clan, since they each represent one of the sub-septs of the sept.

After the holder of the senior matai title dies and a new title-holder is chosen, the cultivable lands and house sites which had been used by the extended family of the deceased title-holder are given over to the new title-holder's extended family. Similarly, the extended family of the successor to a sub-sept's matai title inherits the use of those house sites and cultivable lands which are reserved for that sub-sept.

In summary, the three types of descent group found in Samoa are differentiated as follows. The sept is a perpetuating, corporate descent group whose members trace a nonunilinear relationship back to the founder of the group. The sub-sept is a perpetuating, corporate descent group whose members trace a nonunilinear relationship back to a sibling or child of the founder of the sept. The clan is a nonperpetuating, noncorporate descent group which is defined by the fact that its members live on and use the land of the sept. The clan is not perpetuating in that its membership is subject to periodic replacement; at the death of the holder of a matai title which belongs to the sept, the deceased man's extended family is replaced by the extended family of the successor to that matai title. Thus, in contrast to the sept and sub-sept, whose members live in other villages in addition to the home village, the clan is a residential as well as a descent group. Finally, although the sept is the land-owning kin group, its cultivable lands and house sites are used by the clan. One of the constituent extended families of the clan has usufruct rights over certain house sites and cultivable lands because it is headed by the holder of the senior matai title of the sept; that is, the land this extended family lives on and uses is reserved for the senior matai. Each of the other constituent extended families of the clan has usufruct rights over certain house sites and cultivable lands because it represents one of the sub-septs of the sept; that is, the land each of these extended families lives on and uses is reserved for the sub-sept it represents. So that the reader might have a clear picture of how the three types of Samoan descent group are related, Figure 1 provides a diagram of the structure of the sept.

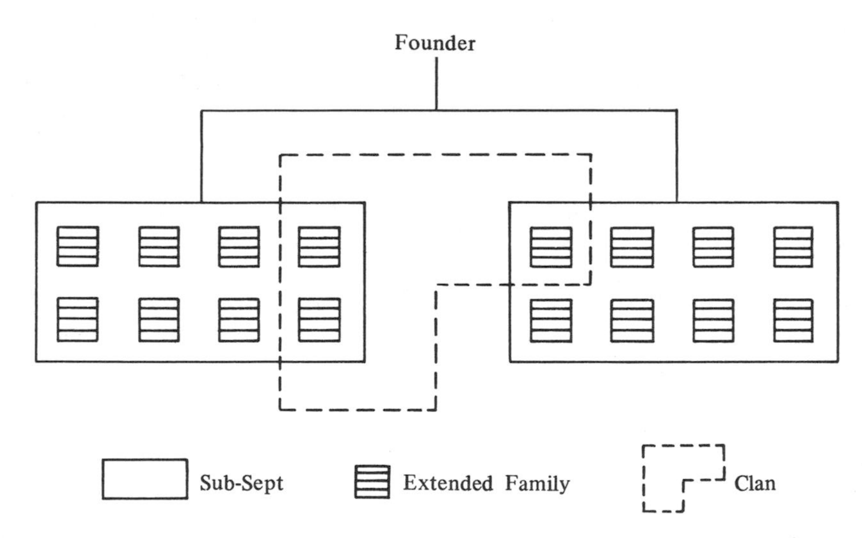

FIGURE 1. *The structure of the sept.*

CONCLUSION

The foregoing analysis of the Samoan descent groups does not hold for recent times. Although the sept and sub-sept still continue to function to some extent as interacting groups, there have been important changes in their residential distribution and relationship to land. Moreover, the clan has all but disappeared, owing to these changes. A complete account of the postcontact changes in Samoan kinship structure, based upon my field study of differential culture change in three villages of American Samoa, will be presented in the near future.

NOTES

1. This paper, in substantially the present form, was read at the 57th annual meeting of the American Anthropological Association in Washington, D. C., November 21, 1958. I am grateful to George P. Murdock and Peter J. Wilson for their constructive suggestions.
2. Field research in American Samoa was conducted between July 1955 and May 1956 under the auspices of the Tri-Institutional Pacific Program.

REFERENCES CITED

MEAD, MARGARET, 1930, Social organization of Manua. Bernice P. Bishop Museum, Bulletin 76.
MURDOCK, GEORGE PETER, 1949, Social structure. New York, Macmillan.
TURNER, GEORGE, 1861, Nineteen years in Polynesia. London.

6

POLITICAL AUTHORITY AND THE STRUCTURE OF KINSHIP IN ABORIGINAL SAMOA[1]

Melvin Ember

Aboriginal Samoa did not have a central government. Indeed, political integration of any kind beyond the village level was infrequent and short-lived. And even on the village level political authority was diffused rather than centralized. How this political system was a function of the way kin groups were constituted is the subject of this paper.[2]

I shall suggest that the extent to which political authority could be exercised was so strictly limited by the kinship structure that no centralization of political authority was possible, on the local as well as supra-local level. First, I shall briefly describe the political system. Then, I shall discuss the kinship structure. And, finally, I shall show how that structure entails a diffused system of political authority. The paper will conclude with some comments on how the kinship structure may have developed and why it did not change so as to allow the emergence of a more centralized political system.

The Political System

As I noted above, the 50,000–60,000 people who aboriginally inhabited the Samoan Islands were not politically unified. There was no hierarchy of political officials culminating in a king or paramount chief who was culturally empowered to initiate behavior for the whole society. Moreover, except when several villages would temporarily band together for purposes of war, political integration was usually limited to the individual village. And even when villages would confederate for military purposes, there still was no special type of person who was accorded the right to exercise supreme authority. All decisions as to how the confederation would fight the war had to be unanimously agreed upon by the political authorities of the constituent villages. Lastly, not even on the village level was political authority centralized. Decisions affecting the village could only be made by a council of

Reproduced by permission of the American Anthropological Association and Melvin Ember from the *American Anthropologist,* 64:964–971 (October, 1962).

chiefs, and here again the decisions had to be unanimous. This rule of unanimity did not mean that all of the council members had to agree publicly before a decision could be voiced. But it did mean that no decision was possible if any member disagreed publicly; for each chief represented an alignment of kin which constituted a sizable portion of the village. Thus, council decisions had to be unanimous if they were to result in concerted action by the village as a whole.

In sum, political authority in aboriginal Samoa was centralized neither on the society level nor on the local level. Rather, it was more or less evenly distributed among the various men who had succeeded to the headship of certain kin groups and were therefore accorded the right to participate in decision-making in behalf of the village.

The Kinship Structure

Kinship in aboriginal Samoa was structured by a series of nonunilinear descent groups whose general characteristics have previously been described (Ember 1959). The present discussion will be restricted to two particular features of the kinship structure which have implications for political organization. As we shall see in the next section, it is these features which were responsible for the diffusion of political authority in old Samoa. And, as we shall see in the present section, these same features also have implications for another issue, namely, the classification of linear kinship structures. With this as a background, let me now identify the two features of Samoan kinship structure to which I have been referring.

The first is one which I did not explicitly identify in my previous article. It is that the largest dispersed descent group in the Samoan system (the *'aiga sa* or "sept") contained only one localized segment. That is, the entire sept included only one group of members who lived together and worked as a unit (with their spouses); in Murdock's (1949) terms, each sept had but one "clan." The other members of the sept, who were in the vast majority, lived scattered in the same village and elsewhere, as members of the clan segments of other septs. In other words, the sept only owned land in one village —the place where its founding ancestor reputedly established the line. Since there was no such thing as sept land in more than one village, there could only be one clan segment per sept.

The second feature of interest to us here was briefly described in my previous article. It is that the membership of one sept overlapped with the memberships of other septs. Although at any one time you could only live with the clan segment of one sept, you still belonged to a number of septs, possibly as many as seven or eight in all, and each one possibly located in a different village. Moreover, you could change your residence (and your active sept affiliation) any time you wanted to, so long as the clan you wanted to join had room for you. And your claim to membership in a given sept did not expire unless you wanted it to expire. Only if you did not fulfill your obligations as a member (e.g., by not providing food for such sept ceremonies as funerals and weddings) or if you forgot how to trace your relationship to the sept (because for some reason it was no longer important to you) would the other members ultimately disallow your and your descendants' claim to membership. But this was rare. Normally a person would remember and maintain all of his recognized sept connections because to do so insured that his descendants would always have some claim to land.

In short, although the sept has been classified by myself (Ember 1959) and by others (Davenport 1959, Murdock 1960) as the nonunilinear counterpart of the unilinear sib (Murdock 1949)—in that both are dispersed groups whose members acknowledge an imprecise bond of common descent—it should now be clear that the sept and the sib are actually quite different structurally. For one thing, membership in the sib is much more exclusive. But what differentiates the sept from the sib even more clearly is the way the group is localized. In contrast to the sib, which has a number of clan segments (each localized in a different community), the sept is a dispersed descent group which has only one clan segment.

Now, how does the sept type of kinship structure compare with that other nonunilinear type of structure which Murdock (1960) and Sahlins (1958) have called the "ramage," after Firth (1957, 1936)?

The crucial point here is that the uni-localized nature of the sept not only differentiates it from the unilinear or so-called "lineage" type of kinship structure; it also differentiates the sept from the ramage. For the ramage is the nonunilinear variant, as the lineage is the unilinear variant, of the situation in which there is more than one localized segment of the largest dispersed descent group. In the absence of detailed descriptions of the Samoan type of descent group, it is very easy to confuse it with the ramage, just as in the absence of detailed descriptions of the ramage, it is very easy to confuse that type of group with the lineage. Thus, the fact that we have not previously been aware of the uni-localized nature of the sept probably explains why Murdock (1960), as well as Davenport (1959), fails to differentiate it from the ramage. Sahlins (1958) does distinguish the Samoan type of group (or "descent-line" in his terms) from the ramage; but he does so on a number of other grounds than the presence or absence of more than one localized segment, and no one of his criteria is sufficient by itself, as is localization, to discriminate the two types of group in all cases. Accordingly, in order to define the Samoan type of descent group most simply, and at the same time to avoid confusing it with the ramage type of descent group, I suggest that we might henceforth reserve the term "sept" to that type of nonunilinear dispersed descent group in which there is only one localized segment or clan. This usage, in fact, would return the word "sept" to its original meaning in anthropology. In 1920, Boas first used the term with reference to the Kwakiutl *numaym* (which also was a dispersed but uni-localized nonunilinear descent group), in order to differentiate that group from the then (and still) better known unilinear and multi-localized sib.

The Political Consequences of Sept Organization

An individual is said to have political *power* when he has influence over the affairs of a territorial unit, such as a village, region, or nation. An individual is said to have political *authority* when he "holds political office," i.e., when he is accorded the right to exercise political power. Thus, if we want to understand how the Samoan type of kinship structure entails a diffused or noncentralized system of political authority, we must first understand how that structure limits the extent to which political power can be exercised by a single individual.

There is good reason to assume that, in a relatively simple culture like that of aboriginal Samoa, the power of a given individual depends almost entirely upon the size of the group he can count on for support. For if the ability to get others to do what they would not otherwise do depends ultimately upon the use (or threat of use) of physical force, and if the weapons which might be used to effect such compliance are equally available to every able-bodied man in the society, then clearly the greater the number of men who are willing to fight for a leader, the greater will be his power in the society. Aboriginal Samoa was just such a society; the weapons which the culture provided (spears, clubs) could be made easily enough that they were equally available to every able-bodied man. Accordingly, the power of a chief in Samoa was called his *malosi,* literally the (number of) "arms," i.e., fighting men, who would stand behind him if any conflict he was involved in with another chief ever came to a showdown.

Now, although the chief was selected by the entire sept whose ancestral title he held, it was only the clan (the group he lived with and directed in every-day activities) that he could confidently rely on for support in case of conflict with another chief.[3] The scattered members of the sept owed their primary allegiance in such conflict situations to the chiefs with whom they were respectively living. This is not to say that some of the scattered members of the sept, especially those living in other villages, did not sometimes join with their fellow sept members when the rights of the localized segment (e.g., with regard to land) were threatened by another clan in the village. This would happen at times, but it had little to do with the amount of political authority possessed by a chief. The degree to which the other chiefs of the village permitted a given chief to participate in council decision-making was mostly a function of the size of his clan; the larger it was, the more the other chiefs were obliged to pay attention to his wishes.

Significantly, however, no one clan was ever permanently larger than the others in the village, and so no one chiefly title was ever permanently accorded greater political authority. Although at any one time there usually was at least one chiefly title in the village which commanded greater deference than the others, its holder was still only a *primus inter pares.* He might be accorded the right to voice the final decision of the council, but if even one other chief publicly disagreed with the prevailing sentiment no decision could be voiced. That political power and political authority were distributed more or less equally among the chiefs of the village, because the clans of the village were all more or less the same size, was a direct consequence of the kinship structure.

In contrast to the situation in a lineage or ramage type of system, a person in a sept type of system can change his active descent group affiliation (and, accordingly, his clan residence) very easily, because he always retains membership in a number of different descent groups. And since a person in a clan of excessive size can usually move into another clan whose membership has been unnaturally reduced (by war or disease), the result is that the clans in a sept type of system are not subject to the great fluctuations in size which seem to be inevitable in a lineage system (and in a ramage system as well, to the extent that the descent group memberships are exclusive). In other words, the permanently overlapping memberships, and the redistributions of excess members which are thereby facilitated, keep the clans in a sept type of system at more or less the same size over time (cf. Goodenough 1955:80).

Thus, the problem of natural clan increase was normally solved in the Samoan system by regular redistributions of excess personnel from one clan to another. Individuals would be sloughed off principally through the mechanisms of adoption and post-marital residence shifts. If the clan segment of a given sept began to exceed the size which was maximally permitted by its land resources, a child might be given to another clan to which it was related (which wanted another helping hand and could afford another mouth to feed), or a couple might move from the husband's clan (the usual place of post-marital residence) to another clan less pressed for land in which either he or his wife had a claim to membership.

Although the redistribution of excess personnel was the normal response to the problem of natural clan increase, two other responses did occasionally occur: 1) a clan might split into two groups, one moving away from the "home" village of the sept; or 2) a clan might attempt to enlarge its land holdings at the expense of another clan in the village. The splitting of a Samoan clan, while resembling the process of segmentary fission observed in lineage systems, differs from it in two respects. First, the group which would split off from the rest of the clan would move to another, already existing village—not to a previously uninhabited area, as is typically the case in a lineage system. Second, instead of continuing to acknowledge common ancestry with the original clan (as would the offshoot of a lineage), the new clan in Samoa would consider itself to be the localized segment of a new sept—even though it sometimes retained the old sept name. As for the other occasional response to the problem of natural clan increase—attempting to seize land belonging to another clan—this did not usually solve the problem since the rest of the village would usually intervene and stop the seizure in order to keep the peace.[4] Such action by the village would have the same effect, then, as the regular redistributions of excess personnel and the occasional cases of "segmentary fission"—namely the maintenance of a more or less equitable (i.e., equal) distribution of land holdings among the clans of the village.

In sum, it should now be clear why I suggest that a sept type of kinship structure entails the absence of centralized political authority. One feature of a sept system is that memberships in the dispersed descent groups are considerably overlapping; an individual always retains membership in a number of such groups. Because of this fact, the problem of natural increase in the localized segments of the septs is normally solved by regular redistributions of excess personnel from one clan to another through the mechanisms of adoption and post-marital residence shifts. These mechanisms, together with occasional cases of "segmentary fission," maintain a dynamic equilibrium in which the clans of the village are more or less the same size over time. Given that the power of a chief in the village is largely a function of the size of his clan (since the only discrete group which can stand unequivocally behind a chief is the localized segment of the sept whose title he holds), the fact that there is no appreciable variation in the size of clans means that no chief occupies a dominant power position in the village. And, since there is no other way to acquire the right to exercise power in village affairs except through succession to chiefship, the fact that power is more or less equally distributed among the chiefs of the village means that political authority must also be so distributed.

Lastly, if a sept type of kinship structure entails a noncentralized distribution of political authority on the local level, it likewise entails a noncentralized distribution of political authority on the supra-local level. In a lineage or ramage type of society, political integration may embrace more than one community, and political authority may be centralized in such a territorial unit, because a given dispersed descent group (and its chief) can acquire a dominant power position by virtue of having clan segments in more villages (and, accordingly, more control over land and other natural resources) than other descent groups. The more resources controlled by a dispersed descent group, the more people it can include and therefore the more powerful its chief can be. But in a sept type of society, political integration cannot permanently embrace more than the single community. For no one descent group (and its chief) occupies a dominant power position in more than one village (and not even there, as we have seen) since the group only has a localized segment and, accordingly, only controls land and other natural resources in its "home" village.

HISTORICAL SPECULATIONS

This paper has been addressed to the functional problem of how the Samoan type of kinship structure entails a diffused distribution of political authority. The historical problems still remain: How did that kinship structure develop? And why didn't it change so as to allow the emergence of a more centralized political system? Although I am not prepared at this time to offer solutions to these problems, I do want to suggest two ways we might approach them.

The first way is to conceive of sept organization as an early form of lineage and/or ramage organization. We might then hypothesize that only when the sept becomes a sib or a ramage might a given dispersed descent group and its chief acquire a dominant position with respect to wealth (in a number of communities as well as in its "home" community) so that the uneven distribution of power which would result might be transformed into a centralized system of political authority. Accordingly, we would need to know more about those factors: 1) which allow multi-localized descent groups to develop; 2) which allow one such group to proliferate faster, and hence acquire control over more land and other natural resources, than other such groups; and 3) which allow the resulting uneven distribution of power to be transformed into a centralized political system.

The second way we might approach the historical problems, and the way which I favor at the present time, is to conceive of sept organization as a collapsed form (rather than as an early form) of lineage and/or ramage organization.[5] Given the fact that most Polynesian societies had ramage organization at the time of contact (Sahlins 1958), we might hypothesize that Samoa also had such a system at one time but that it eventually collapsed into a sept system because of limiting local conditions.

One such limiting condition might have been the scarcity, after a time, of land which could be easily brought into permanent cultivation. Frake (1956:172) has suggested that descent group systems (such as the Samoan), which are characterized by overlapping memberships and regular readjustments in the man-land ratio, will occur only in environments (like the Samoan) which have a limited amount of permanently cultivable land (or, more precisely, a limited amount of permanently cultivable land already cleared of primary forest—cf. Goodenough 1956:174–75). Except for the coastal flats and slight slopes immediately behind them, and the valleys of a few small streams, most of Samoa is extremely mountainous and unsuitable for permanent cultivation. Thus, after the limited supply of fairly flat land had been cleared, new land which could be brought into permanent cultivation must have been extremely scarce.

In such a "closed" ecological situation, a sept type of system may be more adaptive than a ramage type of system, if only because the man-land ratio could be more easily (i.e., peacefully) readjusted in a sept than in a ramage system. In a ramage system, membership in a given dispersed descent group wipes out all possible memberships in other descent groups (at least after a generation), but this is not so in a sept system. The continuing possibility of affiliating with a number of descent groups, in addition to the one in which you live, is maintained in the Samoan type of system. And this greater flexibility with regard to an environment in which cleared land was at a premium also expressed itself in the way men succeeded to chiefly authority. In contrast to the ramage type of system, there was no regular rule of succession in Samoa, much less a rule of primogeniture which seems to have been characteristic of ramage systems.

This last-mentioned difference between the two types of system, taken together with the other differences discussed in this paper, suggests that ramage organization may ultimately be found to occur only in societies which are still expanding, both numerically and territorially (as seems to be the case with the classical examples of segmentary lineage organization—see Sahlins 1961), while sept organization may ultimately be found to occur only in societies which have reached the point where no new land (resources) can be brought into permanent cultivation (production) and further population increase is therefore precluded.

NOTES

1. This paper is a slightly revised and expanded version of one which was read at the meeting of the Central States Anthropological Society, May 4, 1961, in Columbus, Ohio. The occasion was a symposium, organized by Millicent Ayoub, on the implications of nonunilinear kinship.

2. The data upon which this paper is based were collected in Samoa during 1955–56. I am grateful to the Tri-Institutional Pacific Program for sponsoring the field work.

3. The word "chief" refers here only to the senior titleholder of a sept. That is, I am not dealing here with the junior title-holder in a sept, who headed a sub-sept, because he did not have any appreciable political authority. (See Ember 1959 for additional information on the junior title-holder.)

4. The fact that feuds over land did occur in aboriginal times, and that land sometimes passed thereby from the control of one clan to another, probably explains why the parcels of land which were cultivated by a clan were not all continuously distributed.

5. The reader is referred to a paper by Lane (1961), published after the present paper was submitted, which suggests that the "bilateral" systems of Polynesia represent breakdowns of "lineage" systems, owing to demographic factors associated with the risks of oceanic canoe voyages and settlement in marginal environments.

REFERENCES CITED

BOAS, FRANZ, 1920, The social organization of the Kwakiutl. American Anthropologist 22: 111–26.

DAVENPORT, WILLIAM, 1959, Nonunilinear descent and descent groups. American Anthropologist 61:557–72.

EMBER, MELVIN, 1959, The nonunilinear descent groups of Samoa. American Anthropologist 61:573–77.

FIRTH, RAYMOND, 1936, We, the Tikopia. London, Allen and Unwin.

1957, A note on descent groups in Polynesia. Man 57:4–8.

FRAKE, CHARLES O., 1956, Malayo-Polynesian land tenure. American Anthropologist 58: 170–73.

GOODENOUGH, WARD H., 1955, A problem in Malayo-Polynesian social organization. American Anthropologist 57:71–83.

1956, Reply (to Frake 1956). American Anthropologist 58:173–76.
LANE, ROBERT B., 1961, A reconsideration of Malayo-Polynesian social organization. American Anthropologist 63:711–20.
MURDOCK, GEORGE PETER, 1949, Social structure. New York, Macmillan.
1960, Cognatic forms of social organization. *In* Social structure in southeast Asia, George Peter Murdock, ed., pp. 1–14. Chicago, Quadrangle Books (Viking Fund Publications in Anthropology, Number 29).
SAHLINS, MARSHALL D., 1958, Social stratification in Polynesia. Seattle, University of Washington Press.
1961, The segmentary lineage: an organization of predatory expansion. American Anthropologist 63:322–45.

7

SOME OBSERVATIONS ON KINSHIP AND POLITICAL AUTHORITY IN SAMOA

Derek Freeman

In the study of Polynesian social systems Samoa has long occupied a position of importance. Of late, however, it has become a confused position, for Marshall D. Sahlins and Melvin Ember have, in recent years, published views (Sahlins: 1958; Ember: 1959 and 1962 a, b) which diverge markedly from the consensus reached by other scholars. It may then be of value to subject the views of these two writers to brief critical scrutiny.

Let me begin by considering the views of Drs. Ember and Sahlins on the nature of the Samoan descent system. Ember has claimed that his own conclusions support those of Sahlins, but concerning descent in Samoa they are scarcely in semantic accord. Sahlins, in his book *Social Stratification in Polynesia,* consistently describes the Samoan descent system as "patrilineal" (1958:181 seq.), and writes of the local pattern of grouping as being one of "patrilineages." Ember, in contrast, asserts that Samoa "lacks unilinear descent groups" (1959:573), and is a "bilateral society" in which all the descent groups are "nonunilinear" (1958:61).

It is salutary to reflect that these logically irreconcilable definitions refer to the same reality, for, as this suggests, it is no simple reality to be subsumed under a single logical principle, but rather a complex reality calling for somewhat more subtle understanding.

I would like to illustrate this by considering briefly Samoan customary law as it applies to succession to the titled headship of descent groups, for on this topic we are fortunate in having for our guidance the pronouncements of two learned jurists, Imperial Justice Dr. E. Schultz and Judge C. C. Marsack, each of whom was for many years President of the Land and Titles Court (or Commission, as it was called in German times) of Western Samoa.

Sahlins, we have seen, defines the Samoan descent system as "patrilineal." In this he is acknowledging the strong emphasis on patriliny

Reproduced by permission of the American Anthropological Association and Derek Freeman from the *American Anthropologist,* 66:553–568 (June, 1964). Revised by the author for this publication.

which characterizes Samoan society. Somewhat similarly, Schultz, in discussing succession to the headship of descent groups, writes: "the Samoan law of inheritance rests upon relationship in the sense of the German legal term agnation" (1911:51). However, having pointed to this agnatic basis, Schultz at once goes on to say that there are contingencies in which cognates may succeed, so indicating that we are not dealing with an absolute rule of agnatic succession, but rather with a predominant principle to which, in certain circumstances, exceptions are possible.

Marsack (1961:10) makes the same kind of point in his discussion of succession to *matai* titles when he writes: ". . . no one has a vested right to a title by way of inheritance. The old Samoan principle *"toe 'o le uso"* —the right of the surviving brother—is entitled to respect, but confers no binding obligation. In the same way the eldest or any other son of the deceased matai cannot demand, as a matter of right, that he step into his father's shoes. Close blood relations are usually the first to be considered for appointment to a title which has fallen vacant; but the mere fact of the blood tie gives them no pre-emptive right."

In other words, under Samoan customary law, there is no prescriptive rule of patrilineal succession. However, this *de jure* situation does not entitle one to infer that succession in Samoa is, in consequence, "bilateral" or "nonunilinear," for this lack of prescription is accompanied by a pronounced *de facto* emphasis on patriliny.[1]

This feature of the Samoan descent system has been clearly grasped by Firth (1957:5) in his distinction between definitive and optative descent groups in Polynesia. Thus, Firth contrasts definitive descent group systems (for example, Tikopia, where patriliny is "operative in practice for all normal occasions") with optative systems "such as those of the Maori, Tonga or Samoa, in which the major emphasis is upon descent in the male line, but allowance is made, in circumstances so frequent in some societies as to be reckoned as normal, for entitlement to membership through a female."

We may say then that for Samoa the anthropologist's task is to study options as they actually happen, so that the predominant emphasis upon descent in the male line may be accurately gauged and exceptions to it analyzed to reveal the nature of the situations in which they occur. It is also obvious that it is futile to suppose that the Samoan descent system can be comprehended by classifying it definitively as either "patrilineal" or "bilateral," for it is, in fact, neither of these things, but rather, as Firth has indicated, an optative system with a major emphasis on patriliny.

Despite their divergent definitions of descent, Sahlins and Ember do appear to be in agreement in claiming that Samoa is characterized by the absence of any kind of ramified structure: Sahlins (1958:251) has contended that Samoan society is composed of "small, unrelated descent lines"; and Ember (1962b:968) has stated that when segmentation occurred in aboriginal Samoa, the segment breaking away "instead of continuing to acknowledge common ancestry" with the descent group it was leaving, would consider itself to be a new localized unit. In short the existence of any kind of ramified descent system in Samoa is specifically denied by both Sahlins and Ember—though without any kind of empirical documentation. What then of the ethnographic evidence?

In Samoa, as elsewhere in Polynesia, genealogies *(gafa)* are accorded especial significance, for they constitute the *memoria technica* of the descent system, tracing both agnatic and cognatic linkages. "In Samoa," writes Ella (1895:598), "the genealogy of chiefs, especially of high chiefs, was preserved with great care, and the custody was committed to a select class, who were very careful and jealous of the honourable and responsible function they held." That these genealogies do in fact exist may be confirmed by consulting Augustin Krämer's classic monograph *Die Samoa-Inseln,* the first volume of which (published in Stuttgart in 1902) contains extensive genealogies from all parts of the Samoan archipelago, both western and eastern, and which, in Krämer's words (1902:6), "show the origin of the principal families."[2] Similarly, though they are not to be found in Krämer (it would take many scores of volumes to record them), there are the genealogies of the lesser families, many of which, as Grattan has observed (1948:172), are to-day preserved in writing in family books. However, as Grattan (who was for many years Secretary of Samoan Affairs in Western Samoa) has also noted (1948:67): "it is a grave offence in Samoan custom to 'open' or recite genealogies without authority." "This," continues Grattan, "is so important that it has actually been written into the statute law of the Territory." This law exists because, given the intense rivalry of families, the "facts" of genealogy readily become the subject of heated dispute. As Mead (1930:135) has remarked: "The recital of another family's genealogy is always regarded as an insult."

In this situation the ethnographer is faced with difficulties, and Krämer has written entertainingly of the stratagems he himself had to use in collecting genealogies. At the outset of my own field study of Sa'anapu (on the southern coast of Upolu), which I began with a good knowledge of the Samoan language, I was informed by the assembled chiefs of the village that I must never inquire into genealogies, and it was not until about 15 months later that one of the leading orators *(tulafale),* as an act of especial friendship, surreptitiously made available to me his own genealogy book of the village. From this point my understanding of the descent structure of Sa'anapu progressed rapidly and I was eventually able to discuss genealogical questions with several of the chiefs.

There is, then, abundant evidence that, to use the words of Mead (1930: 135) "genealogies of Polynesian type" are kept in Samoa. Again, as Firth has pointed out (1936:581; 1957:5), the type of descent system existing in Samoa also occurs in Tonga and other parts of Polynesia, with, as one of its principal features, descent groups with a "branching character," to which

Firth has applied the generic term "ramage." It is this ramified system which Sahlins and Ember have asserted to be non-existent in Samoa.

In contrast, many other scholars, on the basis of long and close acquaintance with Samoan society, have described Samoa as possessing a ramified descent system of the general kind defined by Firth. Schultz (1911:43) writes of the Samoan people being "divided like a clan into families, *āiga,* which again are split into groups or branches." Krämer (1902:476) notes that if a family is very large, it divides into sub-families called *itū'āiga,* each of these sub-families having its own titled head under the principal chief of the family. Pratt (1911:53) gives itū'āiga as the term for "a division or branch of a family." Buck (1931:70), in evidence submitted to the Presidential Commission on American Samoa, at a session held in Honolulu, Hawaii, on September 20, 1930, stated, with regard to the families *('āiga)* into which the Samoan people were divided: "In the course of time, the families split up into branches which preserved their connection with one another through the oral transmission of their genealogical tables. The branches might occupy the same village or spread to other villages."

Marsack (1961:8), in discussing the splitting of matai titles, a practice which, with the rapid increase in the Samoan population, has become a common occurrence, states that the attitude of the Land and Titles Court is that "there should be one title-holder only, or possibly one title-holder to each well known and generally accepted branch of a large family: such as occurs in the Asi family, where the branches Asi Sagaga, Asi Falana'ipupu, Asi Leuluaiali'i and Asi Tuiataga are universally recognized." Mead (1930:134), in discussing descent in Manu'a, writes of the "splitting up" of families into "branches." J. W. Davidson (1963:Ms.), who was Chairman of the official Commission which in 1950 conferred with chiefs and orators throughout Western Samoa on village and district government, has described "the fundamental facts of genealogy" as "the most important key to an understanding of the balance of power in village politics," and has expressed the view that the character of Samoan social structure, and the complexity of Samoan politics, can only be understood in relation to "processes of progressive segmentation and of consolidation through the creation of new family linkages."

From my own researches I am in full agreement with these depictions of the descent structure of Samoa. I have already referred to the genealogies of Sa'anapu. These genealogies are complicated, and I have no intention of embarking on their exegesis here, but I do want to record that these genealogies demonstrate the existence of a ramified descent structure, which is, moreover, a structure in terms of which the people of Sa'anapu, in various ways, order their social behavior.

For example, in Sa'anapu, the main grouping of titular 'āiga (local descent groups or ramages) are the To'alima. In 1943, this grouping consisted of ten related 'āiga, each with a matai whose tenure of his title had been ratified by the village *fono,* and all of these 'āiga variously claimed descent from a common male ancestor named La'a (see my note, dated June, 1968, at the end of this paper). The fact that the To'alima were related by descent was recognized in the seating plan of the fono by their entitlement to occupy a set of posts in any *fale tele* (ceremonial round house) of Sa'anapu; as also in the *fa'alupega* (honorific titles) of the village.

A similar kind of ramified structure also exists at supra-village levels. For example, as is recorded in the genealogy book of one of the orators of Sa'anapu village, the local 'āiga of the high chief 'Anapu is a branch of a great 'āiga (of about ten generations depth), the Sā Tunumafonō, branches of which (said to be descended from the sons of Tunumafono) also exist in the neighboring villages of Sataoa, Lotofagā, Nu'usuatia and Vaie'e, and all of which, as is confirmed by Krämer (1902:235), are referred to throughout Samoa as the Sā Tunumafonō.

To point to the existence of a ramified structure at village and supra-village levels is not, however, to contend, as Ember would seem to think (1962a:124), that Samoa possessed "an overarching, genealogical hierarchy of descent groups." To so contend would be to ignore the patent facts of Samoan history: one of the cardinal points about Samoa is that while there were a number of high chiefs supported by ramified groupings of considerable scale, there was no overarching genealogical hierarchy, and, as I noted some years ago (1947:295), "no system of centralized political authority."

However, I do not regard "an overarching, genealogical hierarchy" as intrinsic to a ramified descent system. This condition is not even met in Tikopia, where, in 1929, with the small population of 1,281, there were four different clans (Firth, 1936:366). In Samoa, with a total population (in 1853) of 33,901, and as many as 15,587 and 12,444 respectively on the islands of Upolu and Savai'i,[3] the situation, as might be expected, was rather more complicated with nothing approaching an "overarching, genealogical hierarchy."

Again, it does not even happen, in Samoa, that all of the 'āiga of a village are contained within a single genealogical hierarchy. As can be discerned from the fa'alupega books compiled by the Samoans themselves for the use of orators and others (1915:5 seq.), Samoan villages, being the outcome of unique historical processes (such as conquest and alliance), exhibit in their composition considerable variation and complexity; however, in all of the villages and districts known to me, ramified descent groups, of greater or smaller range, are basic to the social structure.

The principal word used by the Samoans to describe their descent groups is " 'āiga."[4] In addition there is the particle *sā̧* which when prefixed to a personal name or title (commonly that of a male ancestor) signifies a family or descent group, as, for example, *Sā Faoā̧*[5] meaning the family of Faoa.[6]

The terms 'āiga and sā are used by the Samoans to refer to groupings at all levels in their society, a fact which, in itself, indicates the presence of a ramified structure based on descent. Thus, in Sa'anapu village the term 'āiga is applied to all of the different descent groups and groupings within the village. I have already referred to the fact that the 'āiga of 'Anapu is a branch of the Sā Tunumafonō, a major grouping of about ten generations depth. The Sā Tunumafonō is also referred to in fa'alupega and elsewhere by the term 'āiga. At even higher levels, as Krämer notes (1902:476), the word 'āiga is applied to villages and districts which "are accustomed to taking the side wholly or in part of a great chief, to whom they are related." For example, there are a number of districts and villages in different parts of Upolu and Savai'i which are known as the 'āiga of the high chief Malietoa. Again, high chiefs, like Malietoa, are traditionally known as *Tama'āiga,* a phrase which is commonly translated as "Royal Son," but which has the literal meaning (Pratt 1911) of "Son with many family connections." At this level the facts of relationship by descent have been modified in various ways by the events of history (and particularly by the wars which were endemic in former times), but it is significant to note that 'āiga is still the term employed.

I would suggest that detailed study of the referents of the word 'āiga, at all levels, would contribute greatly to the understanding of the complex ramifications of the Samoan descent system.

Dr. Ember (1959:574) has applied to the Samoan descent group the "generic name" of " 'aiga sa," and this has been taken up by other anthropologists (e.g. Davenport 1959 and Leach 1962). Before this usage becomes more widely adopted it should be recorded that it is catachrestic. The particle *sā* as in Sā Faoā (meaning the family of Faoa), can only be used as a prefix; it is never used alone and is never the attribute of a preceding word. When the morph *sā* is made to follow a noun it becomes an adjective with the entirely different meaning of forbidden or holy (Pratt 1911:261). Thus the form " 'aiga sa," created by Dr. Ember, means forbidden or holy family, a conceivable theological usage, but not a term that any Samoan in his right mind would apply to his own, or any other, descent group.

I would next like to consider Dr. Ember's article "Political Authority and the Structure of Kinship in Aboriginal Samoa" (1962b:964–971). The object of this article is to demonstrate how the political system in ancient Samoa "was a function of the way kin groups were constituted." Now, as we have seen, Dr. Ember believes (with Dr. Sahlins) that Samoan society was composed of localized descent groups that were not part of any kind of ramified structure. From this and other assumptions, Dr. Ember argues that a certain type of political structure is logically entailed. We are thus presented with a hypothesized functional relationship between descent groups and political structure. This hypothesized functional relationship is of a kind that can be readily tested. I propose to do this by presenting evidence to show that Dr. Ember is at error both in his assumptions and his conclusions, and I shall argue that on these grounds his hypothesis ought to be rejected.

Let me begin by stating Dr. Ember's own argument (all references are to Ember's article in the *American Anthropologist* [1962b]). The largest dispersed group in the Samoan system, asserts Ember (1962b:965), "contained only one localized segment."[7] Further, if one of these localized groups split or segmented, the section breaking away, "instead of continuing to acknowledge common ancestry" with the group from which it had originated (1962b:968), considered itself a new localized unit.

The power of a chief, according to Ember (1962b:966), depended almost entirely upon the size of the group he could count on for support. Further (1962b:967), it was only the localized descent group ("the group he lived with and directed in everyday activities") that a chief could rely upon for support in case of conflict with another chief; and these localized groups were (1962b:967) "all more or less the same size."

Therefore, concludes Ember, because the power of a chief was the function of the size of his localized descent group, "political power and political authority were distributed more or less equally among the chiefs of a village" (1962b:967), and political integration could not permanently embrace "more than a single community" (1962b:969).

I have already presented evidence to show that Samoa, contrary to the beliefs of Drs. Ember and Sahlins, did possess a ramified descent structure both at village and supra-village levels. Let me now go on to examine Dr. Ember's assertions about the nature of chieftainship in early Samoa.

The first thing to be said about Dr. Ember's depiction of Samoan chieftainship is that it ignores the elementary facts of Samoan history and ethnography. As can be ascertained by studying the historical sources, the chiefly titles of ancient Samoa varied greatly in rank, ranging from those of insignificant matai to august titles such as *Tui Manu'a* in the easternmost islands and *Tui Atua, Tui Ā'ana* and *Malietoa* in the west, titles which were of culminating religious and political importance. The other high titles which, at various times, assumed political importance are too numerous to mention here, but accounts of them have been given by many early authorities, and particularly by Stair (1897), Pratt (1890), and Ella (1895), each of whom was long resident in Samoa and studied at first hand the intricacies of the traditional system of chieftainship. Ella's paper "The Ancient Samoan Government," incorporating notes by Stair, and presented to the Sixth Meeting of the Australasian Association for the Advancement of Science in 1895, is perhaps the best account from the early period of observation beginning in the late 1830's. An illuminating and scholarly survey of the principal titles and their complex interrelationships is also given by Krämer (1902:7 seq.).

The holders of the highest titles in ancient Samoa were called *ali'i pa'ia*, or sacred chiefs, and in the political life of the islands they occupied positions of paramount importance. Each of the great chiefs was connected by descent and history with a number of different villages and districts, and in warfare and manifold other activities the people of these places identified closely with their principal ali'i pa'ia, holding him in veneration and regarding themselves as his āiga.

Williams (1837:334) describes how in July, 1830, he witnessed the chief Fauea (himself of considerable rank) salute his ali'i pa'ia, Malietoa Vai'inupō, to whom he was related, with "the greatest possible respect, bowing sufficiently low to kiss his feet and making his child even kiss the soles of his feet."[8] And Hardie (1842: Ms.) reports how, when Malietoa Vai'inupō was ill at Sapapali'i, "his family and many others came from all parts of Savai'i, Manono and Upolu, to visit him in his sickness, bringing presents with them." Such incidents, which are very commonly reported by early observers of Samoan behavior, give an indication of the deep devotion and widespread allegiance on which an ali'i pa'ia could depend.

Of two other ali'i pa'ia, the Tui Atua and the Tui Ā'ana, Ella (1895:597) states that they were supreme in their districts, all the settlements of which rendered allegiance to them. And Krämer (1902:10) writes that in the event of the Tui Ā'ana declaring war against another district (e.g. Tuamasaga) he could be certain that the whole of the district of Ā'ana would flock to his ranks, if there were not any internal dissension between sub-districts.

As I have already noted there was in ancient Samoa no system of centralized political authority. There was, however, an institution which, unstable though it was, represented a powerful striving in this direction. Thus, if an ali'i pa'ia came to possess all of the highest titles of the ruling districts, he became known as the *Tupu*, or King of Samoa. These titles, in the early 19th century, were *Tui Atua*, *Tamasoāli'i* and *Gatoaitele* (of the Tuamasaga district), and *Tui A'ana* (these four *pāpā* being known collectively as the *tafa'ifā*); and *Le Pule 'o Salafai* (representing the whole of Savai'i); and they could be either conferred at the disposition of the respective districts, or secured by conquest in war (Ella 1895:597; Krämer 1902:12 seq.).

Malietoa Vai'inupō, the ali'i pa'ia to whom reference has already been made, was the first holder of the Malietoa title to be generally acknowledged as king, though there had been many other *Tupu* before him, mainly from the Sā Tupuā. Nightingale, an enquiring Lieutenant of Artillery who visited Samoa in 1834 to study natural history, describes Malietoa Vai'inupō as then possessing "an absolute sway over the whole group," and was much impressed by his venerable appearance (1835:79): " . . . encircled by numerous chiefs, his long grey hair flowing around him, his countenance, naturally stern, rendered still more austere by the furrows of age, he seemed the personification of despotism." Malietoa Vai'inupō died in 1842, and Samoan history during the rest of the 19th century is very largely the story of the struggle for the kingship, by the chiefs of three of the great families of Samoa: the Sā Malietoā, the Sā Tupuā, and the Sā Matā'afā, supported by their various 'āiga. These are the three families which, in Stair's words (1897:77): "comprise the aristocracy of Samoa, whose ramifications spread more or less through the whole group, and to one or other of which every chief is referable, no matter what his rank or title may be." In 1878, Maudslay (1930:205), a perceptive and experienced observer and then British Consul in Samoa, wrote (in a letter to his sister): "the essence of native politics is to be found in the 'King Question,' that is, whether Malietoa or Tupua shall be nominally King of all Samoa"; adding that a success in either case would be "a triumph of family pride." With the attainment of independence, Malietoa and Tamasese (of the Sā Tupuā) became jointly Head of the sovereign State of Western Samoa, while Matā'afa became its Prime Minister.[9]

It will be seen then that Dr. Ember's assumptions, which would confine the power and authority of chiefs to small descent groups within a single village community, are of a kind which completely fail to comprehend the realities of Samoan political organization—both ancient and modern.

Furthermore, his assumptions are not even accurate for purely village titles, for within villages matai titles also vary considerably in rank. Because each is the outcome of unique historical processes, the rank structures of Samoan villages vary greatly, which is why the Samoans themselves find it necessary to record these structures, village by village, in their fa'alupega books. However, differential rank there always is, and in some villages the rank of one chief far exceeds that of all others. It happens that Sa'anapu is a village of this kind (Freeman 1948, 1961). Under Samoan custom one of the principal ways of giving expression to rank is in the seating plan of the fono, or assembly of chiefs, which takes place in a *fale tele*, or round house. In the formal and traditional seating plan of the *fono* of Sa'anapu village, the premiership of the 'Anapu title is expressed by allotting to its holder the central post on one of the rounded sides (*tala*) of the house. Moreover, the post directly facing that of 'Anapu is by tradition left vacant in added recognition of his high rank. And, in the fa'alupega, or honorific phrases of the village, 'Anapu is saluted by the words: *Afio mai lau Afioga le Sa'o: 'o le Tama a le Mālō* (Honour to the Noble and Principal One: Born of Conquerors).

The term *sa'o* in this fa'alupega offers a good indication of 'Anapu's rank. Pratt (1911:263) gives as the meaning of *sa'oali'i:* "the principal chief, who has the right to determine what is proper (*sa'o*) to be done"; and this reports accurately the role of 'Anapu in the fono of Sa'anapu village as I observed it some 20 years ago.[10]

In many villages there is no one chief of principal rank as in Sa'anapu, but always there are well marked gradations in rank of one kind or another. In short, the ethnographic facts do not support Ember's conclusion that "political power and authority were distributed more or less equally among the chiefs of a village."

One of the weakest links in Ember's hypothesis is his simple supposition that the power of a chief was the function of the size of his localized descent group. To suppose this is to misunderstand almost entirely the nature of chiefly rank in ancient Samoa, which was based on a complex of religious and other values associated with the ramified descent system and its predominantly patrilineal ideology. I cannot present here an analysis of this complex, but its existence may be seen in the fact that chiefs of high rank were looked on as *pa'ia*, or sacred, and hedged about by all kinds of ritual observances.

Within villages, certainly, there was no simple co-relation between a chief's rank and the size of his local 'āiga. In Sa'anapu, for example, the local 'āiga of the high chief 'Anapu was, in 1943, one of the smallest in the village. And the same was true, *a fortiori*, of the great district chiefs. The "localized descent group" of an ali'i pa'ia like Malietoa Vai'inupō was no more numerous than that of many other chiefs, yet, because he held august and sacred titles with which the people of many different villages and districts identified, Malietoa Vai'inupō, as history records, could summon to his cause thousands of followers from all parts of Upolu, Manono and Savai'i.

Let me now turn to Dr. Ember's assertion (1962b:964) that in ancient Samoa "political integration of any kind beyond the village was infrequent and short-lived," which is one of the assumptions associated with his conclusion that in a society of the Samoan type "political integration cannot permanently embrace more than the single community."

Once again, Dr. Ember ignores the elementary facts of Samoan political history and geography. In one of his papers (1959:575) Ember cites an estimate of the size of the co-resident family from page 280 of Turner's *Nineteen Years in Polynesia*, a volume first published in 1861. On pages 287-292 of this same book (Turner 1861) there appears one of the earliest and best accounts of the organization of district government in Samoa. Thus, Turner (1861:287) describes how "villages, in numbers of eight or ten, unite by common consent, and form a district or state, for mutual protection. Some particular village is known as the capital of the district; and it was common of old to have a higher chief than any of the rest, as the head of that village, and who bore the title of King. . . . When war is threatened by another district, no single village can act alone; the whole district, or state, assemble at their capital, and have a special parliament to deliberate as to what should be done." In a book written some years later, at the conclusion of over 30 years' residence in Samoa, Dr. Turner devoted two chapters (1884:232 seq.) to the delineation of the political divisions and districts of Upolu and Savai'i.

Stair (1897:81), another early observer, has written:

The Samoan islands are divided into districts, which are subdivided into settlements, and these again into villages. The great divisions or districts are quite independent of each other, their boundaries being well known, and the care of them committed to the two nearest villages on either side, the inhabitants of which were called *Leoleo-tuā'oi*, or boundary keepers. . . . Each district had a leading settlement called its *Laumua.* It was the province of the Laumua to convene the fono, or general assembly of its respective districts, to announce the object for which it had been summoned, to preside over its deliberations, to arrange disputed or knotty points, as well as to sum up the proceedings and dismiss the assembly; in fact, to sustain the office of chairman. These meetings were usually conducted with much formality and decorum, the general fono of the district being always held in the open air, in the great *malae* of the leading settlement, or Laumua.

All of the other pioneer missionaries who have written about political organization have reported in similar terms. They include, in addition to Stair (1838-45) and Turner (1841-82), Heath (1836-48), Hardie (1836-54), Murray (1836-70), Pratt (1839-79), Harbutt (1840-1858), Powell (1845-85), and Ella (1848-62), all of whom, as will be seen, were long resident in Samoa, and whose collective experience of the archipelago extended from Ta'ū in the east to Falealupo in the west. For the most part, however, their observations remain in manuscript."[11]

Commander Wilkes, U.S.N., of the United States Exploring Expedition which visited all the islands of the Samoan archipelago in 1839, records (1845: Vol. 2., 93 seq.) the political districts into which the island of Upolu is divided, noting that each was governed by a "separate and independent chief, styled *Tui*";[12] and describes a fono held in the fale tele at Apia on November 4, 1839, attended by officers of the Expedition and "the highest chiefs" of the *mālō,* or ruling districts, and presided over by Malietoa Vai'inupō, "the principal chief of the *mālō,* or conquering party," and who, in his appearance and bearing reminded the American explorers of General Jackson.

W. T. Pritchard, who resided in Samoa for ten years from 1848 onwards (he succeeded his father as British Consul in 1856) has described (1866:51 seq.) the war in which the great political districts of Samoa were joined from 1848 to 1854, and written of the "district gods" that "presided over the various political divisions of the islands."

In more recent years authoritative accounts of the traditional political organization of Samoa have been given by Krämer (1902) particularly, and (in a useful survey) by Keesing (1934:48 seq.), both of whom have published maps showing the principal political districts. Krämer, indeed, in the first volume of *Die Samoa-Inseln,* having surveyed their historical origins, discusses all of the political districts of both western and eastern Samoa in great detail. By way of example, let me refer to his account (1902:148-221) of A'ana, one of the three principal districts of Upolu, which includes discussions of the constitution of the whole district (as expressed in its fa'alupega), the organization of its great fono held at the capital, Leulumoega; the location of its various sub-districts and villages, and the genealogy and history of the Tui Ā'ana (the high chief of the district), and its other most important families of rank.

The evidence I have cited demonstrates beyond question that political integration in ancient Samoa did embrace more than the single community. There is also conclusive evidence that this integration was neither "infrequent" nor "short-lived." When Williams and Barff first arrived in Samoa in July, 1830, a major war was raging which led to the defeat of Ā'ana by several other districts led by Malietoa Vai'inupō. During the decades that followed there was constant political activity at district level, of which we have a detailed record in the letters and journals of the early L.M.S. missionaries. Heath (1838:Ms.), for example, has described the great fono held in Savai'i in September, 1836, at which the victorious districts comprising the mālō decided to permit the people of Ā'ana to return to their settlements; Harbutt (1841:Ms.), "a large assembly of chiefs from all parts of Ā'ana" which he attended in 1841, at which it was decided (despite a serious affray) that Ā'ana should not go to war with her erstwhile enemies; and Hardie (1848:Ms.) and others, the political activity at district level which culminated in the war of 1848-1854, which again involved the Ā'ana district. In 1867, indeed, as Whitmee (Ms.) has recorded, the chiefs of Ā'ana succeeded in gaining the approval of the British, American and Hamburg consuls for an independent constitution for their district, or "state" (as Whitmee calls it).

The well defined district organization which European observers first reported in the 1830's has been one of the principal realities of Samoan political history ever since, and is still of great importance in Samoa today.[13] As to its earlier history, the Samoans aver that it is of great antiquity, and Krämer (1902:17), our greatest authority on Samoan traditions, came to the conclusion that in its main outlines the body politic of Samoa as it existed in the 19th century was "a comparatively recent one, i.e. about 500 years old."

Believing as I do that history always involves change, I have no desire to debate the "permanence" of the political districts of ancient Samoa; however, I think it can be said, on the evidence, that they were of no small importance and far from being "short-lived."

Dr. Ember (1962a:124) has suggested that there may possibly have been major differences in kinship and political structure between American and Western Samoa. On historical evidence this possibility can be dismissed. First, it should be noted that the division between American and Western Samoa, which came into being with the tripartite agreement between Germany, Great Britain and the United States of America of 1899, was no more than a demarcation of the colonial and strategic interests of these great powers, and did not represent, at that time, a division into ethnographic regions. I have no doubt that family and village life in American Samoa (and especially in Tutuila) have undergone drastic change after over 60 years of government and development by the United States, but Dr. Ember's formulations refer specifically to "aboriginal Samoa," and so to a period before the establishment of American influence in Tutuila and Manu'a.

Now, in ancient times, the easternmost islands of Ta'ū, Olosega and 'Ofu, did possess their own sacred chief of exalted rank, the Tu'i Manu'a, surrounding whom were special myths and rituals accompanied by other divergences from the practices of the western islands. However, they were, judging from the accounts of early missionaries like Powell (1857-61), and of Mead (1930) and Holmes (1958), no major differences of the kind suggested by Ember.

Tutuila, moreover, was, both politically and ethnographically, associated with the western islands, and particularly with the powerful district of Atua, at the eastern end of the island of Upolu (Ella 1895:597; Krämer 1902:312; Freeman 1943:109). That there were no great differences in the essentials of kinship and political authority as between Tutuila and the western islands is made plain in the writings of the pioneer missionaries, who were in a unique position to study aboriginal Samoa, and, particularly, in the papers of Thomas Powell. Powell arrived in Samoa in 1845, and in November of that year, visited and described the "three remaining heathen villages" on Tutuila. He was then stationed for some six years at Samata on the remote south-western coast of Savai'i, before returning to Tutuila, where he lived for nearly three decades with frequent visits to Manu'a before retiring in 1885, after 40 years' residence in Samoa. The observations of the Rev. Thomas Powell provide no support for Dr. Ember's statements that political organization beyond the village was lacking in aboriginal Tutuila, and that no chief there occupied a dominant power position. In his "statistical report" for the year ending July 12, 1853, Powell (Ms.) presents an analysis of the village composition of four of the nine political districts (Krämer 1902:313) into which Tutuila was traditionally divided.[14] The "principal chiefs" of these districts are also recorded. For example, Mauga is given as the principal chief of the Fagaloa district, and Le'iato as the principal chief of the district immediately to the east, the Alataua. In a footnote to his report, Powell states: "The principal chief has the nominal power to disannul any measure which may be enacted in the district to which he belongs." These observations by Powell are fully confirmed by Krämer (1902:320 seq.), who states that Mauga and Le'iato are "the most powerful chiefs in Tutuila," records their genealogies, figures a fine photograph of Togiola, who held the Le'iato title at the end of the 19th century, and remarks of Mauga that as a high chief, he "rules the whole of the Fagaloa district absolutely."[15]

We may say then that political authority and the structure of kinship in ancient Samoa were, in fact, markedly different from the descriptions that have been given of them by Dr. Ember; and this being so, the hypothesis he has formed on the basis of these erroneous descriptions must be rejected —at least for Samoa. Hypotheses, however immaculate their internal logic, are but figments if they fail to take account of the facts of the real world to which they purport to apply.

Many observers of Samoan political life have commented on the autonomy of the village *qua* village and of the intense rivalry between some villages. Of this state of affairs there can be no doubt, but it is a state of affairs, it is important to realize, not inconsistent with the existence of formal district organization for wider political ends. The rivalry of villages is but one aspect of the way in which Samoan society is segmented: within a family brothers compete; within a village, related families; within a sub-district, contiguous villages; within a district, sub-districts; and within Samoa, one great district with another. Thus, as J. W. Davidson (1963:Ms.) has remarked: "In structure, the larger political units, the sub-districts, the district and the whole of Samoa resembled the individual village in that, at each level, there was an appropriate fa'alupega and fono."

But these structures, it must be added, have been modified by the vicissitudes of history to produce a complex living society in which Samoan orators find unending diversion, and for the reason that even the most erudite of them is quite unable to master all of its intricacies and subtleties. And this is no hypothesis.[16]

NOTES

1. Pratt (1890:655) states: "a brother, often, nay generally, succeeds a brother." In Sa'anapu, in 1943, approximately 80% of titles (including all of the principal titles of the village) had been acquired by agnatic succession.

2. See also: G. Pratt, "The Genealogy of the Kings and Princes of Samoa," a paper presented at the Second Meeting of the Australasian Association for the Advancement of Science, Melbourne, 1890.

3. I am here citing figures from the first census of Samoa which was completed by George Turner in July, 1853, and published in the *Samoan Reporter* in January, 1854. Ember (1962b:964) has given the population of aboriginal Samoa as 50,000–60,000, which would seem to be an over-estimate.

4. There is, among Samoan scholars, a lack of agreement regarding the orthography of this word. Pratt (1911:6), who is followed by numerous others, gives *āiga* (i.e. a long initial vowel but no glottal stop). Mr. G. B. Milner, of the London School of Oriental and African Studies, who for some years has been working on a new dictionary of the Samoan language, prefers *'āiga*, on both phonetic and comparative grounds (1962: personal communication), which is the spelling I have here adopted.

5. When the particle *Sā* is used in this way the final vowel of the family name is lengthened.

6. This usage, incidentally, indicates plainly the etymology of the name Sa'anapu—the village being named in honor of the family of its high chief, 'Anapu.

7. The term which Dr. Ember has proposed for this "localized descent group" (which averages about 12 members in size) is "clan"; and the *larger* dispersed grouping of which the localized group is a segment, he calls "sept." I have refrained from using this idiosyncratic terminology in which clans become segments of septs, as I judge it to be of a kind unlikely to advance comprehension of the Samoan descent system.

8. See Milner 1961 for the special vocabulary of respect which was reserved for chiefs of "high, or very high rank."

9. The fourth high title recognized in Western Samoa is that of Tuimaleali'ifano (of the Tui A'ana line). See Davidson, *The Transition to Independence in Western Samoa: The Final Stage*, 1961a and b, for a report on the discussion of the four high titles—Malietoa, Tamasese, Mata'afa and Tuimaleali'ifano (the holders of which are known to the Samoans as the *Tama-'āiga*)—that took place during the Constitutional Convention of Western Samoa, held at Mulinu'u, Upolu, in 1954.

10. Until his recent death the Hon. 'Anapu Solofa was Minister of Justice in the Government of Western Samoa.

11. These manuscripts are to be found principally at Livingstone House, London, and the Mitchell Library, Sydney.

12. In Samoa, the title *Tui* was applied, in particular, to the paramount chiefs of Manu'a, and of Atua and A'ana (two of the principal districts of Upolu). It is said (Pratt 1911:345) to have been a title that originated in Tonga, where it was used to designate the paramount chief of those islands. By Samoan scholars the title Tui has been commonly translated as King, or Principal Chief.

13. See: *Report of the Commission to Inquire into and Report upon the Organization of District and Village Government in Western Samoa*, presented to His Excellency the Acting High Commissioner of the Government of Western Samoa, on 30th. November, 1950 (Wellington, 1951).

14. These were the four districts with which Powell was, in 1853, concerned as an L.M.S. missionary.

15. In letters written during the years 1857–1861, Powell gives a detailed account of the hostilities in which the "principal chiefs" Mauga and Le'iato, supported by their respective districts, were the main protagonists, and in the course of which the villages of Le'iato's district were laid waste, "the houses burnt, the plantations destroyed, the bread-fruit and coconut trees cut down and the graves desecrated"; and warriors of both districts killed, and, on occasion, scalped, in a protracted series of skirmishes. Many fono at district level had to be held before peace was finally restored on September 11, 1861; for, as Powell truthfully remarks, "the Samoans are peculiarly sensitive of domination and oppression."

16. I wish to thank Raymond Firth and G. B. Milner (of the University of London), and J. W. Davidson (of the Australian National University) for having read and commented on this paper while it was being prepared for publication.

REFERENCES CITED

BUCK, PETER, 1931, Samoan system of chieftainship. Exhibit No. 12 (pp. 70-73). American Samoa. Hearings before the Commission appointed by the President of the United States, in accordance with Public Resolution No. 3, Seventieth Congress, and Public Resolution No. 3, Seventy-First Congress. U.S. Government Printing Office, Washington.

DAVENPORT, WILLIAM, 1959, Nonunilinear descent and descent groups. American Anthropologist 61:557–72.

DAVIDSON, J. W., 1961a, The transition to independence in Western Samoa: the final stage. Canberra, Australian National University.

1961b, The transition to independence: the example of Western Samoa. Australian Journal of Politics and History 7:15–40.

1963, Samoa mo Samoa, Ms. Published in 1967 by Oxford University Press, Melbourne.

ELLA, S., 1895, The ancient Samoan government. Reports, Australasian Association for the Advancement of Science 6:596–603.

EMBER, MELVIN, 1958, Commercialization and political behaviour in American Samoa, Ph.D. Thesis, Yale University.

1959, The nonunilinear dèscent groups of Samoa. American Anthropologist 61:573–77.

1962a, The nature of Samoan kinship structure. Man 62:124.

1962b, Political authority and the structure of kinship in aboriginal Samoa. American Anthropologist 64:964–71.

FIRTH, RAYMOND, 1936, We, the Tikopia. London, G. Allen & Unwin ltd.

1957, A note on descent groups in Polynesia. Man 57:2.

FREEMAN, DEREK 1943, The Seuao Cave. Journal of the Polynesian Society 52:101–9.

1947, The tradition of Sanalālā. Journal of the Polynesian Society 56:295–317.

1948, The social structure of a Samoan village community, Ms., London.

1961, Review of Social stratification in Polynesia by Marshall D. Sahlins. Man 61:180.

GRATTAN, F. J. H., 1948, An introduction to Samoan custom. Apia.

HARDIE, C., 1842, Letter dated Sapali'i, Savai'i, 9th. February, Ms. Livingstone House, London.

1848, Letter dated Malua, Upolu, 5th. August, Ms. Livingstone House, London.

HARBUTT, W., 1841, Letter dated Upolu, 20th. July, Ms. Livingstone House, London.

HEATH, T., 1838, Letter dated Manono, 16th. April, Ms. Livingstone House, London.
HOLMES, LOWELL D.,1958, Ta'ū. Wellington, N.Z.
KEESING, FELIX, 1934, Modern Samoa: Its government and changing life. London, G. Allen & Unwin ltd.
KRÄMER, AUGUSTIN, 1902–3, Die Samoa-Inseln, 2 vols. Stuttgart.
LEACH, EDMUND, 1962, On certain unconsidered aspects of double descent systems. Man 62:214.
MARSACK, C. C., 1961, Notes on the practice of the court and the principles adopted in the hearing of cases affecting 1. Samoan Matai titles 2. Land held according to the customs and usages of Western Samoa, Justice Department, Apia, Western Samoa.
MAUDSLAY, ALFRED P., 1930, Life in the Pacific fifty years ago. London.
MEAD, MARGARET, 1930, Social organization of Manu'a. Honolulu, Bishop Museum.
MILNER, G. B., 1961, The Samoan vocabulary of respect. Journal of the Royal Anthropological Institute 91:296–317.
1962, Personal communication.
NIGHTINGALE, THOMAS, 1835, Oceanic sketches. London.
O LE TUSI FA'ALUPEGA O SAMOA, Malua, 1915
POWELL, T., 1853, Report dated Pagopago, Tutuila, 14th. July, Ms. Livingstone House, London.
1857–61, Letters from Pagopago, Tutuila, Mss. Livingstone House, London.
POWELL, T. AND PRATT, G., 1890, Some folk songs and myths from Samoa. Journal of the Royal Society of New South Wales 24:195–217.
PRATT, G., 1890, The genealogy of the kings and princes of Samoa. Reports, Australasian Association for the Advancement of Science 2:655–63.
1911, Grammar and dictionary of the Samoan language, 4th. Edition. Malua, Samoa.
PRITCHARD, W. T., 1866, Polynesian reminiscences: or life in the South Pacific islands. London.
REPORT OF THE COMMISSION TO INQUIRE INTO AND REPORT UPON THE ORGANIZATION OF DISTRICT AND VILLAGE GOVERNMENT IN WESTERN SAMOA, 1950, Wellington, N.Z.
SAHLINS, MARSHALL D., 1958, Social stratification in Polynesia. Seattle, University of Washington Press.
SCHULTZ, E., 1911, The most important principles of Samoan family law, and the laws of inheritance. Journal of the Polynesian Society 20:43–53.
STAIR, JOHN B., 1897, Old Samoa. London.
TURNER, G., 1854, Statistics of the Samoan group. Samoan Reporter, January.
1861, Nineteen years in Polynesia. London, J. Snow.
1884, Samoa a hundred years ago and long before. London, Macmillan and Co.
WHITMEE, S. J., 1867, Letter dated Saluafata, 7th. August, Ms. Livingstone House, London.
WILKES, CHARLES, 1845, Narrative of the United States exploring expedition during the years 1838–1842. 5 vols. Philadelphia, Lee and Blanchard.
WILLIAMS, JOHN, 1846, A narrative of missionary enterprises. London, J. Snow.

AUTHOR'S NOTE, JUNE, 1968

Since the first appearance of this paper, I have (from December, 1965, to January, 1968) undertaken further field research in the Samoan islands. The center of my investigations was the island of Upolu, but I was also able to extend my enquiries to Tutuila, Manu'a, and Savai'i, and to devote more than 500 hours to the observation of behaviour at *fono,* and on other formal chiefly occasions, at both village and district levels. In due course I shall be publishing accounts of these researches and of those which I carried out in Samoa during the years 1940–1943 and in 1946. I have, meanwhile, agreed to the republication of this present paper (with minor deletions and emendations), for the reason that its conclusions have, in general, been sustained by my recent investigations. Additional enquiry has revealed that the To'alima grouping of Sa'anapu is internally segmented and that the claim of descent from a common male ancestor is, on this evidence, best interpreted as, in part, a political expedient couched in terms of the prevailing idiom of descent. This, however, is but a slight modification, and beyond those now made there are no other emendations that I presently wish to make to this paper as it was published in 1964.

8

NONEXCLUSIVE COGNATIC DESCENT SYSTEMS: A POLYNESIAN EXAMPLE

F. Allan Hanson*

According to E. R. Leach:

A system in which all children inherited equal rights from both parents would plainly lead to total confusion, but a system in which children could choose to take particular rights from either the father or the mother (though not from both at once) would not, in principle, lead to a structure any more complex than one of straight unilineal descent (Leach 1960:117).

The purposes of this paper are to underline the fact that systems in which children inherit equal rights from both parents do exist, and to argue that they need not result in chaos. Our main source of data is the modern system of descent and property ownership in Rapa, an island in French Polynesia.[1] First we will define the general characteristics of this type of descent system and point out some of the theoretical problems which have been raised concerning it. Then we will describe the Rapan system and demonstrate how, in this case, those theoretical problems are solved or avoided.

I

In cognatic or nonunilinear systems where descent groups are not totally endogamous, persons may trace their ancestry in two or more groups. Yet in many systems, labeled "exclusive" by Davenport (1959:566) and "optative-exclusive" by Murdock (1960:11), the individual may exercise rights and duties of membership in only one of these groups at any given time. Other cognatic systems are classified as "nonexclusive" or "optative-nonexclusive" (Davenport 1959:566, Murdock 1960:11). Here, individuals who

*Grateful acknowledgment is made to the National Science Foundation for the fellowship which supported the field research on which this paper is based. Parts of it were read at the 1966 Annual Meeting of the Central States Anthropological Society in Chicago. I am grateful to Ernest Burch, William Douglas, Ben Finney, Bernd Lambert, Henri Lavondès, Donald Marshall, Scott Robinson, Harold Scheffler, and Martin Silverman for valuable comments on an earlier draft of the paper.

Published by permission of Donald S. Marshall, editor of *Anthropology and Austronesia*, a forthcoming volume in which this article will appear.

trace descent in several different groups may hold membership in two or more of them simultaneously.

Given the empirical diversity of cognatic descent systems, it does not seem accurate to classify all examples into one of two internally undifferentiated categories labeled "exclusive" and "nonexclusive." Preferably, these concepts may be viewed as the opposite poles of a continuum along which the various examples of cognatic systems may be located. Very near the exclusive pole might be placed organizations like the Japanese household and *dōzoku* and the Iban *bilek* family, where the individual acquires rights of membership by descent in one group only—that of his birth (Brown 1966:1139–40, Freeman 1960:67).

The intermediate range of the continuum would be occupied by cognatic systems which I term "semi-exclusive." In these, most individuals are associated primarily with one descent group (usually that of their residence) but may also hold secondary rights of membership in one or more other groups. Viewed from the perspective of the group, one can distinguish between a resident core of primary members and a nonresident periphery of secondary members. Often in such systems there is a bias toward unilineal descent such that persons who trace a unilineal pedigree of the preferred type in the group enjoy higher rank in it than do other resident descendants. The Maori *hapu* and the Choiseulese *sinangge* are examples of semi-exclusive cognatic descent groups in which the preferred mode of tracing descent is patrilineal (Firth 1963; Scheffler 1963, 1965), while a matrilineal bias is found in the *butubutu* of Simbo (Eddystone) Island (Scheffler 1962).

These "semi-exclusive" cases seem nearly to exhaust Murdock's "nonexclusive" category.

> Wherever kin-group affiliation is nonexclusive, an individual's plural memberships almost inevitably become segregated into one primary membership, which is strongly activated by residence, and one or more secondary memberships in which participation is only partial or occasional (Murdock 1960:11).

There are, however, a number of systems in which the majority of individuals regularly exercise primary rights of membership in two or more descent groups simultaneously. These I would place at or near the nonexclusive pole of our continuum. In some cases it is still possible to distinguish between a core of primary members and a periphery of secondary members in each descent group. For example, in parts of rural Java the care of an ancestor's grave is the joint responsibility of all his cognatic descendants,

> who are known collectively as the *alur waris.* The members of this group who live in the village where the grave is located are responsible for keeping it clean and for performing *slametan* ceremonies at fixed intervals. Those who reside in other villages or have migrated to another region are expected to make money contributions whenever the grave requires major repairs (Koentjaraningrat 1960:105).

The important difference between this and those semi-exclusive cases cited above is that presumably most persons have several ancestors buried in their own village and thus are primary members of more than one *alur waris.* That is, the descent group cores do not form discrete segments of society.

A few other examples of nonexclusive cognatic descent groups have appeared in the literature. The groups holding rights over hillside land and stands of pine trees among the Sagada Igorots conform to this pattern (Eggan 1960:29–30). So do the land-owning ramages in the modern Northern Gilberts (Lambert 1966:654–60) and among the Molima of Fergusson Island (Chowning 1962:92). Finney describes a nonexclusive cognatic system of inheritance and land ownership for rural Tahiti and the nearby island of Mai'ao (1965:310–20). The Family Circles and Cousins' Clubs of New York City Jews represent a further case in point (Mitchell 1961). Three examples which might be placed near but not quite at the nonexclusive pole of the continuum are Bella Coola ancestral families (McIlwraith 1948 I:119–39), southern Yoruba descent groups (Lloyd 1966), and modern land-owning groups in the Cook Islands (Crocombe 1964:117–28, 155–57).

While some theorists (e.g. Leach 1962:131, Goody 1959:66) prefer to restrict it to unilineal reckoning, others have found no difficulty in subsuming exclusive and semi-exclusive cognatic systems under the concept of descent. As Firth (1963:36) puts it:

> If the group under discussion is of a continuative, corporate type, comprising persons organized and united primarily on a consanguineal kin basis, with a collective name transmitted from one generation to another; if it is a significant structural unit of the society, performing multiple social tasks, then there seems no good reason to deny it the character of a descent group. Hence I would say that ambilateral groups of the *hapu* type use residential and land use criteria as demarcating instruments to close their consanguineal kinship status for operational purposes, and so constitute descent units.

Goodenough argues that when descent systems are restricted to the point that they generate discrete groups, such restrictions being accomplished either by unilineal reckoning or by other criteria operating in conjunction with a cognatic rule, the groups are so similar structurally and functionally that they should be classed as a single type (Goodenough 1961:1344).

When, however, we turn to those systems we have placed at the nonexclusive pole of the continum, serious theoretical problems arise. First, there is the question of stability over time. If the descent groups are not endogamous and if everyone is allowed to activate full membership in all groups to which both parents belong, then with each passing generation individuals will belong to more and more descent groups. In the absence of restricting factors not inherent in the rule of descent, this would mean that over time the average descent group size would increase drastically, both absolutely and relative to the total population. I shall use the term "augmentation" to refer to this progressive increase in descent group size. Augmentation is inherent in a nonexclusive cognatic system, and it is clearly an unstable process. Beginning at a point where the descent groups are very small, logically an augmentative system would eventually culminate in a situation where each descent group is made up of the entire population.[2] Uncontrolled augmentation would certainly result in the "total confusion" Leach anticipates in nonexclusive cognatic systems, and Finney has given us an empirical example. In 'A'ou'a, a rural area of Tahiti, much land is owned by all cognatic descendants of individual holders who lived a century ago. Some of this land is immensely valuable today, for lots facing the lagoon and suitable for dwellings can be sold to wealthy Europeans for as much as $20,000 or $30,000. Yet due to imperfect genealogical memory and various other problems, it often is not clear exactly who belongs to the large groups of co-heirs which own the land. Disputes over some tracts are so frequent and bitter that they can neither be cultivated nor sold (Finney 1965:310–14, 318–19).[3] In these conditions of economic development and the rising commercial value of land, Finney considers the wide diffusion of ownership rights over undivided lands to be a "grotesque" development which poses serious problems in much of French Polynesia (1965:313–14).

A second and related theoretical difficulty is the problem of overlapping. In nonexclusive cognatic systems the majority of persons simultaneously hold primary membership in more than one descent group. Therefore these groups are not discrete. This in itself has posed a serious problem to some theorists. In Freeman's words (1961:200):

> The difficulty posed by cognatic or non-unilineal descent is that collateral cognates (from first cousin onwards) belong to more than one cognatic stock. This means the cognatic stocks, at this level, overlap; and consequently, unless some criterion other than, and in addition to, descent be brought into operation, it is impossible to achieve the division of a society into discrete groupings. No account of a bilateral or non-unilineal system can be considered complete until the way in which this difficulty is solved has been demonstrated in detail; and this, in my view, has yet to be achieved for the ambilateral *hapu* of the New Zealand Maori, as for the "non-unilinear descent groups" postulated by Goodenough for the Gilbert Islands and other parts of Malayo-Polynesia.

The data from Rapa provide an excellent opportunity to evaluate the problems we have mentioned—which stem for the most part from deduction—in the light of an empirical nonexclusive cognatic descent system. Rapan descent groups, for example, are far from discrete and yet they are corporate and control a rather wide range of resources, in that they own most of the real property on the island. Most interesting, things work out in Rapa in such a way that in certain contexts the predicted problems actually materialize while in other contexts they are resolved or avoided. Thus, by examining this single system we may isolate factors which can impart stability and viability to a potentially unstable and unworkable situation.

II

Lying some 700 miles south of Tahiti, Rapa is the most remote island of the Austral group and the southern gateway to French Polynesia. The island is volcanic in origin and rugged in appearance. It covers about fifteen square miles and the highest peaks attain 2000 feet. The population of 360 Polynesians is clustered in two villages on either side of a large bay. The people subsist mainly by fishing and farming. The staple is taro, grown in irrigated terraces found primarily in the lower reaches of Rapa's numerous valleys. Coffee is a second major crop. Some coffee is consumed locally, but most is exported. Although the island exports only eight to ten tons annually, coffee represents one of the major sources of cash income.

Rapa was discovered by Vancouver in 1791. At that time the population, which was in the neighborhood of 1500 to 2000,[4] was divided into fifteen or twenty semi-exclusive cognatic descent groups or ramages not unlike the Maori *hapu.*[5] After a chaotic century in which the population was nearly eradicated by imported disease,[6] France brought Rapa effectively under its control in 1887. The French replaced customary law with the Civil Code, and the king and chiefs with a native District Council elected by the population at large. As far as the descent system is concerned, the year 1889 inaugurated the modern era. Prior to that time the land apparently was still in the hands of the remnants of the pre-European ramages. In 1889, however, the District Council redistributed the land, awarding tracts to individual owners. For the most part, these beneficiaries of land distribution are regarded as the founders of the oldest modern descent groups.

Rapan descent groups, termed *'ōpū,*[7] do not operate in a wide range of contexts. Legal and political life, religion, recreation, residence, and patterns of mutual aid are founded on principles of colonial government, voluntary association, or considerations of kinship which do not directly involve the *'ōpū.* The *'ōpū* operate exclusively with reference to property. Each *'ōpū* owns an estate, and undertakes no activity which is not directly concerned with it. An estate, then, is an essential element in the definition of an *'ōpū;* outside its estate an *'ōpū* has absolutely no *raison d'être.* An indication of property arrangements and ideology is therefore necessary to an understanding of this descent system.

We may isolate two distinct orders or classes of real property: territory and improvements. The island is divided into a great many named tracts of territory *(fenua)* of diverse sizes. Each of these is owned by an *'ōpū.* Located on these tracts are various improvements, the most important types being houses, taro terraces and other kinds of gardens, and planted groves of trees. In Rapa, territory and improvements are conceived to exist separately and may therefore be owned independently. It is no exaggeration to state that the great majority of improvements are owned by persons or *'ōpū* other than those which own the territory on which they are located.

Typically a tract of territory contains some unexploited areas plus numerous improvements which are owned by several different *'ōpū*. As we shall see below, the activities undertaken by an *'ōpū* vary according to the type of property in question.

All property is thought to have been owned originally by individuals or, infrequently, by very small groups such as a pair of spouses or a set of siblings. For territory, the original owners were those individuals who were awarded tracts in the land distribution of 1889.[8] The original owner of an improvement is the person who created it: he who built the house, made the taro terrace, or planted the grove. An individual owner may dispose of his property as he sees fit. He may choose to bequeath some or all of the improvements in his personal estate to individual recipients. Thus most adults have a few taro terraces, and some a coffee grove or two, which they may call their own. Some of these may have come to them through two or three generations of individual owners.

But invariably in the case of territory, and often for improvements, property is left jointly to all heirs. In the next generation, these pass it on to their own heirs. With the passage of time, then, groups of owners grow up around the various estates. These groups are the *'ōpū*. Each *'ōpū* is named for its founder: the ancestor who owned its estate individually. Depending on the property awarded to and/or created by its founder, an *'ōpū* may own one or more tracts of territory, or a house or two, or taro terraces, or groves of trees, or any combination of these forms of property.

An *'ōpū*'s estate is often not concentrated in a single location. In the territorial distribution of 1889 it sometimes occurred that two or more tracts in widely separated areas were awarded to a single individual. Furthermore, anyone may create (and hence own) an improvement anywhere, regardless of whether he is an owner of the territory on which it is located. When a Rapan decides where to establish an improvement, he is interested primarily in the fertility of the soil and convenience of access. He builds his house in one of the villages, makes taro terraces in the lowlands near a river, and plants trees in the higher reaches of the valleys. All of these improvements pass into the possession of the *'ōpū* he founds. Thus it is common that different parts of an *'ōpū*'s estate are located at diverse points around the island.

New improvements—houses, taro terraces, groves—are created every year. These are not added to the estates of already-existing *'ōpū*. Rather, consistent with the principles set forth above, they belong to the individuals who made them. If such a person leaves the improvements he created to his heirs in joint possession, he becomes the founder of a new *'ōpū*. In this way, new *'ōpū* with estates composed solely of improvements are founded in each generation.[9]

An *'ōpū* comes into being when an individual leaves his personal estate jointly to his heirs. These heirs are his legitimate children: those biological and adopted children whom he has recognized by French law.[10] All legitimate children—regardless of sex, order of birth, place of residence, or any other distinctions which may be drawn among them—inherit full and equal rights in the estates of both parents, and they all pass these rights on to their own legitimate offspring. Thus the *'ōpū* is a nonexclusive cognatic descent group. Looking down, from the point of view of the founder, the *'ōpū* is composed of all those persons who are legitimately descended from him through any combination of male and female links. Looking up, from the perspective of an affiliating individual, he belongs to any and all *'ōpū* which were founded by ancestors from whom he traces legitimate descent through any combination of male and female links. *'Ōpū* membership is strictly limited to legitimate descendants of the founder. Members' affines or cognates who do not themselves trace descent from the founder do not belong.[11]

There are no restrictions on the basis of residence or any other criterion which operate to the extent that most or all persons are limited to primary membership in a single *'ōpū.* A distinction between primary and secondary members is of limited applicability to the Rapan case. Persons who have emigrated from the island can be viewed as secondary members in that they do not and obviously cannot participate actively in the affairs of the *'ōpū,* although they or their legitimate descendants reactivate full membership rights should they return to Rapa. For people living in Rapa, everyone who traces legitimate cognatic descent from the founder enjoys full and equal rights in the *'ōpū.* Henceforth our discussion will be limited to residents of the island.

Very few Rapans belong to less than three different *'ōpū;* most contemporary adults hold membership in five or more. Clearly, then, the *'ōpū* do not form discrete segments of society.

We may gain an idea of how their system of overlapping *'ōpū* works in practice by examining the affiliation of two sibling groups related to each other as first cousins. These sibling groups bear the surnames Natiki and Nāri'i,[12] and their genealogy is presented in Figure 1. This genealogy has been simplified in several respects. First, three or four collateral kinsmen who had no descendants and who are not important in matters pertaining to the *'ōpū* have been omitted. Second, in the sibling set which terminates each descent line I have included only those members currently living in Rapa. Finally, these sibling groups are composed of adults ranging in age from twenty to fifty. Members of all of these sibling groups have children, and members of some have grandchildren.[13] Were these further descendants included, the genealogy would cover a total span of seven generations rather than the six shown here. It should be remembered that these additional siblings, children, and grandchildren all belong to the *'ōpū* listed below, although for the sake of simplicity we will not consider them.

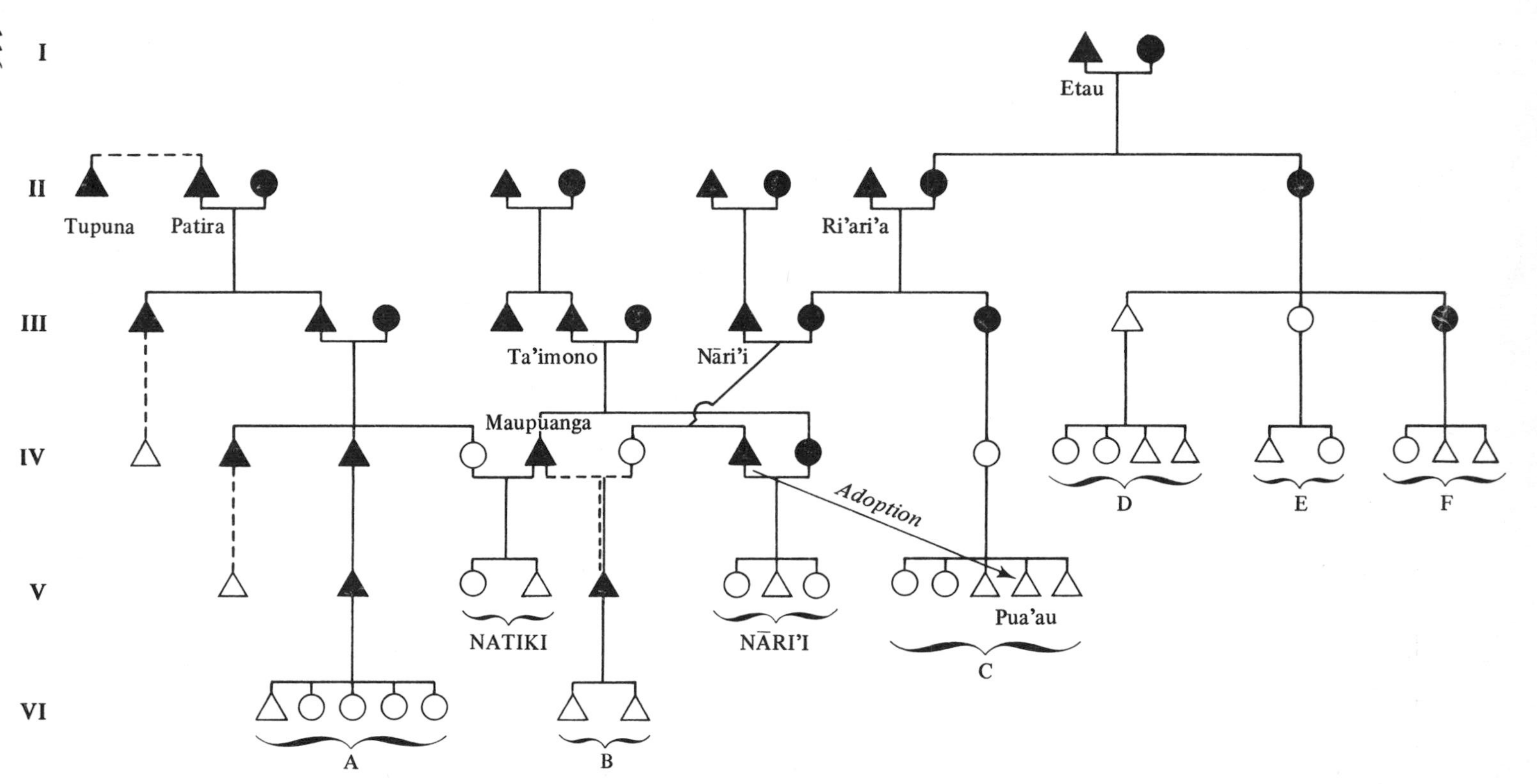

FIGURE 1. *Genealogy of the Natiki and Nāri'i sibling groups.* Solid symbols refer to deceased persons. A solid line connecting spouses signifies marriage; a dotted line, cohabitation. A dotted descent line signifies lack of legal recognition of the child by the parent. The half-brother of the Natiki siblings was recognized by his mother, but not by their common father.

We may now list the various *'ōpū* to which either or both of the Natiki and Nāri'i sibling groups belong.

1. *Tupuna.* This *'ōpū* was founded jointly by Patira, the mother's father's father of the Natiki sibling group, and a contemporary of his named Ava-e'oru. Tupuna, a collateral kinsman of Patira of unknown degree (connected with Patira by a dotted line on the genealogy) was awarded several tracts of territory in 1889. Having no children, his property went to his collateral kinsmen, and two of the tracts were given jointly to his kinsmen Patira and Avae'oru. These tracts of territory make up the estate of this *'ōpū.* Its present members are all legitimate descendants of Patira—the Natiki siblings, their mother, and sibling group *A*—plus all legitimate descendants of Avae'oru, who are not shown on our chart.

2. *Patira 1.*[14] This *'ōpū* was founded by Patira, mother's father's father of the Natiki siblings. Its estate is made up exclusively of territory. It includes six tracts awarded to Patira in 1889, plus four tracts which Patira received individually from Tupuna. At present this *'ōpū* is composed of all legitimate living descendants of Patira: the Natiki siblings, their mother, and sibling group *A.*

3. *Patira 2.* Founded by the mother of the Natiki siblings, this *'ōpū* owns those taro terraces and coffee groves which formed her personal estate. Its membership is composed of the Natiki siblings and their mother.

4. *Ngate Mato.* This is one of three or four *'ōpū* which own only territory and which are historically special cases. They bear the names of pre-European ramages; no member can trace his pedigree to their founders; and they are much larger than the other territory-owning *'ōpū.* According to Stokes (1930:728–29) a few tracts of territory were not included in the distribution of 1889, and may informants corroborated the point. Probably these tracts remained in the hands of the ramages which owned them prior to the distribution, and since they continued to hold property, these old ramages have retained their names and have continued to exist down to the present as modern *'ōpū.* The large size of these *'ōpū* may be explained by the fact that the members of each trace cognatic descent from any one of a group of persons who lived in 1889 rather than from an individual of that period. Returning specifically to Ngate Mato, the Natiki siblings belong to this *'ōpū* but are unable to demonstrate their pedigree in it beyond stating that it is through their mother's mother. Sibling group *A* affiliates through the same individual. I am not certain if the Nāri'i siblings and groups *B, C, D, E,* and *F* belong to this *'ōpū.*

5. *Okopou.* Here is another example of an extremely large and historically special *'ōpū;* this one probably includes the majority of Rapa's population. Like Ngate Mato, it owns only territory. The Natiki siblings affiliate to Okopou through their mother's father's father, and sibling group *A* through the same person. The Nāri'i siblings also belong, probably affiliating

through their father. For sibling group *B*, then, the link would be through their father's mother. I am not certain how or if sibling groups *C*, *D*, *E*, and *F* affiliate, but very likely some or all of them are members. Pua'au, the second male of sibling group *C*, is a member by merit of his adoptive link through the Nāri'i siblings' father.

6. *Natiki 1.* Ta'imono Natiki, father's father of the Natiki siblings and mother's father of the Nāri'i siblings, founded this *'ōpū.* Its estate is composed of a tract of territory awarded probably to Ta'imono in 1889, a coffee grove planted by a brother of Ta'imono (which, the brother being childless, passed to his closest kinsmen, Ta'imono), and numerous taro terraces. Some of these terraces were made by Ta'imono and others by his father, but since Ta'imono was the only heir of his father who had descendants, they are all considered to have been included in his personal estate. This *'ōpū* is composed of the Natiki and Nāri'i sibling groups.

7. *Natiki 2.* Here the founder was Maupuanga, father of the Natiki siblings. This *'ōpū* owns two masonry houses and several taro terraces and coffee groves, all of which formed Maupuanga's personal estate. The *'ōpū* is composed of the Natiki siblings.

8. *Nāri'i 1.* This *'ōpū* was founded by Nāri'i, father's father of the Nāri'i siblings. Its estate consists solely of territory. Present members are the Nāri'i siblings, their father's sister and her grandsons (sibling group *B*), and Pua'au, the second male of sibling group *C*, who was adopted by the Nāri'i siblings' father.

9. *Nāri'i 2.* The estate of this *'ōpū* indicates a masonry house, coffee groves and taro terraces. These formed the personal estates of the father and mother of the Nāri'i siblings which have merged by coming into the joint possession of their children. Members of Nāri'i 2 are the Nāri'i siblings.

10. *Ri'ari'a.* Founded by Ri'ari'a, father's mother's father of the Nāri'i siblings, this *'ōpū* owns only the territory awarded its founder in 1889. Its membership consists of the Nāri'i siblings, sibling group *B* and their father's mother, and sibling group *C* and their mother.

11. *Tinohuri.* This *'ōpū* was founded by Etau Tinohuri, the only male on generation I of our genealogy. It owns the territory awarded to Etau in 1889. Except for Okopou and Ngate Mato it is the largest of the *'ōpū* here listed. Its membership consists of the Nāri'i siblings, sibling group *B* and their father's mother, sibling group *C* and their mother, sibling group *D* and their father, sibling group *E* and their mother, and sibling group *F*. Incidentally, the children of Pua'au (second male in sibling group *C*) affiliate to the Tinohuri *'ōpū* in three different ways. One is through their father's mother, and a second is through their father's adoptive father. The third is through their mother, for Pua'au is married to his mother's mother's mother's sister's daughter's daughter, the female of sibling group *F*.

It may have been noticed that of the six grandparents of our two focal sibling groups, descent for purposes of *'ōpū* membership is traced from or through five of them. The sixth, father's mother of the Natikis and mother's mother of the Nāri'is, was an immigrant from Ra'ivavae, and therefore inherited no property in Rapa. However, these sibling groups claim they share property interests in Ra'ivavae, and very likely they trace their rights through this woman.

TABLE 1. 'OPU AFFILIATIONS.

	Sibling Group							
'Opū	*Natiki*	*Nāri'i*	*A*	*B*	*C*	*D*	*E*	*F*
Patira 2	+	−	−	−	−	−	−	−
Natiki 2	+	−	−	−	−	−	−	−
Tupuna	+	−	+	−	−	−	−	−
Patira 1	+	−	+	−	−	−	−	−
Ngate Mato	+	?	+	?	?	?	?	?
Natiki 1	+	+	−	−	−	−	−	−
Okopou	+	+	+	+	?	?	?	?
Nāri'i 2	−	+	−	−	−	−	−	−
Nāri'i 1	−	+	−	+	−	−	−	−
Ri'ari'a	−	+	−	+	+	−	−	−
Tinohuri	−	+	−	+	+	+	+	+

Table 1 summarizes the affiliations of the sibling groups here considered to the eleven *'ōpū* we have listed. While this table gives the fullest information for *'ōpū* affiliations of the Natiki and Nāri'i sibling groups that my data allow, the list may not be exhaustive for either of them. The types of property we have considered are only territory, houses, and presently cultivated coffee groves and taro terraces. It is possible that groves of orange or lumber trees or abandoned taro terraces in which one or the other of these sibling groups shares ownership stem from yet other ancestors. The *'ōpū* affiliations of the other six sibling groups mentioned here are of course far from complete. Our purpose was to show the composition of the various *'ōpū* to which the Natikis and/or Nāri'is belong. We have therefore examined each of the other sibling groups only as they articulate with the two focal groups. Had we sufficient data and courage to attempt the tremendously complex job of filling in all of the descent lines for these sibling groups and for the other groups with which they share membership in various *'ōpū*, eventually we would complete the tangled genealogical route that would show the composition of every *'ōpū* on the island.

We may now shift our attention from how the *'ōpū* are structured to how they operate. As stressed above, an *'ōpū* acts only in matters of direct concern to its estate. The activities open to the *'ōpū* vary according to the type of property in question. The range of variation in *'ōpū* operation emerges fairly clearly from a consideration of territory, coffee groves and taro terraces, and here we will limit ourselves to these three kinds of property.

With reference to its territory an *'ōpū* is an extremely inactive organization. Territory has remarkably little utilitarian value in modern Rapa. Improvements are the productive forms of property, and an *'ōpū* exercises almost no control over the improvements located on its territory. Anyone may make a taro terrace or plant a grove of fruit or lumber trees on unused territory anywhere. He is under no obligation to secure the permission of the territory owners, nor need he even inform them of his intention. Permission of the territory owners is required for the establishment of only two kinds of improvements. These are houses[15] and coffee groves. However, an *'ōpū* has little inclination or opportunity to stand in the way of someone who wishes to make such improvements on its territory. Permission is nearly always granted to a house builder, while in the case of coffee no new groves have been planted during the last two decades because all locations suitable for the crop are already under cultivation.

Once an improvement has been established, it belongs exclusively to its maker and the *'ōpū* he founds. The territory owners have no rights to any portion of its produce, nor may they confiscate it or demand that it be destroyed or removed in order to put the land on which it is situated to some other use. Again, houses and coffee groves represent minor exceptions to this rule. Theoretically the territory owners may order a house owner to take his house and get off their land. Threats of this nature have been made in the heat of argument, but never in the memory of my informants has an eviction been seriously pressed. In an especially complex dispute over the ownership of a coffee grove the District Council, acting as mediator, may advise the territory-owning *'ōpū* to confiscate the grove.[16] Such a procedure, however, has always been rare and apparently especially so in the last decade. Usually such disputes are settled by dividing the grove among the rival claimants.

The jurisdiction of an *'ōpū* over its territory is essentially limited to the wild vegetation which grows on it. Rapans use many varieties of wild plants and trees in the construction of houses, boats and canoes, for basket-making, and for firewood. In the native ideology, since these products were planted by no one they belong to no one, or to everyone. They may be freely cut and used by anyone. Territory-owning *'ōpū* may, however, exercise some control over a few species of wild trees especially valuable as lumber, and over basket wicker. The *'ōpū* may prohibit the cutting of these products on its territory to all but those who have secured its express permission. Normally this is done if some *'ōpū* member wishes to reserve certain trees ideally suited for a boat or canoe he plans to build, or as a conservation measure to ensure that the supply of wicker will not be exhausted.

Most *'ōpū* which own territory have one individual who is charged with overseeing the affairs of the group. He is called the *ha'apa'o* or "manager" and his term is for life. Ideally the manager is elected in a meeting of the *'ōpū*, but often a manager approaching death appoints his successor and the other members rarely dispute his decision. Preferably, the manager is the senior male of the *'ōpū;* the man of the eldest generation of the *'ōpū* who traces the most senior line of descent from the founder. A diagram (Figure 2) should make this order of succession clear. It is not rare that a man is the senior male in two or more *'ōpū* to which he belongs. In such cases he holds the office of manager in all of these simultaneously.

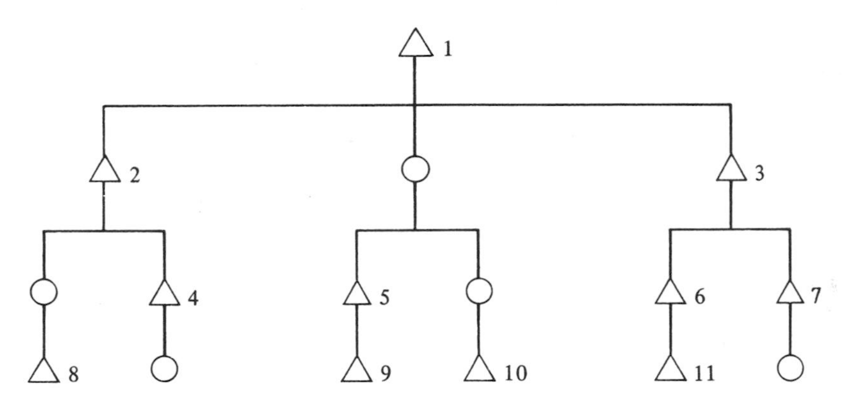

FIGURE 2. *Order of succession to the office of* 'ōpū *manager.* Elder siblings are placed to the left. The numbers denote the ideal order of succession.

All matters relating to the *'ōpū* territory are brought to the manager. He makes the announcements concerning prohibitions on cutting lumber trees or wicker. If some matter of special importance comes up, he may call a meeting of the entire *'ōpū*, and he presides at such meetings. The manager is essentially a coordinating official who has no special authority. In a meeting his opinions carry no more weight than those of other adult members. When no consensus is clear on some matter under discussion, it is decided by a ballot in which each adult member, including the manager, has a single vote. Because its range of activity is so narrow, an *'ōpū* rarely meets to deliberate matters concerning its territory. During the eleven months of my stay on Rapa, to my knowledge only one such meeting was held.

In contrast to the situation with reference to territory, the *'ōpū* are fairly active in matters concerning coffee groves. An *'ōpū* maintains and exploits its coffee groves as a unit. Rapans wait until the berries have fallen from the trees and the pulp has rotted away, and then they gather the beans from the ground. Often it is decreed that no *'ōpū* member may gather its coffee until an appointed day when they all go to harvest a particular grove together. This ensures that all members share equally in the profits. In some *'ōpū* each member keeps the coffee he or she personally gathered after a day's joint work. In others, the coffee beans are pooled at the end of the day and measured out in equal portions to all those who participated in the harvest.

Still other *'ōpū* sell their coffee jointly and divide the cash proceeds among their members. In a few *'ōpū* those members who have emigrated from Rapa are sent a share of the earnings from the coffee. The prevalent attitude, however, is that only those who have participated in the work of maintaining and harvesting the grove should profit from it, so absent members receive nothing.

Each *'ōpū* which owns coffee groves has a manager who coordinates its joint activity. The manager determines when a grove should be cleaned of underbrush and organizes the job. He appoints the day when a particular grove will be harvested, supervises the work, and oversees the division of profits. A manager for coffee groves is chosen according to the same criteria we discussed in our consideration of territory. Therefore, in those few *'ōpū* which own both territory and coffee groves the same individual acts as manager over both forms of property.

When our attention turns to taro terraces a new social grouping—the household—must be considered. A Rapan household is composed of those persons who eat in the same cookhouse. Usually households consist of nuclear or extended families. They range in size from two to fifteen members, with an average of 6.7. The household operates as a unit in subsistence economy, and one of its main tasks is the cultivation of taro.

Depending on factors such as the size of the household, the size of the terraces it cultivates, and the ages and energy of its members, a household may cultivate anywhere from about ten to over fifty different taro terraces. These are often located at widely separated points around the island. Some of these terraces may belong to individual household members, while the rest belong to several different *'ōpū.* Rights to use a terrace belong to the members of the *'ōpū* which owns it. For each terrace that a household cultivates, usually at least one household member belongs to the owning *'ōpū.* By merit of this individual the household has the right to cultivate that terrace. This person is considered to be the manager of all terraces belonging to the *'ōpū* which are cultivated by his or her household.[17] It will be noted that here the office of manager is defined differently than in the case of territory and coffee groves. An *'ōpū* has a single manager for all property of the latter types which it owns, but there may be several managers for its taro terraces: one from each household which cultivates them.

A terrace made in especially good soil may produce high quality taro for twenty to thirty years of continuous cultivation. Where the soil is less fertile the terrace may yield well for only four or five years. When the quality of taro produced by a given terrace diminishes, the terrace is abandoned and replaced with another. A new terrace may be made, or else an abandoned terrace which has regained its fertility is renovated. Abandoned terraces have managers exactly as do those under cultivation. The *'ōpū* member whose household last cultivated a terrace continues to be its manager after it is abandoned.[18] Should another *'ōpū* member desire to renovate that terrace, he goes to its manager. If the manager also has plans to cultivate the terrace, his are the prior rights. If not, the other person begins to use the terrace and he becomes its new manager. One important function of the office of manager over taro terraces, then, is to provide an orderly procedure for the renovation of abandoned terraces.

To summarize, an *'ōpū* retains exclusive rights of use over its coffee groves and the *'ōpū* exercises these rights jointly. Rights to cultivate taro terraces are also restricted to members of the owning *'ōpū*, but these are exercised by the households to which members belong rather than by the *'ōpū* as a unit. Anyone may freely establish and own most types of improvements on unused territory anywhere, or gather wild products from it. An *'ōpū*'s jurisdiction over its territory is limited essentially to the right to prohibit the gathering of certain wild plants which grow there.

III

As stated in the first section of this paper, the two major theoretical problems with nonexclusive cognatic descent systems are (1) that such systems tend to be unstable over time, and (2) that they generate nondiscrete descent groups. We may now explore these problems in turn and discuss their implications for the Rapan system.

We have seen that the problem of instability is rooted in augmentation: the process whereby in each generation descent groups increase greatly in size, both absolutely and in proportion to the total population. The Rapan system is especially interesting in this regard, for in some *'ōpū* augmentation is not controlled while in others the process is contained within certain bounds. This may be explained with reference to the basic distinction between territory and improvements.

Since augmentation develops over time, its progress may be measured by the generational depth of descent groups. Clearly augmentation is more advanced in groups which span eight or ten generations than in those only two or three generations in depth. *'Ōpū* which own improvements augment only within a certain range. The upper limit of this range is represented by a few *'ōpū* which span as many as five generations from founder to most remote descendant and which contain adults as distantly related as first or second cousins. The bulk of the improvements in Rapa are owned by individuals or *'ōpū* up to three or four generations in depth. One reason for the containment of augmentation within this range may be found in the nature of the property itself. New improvements are made, and therefore new *'ōpū* are founded, in each generation.[19] The estates of many *'ōpū* are composed entirely of improvements created within the last few generations, and so these *'ōpū* have not been in existence long enough to augment beyond the range specified above. Furthermore, improvements do not last forever. Taro terraces revert to the status of unused territory if left uncultivated for fifteen or twenty years, groves of trees are cut down, houses are dismantled or destroyed in hurricanes. It sometimes occurs that all of the property in the estate of an *'ōpū* ceases to exist before five generations have elapsed from its founding. In such a case, the *'ōpū* itself vanishes before it has augmented beyond the specific range.

The second mechanism which controls *'ōpū* augmentation with respect to improvements is property division. Occasionally it is thought that an *'ōpū* is getting too large for effective administration of its estate, and so a decision to divide its improvements is reached. Usually the impetus to division stems from matters involving coffee groves. As we have seen, an *'ōpū* is by far the most active with reference to its coffee groves, for these are exploited by the *'ōpū* as a whole. When an *'ōpū* becomes fairly large internal friction may erupt because some members feel they are doing more than their share of the work of keeping the groves free of underbrush, or are receiving less than their share of the profits. Thus, property divisions may be preceded and accompanied by heated disputes. Not infrequently, far-sighted elders effect the division in order to forestall future ill-feeling among their descendants.

Although coffee groves provide the catalyst, all other improvements owned by the *'ōpū* are usually included in the division. The property is distributed among two or more sections of the *'ōpū*, each section consisting of the descendants of a child (or perhaps a grandchild) of the original *'ōpū* founder. When property is divided, it is divided absolutely. Each section of the *'ōpū* gains full and exclusive rights over the improvements allotted to it, and forfeits all rights over the property awarded to other sections.[20] Having thus gained possession of an estate of its own, each section becomes a new and autonomous *'ōpū*. The separation of these new *'ōpū* is complete; after property division no special relations obtain between them because of their common origin. Following Freeman (1960:68–69), we may term this process *'ōpū* partition.[21] Depending on matters such as the rate of membership increase and how well the members get along together, partition may occur at any point in the history of an improvement-owning *'ōpū*. Yet very few such *'ōpū* have attained (and, to my knowledge, none have exceeded) a total depth of five generations before partitioning.

Although augmentation does operate with improvement-owning *'ōpū*, then, it is controlled by the impermanent nature of the property and by *'ōpū* partition. Given these restricting mechanisms, the nonexclusive cognatic system of descent could persist indefinitely but improvements would never be owned by *'ōpū* more than about five generations in depth. The average size of these *'ōpū* would remain fairly constant over time, and therefore we may conclude that with respect to improvements the Rapan descent system is stable.

Turning to territory, we find a very different situation. Improvements may be created at any time and they are finite in duration but, for sociological purposes, territory is eternal. Moreover, Rapans do not divide their territory. Therefore the two major limiting mechanisms which we isolated in the case of improvements do not operate for territory. Here augmentation proceeds unchecked.

The course of augmentation and the instability it imparts to the descent system is clearly visible in the history of those *'ōpū* which own territory. Immediately after the territorial distribution in 1889 most tracts of territory were in the hands of individuals, while today, as a glance at the list of *'ōpū* presented above indicates, these are owned by sizable groups. Since only three-quarters of a century has elapsed since distribution, at most the *'ōpū* founded at that time cover a span of seven generations.[22] More time will be required before augmentation approaches its logical culmination wherein everyone belongs to every territory-owning *'ōpū*. A glimpse of the future, however, is provided by those historically special *'ōpū* such as Okopou and Ngate Mato, discussed above. Members of these *'ōpū* trace descent from groups rather than individuals who lived in 1889. Therefore these *'ōpū* had a head start in augmentation, and they are at an advanced stage of the process today. They are much larger than other *'ōpū* which own territory; Okopou probably contains a clear majority of the population.

As this discussion implies, most *'ōpū* own territory or improvements, but not both types of property. There are, however, exceptions such as Natiki 1,[23] whose estate includes territory, taro terraces, and coffee groves. Two and three decades ago it was not uncommon for territory and improvements to be held jointly, but since that time there has been a marked tendency for these types of property to come into the ownership of distinct *'ōpū*. A concrete example will illustrate how this occurs.

Referring again to our genealogical chart (Figure 1) and list of *'ōpū*, originally there was a single Patira *'ōpū*. It was founded by the mother's father's father of the Natiki siblings and its estate was composed of the territory which currently belongs to Patira 1, the improvements now owned by Patira 2, and a number of other terraces and groves. About twenty years ago all of the improvements were divided between the Natiki siblings' mother and her brother. They continued, however, to hold the territory in common. Because of this division the original Patira *'ōpū* partitioned into three separate *'ōpū*. One of these, which we have called Patira 2, owns the improvements allotted to the Natiki siblings' mother in the division. It is composed of the Natiki siblings, their mother, and their legitimate descendants. The second *'ōpū* does not appear on our list. We may label it Patira 3. It owns the improvements awarded to the Natiki siblings' mother's brother in the division, and its current membership consists of sibling group *A* and their legitimate descendants. The third *'ōpū* is that we have termed Patira 1. It owns the territory left undivided, and thus its membership is composed of all members of the other two Patira *'ōpū*.[24] The case of the Patira *'ōpū*, typical of what has happened in several *'ōpū* in recent decades, provides a particularly clear example of the two paths along which the Rapan descent system proceeds. Augmentation is limited with reference to improvements and so in this area the system is stable, whereas with respect to territory augmentation is uncontrolled and here the descent system is unstable.

We turn now to the problem of overlapping. Of course, this is closely related to the problem of instability because an augmentative system necessarily produces nondiscrete descent groups. In some quarters, however, the fact that descent groups might overlap in membership poses a theoretical difficulty in itself. Such a position, for example, appears to underlie the passage by Freeman quoted in the first section of this paper (p. 112). Leach is explicit on this point: descent groups are discrete by definition; to include nondiscrete groups only results in confusion (Leach 1962: 131). He registers hearty agreement in these matters with Rivers, whose position he summarizes in the statement that the "notion of 'descent group' could only be useful if the groups in question were discrete and did not overlap; he [Rivers] therefore insisted that in practice a *descent group* should always be a *unilineal descent group*" (Leach 1962: 130–31, Leach's emphasis). Perhaps others who prefer to restrict "descent" to "unilineal descent" (e.g. Goody 1959:66, 1961:7–8; Radcliffe-Brown 1929a:50–51, 1929b) are also motivated by the idea that descent groups must be discrete. In this connection Fortes may represent the exception which proves the rule, for he speaks of "bilateral descent groups" only if they are totally endogamous, and hence, discrete (1959:206).

As I understand it, "descent group" is a purely structural concept. It refers to a type of group defined by a particular means of recruiting members. The specific activities and responsibilities which fall under the jurisdiction of descent groups are *operational* considerations, and they vary tremendously from society to society. They have no place in the definition of a structural concept which aims at cross-cultural validity and utility.[25] Yet when the problem of overlapping leads us to limit descent groups to discrete groups by definition I think exactly this has occurred, for the problem of overlapping is rooted in operational considerations. This may be seen clearly in the curious but instructive fact that many of those theorists who seem most committed to the notion of discrete descent groups have for years been dealing with nondiscrete groups without sensing any particular difficulty. I refer to double unilineal systems. If each individual belongs to one patrilineage and one matrilineage, then descent groups of these two types overlap (or "cross-cut") one another in membership. No problems have been perceived in such systems because, in the most frequently discussed cases, while descent groups are nondiscrete *structurally* they are discrete *operationally*. That is, matrilineages and patrilineages engage in different spheres of activity, with the result that what the individual should do as a member of his patrilineage never conflicts with—indeed, is not even relevant to—what he should do as a member of his matrilineage. As Fortes phrases his idea of double descent systems strictly defined, "the total universe of rights, duties, claims and capacities in relation to property, office, rank and ritual status are partitioned into equal and opposite categories for a person" (Fortes 1963:60). Leach puts the same idea in the form of the hypothesis that "in all double unilineal systems the two sets of unilineal corporations, the patrilineal and the matrilineal, represent entirely different and sharply contrasted functional interests" (Leach 1962:134). (There seem to be exceptions to these statements, however, and our understanding of double descent might be deepened if more attention were paid to cases in which patrilineages and matrilineages do not operate in totally distinct realms. In Pukapuka, for example, the two types of lineage overlap operationally to at least some degree in that they both own taro beds [Beaglehole 1938:44].)

Having argued that overlapping poses purely operational problems, we may explore just what these problems are. As Schneider summarizes the position of those who demand that descent groups be discrete,

> the whole person as an aggregate of different commitments must be able to provide unqualified solidarity with the unit to which he belongs. . . . But if a single person's solidarity is qualified by membership in two or more different units *of like order*, then his commitment to, his solidarity with, one of them is qualified by the claims of the other upon him (1965:46, Schneider's emphasis).

From this it is clear that at bottom the problem of overlapping is the possibility that the individual may be faced with conflicting obligations to the different descent groups to which he belongs. It can be solved only by defining the individual's commitment to the descent group in such a way that he may belong to several without compromising his obligation to any.

It does appear that nondiscrete descent groups would pose an insoluble problem in the classic descent systems—such as many reported from Africa —which anthropologists most frequently discuss. Where descent groups are of great significance in a wide range of economic, political and religious affairs, and where much of the individual's activity is directly related to his descent group membership, to be equally committed to several groups of the same kind would inevitably place incompatible obligations upon him. Firth (1963:25–26) has suggested, however, that a system having nondiscrete descent groups could exist if these groups were restricted operationally to a specific resource or a specific activity or occasion. In this manner the problem of overlapping is solved—rather, avoided—in Rapa. As I have stressed repeatedly, an *'ōpū* undertakes no activity which is not directly related to its estate. We have seen that, for the most part, these activities are very few. Because a Rapan is rarely called upon to act in the role of member of an *'ōpū*, and because his commitment to it is so narrowly defined, it is unlikely that his obligations as a member of one *'ōpū* would conflict with his obligations as a member of several others. In Rapa, then, the problem of overlapping is solved by reducing it to the vanishing point.

But let us be more specific. As I see it, there are only two ways in which the individual's obligations to different descent groups may be thought to conflict. First, two groups to which he belongs might come into opposition, such as a feud or dispute. It might be thought that this could place him in a quandry as to which group to support. Second, the groups themselves may not be in opposition but the individual may be faced with incompatible duties to them. For example, he might be required to join with one group in one place and, at the same time, with another group in another place.

Although the narrow range of activities available to the *'ōpū* renders it unlikely, both of these types of conflicting obligations could occur in Rapa. Occasionally two *'ōpū* dispute the ownership of a piece of property, most common being arguments over the boundary separating adjacent coffee groves. It is possible that some persons may belong to both disputing *'ōpū*. Yet there seems to be no reason to anticipate that these circumstances would place the individual in an impossible situation. Among the Kalingas, who are reported to have a special fondness for killing, blood feud is the province of so nondiscrete an organization as the personal kindred. In this society persons who are tied to both sides of a feud are often instrumental in negotiating the peace (Barton 1949:70–71). Similarly, it appears as if a Rapan who belongs to two disputing *'ōpū* need not be torn irrevocably between conflicting obligations. It is just as reasonable to assume that he would be ideally situated to arrange an amicable settlement. As for the second type of conflicting commitments, in Rapa this would be limited to activities concerning coffee groves, for only here does the *'ōpū* act as a unit with any regularity. If two *'ōpū* to which he belongs appoint the same day for joint maintenance or harvesting of their coffee groves, the individual would encounter a conflict in that he could not join both parties. But Rapans solve this problem easily by recognizing the right of anyone involved in a joint activity to send a proxy in his stead. In this way our individual with conflicting obligations could be represented in two or more work groups simultaneously.[26]

IV

Certain operational and structural problems are inherent in a rule of nonexclusive cognatic descent. The descent groups are nondiscrete, and this sets limits on the activities they may undertake and the commitment they may expect from their members. Moreover, such systems are threatened by an intrinsic structural instability. With each succeeding generation individuals would belong to an increased number of descent groups, and therefore each descent group would contain a progressively larger proportion of the population. The confusion anticipated by Leach would be an increasingly apparent fellow-traveler along this road of augmentation.

Yet these problems do not render the existence of nonexclusive cognatic systems impossible, for they can be solved. In these pages I have tried to explain the nature of the solutions in Rapa. Nondiscrete descent groups pose no insurmountable difficulties in this society because they operate in such a way that people rarely encounter conflicts of interest or obligation stemming from plural membership. Augmentation is controlled with respect to improvements in part by the temporary nature of these forms of property, and most importantly by property division and the resulting *'ōpū* partition. It is true that augmentation does proceed freely with respect to territory, but so far at least this has not resulted in confusion. Probably this is partly because most territory-owning *'ōpū* have been in existence for only seventy-five years or a maximum of seven generations, and so the system is not yet at an advanced stage in the process of augmentation. However (and here the situation in Rapa contrasts sharply with that in Tahiti mentioned above), confusion seems to have been averted primarily because territory is a remarkably unproductive form of property and is therefore of little significance in modern economic life.[27]

One of the most interesting characteristics of nonexclusive cognatic descent systems, at least when they are concerned with transmission of property, is that they may vary tremendously in structure, and that this variation results from the simple mechanism of the rate of property division. At one extreme, if property is never divided the descent groups rapidly increase in size and logically the system could result in the communal ownership of all property. At the other, if property is divided in nearly every generation, individual ownership will be the rule and the system will almost lack descent groups entirely. (Our own society is of course an excellent example of this possibility.) Between the extremes, the system can contain descent groups of any size and generational depth, according to the point at which property is divided. The Rapan case is especially instructive in this regard, for here we can observe nearly the full gamut of means of ownership within a single society. Territory is not divided, and here a progression toward communal ownership is clear. Individual ownership may also be found, for often parents divide some of the taro terraces and coffee groves in their personal estates among their children. Other terraces and groves are owned by *'ōpū* which partition at a fairly regular rate, resulting in many descent groups which do not exceed a depth of about five generations.

NOTES

1. My wife and I carried out research in Rapa from December, 1963, to November, 1964.
2. The amount of time required for the completion of the process would depend on the size of the population and the frequency of intergroup marriage.
3. Barrau (1959:160–61) has also noted the confusion which results from undivided lands in Tahiti.
4. See Vancouver (1801 I:216–17) and Ellis (1829 I:48–49) for early population estimates.
5. See Stokes (1930), Caillot (1932), Heyerdahl and Ferdon (1965), and Hanson (1970) for information concerning the pre-European society.
6. On the basis of missionary estimates the population fell from 2000 to 500 between 1826

and 1829. In 1851, the lowest point, only seventy people lived in Rapa. Detailed tables of population size at various points in the island's history may be found in Caillot (1932:25) and Hanson (1970:30).

7. Tahitian, with a few Rapan words thrown in, is currently spoken on the island. *'Ōpū* is a Tahitian word which also means "abdomen."

8. There are a few exceptions, to be discussed below.

9. These remarks apply only to improvements for there has been no redistribution of territory since 1889. Therefore, with the exception of a few which are even older, all *'ōpū* which own territory were founded in that year.

10. The reference here is to the Rapan understanding of French law. This differs from the French understanding in a few respects not central to the purpose of this paper. See Hanson (1970:50) for details.

11. It may be added that the *'ōpū* is an agamous social unit. Persons may marry without disapproval if they are related more distantly than second or third cousins, reckoned bilaterally, regardless of whether they share membership in one or more *'ōpū.*

12. Surnames pass from father to recognized children as in our own system.

13. For example, there were originally thirteen Natiki full siblings. Of the eleven not included on the genealogy, six are dead and five have emigrated to Tahiti. This sibling group has nine children and two grandchildren in Rapa, and seventeen children and five grandchildren in Tahiti.

14. Occasionally different *'ōpū* bear the same name. In such cases, I have added numbers in order that we might distinguish them.

15. An individual need gain permission to build a new house only when it is to be located in a place where he did not reside previously.

16. Perhaps territory-owners might confiscate a disputed taro terrace, orange grove, or other type of improvement in similar circumstances. However, serious disputes are limited almost exclusively to coffee groves (probably because these produce the cash crop), and so this is the only type of property Rapans mention in this context.

17. If several household members belong to the *'ōpū,* usually the senior male of these is the manager.

18. Should this individual die, the office passes to his or her senior male cognatic descendant.

19. With the exception, already noted, that coffee groves have not been planted during about the last two decades.

20. Should one of the sections die out sometime after the division, for example, its property would not revert to the other sections of the original *'ōpū.* It would be considered as the personal estate of the last survivor, and should he die intestate it would pass to his closest collateral kinsmen regardless of whether they trace descent from the founder of the original *'ōpū.*

21. Firth (1957:7) has advanced the terms "definitive segmentation" or "gemmation" for this process, while Middleton and Tait (1958:7–8) label it "fission."

22. As many as seven generations have elapsed in seventy-five years because many of the beneficiaries of territorial distribution were old enough to be grandparents in 1889. Thus the *'ōpū* they founded were already three generations deep the moment they were established.

23. Natiki 1 is included in the list of *'ōpū* presented above.

24. Alternatively we could state that we are dealing with a single *'ōpū* on one level of organization, which is divided into two segments on the next lower level. Elsewhere I have discussed why I prefer not to analyze the Rapan case as a segmentary system (Hanson 1966:48–53). Suffice it here to state that since each of these *'ōpū* is concerned solely with an estate of property, and since each owns its estate autonomously, they all operate on the same level and there are no special relations between them. Hence it seems preferable to consider them as three distinct *'ōpū.*

25. In some respects my position on this point is similar to that more elaborately developed by Scheffler (1966, see especially p. 545).

26. Overlapping membership probably imposes limits on the range of activities which descent groups may undertake. A problem for further research is to determine what those limits are. For a discussion of the effects of overlapping in a system where descent groups engage in a wider range of activities than the Rapan *'ōpū,* see Lloyd (1966).

27. From the data given in this paper it appears as if territory ownership has little or no meaning to the Rapans. Nothing could be further from the truth. There is evidence that they value territory above all other forms of property; in fact, one reason territory is not divided may be that no one is willing to give up any rights he may have in it. Today the value placed on territory is purely an ideological matter which finds little manifestation in economy or in the activities of the *'ōpū*, and therefore we have not discussed it here. A few thoughts on this very difficult subject may be found in Hanson (1970:42–48).

BIBLIOGRAPHY

BARRAU, JACQUES, 1959, "L'Agriculture Polynésienne au Contact des Étrangers." *Journal de la Société des Océanistes*, 15:147–164.

BARTON, R. F., 1949, *The Kalingas.* Chicago: University of Chicago Press.

BEAGLEHOLE, ERNEST, AND PEARL BEAGLEHOLE, 1938, *Ethnology of Pukapuka.* Honolulu: Bernice P. Bishop Museum Bulletin No. 150.

BROWN, KEITH, 1966, "*Dōzoku* and the Ideology of Descent in Rural Japan." *American Anthropologist*, 68:1129–1151.

CAILLOT, A-C EUGENE, 1932, *Histoire de l'Île Oparo ou Rapa.* Paris: Leroux.

CHOWNING, ANN, 1962, "Cognatic Kin Groups among the Molima of Fergusson Island." *Ethnology*, 1:92–101.

CROCOMBE, R. G., 1964, *Land Tenure in the Cook Islands.* Melbourne: Oxford University Press.

DAVENPORT, WILLIAM, 1959, "Nonunilinear Descent and Descent Groups." *American Anthropologist*, 61:557–572.

EGGAN, FRED, 1960, "The Sagada Igorots of Northern Luzon." In G. P. Murdock, ed., *Social Structure in Southeast Asia.* Chicago: Quadrangle Books.

ELLIS, WILLIAM, 1829, *Polynesian Researches.* 2 vols. London: Fisher, Son, and Jackson.

FINNEY, BEN R., 1965, "Polynesian Peasants and Proletarians." *Journal of the Polynesian Society*, 74:269–328.

FIRTH, RAYMOND, 1957, "A Note on Descent Groups in Polynesia." *Man*, 57:4–8.

1963, "Bilateral Descent Groups: An Operational Viewpoint." In I. Schapera, ed., *Studies in Kinship and Marriage.* London: Royal Anthropological Institute.

FORTES, MEYER, 1959, "Descent, Filiation, and Affinity: A Rejoinder to Dr. Leach." *Man*, 59:193–197, 206–212.

1963, "The 'Submerged Descent Line' in Ashanti." In I. Schapera, ed., *Studies in Kinship and Marriage.* London: Royal Anthropological Institute.

FREEMAN, J. D., 1960, "The Iban of Western Borneo." In G. P. Murdock, ed., *Social Structure in Southeast Asia.* Chicago: Quadrangle Books.

1961, "On the Concept of the Kindred." *Journal of the Royal Anthropological Institute*, 91:192–220.

GOODENOUGH, WARD H., 1961, "Review" of *Social Structure in Southeast Asia. American Anthropologist*, 63:1341–1347.

GOODY, JACK, 1959, "The Mother's Brother and the Sister's Son in West Africa." *Journal of the Royal Anthropological Institute*, 89:61–88.

1961, "The Classification of Double Descent Systems." *Current Anthropology*, 2:3–12.

HANSON, F. ALLAN, 1966, *Continuity and Change in Rapan Social Organization.* Unpublished Ph.D. dissertation, University of Chicago.

1970, *Rapan Lifeways.* Boston: Little, Brown.

HEYERDAHL, THOR, AND EDWIN N. FERDON, JR., EDS., 1965, *Reports of the Norwegian Archeological Expedition to Easter Island and the East Pacific. Vol. 2: Miscellaneous Papers.* Monograph of the School of American Research and the Kon Tiki Museum No. 24, Part 2.

KOENTJARANINGRAT, R. M., 1960, "The Javanese of South Central Java." In G. P. Murdock, ed., *Social Structure in Southeast Asia.* Chicago: Quadrangle Books.

LAMBERT, BERND, 1966, "Ambilineal Descent Groups in the Northern Gilbert Islands." *American Anthropologist*, 68:641–664.

LEACH, E. R., 1960, "The Sinhalese of the Dry Zone of Northern Ceylon." In G. P. Murdock, ed., *Social Structure in Southeast Asia.* Chicago: Quadrangle Books.

1962, "On Certain Unconsidered Aspects of Double Descent Systems." *Man,* 62:130–134.
LLOYD, P. C., 1966, "Agnatic and Cognatic Descent Groups among the Yoruba." *Man* (N.S.), 1:484–500.
MCILWRAITH, T. F., 1948, *The Bella Coola Indians.* 2 vols. Toronto: University of Toronto Press.
MIDDLETON, J., AND D. TAIT, EDS., 1958, *Tribes without Rulers,* London: Routledge & Kegan Paul.
MITCHELL, WILLIAM, 1961, "Descent Groups among New York City Jews." *Jewish Journal of Sociology,* 3:121–128.
MURDOCK, G. P., 1960, "Cognatic Forms of Social Organization." In G. P. Murdock, ed., *Social Structure in Southeast Asia.* Chicago: Quadrangle Books.
RADCLIFFE-BROWN, A. R., 1929a, "A Further Note on Ambrym." *Man,* 29:50–53.
1929b, "Bilateral Descent." *Man,* 29:199–200.
SCHEFFLER, HAROLD W., 1962, "Kindred and Kin Groups in Simbo Island Social Structure." *Ethnology,* 2:135–157.
1963, "Choiseul Island Descent Groups." *Journal of the Polynesian Society,* 72:177–187.
1965, *Choiseul Island Social Structure.* Berkeley: University of California Press.
1966, "Ancestor Worship in Anthropology; or Observations on Descent and Descent Groups." *Current Anthropology,* 7:541–548.
SCHNEIDER, D. M., 1965, "Some Muddles in the Models." In *The Relevance of Models for Social Anthropology.* A. S. A. Monograph No. 1. New York: Praeger.
STOKES, JOHN F. G., 1930, Ethnology of Rapa. Unpublished manuscript in the Bernice P. Bishop Museum, Honolulu.
VANCOUVER, CAPTAIN GEORGE, 1801, *A Voyage of Discovery to the North Pacific Ocean.* 6 vols. London.

9

THE FIJIAN SYSTEM OF KINSHIP AND MARRIAGE[1]

Rusiate R. Nayacakalou

PART I

Most modern anthropologists would agree with the view expressed by Dr. H. T. Fei that "a structural analysis of relationship terms, at best, covers only a part of the whole problem of kinship system and that a mere presentation of a chart of terms is of little use by itself because it fails to show their sociological implications."[2] The present study therefore is not only an attempt to formulate the rules by which the Fijian native classifies his kin logically; it is also an attempt to relate the linguistic usages of kinship to actual social behavior.[3]

Fijian kinship terminology varies considerably with locality; but the basic principles underlying the kinship structure vary in comparatively small degree. The aim of Part I of this article is to study these basic principles. But for explanatory purposes and, more importantly, in order that the study should be based upon actual behaviour, it is necessary to discuss these principles with specific reference to a particular locality. For this purpose I have selected Tokatoka in Tailevu Province. I was born and bred there and I am one of the persons who sustain its kinship system. My knowledge of this system and of the associated behaviour patterns is thus the result both of actual coaching during my earlier years and of the continual application of the principles which I am now attempting to study and analyse.

Tokatoka is a group of six villages bordering the banks of the Rewa and Wainibokasi Rivers some five miles down the Rewa from Nausori township where the local District Officer is stationed. In 1948 the Tokatoka buliship[5] had been abolished and merged with Nakelo *tikina* which, with four other *tikina*, now combine to make up Tailevu Province which is administered from Bau Island. Tokatoka is a comparatively large, but sufficiently integrated, unit to serve as the focal point of the discussion.

Reproduced by permission of Rusiate R. Nayacakalou from the *Journal of the Polynesian Society*, 64:44–55 (1955) and 66:44–59 (1957).

Table I contains all the kinship terms commonly used in Tokatoka, and in our discussion of them we begin with the patrilocal monogamous family. The father is called *tama* and the mother *tina;* the husband and the wife are each called *wati;* the children are called *luve.* While the last term refers specifically to progeniture, it does not distinguish between the sexes. The separate qualifying term *tagane* (male) and *yalewa* (female) are sometimes used to differentiate between son and daughter.

All these terms, however, rarely appear in these forms, being normally used possessively with suffixes, with which they are compounded. The suffixes most commonly used are *-qu*, *-mu*, and *-na* signifying the first, second and third person singular respectively.[6] *Tamaqu, tinaqu, waitqu, luvequ* are therefore the terms for my father, my mother, my spouse and my children respectively. Similar applications of the relevant possessive suffix can be made to cover most of the other relatives.

In addition to these possessive constructions of kinship terms, there are also special constructions to cover situations of reciprocal kinship. Thus a husband and his wife are said to be *veiwatini,* i.e. they are husband and wife. Similarly a father and child are *veitamani,* and a mother and child are *veitinani.* The two latter terms are perfectly substitutable by the alternative term *veiluveni* (parent and child).

The father's father is called *tubu,* and the mother's father is called *tuka.* All women in the second ascending generation are called *bu.* These three terms also form the basis for classifying all blood kin above the second ascending generation. Thus my grandmother's mother is *buqu vakarua* (grandmother twice over); my grandmother's grandmother is *buqu vakatolu* (grandmother three times over); and so on. Similarly with the father's father's father's . . . The reverse relationship between alternate generations, viz. grandchild, is expressed in a single term—*makubuqu.* This term is used by father's father, father's mother, mother's father and mother's mother to both grandson and granddaughter. A person in the third descending generation is called *makubuqu vakarua,* in the fourth descending, *makubuqu vakatolu,* and so on. However, in Tokatoka, the great grandparent simply addresses the great grandchild as *makubuqu;* conversely the great grandchild simply addresses the great grandparent as *tubuqu, tukaqu* or *buqu* as the case may be. This is purely a matter of convenience, and in a descriptive context requiring exactitude the full description is always given.

At this point we isolate two fundamental unifying principles within the total kinship structure. The first is common descent, which binds together the members of what may be termed the lineage group.[7] Membership of this group is automatically determined by the principle of patrilineal descent. Female members do not lose their membership merely by marrying into another group, but their children must, obviously, belong to the group of their own fathers. The second principle is that of common parentage, which

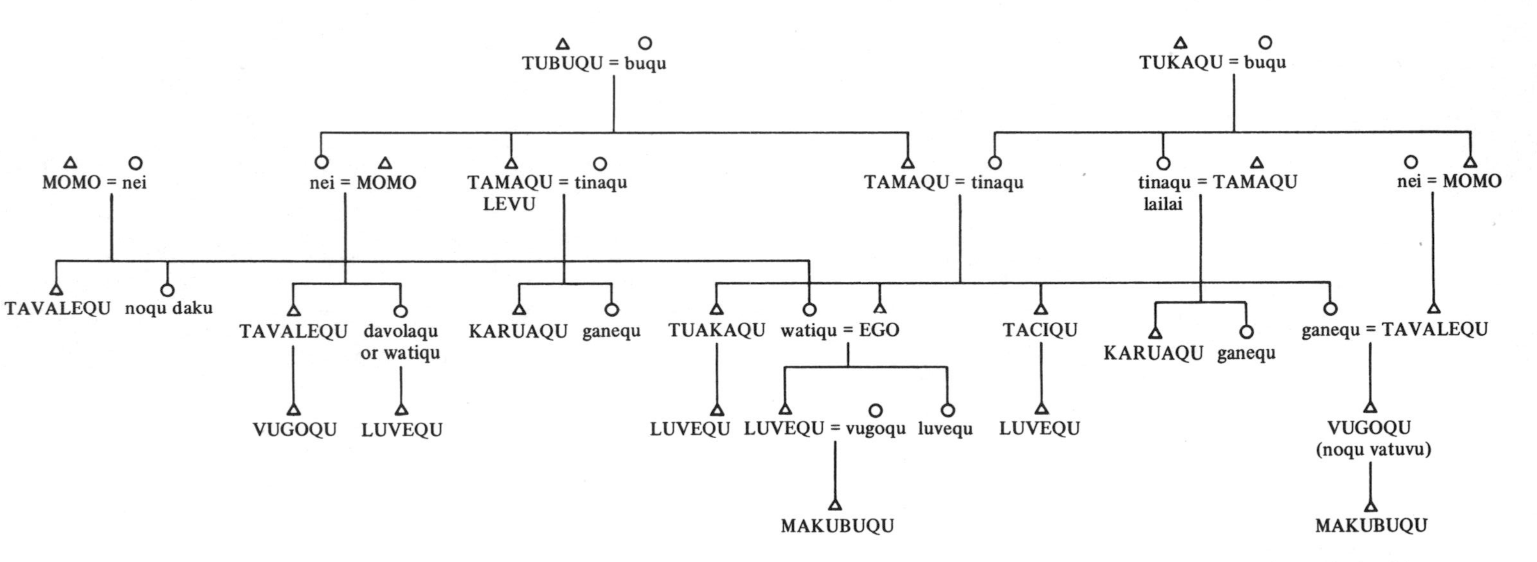

TABLE I. SUMMARY OF KINSHIP TERMS CURRENT IN TOKATOKA, FIJI. *Note:* The following genealogical table contains all the kinship terms commonly used in Tokatoka today. The standard symbols Δ and O have been used, together with capitals and small letters respectively to designate males and females, and the terms are those of EGO's reference.

TABLE II. LIST OF KINSHIP TERMS. *Note:* The abbreviations used are: F—father; m—mother; B—brother; s—sister; H—husband; w—wife; S—son; d—daughter; x-c—cross-cousin; e—elder; y—younger; tekn.—teknonym; pn—personal name; (bs)—man speaking; (ws)—woman speaking; combinations such as mB—mother's brother; FF—father's father.

English	*Fijian Description*	*Address*	*Elaboration*	*Notes*
FF	TUBUQU, TUBUQU O . . . (pn)	TUBUQU	Includes FFB, FFFBS, etc.	
mF	TUKAQU, TUKAQU O . . . (pn)	TUKAQU	Includes mFB, mFFBS, etc.	
mm, Fm	buqu, buqu o . . . (pn)	buqu, bu	Includes mms, Fms, mmmsd, Fmmsd, etc.	
F	TAMAQU	TAMAQU, NAU, TATA		For terms for FB, see text
m	tinaqu	qei, tinaqu, nana		For terms for ms, see text
mB	MOMO, MOMO . . . (pn)	MOMO	Also FsH, wF, HF	
Fs	ganei, nei, nei o . . . (pn)	ganei, nei	Also mBw, wm, Hm	
eB(ms)	TUAKAQU, pn	pn		
es (ws)	tuakaqu, pn	pn		
yB (ms)	TACIQU, pn	pn		
ys (ws)	taciqu, pn	pn		
B (ws)	GANEQU, tekn.	—		Brothers and sisters do not address each other[1]
s (ms)	ganequ, tekn.	—		
FsS, mBS (ms)	TAVALEQU, tekn., rau o . . . (adding pn or tekn.)	IE, KEMUDRAU, TAVALE, tekn., very rarely pn	Also wB, or sH (ms)	
Fsd, mBd (ws)	raivaqu, tekn.	ie; kemudrau, raiva, tekn., very rarely pn	Also Hs, or Bw(ws)	The term *dauve* is sometimes used meaning Hs or Bw(ws).
FsS, mBS (ws)	DAVOLAQU, pn	pn, TAVALE, DAVOLA, NA WATIQU		

Fsd, mBd (ms)	davolaqu, pn	pn, tavale, davola, na watiqu	
H	WATIQU, pn	pn	Also any x-c of opp. sex
w	watiqu, pn	pn	
ws, Bw (ms)	noqu, daku, pn	pn	
HB, sH (ws)	NOQU DAKU, pn.	pn	
classif. B (ms)	KARUAQU, TACIQU, pn	KARUA, pn	
classif. s (ws)	karuaqu, taciqu, pn	karua, taciqu, pn	
S	LUVEQU, pn	NA LUVEQU, pn	Also BS(ms), FBSS(ms), or sS (ws), FBdS(ws) and S of x-c of opp. sex
d	luvequ, pn	na luvequ, pn	Also Bd(ms), FBSd(ms), or Sd (ws), FBdd(ws) and d of x-c of opp. sex
sS (ms), BS (ws)	VUGOQU, pn	NA VUGOQU, pn	Also child's spouse
sd (ms), Bd (ws)	vugoqu, pn	na vugoqu, pn	
sS or sd (ms)	noqu vatuvu, vugoqu	noqu vatuvu, na vogoqu pn	
SS, dS; (m or w s)	MAKUBUQU, pn	NA MAKUBUQU, pn	
Sd, dd; (m or w s)	makubuqu, pn	na makubuqu, pn	

[1] One can talk to a person without having to address that person. Nevertheless, some cross-siblings in Tokatoka are nowadays tending to disregard the social barriers to conversation among themselves, especially where the brother is the younger of the two.

binds together the members of a sibling group. This group forms the prot
type of relationships at each generation level within the lineage group. T
principle of common parentage, by a simple extension using the classific
tory principle,[8] enables all the members of each generation within t
lineage group to be classified together as siblings.

We can also isolate certain principles of differentiation within the syste
The members of a lineage group, for instance, are differentiated firstly
generation, and secondly by sex. Thus all the male members of the fi
ascending generation are classified together as fathers, and the female me
bers as father's sisters; the male members of the contemporary generati
are classified together as brothers, and the females in the same generati
are sisters; the male members of the first descending generation are son
and the females are daughters; the male members of the second descendi
generation are sons' sons, and the females are sons' daughters; and so o
At each generation level all the members of the lineage group stand to ea
other in the simple relation of siblings; but relations between proxima
generations are complicated, as we shall see presently, by the distinction
sex.

Again, siblings are distinguished by age and sex. An elder sibling of t
same sex is called *tuaka*, and a younger sibling of the same sex is call
taci. (This latter term, incidentally, is the generic term which express
siblinghood; persons who are related as siblings are said to be *veitacin*
Any sibling of opposite sex is called *gane*, and siblings of opposite sex a
said to be *veiganeni*. The fact that there is no term to express age distin
tions between siblings of opposite sex may be correlated (although no caus
tive relation is necessarily implied) with the social fact that age distinctio
are important only between siblings of the same sex. These principles
classification lead to more important consequences not only in the deter
nation of positions of leadership and seniority within the sibling group, b
also in the structural alignment of kin in descending generations, and in t
structure of the lineage group.

The importance of age and sex for seniority and leadership within t
sibling group is simple. As descent is patrilineal, marriage patrilocal and t
lineage group exogamous, the female members of the sibling group need n
come into considerations of seniority at all, as they will sooner or later
marry outside the lineage group, and their children will be classified f
seniority in their own patrilineage. Over and above that, women are consi
ered socially inferior to men in Fiji, and any claim they might have had
seniority on the basis of age is thus automatically shelved. This leav
seniority a matter entirely for the male sibling group only, with few, if a
exceptions. Within that group, seniority is conferred in order of bir
Leadership is very closely associated with age, but is not identical with
as it depends on other considerations also. A brother who was insane, f
instance, or who was for some reason unsuitable to occupy the position

leadership cannot be expected to lead the group; but he is still senior to all his younger brothers, and so are his sons to theirs irrespective of age.

It is now necessary for us to delve somewhat more deeply into some of the inner features of the system. We begin with the internal structure of the sibling group, which we recognize is governed by the principle which Professor Radcliffe-Brown has called the principle of unity of the sibling group. This unity "refers not to the internal unity of the group as shown in the relations of the different members to one another but to the fact that the group may constitute a unity for a person outside it and connected with it by a specific relation to one of its members. Thus a son may, in a particular system, be taught to regard his father's sibling group as a united body with whom he is related as their 'son'."[10] Professor Radcliffe-Brown uses this principle to explain the classificatory system of kinship terminology. The principle is at work in Fiji and, no doubt, explains the operation of the classificatory principle there; but its use is significantly modified here in that it covers siblings of the same sex only. Thus a person would be a son to his father and father's brothers only, or to his mother and mother's sisters only, and there is no suggestion that the father's sister belongs to a kinship category somewhat similar to that of the father, or the mother's brother to that of the mother. It appears, however, that this distinction of sex between siblings is ignored when viewed from an ascending generation. Thus there is only one type of relationship between a father and his children irrespective of the sex of the children; and between a father's sister and her brother's children, again irrespective of the sex of the children. The similar relation of a grandparent to his or her grandchildren has already been referred to.

There are two reasons why we have laboured the statement of this principle: it provides a basis for a demonstration of the classificatory principle; and it brings to the foreground the most fundamental cleavage in the Fijian kinship structure, viz., the distinction of sex within the sibling group.

The classificatory principle is based upon the unity principle. Because siblings of the same sex are regarded as constituting a unity, they tend to be addressed by the same term. Thus a child addresses all his father's brothers by a term meaning father, and all the mother's sisters by a term meaning mother. All the father's elder brothers are referred to as *tamaqu levu* (big or senior father), and all his younger brothers are referred to as *tamaqu lailai* (small or junior father). Similarly there are also "big mothers" and "small mothers." Applied somewhat in the opposite situation, this principle leads ultimately to what may conveniently be termed "classificatory siblinghood" in which persons are regarded as siblings if their fathers are brothers or their mothers sisters. The familiar term, of course, is parallel-cousins, but we use the term "classificatory sibling" because it comes much closer to the Fijian interpretation, and would be more useful in this analysis. By simple extension, classificatory siblings include not only persons whose fathers are brothers or whose mothers sisters, but also persons whose fathers are classificatory brothers and whose mothers are classificatory sisters.

When the principle of the unity of siblings ceases to provide a workable basis for the classificatory principle it is supplemented by cold hard logic. Thus a man can be a classificatory brother to another man through a third man if they are both related to the third man in the same type of way. Thus if A is a classificatory father to B, and C is also a classificatory father to B, then A and C are classificatory brothers, even if no genealogical tie can be traced between them. Similarly, if A is a classificatory father to B, and B is husband to C, then A is a classificatory father-in-law to C. In a similar way one can work out relationships involving persons of different sexes in different generations through any number of intermediate connections. This is the way in which the classificatory principle ultimately ramifies right throughout the entire kinship system.

Sex distinction not only delimits the application of the unity principle; it also has repercussions in the relationships between offspring of the sibling group. Thus there is a certain interrelationship between sex differentiation, sibling unity, and lineage unity: sex differentiation within the sibling group affects the kinship structure by reacting upon lineage unity in the first descending generation. The mechanics of how this is brought about can be described, but cannot be adequately explained without reference to brother-sister taboo. Thus there is in the whole of Fiji a certain relationship of very slightly varying degrees of intensity between a brother and his sister, who are said to be *veitabui,* i.e. to be taboo to each other. They may not come into physical contact, and may not address each other except through a third party (although a brother is freer to reproach his sister directly or to command her to perform his bidding). The brother has a corrective and protective authority over his sister—authority which sometimes supersedes even that of the father or mother. The sister regards her brother as sacred to her, and as one who must be obeyed and whose sanctity is supreme. Reference may not be made to some subjects, e.g. sex, in the presence of a brother and his sister. This basic respect for the brother-sister relationship is consistently and rigorously upheld throughout every type of relationship and behaviour pattern in the entire kinship structure. Even the suggestion that the children of a man are *veitatacini* or classificatory siblings with his sister's children is regarded as putting the man and his sister in the category of spouses, and is an insult to the brother-sister taboo. Hence the children of two persons who stand in the relationship of brother and sister to one another must never be ranked as classificatory siblings; but must be separately aligned as cross-cousins or *veitavaleni.* This relationship is at the root of a major cleavage in lineage procreation and to deal with it adequately we need specialised terminology.

We define "cross-siblings" as siblings of opposite sex, and "parallel-siblings" as siblings of the same sex.[11] A "cross-parent" is the cross-sibling of the parent including the spouse of such cross-sibling; it would be a father's sister and her husband, or a mother's brother and his wife. It will be easily seen that a "cross-parent" in this sense would be the parent of a cross-cousin. A "cross-child" is the child of a cross-sibling, or of a cross-cousin of the same sex. A "cross-relative" is a cross-parent, cross-cousin or cross-child in the sense of the above definitions.

The generic term for a cross-parent irrespective of sex is *vugo.* The cross-parent's term for his or her cross-child is also *vugo.* The reciprocal relationship between a cross-parent and a cross-child is called *veivugoni.* The mother's brother is called *momo,* and the father's sister is called *nei.* The children of either a *momo* or a *nei* (i.e. cross-cousins), are referred to by a man as *tavale* if they are males and as *davola* if they are females; by a woman as *raiva* if they are females and as *davola* if they are males. *Tavale* is the generic term for cross-cousins irrespective of sex, but *davola* is the term for cross-cousins of opposite sex only. The cross-parents, cross-cousins and cross-children of an individual constitute to him a lineal unity similar to that of the lineage group. The children of a cross-parent are always cross-cousins; the children of a cross-cousin of the same sex are always cross-children; one's own children are cross-cousins to one's cross-children, and so on down through the generations.

Thus within his own generation a male will distinguish only two major types of male relatives: brothers, real *(taci)* or classificatory *(karua);* and cross-cousins *(tavale),* real or classificatory. In the same way he will classify female relatives of his own generation according to whether they are sisters *(gane),* real or classificatory, or cross-cousins *(davola),* real or classificatory. For a female there is a similar mode of classification of male and female relatives within her own generation. A similar distinction is made in the first ascending generation between parents and cross-parents, and in the first descending generation between children and cross-children. In this way we distinguish two major types of relatives: lineal, and "cross." As will have appeared from our discussion, this fundamental cleavage can be traced back ultimately to sex distinction within the sibling group. Furthermore, being the basis, as we shall see, of determining marriageable relationships within the kinship structure, it is of fundamental import in the social structure.

There is hardly need for us to state that cross-cousin marriage is the custom in Tokatoka as it is in many other parts of Fiji. There are, however, some popular misconceptions here which must be corrected. Cross-cousins of opposite sexes in very many parts of Fiji regard each other as "natural" husbands and wives. In Tokatoka they treat each other as husbands and wives, address each other by the term for spouse *(wati),* and are rather inclined to behave with playful familiarity; but while sexual indulgence between such persons is not subject to taboo, no sexual familiarity is necessarily involved. The relationship is standardised simply at that. Furthermore, while cross-cousin marriage is often practised, we cannot say that this is the "preferred" type of marriage. No marriage is permitted between any two generations (so far, of course, as prospective spouses can be comparably placed within a recognizable generation structure), nor between siblings, real or classificatory. Therefore, strictly logically, no other type of marriage is possible to which cross-cousin marriage can be a preferred alternative; except when the case of unrelated persons is considered. Indeed, cross-cousin marriage is often encouraged, but the preference in fact more often falls upon persons with whom no blood tie can be traced. We must say, therefore, that cross-cousin marriage is not the preferred, but that it is the only permitted, type of marriage between genealogically related persons. However, even if two cross-cousins do not actually marry, they are regarded as husband and wife nevertheless, and their children as classificatory siblings.

We illustrate the whole position of marriageable relatives from the appended table which shows the relationships between a number of descendants of a single male ancestor through four consecutive generations. We use different letters for different generations—capitals for male members and corresponding small letters for female members. We use numerical indexes along with the letters to distinguish males from other males, and females from other females, within a single generation. We underline all males and females who are descended patrilineally from the original ancestor to distinguish them from those who are descended through a female intermediary. We have stated that no marriage is permitted between any two generations; and that within any one generation, marriage is permitted only between cross-cousins. Hence we have A1 and a1 are cross-siblings. Therefore, B1, whose mother is a1, is a cross-cousin to B2, B3 and b1 who are all children of his own cross-parent A1. He is permitted to marry b1, because they are cross-cousins; but in the table he does not marry her. In the third generation, c1, a daughter of B1, marries her cross-cousin C1 who is a son of B2 who is a male cross-cousin of her father B1. C3, son of b1, marries his mother's brother's daughter c3. He could have married c2; but not c1 because their parents B1 and b1 are cross-cousins of opposite sex who could have married, and whose children are therefore classificatory siblings. In the fourth generation, D2 marries his mother's brother's daughter d1. D1 can marry his father's sister's daughter d2 not only by virtue of that relationship, but also because their mothers c1 and c2 are classificatory cross-cousins through their fathers B1 and B2 who are cross-cousins. But D2 could not marry d3 because their mothers are classificatory sisters. Similarly, D4 could not marry d1 because their fathers are classificatory brothers. It is perhaps as well to point out here that in Takotoka the distinction by degree between cross-cousins is hardly worth making, the different degrees being largely classified together.

Table III effectively illustrates the way in which sex differentiation affects lineage unity. If in the present context we are to identify the "lineage group" with the *mataqali,* we may say that the lineage group is both patrilineal and

TABLE III.

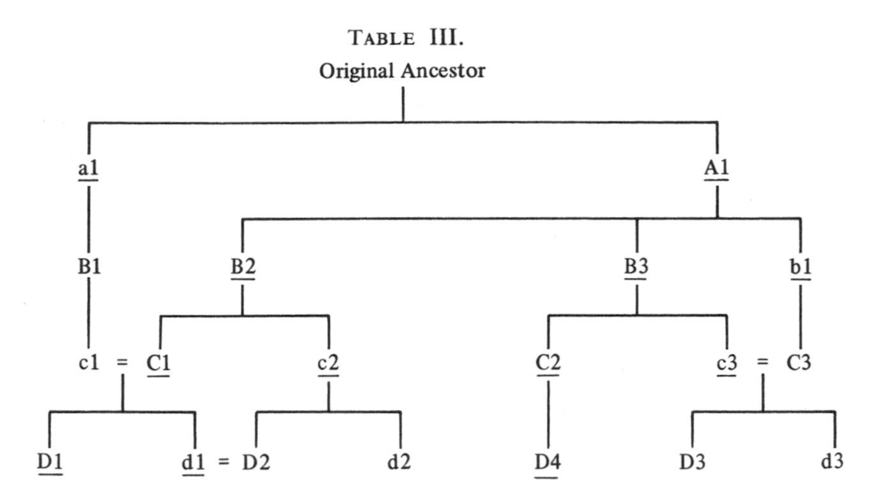

exogamous. Therefore, the children of the female members of an original lineage group must belong to a different lineage group from that of their mothers. We can distinguish, by means of underlining patrilineal descendants, those persons within each generation who are true members of, and those who must eternally be excluded from, the original lineage group.

The marriageability or otherwise of two genealogically connected persons depends primarily upon whether they are cross-siblings, real or classificatory; or cross-cousins, real or classificatory. They are marriageable in the latter case, not in the former. Whether they are cross-siblings or cross-cousins depends primarily upon the relevant relationships in the first ascending generation. Thus if they are respectively descended from two parents who are siblings of the same sex, real or classificatory, or from parents who are cross-cousins of opposite sex, they are classificatory siblings. If, on the other hand, they are respectively descended from two parents who are cross-siblings, real or classificatory, or who are cross-cousins of the same sex, they are cross-cousins and are therefore marriageable. The relationships in the parent generation will, of course, depend in turn upon the relevant relationships in the second ascending generation, and so on *ad infinitum.*

The manner in which the sex principle operates on succeeding generations to determine kinship relationships, and hence marriagability among genealogically connected persons may be more generally stated with the aid of the following illustration. We show two members of a single sibling group procreating separately over seven generations, each time through a single child. So long as the sexes of the procreating parents[12] in any one generation is the same in both lines, the relationship between those parents, whether that of sibling (real or classificatory), or of cross-cousins, is retained between their respective children. This holds irrespective of changes of sex as between one generation and another in either line, such as between generations 1 and 2 or between 4 and 5, in Table IV. If, on the other hand, the sexes of the relevant procreating parents in any one generation differ in the two lines, the relationship between them will not be sustained between their respective children in the following generation; i.e. if the parents are cross-siblings, their children will be cross-cousins; but if the parents are cross-cousins, then their children will be classified as siblings. Examples are found between generations 3 and 4 and between 6 and 7 in the table.

TABLE IV.

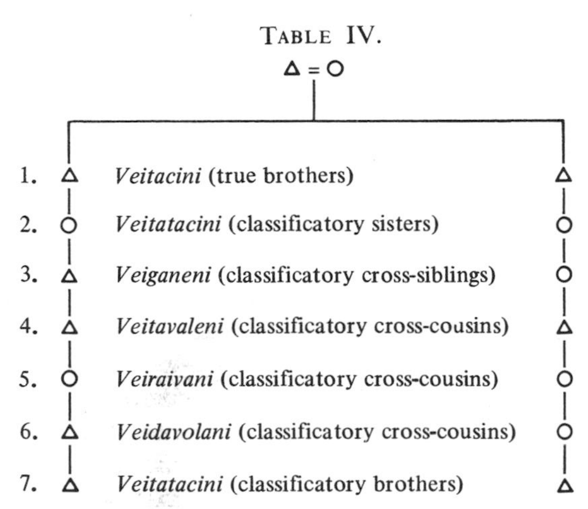

Turning now to the classification of affinal kin, we recall that in discussing the position of cross-relatives, we said that a *tavale* is always the son of a *momo* or of a *nei*, and also the brother of a *davola* who is also addressed by the term for spouse. The principles which govern the classification of affinal relatives proceed from this set of terms. The first necessary observation is that while the spouse is not addressed by the term *davola*, he (she) is nevertheless placed in exactly the same structural position as a *davola*. Immediately after consummation of the marriage[13] the spouse's cross-siblings become *tavale* (or *raiva* as the case may be); i.e. the spouse's sibling group immediately becomes a cross-cousin group. In the case of a man[14] the wife's father becomes *momo* and her mother *nei;* i.e. her parents become his cross-parents. Similarly, her sister's children become his children in the classificatory sense, and her brother's children become his cross-children, i.e. he and his wife now become cross-parents to them. The wife's sisters become *noqu daku* to the husband and the husband's brothers become *noqu daku* to the wife. Even if in fact the kinship terms which arise from a marriage are not used at all (see footnote 12 . . .), it is important to recognize that the terms used reciprocally with cross-relatives apply nevertheless, and are in fact used. A man becomes, on marriage, *veivugoni* with his wife's parents and they with him; he becomes *veitavaleni* (cross-cousins) with her brothers and they with him; and he becomes *veivugoni* with her brother's children and they with him.

It is convenient at this point to elaborate the position of cross-parents a little further. We stated that if the children of a man were ranked as classificatory siblings with the children of his sister, this would be regarded as putting him in the position of husband to his own sister. This attitude illustrates an important principle, viz., that the principle by which marriageability in any generation is determined by reference to the next ascending generations applies reciprocally as between those two generations. Thus, if we can say that two members of a generation are not marriageable because the father of the one is a marriageable relative of the mother of the other, then reciprocally we must say that because a man and a woman of the same generation are unmarriageable, any classificatory father of the one is marriageable to any classificatory mother of the other.[15] Conversely, if two children are marriageable, any classificatory father of the one is unmarriageable to any classificatory mother of the other. Therefore, by virtue of the marriage between any two spouses, the husband's father is an unmarriageable affinal kin to the wife's mother, i.e. the wife's mother is regarded as a classificatory cross-sibling of the husband's father. This establishes the application of the term *nei* to both the father's sister and the wife's mother: they are kin of the same general category. Following a similar line of reasoning, we can establish the application of the term *momo* to both the mother's brother and the wife's father. Again, using the principle of the unity of the sibling group, we can see that by virtue of the marriage between the father and mother, there is a marriageable relationship between the father's sister and the mother's brother, i.e. *nei* and *momo* are marriageable relatives. Hence, the general principle that whenever a *momo* marries, his wife is called a *nei* and vice versa. This establishes the extension of the term *momo* to cover not only the mother's brother but also the father's sister's husband; and the extension of the term *nei* to cover not only the father's sister but also the mother's brother's wife. In both cases, the *momo* is a *tavale* to the father and the *nei* a *raiva* to the mother. This can be checked in another way. We have seen that the type of relationship between two progenitors or between two progenitrixes, whether the relationship of sibling or that of cross-cousins, will be reproduced in their respective children. Therefore, because the relationship between two spouses is of the cross-cousin type rather than the cross-sibling type, such relationship is a faithful reproduction of the relationship between their respective fathers and, similarly, between their mothers. The wife's father is therefore a *tavale* to her husband's father; her mother is a *raiva* to her husband's mother. Hence our final definitions: a *momo* is a man who stands in the relation of cross-cousin to the father; a *nei* is a woman who stands in the relation of cross-cousin to the mother.

While the principles discussed above appear to be admirably self-consistent, we must never lose sight of the fact that certain inconsistencies do arise, mainly as a result of irregular marriages which take place when classificatory ties loosen. Men have been known to marry relatives of an unmarriageable type such as classificatory sisters or daughters, in cases where they are distant enough.[16] These irregular marriages give rise to further conflicting situations, e.g. a man may thereby become related to a woman both as a brother and as a cross-cousin, in the classificatory sense, by different genealogical paths. If two such persons desire to marry, the brother-sister relationship is simply quietly ignored in favour of convenience, possibly making some relationships in other areas of the same kinship structure even more confusing. However, as such marriages would appear to indicate a sufficient loosening of the older ties with which they are in conflict, they give rise to a new principle: the affinal relationships which are immediately connected with a marriage which is in conflict with established consanguineous relationships must always be accorded precedence over such consanguineous ties.

PART II

Part I of this article[1] was a structural analysis of the Fijian kinship system. It had been stressed there that a purely structural analysis is of little value because it fails to show the sociological implications of the structure. This Part is therefore designed to illustrate the way in which Fijian kinship serves as a principle of social organisation, i.e. how it is that on the basis of it, people organise the major aspects of their social life. This task I propose to carry out at two major levels. In the first place, I shall attempt to describe the type attitudes and behaviour patterns associated with the terminological structure; and in the second place I shall attempt to show how the kin-group as a whole is socially distinguishable from the general "out-group" of non-kin. At the end of the study I hope to be able to show that, while kinship is one of the most persistent (in the sense of being resistant to change) features of primitive social organisation, it is nevertheless susceptible to change as a principle of social organisation under the conditions of a culture contact situation.

Type Attitudes and Behaviour Associated With Kinship

This section attempts to describe the general types of attitude and behaviour adopted towards relatives by virtue of the kincategory to which they belong. Such a category is always designated by a kinship term, and one could therefore say that attitudes and behaviour towards kin "follow the terms."

1. *Grandfather, grandmother (tubuqu, tukaqu, buqu).* For all practical purposes there is no difference in attitude or behaviour between that adopted towards the father's father and that adopted towards the mother's

father. Both are members of the second generation ascending and therefore separated not only by one intervening generation but also by a great difference in age. They are persons from whom the child expects special favours and to whom he may turn for comfort when he is punished or scolded by his father or mother. They are not directly responsible for the discipline of the child, so that the child can more easily identify himself with them than with the parents.[2] Substantially the same can be said of the father's mother and the mother's mother, except that these relatives are even more lavish in bestowing their favours on their grandchildren.

One point calls for comment here. There is a terminological distinction between the father's father and the mother's father, but none between the father's mother and the mother's mother. Here it appears that emphasis on male sex in the lineage structure provides an explanation. In the first place, the male members are distinguished while the female members are not; and in the second place, the distinction between the male members is on the basis of sex in the intervening generation. Hence the suggestion that the distinction arises because of the emphasis on patriliny in the lineage structue.[3]

2. *Father, mother (tamaqu, tinaqu).* The father and mother are the persons directly responsible for the welfare and training of the child. They are not only persons from whom the best things in life can be expected, but also persons who have authority to wield the rod when occasion demands. They are therefore regarded with hope on the one hand, and with awe and respect on the other. Both may be addressed by the terms of endearment *tata* and *nana,* but neither may be addressed by personal names. Attitudes on the two sides of this relationship are not symmetrical; there is only superordination from the parent generation and complementary subordination from below. Even here, however, there is some difference between the father and the mother, for there tends to be a greater degree of indulgence from the mother, favouring greater familiarity with her than with the father.

3. *Siblings (tuakaqu, taciqu).* Brothers, like sisters, are largely free with each other. A brother may be freely spoken to, be addressed by his personal name, and his personal belongings may be taken without his knowledge and, as sometimes happens, be even given away at a ceremonial exchange of wealth. Buell Quain, for instance, records the case of a man who, after helping himself to *taros* from his bother's *taro* garden, later informed him casually, and without embarrassment, of what had happened.[4] Brothers are often seen planting the same piece of ground together, especially if they are still under the father's authority; and normally freely lend assistance to each other in housebuilding or gardening, material reward being unnecessary. All this freedom between brothers expresses itself in a lack of inhibition in all forms of behaviour—in work, play and laughter. Brothers feel free enough with each other even to be able to allow their quarrels to develop into fist

fights—something almost totally impossible in the case of, for instance, cross-cousins.[5]

Be that as it may, however, we remember that kinship terminology distinguishes between senior and junior brothers. Senior authority rests with the elder brother by reason of age, and this can be exerted and respected in cases where the younger brother sufficiently values the community sentiments which condemn the unmannerful junior. This principle does impose a limitation on the wide range of modes of behaviour possible between brothers. Nevertheless, it remains true that this range is wider than in the case of any other relationship in the entire kinship structure. As a general description of a type relationship, this holds also in the case of sisters among themselves, except perhaps that they are more gentle with each other.

4. *Cross-siblings (ganequ).* It was stated in Part I that the cross-sibling relationship involves considerable restraints; that it is a taboo relationship and is called *veitabui.* This is the exact antithesis of the relationship of parallel-siblings, and is especially compelling after puberty when, for instance, neither may refer to the other by name, but must either resort to teknonymy or to some other form of indirect reference. Indeed, the relationship might even be termed one of avoidance. At every point, the conduct and behaviour of each towards the other is pregnant with the greatest caution and restraint.

Once again, however, the principle of seniority by sex intervenes here. The brother is always understood to have authority, and powers of protection and discipline, over his sister. If they come accidentally into the presence of each other, it is the sister who must retire from sight. The brother can speak to his sister with authority while her doing likewise would constitute the most unthinkable act of gross insolence. He is the one to whom she looks for protection and comfort when her father has died; and she must return to his care and protection on the death of her husband. In some circumstances even important decisions relating, for instance, to her marriage may finally rest with him. Apart from her husband, he has first claim to her assistance or services at crises such as sickness or ceremonial occasions.

5. *Cross-parents (momo, nei).* The basic pattern of attitude and behaviour exhibited by a sister towards her brother is reflected in almost every detail in the attitude and behaviour of a child towards his mother's brother. The mother's brother is one who must be treated with the greatest respect, caution and restraint. He must not be addressed or referred to by name (except when the addition of his personal name becomes necessary as an index identification), and if spoken to at all, he must be addressed slowly and deferentially. His sister's child must not make unprompted addresses or advances towards him, and must obey his commands to the last detail. This is the case also in respect of any decision which he may make in regard to the choice of a spouse.

The mother's brother is definitely superior in rank to his sister's children. Marks of respect for him, such as refraining from standing up while he is seated, from reaching for any object above his head, drinking from the same cup, and even sitting near him in the house, are required from the sister's children. Indeed, the term *momo*, used in Tokatoka to designate the mother's brother, is used in Nandi on the Western coast of Viti Levu to mean "chief"; and in one area it is employed by children to refer to the father only if he is a chief, in the same manner that the term *Ratu* (prefix to a chief's name) is used to designate a chiefly father in other areas.

Reciprocally, the mother's brother, recognising his position of authority in relation to his sister's children, bestows considerable favours on them, and regards them as his charge almost as much as his own children. He is the popular relative to whom the child may turn in case of need, and who it is understood will always do his best to satisfy the child's desire.

A man's sister's children are said to be his *vasu*, but this is not strictly a kinship term, because it expresses the relation of a child to his mother's patrilineage. We said that the sibling group must treat their mother's brother with respect, and must not take any liberties with him. But the *vasu* relationship enables them to take certain liberties against the whole of the mother's lineage group. On ceremonial occasions, for instance, when that group has accumulated property and food, they may take any movable property, food, pigs, cattle or anything else they may fancy. The only exceptions are persons and the personal belongings of the mother's brother himself. This power of acquisition is decidedly clear-cut over property owned by the whole group; but while there are cases where it has been applied to individually owned items, it seems to me that this is an illegitimate extension of the custom. When an item is acquired in this way, there is always an obligation that a small feast called *vakatakata ni liga* should be presented to the mother's group, never to the individual owner.[6]

The position of the father's sister is, on the other hand, somewhat anomalous. Although in any final generalization about her position, based upon the detailed and factual examination of her relationship to her brother's children, it will be difficult (I think) to distinguish her sufficiently from the mother's sisters, she is not identified with them, nor can she be classified as a kind of female father. Conceptually she stands all alone in the mind of the Fijian child, although if she must be classified with anyone at all in her generation, then she would belong to the same category as the mother's brother, with whom she is classified as a "cross-parent". The extent of her authority over her brother's children, the kinds of favours and punishment expected from her in earlier years, and the comparative ease with which she may be addressed or approached, are not markedly different from what they are in the case of the mother's sisters. There is, however, this difference that in later life there seems, from my general observation, to be greater dependence on her part upon her brother's children than upon her sister's children for the minor favours which they are in a position to give.[7] If she has to administer punishment upon her brother's children, she does so with greater restraint than she would maintain in the case of her sister's children; and in later life she tends to look upon them with greater respect than upon her sister's children, whom she can treat much as her own children.

6. *Cross-cousins (tavale, davola, raiva).* A man's attitudes and behaviour towards his male cross-cousin vary slightly between different parts of Fiji. For instance, in Nadroga, Gau Island, Kadavu, and among the Waimaro people of Naitasiri, the *tavale* is a person towards whom one is expected to display joking familiarity; but in Tokatoka, as in Nakoroka village in Vanua Levu, he is the most "heavy and difficult"[8] of all relatives, and must be treated only with respect. In Tokatoka he is never addressed or referred to by his personal name, and, as a mark of respect, must be spoken to using the dual number as though he were two persons. A person does not use harsh language towards his *tavale*, in whose presence he is obliged to avoid referring to topics such as sex. As Quain has recorded, a man is prepared to sacrifice clan allegiance in times of war in order to ensure the safety of his cross-cousin. Thus the male cross-cousin is a relative not to be failed in any way, but must always be treated with courtesy and, if any joking takes place, this can only be of mild character. These statements apply also to female cross-cousins as amongst themselves.

In the case of cross-cousins of opposite sex, there is again a difference in attitude and mode of behaviour as between different areas in Fiji. While it is generally accepted that cross-cousins are "natural husbands and wives," some areas, such as Kadavu, modify this marriage rule to make it apply only to second and more distant cousins. In Tokatoka, the familiarity and joking between cross-cousins of opposite sex are so intimate that some people even argue against cross-cousin marriage on the ground that the wife will be difficult to control.

7. *Noqu Daku.* Another important class of relatives comprises those persons of opposite sex who are *veidakuni* with one, i.e. a man's brother's wife or wife's sister; or a woman's husband's brother or sister's husband. These are a man's sisters-in-law, or a woman's brothers-in-law. Attitudes towards these relatives differ from one part of Fiji to another. In Tokatoka they are placed in the same category as a wife or husband, which is equivalent to placing them in the same category as a cross-cousin of opposite sex; with this difference, however, that they are subject to the same joking relationship as are ordinary *tavale* of opposite sex. Although a man may sometimes be noticed to pass mild joking remarks with his *daku*, he may not make obscene or unpleasant remarks or engage in any discussion of sex in her presence. A man speaks to his sister-in-law with firmness and perhaps aloofness; while the woman must be straightforward and respectful. A woman may even be regarded as a wife, provided the sexual bar is strictly maintained; and she may cook and launder and perform

such other services as might be expected of a wife.

A case, however, once came to my notice where a young girl of barely fourteen had a child by her elder sister's husband while the sister was away in hospital; and another where a man's wife had a child by his elder unmarried brother while he was away in the army. These, however, are extremely unusual cases which shocked the public conscience when they took place. In yet another case a widower was happy in marrying his elder brother's widow, so that she might assist him rear all their children who, in any case, were already a large community of "brothers and sisters". Thus while there is a duty upon persons related as *veidakuni* to treat each other with restraint and control, having due regard to the exclusive rights of the relevant husband or wife to the sexual favours of a *daku*, there do exist in rare circumstances certain incentives for the relationship to be merged in the more general category to which cross-cousins of opposite sex and spouses also belong; so that much the only consolation in irregular cases such as those quoted is the conniving comment: "Oh well, it is the same—they are spouses too!"

In some areas of Fiji, such as in Lau, on Gau Island, and in Nadroga, there is an extremely strict avoidance relationship between persons who are related as *veidakuni*, especially between a woman and her husband's brother. In Nadroga, where I had the opportunity of observing this particular relationship in action, several pairs of *veidakuni* have simply reached perfection in conforming to the rule. They must certainly not talk to each other, and the women are always more or less obliged to slip out when their husband's brothers come in; if they must remain, they do not utter a word unless absolutely necessary—and then only as softly as possible—and withhold their laughter if a joke is afoot. When asked if any irregularities in this pattern of behaviour have ever occurred, the people reply that irregularities are simply not possible.

These are the main types of attitude and behaviour which a child is taught to observe, and which regulate the everyday relationships of kin. As the child grows up he learns to classify his more distant relatives according to the principles stated in Part I of this article; and to apply to them also, though to a less marked extent, the attitudes and behaviour stated here. At this point we turn to the second major task of this Part.

KIN-GROUPS AND THE WIDER EXTENSIONS OF KINSHIP[9]

Social segmentation in Fijian society is based on patrilineal kin-groups, the widest of which is known as the *yavusa*. In Part I we referred to these groups generally as lineage groups; we may say therefore that the formal social structure (in the sense of social groupings) comprises numerous lineages or lineage groups. From the point of view of kinship we said that these are groups of persons of both sexes who consider themselves to be patrilineally descended from a known or unknown common ancestor. This differs from the definition given for the Tallensi by Professor Fortes[10] because it has to take account of the actual variations found in Fijian lineages today:[11] a definition of the "ideal" structure would be much the same as for the Tallensi. The essential fact for our purposes is that in such a lineage structure all the members of a generation are parallel-cousins. Fijian kinship classifies parallel-cousins as "classificatory siblings". Hence lateral unity within the lineage is particularly strong, being merely an extension of sibling unity.

The size of *yavusa* varies greatly from one to the next. Generally each village would contain two or three, possibly even four *yavusa.* Some *yavusa* are larger and may occupy a whole village. Others, larger still, may occupy a number of different villages, possibly sharing some of these with other *yavusa.* Nabukebuke *yavusa,* for instance, occupies thirteen villages in three different districts in Namosi province.

Each *yavusa* comprises a number of lesser branches known as *mataqali.* In the "ideal" *yavusa* there are five *mataqali,* the most senior of which provides the chiefs, and the others the chief's executives or henchmen, the heralds, the priests, and the warriors respectively in order of seniority. The *mataqali* is exogamous[12] and is the fundamental landowning group.[13] It may itself have lesser branches—arranged in order of seniority in a way similar to the constitution of the *yavusa* itself—known as *i tokatoka.* These are best termed extended families.

These kin-groups—*yavusa* and *mataqali*—can be identified and observed in every village in Fiji. Each one is named and normally occupies a definite section of the village. Through the operation of the classificatory principle, its kinship-basis is an extension of the vertical and lateral ties found in the elementary family. With patrilineal descent, patrilocal residence, and common ownership of land in the patrilineal line, each patrilineage is a persistent and well-defined group. The kinship ties which bind its members together are expressed not only in the attitudes and behaviour described earlier, but also in economic co-operation in matters such as housebuilding and gardening, on ceremonial occasions, and more generally in the operation of reciprocal obligations. Before we factually demonstrate these statements, one further point needs making. While ties in the male line tend to be emphasized in comparison to those in the female line, the latter are not necessarily any more tenuous. Indeed, from the point of view of marriage rules, "classificatory siblings" are equally taboo whether traced in the male or in the female line. Moreover, co-operation with matrilineal relatives is no less necessary or binding. On the basis of ties with them, social co-operation is necessarily carried outside the immediate confines of the local patrilineal group, as matrilineal relatives are, through exogamy, diffused throughout other groups in the society.

Social and Economic Co-operation Within and Beyond the Patrilineal Kin-Groups

From the point of view of the individual household, the assistance of relatives can be sought either to secure an adequate labour supply for a particular undertaking or to secure wealth and food for occasions such as marriages or death. In the former case a person can be quite informal, asking whatever brothers or cousins he considers able to complete the task in hand. When his yam gardens are being planted up, for instance, he sends a woman or other member of the household around to the members of the *mataqali* or *yavusa,* asking them to come and help on a certain day. Such planting rarely ever takes up more than one day, very often only one afternoon. On completion of the task all those who have participated come together and are given a common meal known as *oco,* followed by *kava* drinking. A similar procedure is followed when a house is repaired or a kitchen built. But when a house needs to be built, the task is usually too big for the *yavusa* only; the village therefore usually does it.

In the case of marriages and deaths, and other social or ceremonial occasions affecting the life cycle of a member of the *mataqali* or *yavusa,* the group co-operates as a group; all the members are affected. The distinguishing feature of these occasions is that they require formal handling. There is no casual asking such of a man's relatives as he wishes; he is obliged to give all of his relatives an opportunity to participate. Co-operation within the whole *yavusa* is necessary, and its direction is placed in the hands of the senior member. He should ensure that no matrilineal relatives are left out, for an oversight in this matter can be a source of irritation for years. Sometimes the affair is too important or too big, so that even the whole *yavusa* is not big enough to cope; then it may be placed in the hands of the village as a whole.

At this point I wish to draw three examples from my field study[14] to illustrate factually the meaning of these statements. The first comes from Lomawai village in Nadroga province on the south-western corner of Viti Levu Island. This village contains three *yavusa* known as Nalolo, Nakurasiga and Varaga, in that order of precedence. Each group is a compact unit, the members of which co-operate on social occasions such as marriages. Thus Manoa Kucuve, head of Household XV and a member of *yavusa* Nakurasiga, told me that if there was a marriage ceremony involving his wife's *mataqali,* she would be asked to participate in the ceremonial exchanges of wealth and food, and this meant him. If he considered that the occasion demanded, he might get the support of his *mataqali.* To do that he would make a formal presentation of *yaqona* to Peni Narube (head of Household XVI) and Savenaca Veikoso (head of Household XIV), asking them to accompany him to the marriage ceremony. Peni is father of Filimoni of Household XVII, and Savenaca of Peniasi Naqau in Household

XIII. Through these fathers their sons are also involved, and this is the whole *mataqali.* On the appointed day, all members of the *mataqali,* comprising the five households XIII–XVII, would pool together the resources they have available for the occasion, and go off to the ceremony in Manoa's wife's village.

If this *mataqali* wishes to enlist the assistance of the whole village in any social or ceremonial activity such as this the procedure is for them to make a formal *yaqona* presentation to *yavusa* Varaga first, asking for their co-operation. Then the two *yavusa* together make a further presentation of *yaqona* to *yavusa* Nalolo, asking for the assistance of the whole village.

This procedure was adopted when Jonetani, a member of *yavusa* Varaga, made preparations for the marriage of his son Eroni. When Eroni told him of his desire to marry a girl from Korovuto village, he took a few *tabua* (whale's teeth) and went to his *vasu vata*[15] at Moala village in Nadi. A few of the elders from that village then accompanied him to the nearby village of Korovuto, where the *tabua* were presented formally to the girl's group, asking her hand in marriage. The suit was accepted and the marriage notice posted within a week. On Jonetani's return to Lomawai he made a *yaqona* presentation to his *yavusa* informing them of what had happened and asking them for a decision as to how the affair was to be dealt with. The *yavusa* decided that it was necessary to ask the whole village for assistance, whereupon *yaqona* presentations were made to *yavusa* Nakurasiga, and to *yavusa* Nalolo. The affair was handled by the whole village which then shared out the responsibility for providing the major presentations of wealth and food among the three *yavusa.* In addition to the three *yavusa,* however, Eroni's mother's *mataqali* from Korokula village also participated, providing the feast for the *kana vata ni vakamau,* which was shared by the bride, the groom, and a small party.

This illustration shows how kinship ties can be utilised for purposes of mutual assistance and co-operation. We see how Jonetani's *vasu vata* at Moala village gave him their support when he went to the girl's village to ask her hand in marriage with his son. These must be very distant relatives as they were not present at the marriage itself. When the marriage took place, people from several villages assisted. First there were the members of Jonetani's wife's *mataqali* from Korokula village; then there were also people from Navutu and Kubuna, two nearby villages; and from Bavu village came Jonetani's sister and the members of the *mataqali* into which she married. Even people from Vagadra and other villages who were present at the marriage had special kinship connections with the groom's *yavusa.*[16]

The second illustration comes from Nakelo district in Tailevu province, at the south-eastern corner of Viti Levu Island. In this district we find the *yavusa* known as Qalisau, the members of which reside in the three villages of Namuka, Naimalavau and Vadrai—villages which themselves embrace other *yavusa*. *Yavusa* Qalisau is of special importance in Nakelo because it has certain powers and privileges. It stands in a special relation to the patrilineage of the Tui Nakelo, the highest chief in the area. Its members are obliged to perform intimate services for the Tui Nakelo, such as cutting his hair. When he dies, they clear a pathway about two fathoms wide to the burial place (plundering any crops which might be growing on the ground traversed by this path); dig the grave, and plant the decorative *vasa* shrub around the grave when the burial is completed. Until the fourth night after the funeral they do not touch their food with their hands, and must be fed by others or use some other method of conveying food to the mouth. They are exempt from the provision of feasts both for the *burua* (burial feast) and for the *vakabogiva* (commemoration of the fourth night after burial); but must prepare a small feast or make some *vakalolo* (pudding) "to wash their hands" with, after which they may resume eating with their hands.

The important thing about this example is that only on these occasions do the members of this *yavusa* come together and perform their function in spite of physical separation over three villages. Each local branch remains very largely unaffected by what is going on in other branches until something of this order of importance comes up, when all the branches will come together.

For a last example I wish to quote a case from Nakorosule village in Naitasiri province. Saiasi Vukitu, a member of this village, is *mata* (ambassador or envoy) to Nawaisomo village further up the Wainimala river—a relationship which involves, at the very least, some distant kinship connection. He wanted his house built, but because his village was too busy at the time with other things, he preferred to call on the Nawaisomo people to come and build his house for him. He took one *tabua* to that village and presenting it he asked the people over. Twenty-six men from Nawaisomo finally participated, taking eight days to get all the materials and build a house measuring 39 feet by 19 feet. Saiasi had to make other presentations of *tabua* and *yaqona* when the men arrived for the work, and when the task was completed; and fed them fairly sumptuously during the building of the house. His final speech of presentation is particularly interesting, reflecting sentiments which take their roots in the past, sustain social relationships in the present, and duly emphasize relationships in the future:—

"In the manner of chiefs to Wailevu, to Nakorovatu, to Togovere. Well now, Sevuloni, a little feast is here, in conformity with my bringing you over to build our (yours and mine) house, and the gentleman there behind you. A little *tabua*, too, is here, your *vakasirovuti* (wealth presentation on completion of housebuilding). This *tabua* is for you to remember our land with. It is not a *tabua* for what is done today; this is the *tabua* of the future, for the customary works of our land—for these will never end. We will depart, and our children will grow up (in our place), for which let this *tabua* be remembered—to be our bond as brothers, as fathers and sons, and as relatives.

"I ask also, if you should return, not to speak badly of me, for very small indeed are the things which I and my children are able to do for you and those behind you. This *tabua* is also the *tabua* of the chiefs of the *yavusa* of Waimaro and the gentlemen of Loma,[17] that they should be remembered in times to come. If at any time they call you again to a work of Waimaro, have patience. Too long is the speech of the feast and the *tabua*, a presentation from the gentlemen of Waimaro, Loma, and my children, and myself too, presented in chiefly manner to Wailevu, Nakorovatu, Togovere, and all the lineages following behind you, and the lesser branches."[18]

In addition to co-operation of the types described in the above examples, there is also a general undercurrent of reciprocity among kin. This is expressed in general helpfulness in minor matters. One form in which this is done is in the custom of *kerekere*, by which a person can ask a member of his *mataqali* to give him a mat, some yams, or any other type of article with which he may not be well supplied for the time being. Such a relative would be obliged to grant such a request, under pain of such sanctions as public opinion against meanness, the possibility of retaliatory refusal when he is in need, or even a social boycott. In return he is assured that a similar request by him in the future would be granted either by the same person or by some other member of the *mataqali*. In effect, this practice is a form of social insurance against times of need, such as old age.

KINSHIP IN THE MODERN CULTURE CONTACT SITUATION

These are the ways in which kinship serves as a principle of social organisation. Because kinship classifications set type attitudes and behaviour patterns, they play an important part in the ordering of interpersonal relations within the kinship setting; on the basis of it people define the possible modes of attitude and behaviour which they may adopt towards particular classes of kin. Viewed from outside, the well-defined patrilineal kin-groups, together with their peripheral matrilineal extensions, form the basis for organising formal relationships with other groups. While in their external relations these kin-groups continue to work much as they did in the past, there are many internal changes in their functioning which should also be considered.

With the growth of commercial influence from the towns, the economic co-operation which used to be a pillar of unity among kinsfolk is drastically affected. By and large, money can be obtained only within the framework of a Western type of economic organisation—to obtain it a man has to give an equivalent value either in goods or in services. He can no longer obtain greater value for less, as was often possible in the traditional economic organisation. This necessitates a certain degree of individualism, which directly contradicts the principle of communalism embodied in kinship obligations. Kinship ties get attenuated and the intensity of kinship unity is rendered less. One does not always look to kin for assistance; the distance which one traditionally traversed along kinship paths to obtain such assistance is reduced, and this limits the circle within which kinship is effective as a continuing principle of co-operation.

Another type of change in kinship organisation is brought about by the use of money as a means of exchange. This is mainly because money is now accepted in many situations in exchange for either goods or services. The crucial point for us is that it is also accepted and used even among kin in their relations among themselves. To illustrate the importance of this point I shall once again refer to my field study.

In Draubuta this acceptance is fairly thoroughgoing. A person, finding it impossible to mobilise enough labour to carry out a big task, often hires labour to do it, both from within and from without the kin-group amongst whom economic co-operation normally existed. No feast is necessarily supplied as in the traditional situation (unless it is specified as a part of the bargain); a set number of working hours is stipulated and adhered to; and the choice of personnel is restricted to persons who, in his evaluation, are worth the price. The transaction is a purely contractual one, in which roles are, in principle, completely "depersonalised," in the sense that the social relationships existing between the employer and workers do not figure in his or their calculations. This type of employer-worker relationship is at present largely applied only in situations where kin did not formally co-operate, particularly in the planting or harvesting of commercial crops. Nevertheless it is also applied in situations of buying and selling of fruits and even garden produce. In effect it ignores the kinship framework within which such needs used to be satisfied.

In Lomowai such acceptance is not so extensive. Work on cane plantations, for instance, is still done on the basis of traditional co-operation. But here the villagers may, at times, ask a cane-grower to provide employment to enable them to raise adequate money for a special purpose, such as when they have to make Church contributions. Ordinarily, however, he asks his relatives to come and help on his cane plantation just as he would on his yam gardens. Acceptance in principle is there, but it is seldom employed. The villagers do not sell garden produce to each other or to outsiders.

In Nakorosule there is a curious arrangement in this regard. Payment in money is made to people who assist in the cutting of bananas, their transport to the packing station, and their packing for export. For the assistance rendered on one, perhaps two, days, payment is usually in the vicinity of 30/-, which is extremely high either by time rates or by piece rates. People normally prefer to assist non-relatives, because in that case they get paid. Banana packers cannot obtain the assistance of their own relatives because the latter are attracted by a money reward from non-relatives; and they cannot exert their authority against public opinion which favours such rewards.

These cases reveal different degrees of change. What they reveal in common is the general acceptance of an alternative principle of organising economic relationships in a situation in which social considerations normally determined them. Such acceptance has already carried economic action outside the traditional framework within which it largely transpired, and to that extent reflects a line of change in the functioning of kinship as a principle of social organisation.[19]

Another important line of change in the kinship organisation is in the way in which it traditionally affected, even determined, residential patterns. With able-bodied men moving towards localities where opportunities for earning money are more easily available, often taking their families with them, a new situation arises. On the one hand we find many "incomplete families" (the situation where, for instance, one old woman and two or three of her grandchildren might be living together largely depending on themselves for their sustenance), where most of the men have been relocated for work elsewhere. On the other, we find the normal patrilocal pattern disturbed to a considerable degree. In Draubuta, for instance, six men from other villages have come to live with their wives because the village is within easy reach of the towns where they work. This sort of development is bound to have a telling effect on the traditional system of social control.

A more serious feature of this development is the urban drift which not only rightly worries the administration, but also creates a dilemma for those who leave their villages. Many of them leave in order to escape the social obligations of village life (most of these are kinship-based). When they successfully evade these obligations, they are weakening their own kinship ties. When they do not, they maintain many connections with the village; in which case they have an assured place where they can return in their old age, while at the same time they are jeopardising their chances of making good in the commercial world. The question of choosing between the two courses is one which must be seriously faced if the people are to make a success in either direction.

In the last place, even kinship attitudes seem to have become attenuated. In cases where brothers and sisters are continually in contact with town life, for instance, it is particularly noticeable that the rule of brother-sister taboo is not followed to the letter: they talk to each other more freely now than they would have been permitted to do in the past, and the respect and reverence in which they traditionally held each other are in many cases almost absent. In a similar manner, the norms of attitude and conduct formerly expected between kin of every other description are nowadays becoming something of a mere reflection of their past reality.

CONCLUSION

While the structural analysis in this article is restricted to the system of only one area, that system is nevertheless extremely important because it expresses all the central tendencies of the variants found in other areas. As such it is well-suited to serve as the focal point for discussing the main controlling principles in Fijian kinship. Sex, age, generation, lineage and sibling unity are shown to determine the classification of kin in this area of Fiji; by and large they also determine it in all the other areas. While the terminology varies rather much from one area to another, the basic structure varies only a little, and the principles which determine that structure are the same throughout.

The study of kinship, however, is not complete when structure is explained; we still have to show the sociological implications of the structure. This task we have done for Fijian kinship in Part II of this article. Unlike kinship structure, the actual contents of the social relations based upon kinship vary so little in Fiji that we are able to extend our discussion of them freely to other areas much as though we were talking about a single system. Only by a consideration of these aspects of kinship organisation can we appreciate that in primitive society kinship serves as an extremely important principle of social organisation, for on the basis of it people handle their interpersonal relations and organise many of the major aspects of their social life.

One final point remains. As a feature of primitive social organisation, kinship is well recognised by anthropologists as extremely resistant to change—in the Fijian situation we have shown how this creates a dilemma for the Fijians who are caught up in the urban drift. One contribution of this study, however, is to show that even kinship, as a principle of social organisation, may change under the conditions of a culture contact situation, despite the comparatively strong persistence of its fundamental structure.

NOTES FOR PART I

1. This study would not have been possible without the aid of a predoctoral Fellowship in Anthropology granted by the Wenner-Gren Foundation for Anthropological Research, New York, to which body I am gratefully indebted. Acknowledgment is also due to Dr. W. R. Geddes, Senior Lecturer in Social Anthropology at Auckland University College, for continual help and many useful suggestions given to me during the preparation of this article.

2. H. T. Fei, *Peasant Life in China.* London, 1939. Appendix, p. 287.

3. Of the published material on Fijian kinship, the most detailed study is that by Capell and Lester (A. Capell and R. H. Lester, "Kinship in Fiji," *Oceania,* Vol. XV, No. 3, 1945, pp. 171–200; Vol. XVI, No. 2, 1946, pp. 109–143; and Vol. XVI, No. 3, 1946, pp. 234–253). While my treatment of the subject is different and based upon direct study, I am grateful to these authors for increasing my insight into the system as a whole. The local systems of various villages in Fiji have also been studied by other writers, in particular by B. Quain, *Fijian Village,* Chicago, 1948, and by W. R. Geddes, *Deuba; a Study of a Fijian Village,* Memoirs of the Polynesian Society, Vol. 22, Wellington, New Zealand, 1945.

4. [Omitted].

5. Under the system of native administration in Fiji a buliship is a group of an unspecified number of villages under the charge of an administrative official called a *Buli.* There are 5 bulishipss under the Roko of Tailevu province, and 14 Roko in the whole of Fiji. Although bulishipss used to be referred to as "districts," they are now commonly known in government circles by their native name "*tikina.*" The use of the term "district" is now confined only to the three main administrative districts of the Colony—Southern, Northern and Western.

6. We are not here concerned with Fijian grammar. I have illustrated the use of suffixes with respect to one number and three persons only. Actually there are four numbers in the Fijian personal pronoun, with inclusive and exclusive forms of the first person in the dual, trial and plural numbers.

7. In view of the nature of Fijian social structure, it is not possible at this stage to give a precise interpretation of "lineage group." No agreement has yet been reached among the various writers on Fijian social structure as to an unequivocal translation of the terms *yavusa, mataqali* and *i tokatoka.* From the point of view of kinship, however, "lineage group" may be defined as a number of persons of both sexes who consider themselves to be patrilineally descended from a known or unknown common ancestor. Such a group may or may not coincide with any one of the above three Fijian terms.

8. See below.

9. Below the contemporary generation, the relationships given hold only in the case of male members of the contemporary generation.

10. A. R. Radcliffe-Brown, Introduction to *African Systems of Kinship and Marriage,* ed. by A. R. Radcliffe-Brown and Daryll Forde, London, 1950, p. 24.

11. These terms were suggested to me by Dr. W. R. Geddes.

12. Of course there will be four parents in two lines; but there are only two relevant parents for our purpose, i.e. those two, one from each pair, who are genealogically related through the two lines of procreation we are considering. It is possible for the two remaining parents to be related also, but this is irrelevant.

13. The classification of affinal relatives is theoretically irrelevant until after consummation of the marriage. In practice, however, the terms are sometimes used even before marriage. But on the other hand, the spouses very often prefer to resort to teknonymous forms of address. Other modes of accommodation to this problem are found in practice, but at present their description is not strictly relevant.

14. We take the case of a man for the sake of simplicity of illustration. The reader is at liberty to substitute "woman" and make for himself the necessary grammatical changes in the text. Neither terms nor principles will be affected.

15. Because "a man and a woman of the same generation are unmarriageable," they must be cross-siblings (real or classificatory), and not cross-cousins.

16. Distance here is arbitrarily determined. Genealogical distance is basic, but other considerations also come into play, e.g. the plain spacial distance of residence which may indirectly affect the frequency of social relations between kin or the intensity of their feeling of kinship unity.

NOTES FOR PART II

1. This appeared in *J.P.S.,* Vol. 64, No. 1, March, 1955, 44–45.

2. In Nakorosule village, Naitasiri province, the term *tukaqu* is applied also to the elder brother (man speaking) and to the elder sister (woman speaking).

3. In a similar way, Arensberg and Kimball, in *Family and Community in Ireland,* attribute to patrilineal emphasis the fact that the only affinal relative to be designated by a special term is the son-in-law.

4. Quain 1948:250.

5. A young man from Vuci village, Tokatoka, for instance, on a number of occasions brought liquor to his two elder brothers in the village at Christmas, had a drink with them and then picked a fight with both to return the punishments he used to receive at their hands in his younger days.

6. Today, the Fijian Affairs Regulations prohibit the practice of the *vasu* custom.

7. When I first wrote down this statement I was not influenced by the consideration that because she belongs to the same patrilineage as her brother's children, she would have more in common with them than with her sister's children.

8. Quain, op. cit. 262, 264 (fn. 29).

9. The following discussion of social groupings in Fiji is based very largely on the treatment of the subject given by Dr. W. R. Geddes in his *Cultural Change in Fiji* (unpublished Ph.D. thesis presented in the London School of Economics and Political Science, 1948). He was the first to draw the comparison with the Tallensi, and, as far as I know, was also the first to use the concept of an "ideal structure" in connection with Fijian social organisation.

10. ". . . an association of people of both sexes comprising all the recognised descendants by an accepted genealogy of a single named ancestor in a putatively continuous male line." —M. Fortes 1945:30, quoted by Dr. Geddes, *ibid.,* 91.

11. Dr. Geddes distinguishes three types of *yavusa:* (i) those which form a complete lineage;

(ii) those which have a core lineage, but to which lesser branches of other *yavusa* have been incorporated; and (iii) those with no core lineage structure. From a perusal of some of the lists of *yavusa* in the Native Lands Trust Board Office in Suva, I gained the impression that those of type (i), to which Professor Fortes's definition would properly apply, are in the minority. My more casual definition is more appropriate to describe the reality rather than the ideal structure of existing *yavusa*.

12. This is the case only with "composite" *yavusa*, i.e. those of types (ii) and (iii) in fn. 12 above. In the case of *yavusa* of type (i), *mataqali* exogamy is extended to cover the whole *yavusa*, in which case the *yavusa*, not the *mataqali*, is exogamous.

13. The records in the Native Lands Trust Board Office shows that *yavusa* as well as *i tokatoka* may also own land.

14. This field trip, financed by the Wenner-Gren Foundation for Anthropological Research, aimed at studying the impact of economic change on Fijian culture. Three villages were selected which were expected to show different degrees of acculturation—Draubuta, near Suva; Lomawai on the south-western corner of Viti Levu Island; and Nakorosule in Naitasiri province, near the centre of Viti Levu.

15. i.e. "*vasu* together." Jonetani's mother was from Nakurasiga *yavusa*, hence he is *vasu* to that *yavusa*. Other *mataqali* of this *yavusa* are living at Moala village, where there are also men who are *vasu* to the local branch of Nakurasiga. Hence they are classified as clan brothers to Jonetani.

16. A fuller discussion of this material is given in my *Tradition, Choice and Change in the Fijian Economy* (unpublished M.A. thesis, 1955), pp. 98–107. A copy of this is in the Auckland University College library.

17. The three *yavusa* in the village are Waimaro, Loma and Nakoroduadua, in order of precedence. Saiasi is a member of the last named *yavusa*.

18. This is a fairly close translation. Fuller study of this material is given in my thesis, from which the speech itself is quoted, *ibid.*, 183, fn. (1).

19. cf. Raymond Firth, 1951:39-40. Also his statement in 1954:4: "Another way to look at social action is in terms of its organization. The structure provides a framework for action. But circumstances provide always new combinations of factors. Fresh choices open, fresh decisions have to be made, and the results affect the social action of other people in a ripple movement which may go far before it is spent. Usually this takes place within the structural framework, but it may carry action right outside it. If such departure from the structure tends to be permanent, we have one form of social change."

BIBLIOGRAPHY

ARENSBERG, C. M. & KIMBALL, S. T., 1948. *Family and Community in Ireland.* Cambridge, Mass., Harvard University Press.

CAPELL, A. & LESTER, R. H., 1945–6. "Kinship in Fiji." *Oceania,* XV, 3, 171–200; XVI, 2, 109–143; and XVI, 3, 234–253.

FEI, H. T., 1939. *Peasant Life in China.* London, G. Routledge & Sons.

FIRTH, RAYMOND, 1951. *Elements of Social Organization.* London, Watts.

———1954. "Social Organisation and Social Change" (Presidential Address), *Journal of the Royal Anthropological Institute,* Vol. 84, Pt. I.

FORTES, MEYER, 1945. *The Dynamics of Clanship Among the Tallensi.* London, New York, etc., Oxford University Press.

GEDDES, W. R., 1945. *Deuba: A Study of a Fijian Village.* Wellington, Memoirs of the Polynesian Society, Vol. 22.

———1948. *Cultural Change in Fiji.* Unpublished Ph.D. thesis.

NAYACAKALOU, R. R., 1955. *Tradition, Choice, and Change in the Fijian Economy.* Unpublished M.A. thesis presented in the University of New Zealand (copy in Auckland University College library).

QUAIN, B., 1948. *Fijian Village.* Chicago, University of Chicago Press.

RADCLIFFE-BROWN, A. R., 1924. "The Mother's Brother in South Africa." *South African Journal of Science,* XXI, 542–55; reprinted in *Structure and Function in Primitive Society,* by the same author, London, 1952:15-31.

———1950. Introduction, *African Systems of Kinship and Marriage,* ed. A. R. Radcliffe-Brown and Daryll Forde, London, etc., Oxford University Press.

FURTHER READINGS

A sizable theoretical literature has been generated on the question of bilateral descent and its implications. For a useful review of the issues involved, Scheffler's "Ancestor Worship in Anthropology: or Observations on Descent and Descent Groups" should be consulted. Two of the papers which introduced the debate were Goodenough's "A Problem in Malayo-Polynesian Social Organization" and Davenport's "Nonunilinear Descent and Descent Groups." A careful reading of these papers is indispensable to an understanding of recent attempts to describe Polynesian social systems.

In addition to the papers contained in this part, other theoretically relevant analyses of Polynesian descent systems are provided by Ottino's "Early 'Āti of the Western Tuamotus" and Howard's "Land, Activity Systems and Decision-Making Models in Rotuma." Firth's analysis of kinship, in *We, the Tikopia,* is the most extensive treatment of social structure in a Polynesian society and should be read by anyone seriously concerned with the subject matter covered in this part. His paper "A Note on Descent Groups in Polynesia" is also a must.

For those interested in delving more deeply into the complexities of Samoan social structure, Mead's *Social Organization of Manua* should be required reading, while an understanding of Fijian society will be substantially furthered by Sahlins' *Moala* and Groves' review of Sahlins' book.

PART III SOCIAL PROCESS

The vagaries of Polynesian social structure are in part a reflection of cultural commitment to adaptive expediency. Polynesians were more concerned with meeting exigencies of everyday life than they were with upholding an idealized social structure for its own sake; rules were therefore kept flexible enough to permit a good deal of individual manipulation. For this reason, Polynesian societies are best understood in terms of an interplay between ecological requirements, cultural rules, and individual behavior patterns; and the papers contained in this part describe various aspects of these interrelations.

The opening paper, by Margaret Mead, provides a somewhat different slant on Samoan society from that obtained in the part on social structure. Whereas the papers on Samoa in Part II attempt to characterize the social system as a whole—from an "outside" viewpoint, so to speak—Mead presents the picture from the perspective of the individual Samoan—that is, from an "inside" perspective. From her paper one can gain a finer appreciation of the theoretical problems confronting social structuralists.

In the following selection, Raymond Firth describes the process of selecting chiefs in Tikopia, a Polynesian outlier. Although the succession pattern described by Firth cannot be considered typical of Polynesian societies, inasmuch as the Tikopia place a greater emphasis on male primogeniture than do most others, the social context of chieftainship and considerations relevant for selection are characteristically Polynesian.

The relationship between religion, social organization, and the natural environment is the subject of Torben Monberg's analysis. He describes the religion of Bellona, another outlier, in terms of social transactions involving men in a set of mutual obligations with other men and with supernatural figures. Such an analysis is particularly well suited to the societies of Polynesia, for the religious emphasis in this region was predominantly on the maintenance of harmonious relations, both man with man and man with nature, and not on intellectualized, internally consistent theological systems.

Howard then discusses the relationship between Rotuman life style, the socialization processes that are associated with it, and corresponding personality traits. Contrasts between Polynesian and middle-class Western patterns are here made explicit. In Howard's view, the underlying premise of Rotuman culture is that social life should be harmonious and free from conflict; from this follow most of the significant features of the island's life style. The pattern he describes is characteristic of most Polynesian cultures, although there are variations on the theme.

One of the more interesting variations is documented by James Ritchie in the following paper. He describes the development of Maori social character in a rural New Zealand community. Ritchie was trained in psychology, and his presentation is the culmination of many years of intensive work on the development of Maori personality structure in its social context—work that was stimulated by Ernest Beaglehole's pioneering efforts in culture and personality.

10

THE RÔLE OF THE INDIVIDUAL IN SAMOAN CULTURE[1]

Margaret Mead

In the evaluation of the rôle of the individual in culture, it is fair to assume that the importance of the individual as innovator and stylist will be in great measure a function of the particular culture into which he is born. And it is of interest to investigate in what types of culture individual talent is given the freest play. The following study is based upon field-work in the Manu'a Archipelago of the Samoan Islands. The Manu'an culture presents such a striking picture of flexibility, rapid slight changes, easy acceptance of innovation and deviation, that it would seem to give each gifted individual a particularly open field for the exercise of his peculiar talents. This flexibility is probably the exception rather than the rule in primitive cultures, and therefore presents a good test case of the relation between flexibility of culture and individual initiative.

I shall first discuss the attitudes in Samoan[2] society which are relevant to the problem of individual initiative: the logical limitation implicit in the culture, attitudes favourable to individuality, and attitudes unfavourable to it. After which I shall examine briefly the personal life of the Samoans and the opportunities open to the individual in the fields of industry, art, religion and social organization. It must, however, be borne in mind throughout this discussion that social organization is the principal preoccupation in Samoa; industry, art and religion all are dwarfed beside it.

The Samoans regard the social structure, a hierarchy of titles carrying with them specific privileges, as of paramount importance. The individual has neither rank nor sanctity in his own right, nor by virtue of the blood which flows in his veins. It is only as the holder of a title, the accession to which has been validated by large distributions of property, that he is honoured and obeyed. Coincident with this attitude is a disregard of the rules of primogeniture and of direct descent—not to the extent of ignoring

Reproduced by permission of the Royal Anthropological Institute of Great Britain and Ireland and Margaret Mead from the *Journal of the Royal Anthropological Institute*, 58:481-495 (1928). The notes have been renumbered to run in sequence throughout the article.

them entirely, but sufficiently to set them aside in favour of special ability in heirs-aspirant with a weaker blood claim upon a family title. Each large family can hold several titles of varying importance. As a result there is no chiefly class as opposed to a class of commoners. In a family of four brothers one may hold a high chief's title, the second an ordinary chief's title, the third a talking chief's title, and the fourth be a *taule'ale'a*, without the right to sit in the council of the titled, but condemned to associate with the "young men." Yet, in the next generation, the son of the *taule'ale'a* may perhaps hold the high chiefly title if he has shown the greatest promise among the children of the four brothers. Selection for a title is based on two major considerations—personal qualifications of strength, charm, leadership, integrity; and the possession of special abilities: skill as a carpenter, orator, or fisherman.

The possession of special gifts exacts recognition from the society in two ways; a gifted man is more likely to receive a good title early in life (in some cases, if his immediate family have no vacant title which they can confer upon him, the village council takes the matter in hand, and seeks out a title for him which will enable him to sit in the council and profit by the words of the old men); and, also, a man of skill accumulates wealth through which he can advance his prestige by large distributions of property. The social structure further recognizes the master craftsman by according him all the prerogatives of chiefly rank, special terms of address, precedence in the *kava* ceremony, and position in the house, on the occasions when his craftsmanship is concerned. So the chief carpenter is the guest of honour at a house-warming ceremony or the launching of a canoe.

Where there is[3] no system of usury, the initial possession of wealth does not give anyone a disproportionate start. The *Gross-familie* system makes it easy for a young man to borrow a fishing canoe or collect a bride price. The land is only partly under cultivation and it is always possible to clear new land. Wealth consists of houses, canoes, food, bark cloth, and mats. Because the mats and cloth are made only by women, and the canoes and houses only by men, a household is more likely to be crippled by the lack of one *kind* of property, owing to a disproportion of the sexes, than by actual poverty. Before the introduction of the European copra trade there was very little property which could be said to constitute definite permanent capital. Cleared land goes back to a natural state in a very few years. The best houses, constantly repaired and reinforced, last only nine or ten years. The supply of pigs and chickens can be greatly increased in the course of three or four years. Breadfruit trees and coco-nut palms are slower to reach maturity, and are therefore the most valuable property; but here again the system of obligatory mutual aid within a large relationship group makes it possible to translate industry in fishing into breadfruit beams for a new house with very little delay.

The crafts are neither exclusive organizations nor controlled by heredity.

The boy who desires to learn a trade attaches himself to a master craftsman until he has acquired sufficient proficiency to complete a piece of work himself.

So that neither birth, nor wealth, nor inherited craft privilege are sufficiently determining factors to seriously weight the scales as against the possession of natural ability.

Age is a serious handicap to the politically ambitious, for the political affairs of the village are in the hands of the titled men—the *matais*, to which body a man is seldom admitted until he is twenty-nine or thirty years old. But the very postponement of a genuine political majority increases the zest of the struggle to master the intricacies of the social organization, and some special wealth-producing prestige meriting skill.

The fact of being a woman presents more serious obstacles to the free play of individuality. The property owning system is such that, with a few outstanding exceptions, property can only be held by heads of families—*matais*. At the present time there is only one woman *matai* in the Samoan Islands. They seem to have been as rare as European queens and must be regarded as non-typical in every respect. The girls belonging to families of high rank who are given the title of *taupo* receive a great amount of social adulation and ceremonious recognition, but in return more services are demanded from them, and they can neither own property nor openly participate in political affairs. The public rôle of a woman is entirely confined to wire-pulling and the private manipulation of the men-folk within her sphere of influence. That sphere is often very wide, as a woman is able to use her manual skill as well as her knowledge of intrigue in obtaining recognition within the household. The man owes his position in the village organization to the possession of a title, originally conferred upon him by his family; but the duties incident upon holding the title are so onerous that an old man is usually forced to resign it in favour of a younger one. His prestige within the household diminishes enormously, while that of the woman, subject to no such spectacular rise and fall of social position, suffers no such eclipse; and it is as an old woman, relieved of child-bearing and child-tending, famous for her skill as mat-maker or midwife, that a woman finds the freest vent for her individuality.

Physical defect has few far-reaching consequences. Blindness or deafness disqualify an individual for occupations in which the particular lost sense is specifically needed. Ill-favoured boys and girls are debarred from holding the two titles of *taupo* and *manaia* (the title which may be given to an heir-apparent in a high chief's household), but if they possess special abilities these may later be recognized by a good title for the man, and a good marriage for the woman. The society is more likely to give absolution to the disabled in perfectly irrelevant matters than to penalize them unfairly.

There is no rigid series of tests or ordeals which may serve unfairly to eliminate those who, while possessing special abilities, nevertheless lack particular character or mental traits necessary to carry them through preliminary encounters with set tasks. There is scant premium set upon fortitude and endurance. Neither fasting, self-torture, or significant self-denials are enjoined upon young or old. Entrance into the *Aumaga,* the organization of young men, is the social stamp of young manhood; the requirement is a gift from the father or *matai* of the initiate to the group; the initiation ceremony is a feast. Within the *Aumaga,* a tattooed and an untattooed group are distinguished, so that tattooing may be postponed several years beyond puberty. The tattooing itself may be prolonged over several months, and any number of groans are permitted.

No other sharp trials confront the youth. He is left to work out his own salvation slowly, without undue pressure. His choice of a profession is in his own hands, and professionally he is subjected to no atmosphere of harsh and unfriendly criticism. When he has studied carpentry long enough so that he feels capable of building a house himself, some relative will give him his first commission. If he completes the house satisfactorily, he receives the final payments in the stately ceremony of the *Umu Sa* (the Sacred Oven); the chief carpenters of the village all partake of the feast, at which the successful novice is given highest honour. He is then recognized as a *tufuga fau falé* (a master house builder). If, on the other hand, the novice has overestimated his skill and bungled his job, the others will go to his assistance, but neither in triumph nor rebuke, and help him to finish his too ambitious task. His defeat will be glossed over, revamped into a step in his education, and not viewed as a signal and crushing defeat.

Bravery in warfare was never a very important matter in Manu'a. War was a matter of village spite, or small revenge, in which only one or two individuals would be killed. The most dangerous posts were allotted not to those who had watched their arms or seen a vision, but to the young men living in a special division of the village. Where the war-making and war-leading powers were vested in men holding special titles and the service as scouts was residentially determined, any selection on the basis of prowess was of little importance.

No religious experience was demanded of any individual, neither skill in communicating with spirits, nor, in fact, any important communication with them whatsoever. A careful observance of the taboos surrounding special places; the village god—where there was one—and one's family god; a libation poured to the family god[4] at the evening *kava* ceremony, completed one's religious duties.

In only one respect does the society impose an ironclad choice—the acceptance of a title. A man who through self-distrust, laziness, or fear of responsibility refuses a *matai* title is for ever marked as a social backslider; he can never be awarded any other title, and remains a titular "young man" until his death. But only here, where the very base of the social order is rejected, can an act, one moment's failure, damn an individual for life. In all other respects most of a man's life is regarded as a painless, casual sort of novitiate, offering repeated small occasions for making a mark. The reward is a very brief period in which the fruits of these not too strenuous efforts are enjoyed, before old age and decrepitude relegate him again to a cup of *kava* by courtesy and a seat in the back of the house.

In contrast to this flexible scheme there are other attitudes definitely hostile to the cevelopment of individuality or the exercise of peculiar talents. Complementary to the *laissez-faire* attitude toward slow development, toward the awkward gangling boy who gradually finds his tongue and at thirty-five learns to speak in council, is a feeling of rigid intolerance toward precocity, youthful innovators, or short cuts to prestige. All of these crimes were summed up in the expression "*tautala lai titi*" (talking above one's age, or, less importantly, one's status). No stigma, not even the reputation of tale-bearer or thief, can so thoroughly wreck a boy's whole career as receiving this brand. Such an attitude, never relaxed except on the dance floor, serves to discredit the gifted and discourage the prematurely ambitious, and so becomes an even greater levelling force than the social tolerance of tardiness. Where the precocious are execrated and the slow plodders treated gently and rewarded according to their ultimate achievements, titles and positions of equal importance may be held by middle-aged men of very different natural gifts.

The suppression of a whole group because of one common quality like age or sex is as likely to produce undesirable results as the favouring of a whole group because of some common characteristic like rank or wealth. To be young or a woman in Samoa is a sort of guilt in itself, a state of affairs for which perpetual tacit apologies must be made. And the fact that so much of the heavy work, and almost all of the dull, routine and humdrum miscellaneous tasks fall upon the young makes the status of youth a positive and onerous burden.

This attitude toward youth is aggravated rather than relieved in the case of children of men holding high rank. There is rigid chaperonage of the girls, severe and exacting tutelage of the boys. Because there is so little permanent wealth, and a chief's expenditures are heavier than those of men of lesser rank, the young people of a chief's household work harder and have less freedom and less chance for self-expression than the children of households of fewer pretensions. The young relatives of a chief are always liable to more or less compulsory invitations to become members of his household, and must undertake the more exacting responsibilities which such residence implies.

Furthermore, the very democratic nature of the competition for titles has a deterrent effect upon the attempt to attain virtuosity. A man's accession to a title means endless responsibility for ten or fifteen individuals in the household under his charge—responsibility to the village council for their care, guidance and peaceful behaviour; responsibilities in the affairs of the village. Holding a title also carries with it a status fenced about wth prohibitions. A *matai* may not associate with the young men, play games with them, or take light-hearted part in any youthful frolic. Whatever his age, status, not age, determines his behaviour, with the result that many gifted boys, unwilling to accept these responsibilities, hide their lights under bushels; and lights so hidden for years are likely to go out for ever.

But offsetting these deterrent social attitudes are others—most importantly the eager acceptance of the new, and a premium upon the incomprehensible, the esoteric and the elusive. On the dance floor and in the minor industrial arts even very young people are permitted to initiate, and in adult life individual variations of the pattern are accepted with hospitable acclamation. Because all social ceremonials are combinations of a number of relatively independent elements, each one of which is regarded as a unit subject to manipulation and variation, the innovator can give immediate and free play to his desire to make himself felt by introducing some slight change. The native delight in a proverb which no one understands, a change of phrasing, a hint of some knowledge of esoteric lore, results in an atmosphere more favourable to individual variations than the sort of society in which everything is conceived of as having been done in one particular way from time immemorial, and the knowledge of the tradition-sanctified procedure is shared by the entire group.

PERSONAL LIFE

The young child is allowed many startling privileges. The developing individual is conceived of as gradually growing in a quality designated as *māfaufau*—a difficult word to translate, perhaps best rendered as "an ability to exercise good judgment in personal and social matters." Character deficiencies are explained by a lack of this quality; any particular breach of group standards carries with it the accusation *"Lē ai se māfaufau"*—"lack of judgment." Although regarded rather as a unit quality, there is also the suggestion that judgment on particular points may develop at different ages.[5] The natives look upon the development of this quality as a pure matter of growth; they meddle with it neither by magic nor profane formulas.

The enforcement of the most severe and important sex taboo in the society—the brother and sister taboo—is left in the hands of the younger of the siblings. When the younger child has sufficient *judgment* to feel ashamed at any contact—this includes familiar conversation, participation in the same small social events, and use of each other's possessions as well as actual physical contact—then the taboo comes into play. The older child is expected to make no move, but to wait upon the younger's maturing judgment.

The selection of a residence is also very much in the children's hands.

Any child over five or six is an economic asset; little truants are welcomed by any relative, and a ten-year-old may change his or her residence two or three times before settling down. This freedom of choice actually serves as a powerful deterrent of specific adult tyrannies, and the child is often content to remain in one household, serene in the reflection that he can always run away if he wishes.

The selection of tutors is also left to the young people themselves, with the exception of children of high chiefs. These latter must be taught by the talking chiefs and their wives, the education of the chief's children being one carefully defined item in the complicated reciprocal relationship existing between a high chief and his talking chiefs. Social pressure is exerted in indefinite terms—"It is time Tuli learned to weave blinds"; "It is time Lele began a fine mat"; "It is time Palo should be able to go bonito fishing"—and the choice of a teacher who will teach Tuli to weave blinds, Lele to begin her fine mat and Palo to fish, is left to Tuli, Lele and Palo individually. Very often a child's own father and mother are the teachers, especially in the simpler tasks, but as often the *matai* and his wife, as persons of more prestige and skill, are chosen; and the boy in search of a special technique, like carving, netting or lashing, will range far afield to the very edges of his wide relationship-group, and occasionally even beyond it.

Boys are circumcised at puberty; and here again they make their own choice of physician and occasion, two boys usually repairing together to an older man skilled in the operation.

The same freedom is permitted in the matter of personal names. As a name is regarded as a tangible entity, it cannot be both retained and given away. So constant name-changes occur through an older girl or boy "giving away a name" to a younger child and assuming a new one; the younger child in turn "throws away" the old name. In this way there is among the youth of the community a non-significant aping of the important adult mechanism of changing from one title to another. The choice is left almost entirely in the children's hands.

Also, for all the young people, except the daughters of houses of rank, there is comparative freedom of choice of partners in sex-experience. This does not apply to marriage, but it does result in a gradual development of the emotional life free from any warping compulsory factor. The idea of forceful rape or of any sexual act to which both participants do not give themselves freely is completely foreign to the Samoan mind. This applies also to freedom of divorce; marriage is a socio-economic matter, but divorce is not. Either party to a marriage may leave it at any time and return to his or her home. Such freedom is possible because women always retain a claim on their parents' property, which needs only to be validated by actual participation in the labour of the household and on the plantation.

Members of chiefly families are deprived of a great deal of this freedom. The chief's child is named more formally, is educated and circumcised by the talking chiefs, and, in the case of a girl, denied pre-marital sex-experience. Similarly, adultery with the chief's wife is a crime punishable with death. The marriage of women of rank is a source of profit to the talking chiefs; so is the remarriage of chiefs, on whom pressure is often exerted to divorce one wife that his councillors may fatten upon the dowry of a new one.[6] Less definite, but very important in the development of individuality, are the thousand minute rules of etiquette which hedge about those of high rank, from the plight of the *taupo* who is strictly forbidden to scratch mosquito bites in public, to the chief who may not climb his own coco-nut tree if anyone of lesser rank is present to climb it instead.

Fatal to the prosecution of private plans is the lack of power over one's own time. Only the *matais*, subject to the demands of the village council, can make their own times and occasions; everyone else must suffer continual interruptions without irritation. The young child is subject to every single older relative in the village. This ascendancy of age continues throughout life, cut across by accession to a title for a fortunate man, while the young and unfortunate must accede to the demands of the titled as well as those of their elders. Village matters take precedence over household, household over individual, the affairs of the older over the affairs of the younger—and all this constitutes a network of exactions through which the young can seldom count upon escaping for more than an hour at a time.

With the exception of the *matai*, no individual has any privacy or control of personal property. Ten to twelve persons eat and sleep in a one-room house. The *matai* alone can exclude others from his house, and even require someone to wake and keep intruders away while he sleeps. Every word, every act, is the property of an interested inquisitive public. Similarly, a ring, a dance skirt, a fishing-rod might be the handwork or the nominal property of an individual, but it is liable to seizure by the *matai*, or, as an obligatory loan to a relative, or simple confiscation by an elder at any time.

In the selection of his rôle in the social structure the individual is allowed very little positive choice. Marriage[7] is an economic matter ratified by an exchange of property between the two contracting families. The wealthier and more important the family, the less chance the young people have of selecting their mates. No act of theirs, not an elopement resulting in children, could legalize a union from which the customary exchange of property had been omitted. Similarly, a man may refuse a title, but he can never select one and take it for himself. He may aspire to a title, labour zealously to attain the necessary skill, knowledge and wealth; the choice still lies with someone else. The individual is still a pawn on the social chess-board.

ARTS AND INDUSTRIES

There is a virtual absence of formal industrial procedure as far as the artist himself is concerned. He does not need to prepare for his task by a long series of ritual acts, treat his materials with religious deference, nor consecrate the finished object. Work is primarily secular in character. Only when it involves several individuals, a contracting chief and a craftsman of standing, is social ceremonial between the participants introduced.[8] Education in industrial matters is definitely a question of imparting actual techniques. The relationship between pupil and teacher is secular, casual and uninstitutionalized. There are no charms, no secret formulas, to be imparted.[9] Material is regarded unreverentially and as subject to repeated experimentation and manipulation.

There is no symbolic art. Certain kinds of tapa patterns are most esteemed and put on the best tapa, which is worn by those of highest rank. But this implies merely a demand for the best for the highest; rank only plays an indirect rôle. There is no absolute number of tattooing stripes, or house beams or platform terraces permitted to men of different rank. But if several boys are tattooed together, and the chief's son has five bands of tattooing, the sons of the talking chiefs may not have more than four. If the highest chief in the village has only three terraces around his house no other chief may have more than two, but if he has seven the next ranking chiefs may have as many as six. But rank sets no premium upon special designs or special styles of decoration, and so provides no stimulus to development along particular lines. A premium set upon size, breadth, length and thickness, while developing routine craftsmanship of a high order, has much less influence upon individual initiative than would have come from setting a price upon new and original forms of decoration or actual variations in style. While a Maori chief was distinguished by the possession of a carved house, a Samoan chief boasts principally of the possession of the house with the greatest number of cross-beams (this makes it automatically the highest) and the greatest number of pebbled terraces in the village.

In the details of a craft innovations were welcomed. There is no set style from which it is inadmissible to deviate, no stringent taboo against change. On the contrary, there is a strong feeling against making any two things alike, which extends even to a prejudice against making two sides of the same house or both ends of the same piece of tapa cloth exactly alike. The deadening effect of the use of pattern-boards in stamping tapa is continuously and consciously evaded by the introduction of asymmetrical variations in the subsequent free-hand emphasis given to parts of the design. There is a genuine feeling for individual choices in decoration and a vivid distaste for slavish imitation. The innovation tends to become completely identified with the originator, and so the more striking the departure from established usage the more conspicuous becomes any attempt to copy it, and the more likelihood is there of the new pattern's perishing with its author. I once particularly admired a fan in which the usual form was varied with conspicuous success. I tried to persuade some of the women on Taū to make fans like it, but without success: "A woman on Olosega makes that kind." "But why don't you make them too?"—"Because a woman on

Olosega makes them. I make my own kind of fan." Surrounded by the easy social expectancy of at least some slight rearrangement of the old designs, deprived of the flattery of imitators and any social or economic premium upon stylistic variation, the artisans take but little significant advantage of the unusual freedom allowed them. Their audiences are easily satisfied—a new combination of dance-steps; the transfer of a weaving pattern used on baskets to a food platter; a leaf design reversed—these are sufficient innovations. So decided is the set against imitation in dancing, that when I was trying to work out some variation on the pattern for my own dancing, I tried mimicking the peculiarities of well-known dancers. This was sufficiently new and unexpected to satisfy my audience.

In the larger industrial undertakings, such as house and canoe building, the question of departure becomes a socio-economic matter. An additional house post means an additional feast and consequently additional expenditure. Where variations have such far-reaching consequences, the whole craft-group retains a firm control, and unlicensed changes are punished by the village council; the deviating carpenter is deprived of the right to practise his trade. Where changes affect the entire group of carpenters, they decide upon them as a group in the occasional large councils of *tufugas*, where questions like adding to, or reducing the number of, payment feasts are solemnly voted upon.

The practice of medicine presents a somewhat striking contrast to the other arts. Although there are no charms or incantations, the formulas are secret and handed down from an old woman to her daughter or niece. Each formula is regarded as a personal possession: "Lale has a good medicine for the stomach"; "Tofi has a good medicine for the toothache." Sometimes six practitioners have six different medicines for the same ailment; they are regarded as probable equivalents, just as to-day native remedies and white men's remedies are often resorted to indiscriminately. This secrecy, this easy acceptance of the possibilities inherent in half a dozen remedies, militate against the accumulation of any general store of medicinal knowledge. The individual practitioner has the formula she learned from her elders, a knowledge of a few general medicinal herbs with cathartic qualities, and a free field for unchecked, dangerous and profitless experimentation.

In striking contrast is the practice of surgery, which is a public affair—a matter of skill, a technique to be learned; and so efficient have the natives become that mis-set bones come under the care of the American doctors with surprising infrequency.

RELIGION

Institutionalized religion and personal psychic experience were both exceedingly undeveloped in aboriginal Manu'a. Through the existence of the taboo system much of the social ceremonial took on a quasi-religious character, but innovations here really belong in the field of social organization.

When the solemn *kava* ceremonies, in which the *kava* is poured to the gods in a prayer to avert misfortune, and other social functions of the same sort are subtracted from the sum total of religious activity very little remains.

In his relationship to the family god and the spirits of the dead a very free rein was given the individual. The origin of village gods or local gods worshipped by a number of families seems to have been in an extension of the worship of the god of some gifted individual who combined psychic powers with a general worldly success which testified to his possessing much *mana.* Sometimes he assumed the position of a priest or oracle and was richly rewarded by offerings. This prestige he might perhaps transmit to a son, but there it seemed to lapse, resulting in a shifting pantheon and no genuine priestly institution. There were no priestly families.

Aside from this enhancement of his own inherited god's prestige, an individual who possessed special psychic gifts might gain considerable prestige and wealth from their exercise. His services would seem to have consisted in exorcism of evil spirits and ascertaining the cause of disasters. These special gifts range the whole gamut—from the ability to go into a trance, to the medicine-makers who talked to the ghosts as they gathered their herbs, and when the herbs could not be found knew that the patient would never get well. But there was no point in the social life at which the services of such people were absolutely necessary—a priestless *kava*-drinking ceremony would always do just as well. The unstable were rare; they were regarded as gifted, not skilled, and there was no tradition of apprenticeship.

Social Organization

But art and religion and the basic economic operations themselves are all mere background and by-play compared with the social organization. A man holds his title first; his skill, his character and his god are less important. And this very overpowering importance of the social structure, coupled with the fact that the individual and the title never became completely moulded into one unit, makes for flexibility and change.

The titles are arranged in an ideal structure, based on the seating positions to which they entitle their holders in a great ideal council *(fono)* of all the Samoan Islands. This ideal structure is repeated on a smaller scale for each island, island division and village. In each local replica of the great plan, fewer of the great titles appear and titles of smaller and smaller rank are inserted. On the island of Taū there are three village *fonos*—one for Fitiuta, one for Faleasao and one for Taū; a second scheme includes Taū and Faleasao, necessitating the omission of some of the lesser *matais* from the seating arrangement; and a third includes all three villages, in the *Fale Ula,* the great council of the Tui Manu'a.

These titles belong to two main classes—chiefs *(alii)* and talking chiefs *(tulafale).* Within these two groups there are endless shades of rank and precedence, but the two main classes remain distinct; their relationship to each other is an elaborate system of reciprocal services. It is the duty of the talking chiefs to maintain the honour, prestige and public high estate of the chiefs; to act as their ambassadors, spokesmen, grand viziers, bankers and campaign managers. In their hands lie all the traditions, the regulation of etiquette and inter-village social intercourse, the ordering of all important social events such as the marriage or death of a chief of high rank, his princess *(taupo)* or his heir-apparent *(manaia).* For the talking chief of highest rank, called in Manu'a *"to'oto'o"* and *"suāfanu'u,"* these functions are conceived more as services to the whole village, organized as it is around one or more high chiefs, than as personal services. Talking chiefs of lower rank perform definite services, such as preparing the chief's food, or representing him for several months before his marriage in the family of his betrothed. The talking chief must also provide the chief with food upon all important occasions.

In return for these services, they receive fine mats and tapa, payments ranging from the great distribution of the bride's dowry among the talking chiefs of the high-chief bridegroom to the gift of a length of tapa to each talking chief who has danced beside the *taupo.* And, more importantly, they possess great power. Theoretically the chief is a noble figure-head, of too high rank to make his own speeches in council or propose for his own wife. And the talking chief who obsequiously sings his praises also makes most of his decisions for him.

A *matai* title is conferred upon a man by his family group, and carries with it a place in the social structure. Theoretically this place is fixed and invariable; actually, if the holder of the title is poor and unpopular, the position of the title may be radically altered by the powerful and disaffected talking chiefs who wish to exalt some other and wealthier individual instead. Such changes necessitate the manipulation of old myths, or the outright invention of new ones, to validate the claim of the *nouveau riche;* changes in the *Fa'alupega* (the courtesy salutation formally recited by visitors); changes in the geography of the village and even in the dating system. It is customary to refer to events of the past hundred years as happening during the time that such and such a high chief held his title. When a high chief is quietly, insidiously relegated to an inferior position, the conversational habits of the village historians must be revised so that their references are not to his forebears but to the undistinguished forebears of his successful rival. I have one case where this happened in the course of twenty-five years. It is possible to check these local changes by the talking chiefs of distant villages, who visited the now metamorphosed village some twenty years ago and had studied the then existing social organization carefully for the occasion.

Such conditions were made possible by several different factors. The social organization was known in detail to only some twelve or fifteen old men in a village; the more incomprehensible they make it to the rest of the population the greater their prestige. The relationship-group controls the title, and the talking chiefs have, with one exception (the Tui Manu'a), nothing to say about the choice of an incumbent. Not being able to choose the individual, they, instead, manipulate his formal status, greatly increasing the strange disassociation between the individual and the position which he holds.

Furthermore, there are other premiums set upon innovation and originality of social form, quite aside from the desire of the talking chiefs to exercise their power or increase their wealth and the way in which the ambitious *nouveau riche* exploits these desires. Every village seeks to have a different social structure from the neighbouring village, and there is no standard of better or worse. The stress is all laid upon difference. If one village derives its prestige from having seventeen chiefs of such high rank that each one has to be mentioned in the introduction to every formal speech, the next village retaliates by exalting one chief so high that no one else's name can be mentioned with his. If one village has four *to'oto'o*s the next village is unique; it has only one *to'oto'o.* If Fitiuta has the most systematic *fono,* in which each pillar seat is named not only after one *matai* but after others who are entitled to sit in his place during his absence, Ofu can boast of having three entirely different ways in which the *fono* can be arranged. Similarly with the courtesy language, a common word on one island may become the highest chief's word upon another; and the courtesy language also gives wonderful opportunities for the invention of new esoteric phrases known only to the locality and designed to puzzle visiting orators. A talking chief's prestige depends upon his knowledge of the minute details of the social organization not only of his own districts, but of other districts, for upon this knowledge, more even than upon rhetorical skill, depends the choice of orator for great occasions. And a village is proud of the reputation of being *faigata* (difficult) for the visiting orator.

Because of the extreme variety of social ceremonials, composed as they are of the same elements in endless recombinations, the Samoans really see them as combinations, not as fixed sequences. An intelligent talking chief never has to begin at the beginning and go through a ceremony in order to arrive at some detail. It is possible to ask directly, "How many *kava* bowls are used at the marriage of Tui Manu'a?" "What kind of girdles do the *Suafa-nū*'s wear in the funeral ceremony?" and get an immediate answer. (Needless to say, the actual procedure varies enormously from occasion to occasion.) This is also due to the fact that the highest pitch of etiquette is reached not by observing the fixed procedure, but by pointedly reversing or rearranging it. One of the principal reasons for knowing who *should* receive the *kava* cup first is so that one may honour another by giving it to him instead. In this dexterous, graceful play with social forms the Samoans find their chief artistic expression. In the more serious manipulation of the social structure, for purposes of economic gain or political ambition, lies the most powerful dynamic force in Samoan society.

Conclusions

Only by placing Samoa against the Polynesian background is it possible to arrive at a basis of comparison and say, for instance, that the art of Samoa is relatively undeveloped or that the religion plays a minor rôle. Thus, in religious development, Hawaii, Tahiti, New Zealand and the Marquesas all out-distance Samoa in richness and variety of religious forms and beliefs and in the relative importance of religion in the lives of the people. Samoan tattooing is of negligible artistic intent beside that of New Zealand and the Marquesas, as is Samoan woodwork. In tapa-making the Samoans never approach the beauty of Hawaiian tapas. It is for its intricacy and complexity of social organization that Samoan culture is particularly conspicuous.

When the comparison is made, not with other cultures of Polynesia but within the Samoan archipelago, the same result is reached—social organization occupies most of the thought and interest of the community; all other activities are at least partly subordinated to it and made to minister to its ends.

With this preponderance of the social interest in mind, it is possible to ask: How important is the influence of the individual upon the different parts of this flexible culture which is hospitable to innovation, omnivorous of variation?

In the field of personal relationships the freedom of choice allowed the individual is prevented from having more important results by the low level of appreciation of personality differences. Choice is possible among homes, among teachers, among lovers; but the consciousness of personality, the attitudes necessary to make such choices significant, are lacking. So that the freedom in personal choices operates mainly in reducing the poignancy of personal relations, the elements of conflict, the need for making painful choices. The emotional tone of the society is consequently more moderate, and less charged with strain and violence. It never exerts sufficient repression to call forth a significant rebellion from the individual. The suicides of humiliation so common in parts of Polynesia do not exist in Samoa. The individual need commit no murder, need not even muster up a fine rage to escape from a disagreeable situation—he simply slips out of it into the house next door. Such a setting does not produce violent, strikingly marked personalities; it is kind to all and does not make sufficient demands upon any.

In the decorative arts, the freedom given to the individual is rendered nugatory by the absence of cultural recognition of the innovator and by the strong prejudice against active imitation; so the gifted individual receives but passing praise for his work. The variations are taken for granted; they do not become distinguishing marks of high rank, nor do they enhance greatly the economic value of the object. And his ingeniousness is seldom directly perpetuated in the work of those who come after him. Tattooing and tapa designs retain the same fluid, slightly differentiated style, containing endless, non-significant variations, imitation of no one of which permits a real trend in a new direction to develop.

In religion the premium set by society was also very low, giving slight economic gains and only small increase in social prestige; and the man who had been a medium or local priest in his day was still remembered more for the place which he had held in the social structure. The most famous "priest" in Samoan history is probably O le Tamafaiga of Manono, who usurped the great secular title of the family of Muagututi'a.[10] So in religion the same nondescript variation occurs—one village with two gods, another with none, a pile of stones where the god of some family had once been worshipped by the whole neighbourhood. The society contained no mechanism by which an individual religious genius could permanently institutionalize his inspiration. In a generation they were back again to the casual service of their family gods, and the occasional formal recognition of the high gods in the course of social ceremonial.

In the social organization the individual is given the freest hand and meets with the greatest rewards. So flexible is the social structure, so minutely adapted to manipulation, that it is possible to change the appearance of the *fono* in twenty years. But this very sensitivity to slight change proves in the end to be a conservative factor. The social innovator runs against no hard-and-fast wall of caste, no religiously sanctioned ritual, no jealously guarded body of tradition. Would he make a change—a few fine mats, a little judicial diplomacy—the social landscape is completely altered. His ambition, his itch toward manipulation, and his desire for revenge meet with too slender opposition. The social structure offers too slight a challenge; it is too complacent to the innovating hand. And so the recent history of Samoa contains few records of important changes introduced by individuals. The daring coups of the Hawaiian kings and the lonely, dangerous rôles of Maori outlaws are absent from Samoan chronicles. And the ever-yielding, ever-accommodating social structure has remained much the same, generation after generation, while the talking chiefs with original minds and social ambitions slid, sated with too easy victories, into undistinguished grooves.

Without seeking to generalize beyond the limits of the material, it is possible to summarize: In Manu'a the individual plays the most significant rôle in the most complex and important aspect of his culture, the social organization. The whole flexibility of Samoan culture, which at first blush looks so favourable to the display of individuality, so pliant to the moulding hand, is also a powerful conservative force. It possesses all the strength of the tough willows, which bend and swing to every passing breeze but never break.

NOTES

1. I wish to acknowledge my indebtedness to the Board of Fellowships in the Biological Sciences of the National Research Council, whose award of a Fellowship made the field-work, upon which this investigation is based, possible.
2. The term "Samoan" will be used throughout this paper with the explicit understanding that the concrete data were gathered in the Manu'a Archipelago.
3. I use the present tense throughout, although the slow introduction of American civilization is gradually changing the face of Samoan culture, especially in its economic aspects. But in isolated parts of the islands, such as the village of Fitiuta on Taū, in Manu'a, these conditions still obtain.
4. This "family god" had all the elements usually included in the definition of totemism except the theory of descent from the totem. Because so much dialectical confusion centres about the term, I prefer to keep the term used in the earlier literature on Samoa, "family god."
5. The Protestant Church has taken over the word and uses it for "years of discretion."
6. This is a modern development. Before the abolition of polygamy the talking chiefs simply *added* a wife to the chief's household.
7. Church and government are gradually introducing a marriage based on individual choice which is recognized by the community.
8. The one exception to this is the ceremony for burning candlenuts for black tapa dye. Here, although only one old woman participates, an elaborate magical ritual is followed.
9. Except in medicine, which will be discussed separately.
10. Stair, J. B. *Old Samoa,* p. 77.

11

SUCCESSION TO CHIEFTAINSHIP IN TIKOPIA[1]

Raymond Firth

The institution of chieftainship is basic to the Tikopia political system, and traditionally was one of the key features in Tikopia religious performance. It is of interest then to examine the principles and the process of succession whereby the chiefly roles were filled.

Succession in the social sense is a process of replacement, with public recognition, whereby titles, offices, authority, roles and other indicators of status are transferred from one person (incumbent) to another. Succession may be generational, after the socially active span of the incumbent has been completed by retirement or death, or periodic, after a definite interval. Succession to an office or title is very rarely open to every member of the community, without specific criteria demanded in the candidate; usually it is restricted and involves a sex limitation, qualities of maturity, membership of a given social group, etc. Part of the restriction may be in terms of a kin tie, making the succession hereditary.

In Tikopia succession to chieftainship is generational, restricted to males, and hereditary. It normally takes place only on the death of the incumbent; there is no rotation of office and no recognized provision for retirement.

Succession to office and position of authority implies a need by the society for continuity of personnel. In any community it is desirable that the machinery for bringing a new official into being should operate as soon as possible in order that authority and social order shall continue unbroken and that essential services shall have their functionary. Where the official has the authority and the multiple functions of a chief it is particularly important that a replacement should be obtained as soon as possible. An interregnum affords opportunities of disorder in the body politic and may leave the group without its representative towards other groups and putatively (in traditional Tikopia) towards the gods. When a vacancy is caused

Reproduced by permission of the publisher and Raymond Firth from *Oceania*, 30:161-180 (1960); also by permission of the London School of Economics and Political Science, publishers of Firth's *Essays on Social Organization and Values* (Monographs on Social Anthropology No. 28, 1964), in which the article was reprinted.

by retirement, planning for succession is facilitated and the timing can be arranged. When the vacancy is caused by death, planning can only be imperfect and the necessity for succession may arise at any time. Succession at the death of a chief calls for some agreed principle of replacement by the society. The gap may arise at any moment, the emotional tension at the death of a man of rank is likely to be considerable, and it is functionally useful to have some mechanism which can be put into action to ensure that a replacement is obtained as soon as possible.

In some societies this issue has not been very clearly met. A period of confusion ensues on the death of a chief, and factional struggles of a violent order may take place until one person emerges as victor in the succession move. In some other societies it has been customary for the announcement of the death of a leader to be conjoined with the proclamation of his successor, presented in advance. *"Le Roi est mort; vive le Roi."* In Tikopia the system was neither one of confused competition among candidates nor one of automatic succession. It was a somewhat curious system of election, in which the principal role was played by competing "king-makers" rather than by competing candidates.

In examining this system in detail, I want first to consider the type of qualities regarded as desirable in a chief by Tikopia society.

QUALITIES DESIRED IN A TIKOPIA CHIEF

If one asks the question, what has been demanded of a chief in Tikopia, what qualities should be possessed, one does not get a neatly rounded formulation of an ideal personality responding to a clearly demarcated set of obligations. The ideal of what a chief should be can only be extracted piecemeal from the judgments of people expressed upon his behaviour in concrete situations, and from isolated statements of principle often arising from these situations. The most explicit generalizations have come not from the people, but from the chiefs themselves and the members of their families, whose consciousness of the chiefly role has been most acute. From my experience in 1928–29 and 1952 it may be said very broadly that all Tikopia held that the chiefs were the guardians of the interests of their people, and that this demanded from the chief certain types of conduct, including abstention from direct injury to his people through selfish motives, and limitations upon his freedom of action where this freedom might be indirectly prejudicial to them. Traditionally this position was correlative with their function as priests, that is, as representatives and intermediaries with the Tikopia gods. The Tikopia chief could be, in theory, a dictator. In practice, his power and authority were subject to limitations imposed by the very character of that authority. The efficacy of the limitations upon him depended to a large extent on his conception of trusteeship.

This conception of responsibility and trusteeship received explicit expression in statements of the chiefs themselves about their own motivations, and in criticism of the actions of other chiefs in such terms. It was also given concrete manifestation in acts where a chief put himself to inconvenience or economic loss for the sake of his people.[2]

In many contexts it was implied that a Tikopia chief should be a mature man, capable of making responsible decisions. The Ariki Tafua described to me in 1952 how his father when very ill looked on his son who had become a man *(ku tangata)* and was ready then to abandon life, in the thought that it was time he succeeded to the chieftainship. And I think it is significant that although at least one case is recorded of a chief having been elected as a minor there is no case of a chief having been elected *in absentia*—on a sea voyage abroad.

Of the other qualities that were demanded of a chief, one was physical health. If his body was not hale, then he could not serve efficiently as a representative of his people and a medium for his gods. This was exemplified by an Ariki Kafika, Pepe, about nine generations ago, according to tradition.[3] He was said to have been afflicted with severe yaws (framboesia), and therefore to have abdicated in favour of his younger brother, Tuisifo. In comment on this story, one of the senior men of rank in Kafika said, "If a chief dwells and contracts yaws, then he is put on one side to the rear. He is taken to the rear since he has become bad. Even while the yaws is slight he goes to the rear, because it is an evil thing. When the yaws stands in (the body of) a chief, it is the doing of the gods. It is bad, therefore is set to one side that another chief that is good may be taken." The underlying reason for this setting of a chief aside in Tikopia belief was not that the disease itself was physically contaminating or ritually destructive, but that it was a manifestation of the displeasure of the gods towards the chief. There was a suspicion that he had done something wrong. In any case, his power with the gods must have been ineffective, otherwise he would not be suffering. Yet such a general principle was not necessarily carried out in practice. The Ariki Fangarere in 1929, an elderly man, had been afflicted with a debilitating tropical ulcer in his foot for a number of years, but he still carried on his duties as chief, and I heard no suggestion that he ought to retire. He himself had not expressed any wish to abdicate. This may have been due to the fact that he was extremely active in economic and ritual affairs despite his lameness. Occasionally a concession was made to him as when, during the rites of the Work of the Gods, he came by canoe over the lake instead of walking round the shore with his co-chiefs. As I saw in 1952, such a concession could also be made to a chief on account of the weakness of old age. The affliction of the Ariki Fangarere was treated, then, rather as weakness than as fault. Yet that weakness of old age of the Ariki Kafika was regarded as deleterious to the welfare and prosperity of the land was borne out by opinions in 1952.[4]

In addition to physical purity, it was thought that a chief should have a certain moral purity. The ethical side of their religion was not strongly emphasized by the Tikopia, but it was asserted that sorcery should lie outside the province of a chief. In 1929 the Ariki Taumako said to me, "A chief should continue to dwell beautifully only, to make the *kava;* it is made only for welfare, for food to be good." The term translated as "beautifully" could also be rendered as "in proper style," that is, "without evil intent." The sanction given for this kind of behaviour was a reference to the traditional death of the great Tikopia culture hero, the premier deity of the whole community, who was said to have gone sinless to the realm of the gods without revenging himself on his slayer. It was said then that he objected to any "cursing speech" *(taranga tautu),* i.e. any formulae of sorcery, by chiefs who in so many rites and activities were said to have been following the model he created. The Ariki Taumako also told me that his father had said to him, "We who make the *kava,* we follow the one god, the deity of Kafika." His father instructed him that a chief who used sorcery lost his *manu,* the potency of his *kava;* a chief who practised sorcery has done wrong, his *manu* had thereby been directed into sorcery. His *kava* would be efficacious only on occasions of the descriptive ritual itself. At other times the chief would call on the gods but they would not hear him; they no longer would desire him. Rain would no longer fall at his word, nor would the seas grow calm. As it was by the reputed control of such phenomena that the Tikopia chief was helped in maintaining the good opinion of his people, this belief might act as a deterrent against a chief's misuse of his relation to the gods. In 1929 Pa Fenuatara said, "If a chief is angry, he scolds only with good speech; he curses by the father (i.e., 'May your father eat filth'), but he does not use sorcery." He added, however, "It is true indeed, some chiefs are bad." The Ariki Tafua was cited to me (in private) as one who had caused the deaths of several people and the illness of others by invoking his gods against them, and this was condemned as bad conduct by those who told me of it. Pa Fenuatara went so far as to admit that if his father, the Ariki Kafika, had used sorcery against a man, then, "He would die indeed; he would not see the night; there would be no delay; he would die on the instant." But, he said, "The Ariki Kafika has sympathy for the land, that each stands there in his body of belief. If a man is sick anywhere and the news comes to Ariki Kafika, he will recite the formula for the man to get well."

The attitude of the Tikopia chiefs towards sorcery was not one of simple adherence to the traditional ethical code. Where adopted, it was partly in deference to a sense of responsibility and partly through fear of loss of power in ritual directions. Moreover, though given verbal allegiance, either it was disregarded on occasion or there was sufficient lack of faith by the ordinary people in its observance for them to make specific accusations of breach. But the effect of such a code of abstinence from sorcery was promulgated among the chiefly families themselves, and that commoners also held it indicated that it was part of the general concept of the duty which the chief bore towards his people.[5]

But correlative with this attitude of responsibility and obligation towards the people of his clan and the community as a whole was the pride of a chief and his family in his position. In his daily life, each chief was continually subscribing to the thesis of his supremacy and his unique role in his clan. He accepted gifts as a kind of tribute due; he gave largesse as a matter of right; he behaved in ways which in all other men would be described as arrogant; he was quick to criticize the actions of commoners which appeared to him to overstep the bounds of their status; he had outbursts of anger at anything seeming to offer him an affront. Going beyond his immediate personal interests, he spoke in approval of the actions of other chiefs in regard to their clansfolk, maintained their common interests, and on critical occasions was willing to lend his presence and authority in their support. A chief was apt to exemplify his status by special figurative expressions. The Ariki Kafika said to me in 1929, "I who dwell here am the net-ripping *urua,* the man-eating shark"—comparing himself with the furious fish of the ocean. On another occasion he gave me a further set of metaphors. The Ariki Kafika is "The mouth of the land, the confirmation of all things, that to which the land listens, the standing chief indeed." In explaining to me a secret formula, he drew attention to a phrase which occurred in it, "The deity of the land is one." This, he said, was the chief who in his power stands over a commoner like a god. If a commoner of his clan disturbs the peace of the land, then the chief will hear him and will make him pay for it. In terms of the social framework, commoners were regarded by the families of chiefs as of minor importance. Pa Fenuatara said to me in 1929, "The commoner who dwells, his ancestral tale is one, the chief; his deity is not heavy and did not go whither or whither." This meant that the ordinary clansman had no history or traditional origins apart from those of his chief, which subsumed his. The gods to whom he appealed were of small influence ("light"). They performed no deeds of note which demonstrated their power, nor did they have adventures of that variety or interest which would have entitled them to a particular rank in a spiritual hierarchy.

A chief in relation to commoners, then, was expected to be someone superior, somewhat aloof, capable of fierceness when angered, but compassionate. In the family circle of the Ariki Tafua in 1929 I was given a set of honorific phrases for a chief concerned with his bounty towards his people. He was addressed thus: "You are a chief who feeds voyaging sons, a chief of sympathetic appeal, a chief who feeds orphan children." Now it is true that I heard some of these expressions from the lips of commoners and was given examples of songs in which they were used for formal thanksgiving and praise. But it is significant that it was in the family circles of the chiefs that I heard them quoted most.

This stereotype of the ideal of chiefly character and conduct was subscribed to by the commoners, though formulated mostly by the chiefs and their immediate kinsfolk. What was sociologically important about this code was that it put into a moral category, conduct which was of practical service in maintaining the position of the chiefs. Up to a point it could be regarded as a realization of the need for putting a halo round autocracy and making the chief serve public interests if he was to exercise his privileges.

An index to the special position of a chief in Tikopia is the care that is taken over the marriage of the potential heir, a chief's eldest son. The history of the marital unions of the Ariki Taumako of 1952, before he became a chief, illustrates this.

As a young man he was first married to a woman of the lineage of Fetauta. The first wife had been the choice of Pa Tarikitonga, the father's brother's son of the young man's father. The choice was taken up by the agnatic kinsmen, but it had never been approved by the husband—he had never gone to her as his mistress. He had never given her betel materials or tobacco. But the woman was brought to him by his kinsfolk according to the traditional custom of *tukunga nofine.* They settled down together, but after a time the young man objected to her, saying she was no good. So she left him and after a while remarried, having as her husband a man of the district of Rofaea. Then the young man married Tauviitevasa, a girl from Akitunu lineage of Namo. He selected her himself, brought her back, the marriage feast was made, and they settled down. But then his present wife came over from Faea alone to him. He had gone to her as his mistress earlier, and it was said it was by the wish of her father, the Ariki Tafua (formerly Pa Rangifreri), that she went to marry him. Her father wished that his daughter should become the wife of the man who in time would be the chief—that she should be sheltered by Taumako. The young man obviously was willing to accept her as his wife and the marriage feast was made. Then the jealousy of the new wife drove out the earlier wife. This woman returned home and remarried, becoming Nau Te Aroaro. She had no child by the young man; she went home pregnant, but nothing was known of the results —possibly she procured an abortion, it was said.

The young man's father, the Ariki Taumako, then still alive, had been impressed by this second wife and was very angry when she was driven out. She was an instructed person who knew how to run the household affairs and in particular to provide food for members of the clan. The third wife, it was said, did not feed the people properly. "Do you see how we do not go constantly to Motuata?" said my informant in 1952. (Motuata was the principal residence of the chief of Taumako.) "The place of gathering of this clan from of old is Motuata, the place of assembly of the people. The reason why the brothers of the chief and other people of the clan do not go much to the Ariki Taumako is 'because of the woman.' One chief is good, another is so-so *(na atamai e fefea).* His brothers observe and behave accordingly. Each sits in his own house."

When the first two wives remarried, in each case the men of sa Taumako formed a party and went over to demonstrate against the marriage. It was held that a woman who had been the wife of a chief or of a potential chief should remain unmarried—even though he had thrown her off. When I protested, my informant made a face and said, "I don't know, it is the custom of this land."

The marriage feast of the girl from Fetauta was made in the house of Vangatau, that of the girl from Akitunu in the house of Te Aorere and that of the third wife, who remained as Nau Taumako, in Motuata, the chief's own house. In 1952 the chief's three marriages were not popular with some members of his clan. My informant said, "We objected—the valuables disappeared, the sinnet cord and the paddles, because he married three times. The valuables and the food of the clan of Taumako and of us, the lineage of Taumako here, just went and went and went. Bowls and paddles were finished." *(Matou ne teke—ku leku ko te koroa, te kafa ma te fe—ku avanga fakatoru. Poi, poi, poi ko te koroa ma te kai te kainanga sa Taumako ma matou sa Taumako nei—oti ko te kumete ma te fe.)*

Apart from the objection to the triple marriage, two points of importance are embodied in this whole statement. One is that the marital affairs of a chief or even of a potential chief are also the concern of the clan. They regard themselves as entitled to provide him with a wife and bound to protest if that wife leaves him, even although she may have been provoked into doing so. Secondly, the degree of attachment between clan and chief is to some extent dependent upon the hospitality which his wife will exercise. She is responsible for seeing to it that the clansfolk who visit the chief are well received and given food. By her conduct in this respect she can do much to make or mar the reputation of the chief and his relations with his clansfolk, even his close agnatic kin. The interest of the clan in providing the chief with a wife is therefore directly related to the quality of their own future relations with the chief. The Tikopia have no expression equivalent to the African one—"The chief's wife is the wife of the tribe." But in effect their behaviour bears much the same significance.

Principles of Succession

How were such general ideals recognized and put into effect when questions of succession arose? Aristotle laid down three qualifications required for those who have to fill the highest office. These are: loyalty to the established constitution; the greatest administrative capacity; and virtue and justice appropriate to the form of government. Since all these qualities do not necessarily meet in the same person, some selection is necessary. Aristotle advised us to make the choice in the light of the kind of functions the office has to exercise. In selecting a general, for instance, we should choose a man of skill in preference to a man of virtue without skill, since military skill is presumably rare. But we should choose virtue in a man required as a steward, since the administrative capacity required by this office (so he thought) is of a common kind.

In general, the Tikopia way of thinking can be related to Aristotle's conceptions. They have not appeared to feel the need of military skill in the organizational sense. Their leaders in such warfare as they had seem to have been aggressive individual fighters *(toa)* rather than generals. Loyalty to the constitution of Tikopia society might be assumed, since until recent years all Tikopia appear to have shared the same general values and attachment to their way of life, including the traditional social structure. As Westernization has come closer to the Tikopia, the greater interest of some men in modern ways has only just begun to raise the question of basic loyalty as a conscious issue. Administrative capacity the Tikopia have seemed in effect to have disregarded as a criterion for chieftainship—or rather to have assumed (with Aristotle) that all men possess it to a sufficient degree for the office. Moreover, a chief can have good advisers. Virtue they have regarded as an important, though not necessarily final, determinant in selection for office.

This may have been because the Tikopia realistically may have regarded it as simpler to secure virtuous conduct in a chief by demanding it after his election rather than by looking for it beforehand. In other words, with a somewhat cynical view of human frailty, they seem to have placed more reliance on the regulating effect of the social code upon an office-holder than upon any earlier inducement of virtue *per se.* They seem to have attached much more importance to a regular form of succession than to a search for the ideal qualities in the person who would succeed, though such qualities were not ignored. This type of abstract intellectualistic statement is not, of course, that of the Tikopia. It is my inference from the evidence which they produced.

Neither in 1929 nor in 1952 did an actual case of succession to chieftainship in Tikopia occur. But I was given a considerable amount of descriptive data about recent cases, and I had also for consideration the mass of genealogical material about the chiefly lineages of Tikopia. Though this cannot be taken as specifically historical case material, the types of succession there indicated conform to those of very recent occurrence and may be taken as illustrative of Tikopia theory, and probably, practice also.

Succession to chieftainship in Tikopia has been hereditary by descent in the male line. No woman has succeeded to chieftainship,[6] nor has any descendant in the female line. With the exception only of a founding ancestor, no one who was not an agnate in the chiefly lineage could succeed.

Material of succession to Tkiopia chieftainship is obtainable from the genealogies of the four chiefly lineages, and comprised by 1952 a total of 49 cases of succession, 13 each in Kafika and Tafua, 15 in Taumako, and 8 in Fangarere. Succession has been of the following order:

Son succeeded in	27 cases
Son's son	3 ,,
Brother	5 ,,
Brother's son	7 ,,
Other agnates	7 ,,
	49 ,,

The principle of direct hereditary transmission of the office is clear from the material. There was also an emphasis on primogeniture.

In collecting the genealogical material I was told on various occasions that a particular man—usually one lost at sea—had been *te ariki fakasomo*, the "growing chief," *te pupura*, the "shoot" or "seedling," or *te pupura nga atua*, the "seedling of the gods." The terms were used in every case only of the eldest son of a chief, and the analogies with growing plants illustrate how the Tikopia look upon the eldest son as the probable chiefly heir.[7] Special treatment might also be given to such an eldest son, as in taking gifts of food to him, "since he is the coming chief." Primogeniture was thus the normal Tikopia mode of succession.

In 11 cases of the 27 where sons succeeded, it was the eldest son in birth order; in four other cases an only son succeeded; and in the remainder it was the eldest surviving or the only surviving son, other potential heirs having died meanwhile (commonly lost at sea). No case is recorded where a younger son succeeded his father as chief when his elder brother was still alive. (Only one case is recorded, that referred to already in Kafika, where a younger brother succeeded his elder brother, the latter being alive but ill.) The pattern of filial succession was common to all clans. In Kafika and in Tafua son succeeded father in eight cases out of 13, in Taumako in seven cases out of 15, in Fangarere in four cases out of eight. In general, where a son did not succeed, the pattern seems to have been to select a brother or other agnate as close as possible to the dead chief. A problem, however, arose at the death of this man—whether he should be succeeded by his own son or whether the chieftainship should revert to the line of his predecessor? Here the Tikopia seem to have adopted the principle of reversion, but not automatically. It seemed to depend upon the relative availability of likely successors in the different lines, and it was here perhaps that the qualities regarded as desirable in a chief came most to the fore as criteria for selection. But succession in the case of brother's sons was for the most part a reversion to an elder line.

In the records of Kafika there appear to be three cases in which reversion to the senior branch did not occur after the succession had been so broken. The first of these was when the chief Pepe, who abdicated by reason of disease, founded the house of Tavi. No attempt seems to have been made to seek later chiefs of Kafika from this house. The second case occurred two generations later. The chief, Tanakiforau, had succeeded his father; he was the second son, but his elder brother, Mourongo, *te pupura,* the "chiefly seed," had died at sea. As Tanakiforau grew old, he was neglected by his sons. They used to go out and procure food, but they did not bring back to him the little delicacies which were due to an aged parent—forest fruits, land crabs, birds. They selfishly ate them in the woods themselves. Seeing this, one of his younger relatives, Vakauke, an adopted child in the house, used to bring him back such things to tickle his palate. This went on for a long time and one day the chief said to the lad, "When I am gone, that which is hung round my neck shall be yours"—that is, the lad would be given the chiefly necklet of coconut frond which was worn by a chief on ritual occasions. Tanakiforau became ill and was about to die. All his kin assembled. Tereiteata, the Ariki Tafua, was summoned. When he arrived the chief of Kafika was to all appearances dead, but at intervals a long breath still assured the people that he lived. (As a matter of fact, said the Ariki Tafua who was telling me this tale in 1929, the chief really was dead, and it was only the god in his body waiting for the Ariki Tafua to come before leaving the corpse untenanted.) The Ariki Tafua came and asked, "What did he say? Where is the speech he left?" All replied, "He has said nothing." Then he turned to the dying man, now motionless, and said, "Speak to us, make known to whom the chiefly necklet shall be given." The body made no sign of life. He addressed it again and again, but there was no response. Then he began to repeat the names of the dying man's sons, but there was no indication from the old chief whether he favoured one or not. The Ariki Tafua recited the names of all the sons and other close agnates and again repeated, "Tell us who it is that shall have the chiefly necklet." There was no response. At last he turned and said, "It is this thieving thing that sits there?"—indicating Vakauke and using a term which is one of contempt. The apparently lifeless body rose, drew up its head in assent, and fell back motionless, now really dead. Thus the succession was confirmed and Vakauke became chief. He was the ancestor of the present line of chiefs who are thus the offshoot of a junior branch of the lineage of Kafika.

Such is the traditional tale, which has certain odd features, including the unusual specification of a successor by a dying chief. It might be interpreted as in part a moral story to influence sons to behave well to their fathers. But the Ariki Tafua told it to me with emphasis upon the political aspect to explain—and to some extent enjoy—the break in the direct Kafika line. I had in fact found it already impossible to ascertain precisely what was the ancestry of Vakauke; the story might have been a reconstruction originating in Kafika clan to bolster up the election of an outsider. Yet, if this were so, one would expect a more direct link in the succession to be given. In the story told by the Ariki Tafua, his own ancestor plays a most important part, and this entry of another chief in facilitating a decision as to the succession is in accordance with traditional rule. The use of the contemptuous term "thieving thing" by the presiding chief indicates the unexpectedness of the choice. What is not explained is why the choice was left to the expiring chief. It is notable also that in this case the selection of a new chief was regarded as being in effect through a sign from the gods. Since a Tikopia chief traditionally had as primary function the job of serving as intermediary with the gods and at times even as their embodiment, it is interesting that nomally no supernatural approval of the human selection seems to have been sought. What this tale suggests is an anomalous succession, probably because there were no obvious candidates available; it is probably significant that, although mention is made in the tale of the sons of Tanakiforau, I was not able to ascertain their names, which is unusual. As a speculation, one may advance the view that this was an instance of virtual ultimogeniture—that the old chief had no sons of proper calibre, that the senior line as a whole had no one outstanding, and that therefore the chieftainship devolved upon a very junior agnate actually living with and serving the chief. A member of the senior branch—a great-grandson of the Mourongo referred to above, was in fact chosen as chief of Kafika later. When, however, he died the title reverted to a brother of his predecessor and then to his predecessor's son, and not to any descendant of his own.

In Tafua, the direct line of succession was followed closely. The most marked divergence from it was in the case of the predecessor of the Arika Tafua, whom I knew in 1928–29. This man was an F.F.B.S.S. of his predecessor and the product of a third wife. When he died, he was succeeded by the eldest son of his predecessor's first wife, and again the direct line resumed.

There was one case, told me by the Ariki Tafua in 1929, where a former chief of Tafua, Moritiaki, attempted to reserve the chiefly office for his younger son. By an Anuta wife he had Taupe. Though the boy was not his eldest, the chief wished him to have the *kasoa,* the chiefly necklet, because by reason of his mother's alien origin, he had no supporting body of kin in Tikopia. His half-brothers, on the other hand, had standing through their kin ties. But when the brothers heard of their father's proposal they were very angry, and all deserted Uta, where their father lived. Seeing this, Taupe was much ashamed at being the cause of so much disruption, and went to live alone in Namo. There he lived for a long time, catching fish, cooking and eating them, and sleeping, all alone. Finally he married there and became the progenitor of the lineage of Akitunu. At last his father summoned him to Uta. There he gave him a little basket of sacred adze blades *(toki tapu)* to carry and they went together to Maunga Faea. There the chief buried the blades in various spots, as "blocks" *(pipi)* to secure the land for Taupe and his descendants in perpetuity, and ward off any possible encroachment by his brothers or their descendants. After their father's death the eldest of the brothers, Te Urumua, then became chief, but Taupe's economic future was assured.

In Taumako and Fangarere the line of the eldest son was left on one side in a few cases, presumably because there was no available candidate. But it seems that in nearly every case an attempt was made to return to the senior line as soon as possible. In Taumako, where a brother succeeded in three cases, on his death the succession went to a son of his elder brother in two cases and in the other the chieftainship reverted to an older branch. Where a brother's son succeeded, on his death the succession reverted to the elder branch again. In Taumako, primogeniture with the right of the elder branch to succeed has been the dominant principle; save for the one case of refusal, youth or absence seem to have been the only bar.

Normally, a Tikopia chief is a married man at the time of his election. But this is not an invariable rule. Pakimoana of Taumako was elected while still a child (see later), and Tereiteata succeeded as a bachelor. He was lost at sea before he married and left no descendants, but in accordance with a Tikopia practice of respect to a chief he was given a title, Pu Tafua Lasi, equivalent to that of a married man and an ancestor.

The most outstanding exception to normal succession in Tikopia chieftainship was in the case of Fangarere in recent times. As I discovered in 1952, on the death of the Ariki Fangarere I had known earlier, *two* chiefs of the clan had been elected. This was a clear case of factional interests arising from difference of religion. The elder son of the late chief, personally not very desirable, and a Christian, had been made "the Chief of the Gospel" at the instance of the Ariki Tafua. The younger son, personally much better fitted for the office, and a pagan, had been made "the Chief of the Chiefs" by his pagan colleagues. He was the chief of higher status.[8]

Unlike the practice with some African peoples, Tikopia has no provision for a regency. The clan must have a chief as soon as possible after the death of its former leader, and he who leads the clan as chief must have full powers. In the traditional Tikopia society this absence of regency could be correlated with the necessity for the chief to perform ritual functions of direct relation with ancestors and with the understanding that he himself in turn would be incorporated into the ancestral line as an object of spiritual appeal. No one who had not been properly and fully inducted as chief could perform these roles. It might be understood generally that when a chief taken from a junior branch died the succession would probably revert to a descendant of the senior branch. But such a limitation could only be implicit in the Tikopia system. It was not structurally expressed as an explicit limitation; in other words, there were no purely regent's powers.

There is no recorded case of a Tikopia chieftainship ever having been seized by force, though reference is often made in tradition to attempts to seize power as such by violence, and the origin tales speak of contests to gain the office. In quasi-historical times certainly, it seems as though the combination of ritual and social sanctions for chieftainship was such that no legitimacy could be expected by such forcible seizure. (Of course such seizure may actually have happened, and been disguised under a story of normal succession, but this is unlikely since the interlocking kinship ties of the other clans would have probably revealed it.)

MECHANISM OF ELECTION

It is curious that in the Tikopia system of succession despite the emphasis upon primogeniture there is no automatic rule by which a designated heir succeeds to a dead chief. No man, even the eldest son, could claim the chieftainship as his in advance. Instead, by a custom which is almost unique in Polynesia, a chief is chosen by what may be called a system of election.[9] In this system the major active role is taken by leading men of clans other than that whose chief has died.

The election takes place as soon as possible after the death of the reigning chief, usually in the midst of the uproar and wailing which begin the funeral ceremonies. The formal token of conferring office upon the new chief is the demonstration of seizing him and raising him into the air in the arms of his selectors. This public elevation is the notification to him of his election. It also serves as a sign to the people at large that the succession has been renewed. Apart from clothing the newly elected chief in a new bark waist-cloth, this is the only ceremonial act that is necessary to accomplish the election. There is no formal ritual induction by which he is introduced to the ancestors or in any other way consecrated to his new work. The choice of the funeral as the place of election has the advantage that it gives the widest publicity to the occasion, since at the obsequies of a chief a large number of people are present from all clans and from all parts of the island. The act of elevation (which may be performed on the person of the chief on other occasions also) is described by the term *sapai* and expresses in symbolic form the lofty status of the chief in regard to the mass of the people. By this act too those who select the chief acknowledge their own formal inferiority to him.[10]

The point of especial note in this proceeding is that the choice and elevation of the chief are done by people whom he does not rule. Since no chief died while I was on Tikopia, I have no first-hand data, but descriptions given to me make the procedure clear. In 1929 the Ariki Kafika described to me how the then Ariki Taumako had been chosen. He said, "The chief who was living there was taken by me; my chief whom I took. I went where people were crying (i.e. wailing for their chief who had just died). I called out, 'Where is my chief?' The crowd pointed with their fingers." Then the Ariki Kafika went up to the dead man's son, who was wailing for his father near the corpse, and gripped him tight despite his struggles to get free. Then came another man, also a member of the Kafika family, at the back of the Ariki to assist him. The Ariki said, "Hold your chief and lift him into a man's lap." He was held fast and raised from the floor while his kinsfolk strove to release him. Such, said the Ariki Kafika, is the general custom at the *sau ariki*, the taking of a chief. The party which has determined on a choice goes in a strong body of kinsfolk *(paito soa)* to the house of mourning, and while some hold the man they have selected, the others engage in a rough and tumble with the members of his lineage. "The body of kinsfolk of the man taken—to be a chief—object to his being taken. Great is the fighting at a chief-taking. When a chief is taken, it's terrific. Folk are struck and the kin of the new chief wail for their son who has been taken to rule." It must be noted that although a chief making a selection indicates the man to be elevated, he does not himself raise the new chief in his arms. This would be derogatory to his own dignity. The job of elevation is done for him by one or more of his henchmen.

The struggle of the kin of the ruler-elect to dissuade those who would elevate the new chief seems paradoxical. Why should a man's kinsfolk object so strenuously? Why should they want a chief to be chosen elsewhere, as the Tikopia themselves say they do? For this attitude two reasons were given me by the Ariki Kafika. The first was that the body of kinsfolk lose some of the services of their man when he is elected, since he will not go and prepare food as consistently as formerly owing to his new status and obligations. There did not seem to me to be much practical weight in this objection because though a Tikopia chief takes little part in the actual preparation of food, and not at all in the oven work, he does occupy himself in cultivation of the soil, in fishing and in many other economic affairs. Moreover, there are other economic advantages which could compensate for immediate loss of services. The second reason, perhaps more plausible, was that the kin of the chief-elect are afraid lest they be called "a family wishing to be chief" *(paito fia ariki)*—that is, lest they be accused of ambition and greed. Yet both these reasons are probably nominal. The show of resistance seems to be largely a traditionalized move to "save face". This interpretation is borne out by the fact that I obtained no record at all of such resistance having been carried to the point of preventing the election altogether.

It is not only the kinsfolk of the chosen man who object. The man himself usually makes some show of avoiding election by struggle or by flight. I was told in 1929 how the then Ariki Kafika ran away when he thought that his election was near and hid on top of a shelf in a house, carefully arranging around himself a number of wooden bowls. But a man discovered him and announced his whereabouts to the crowd. Whereupon the reluctant ariki-elect got down and ran, but was intercepted by outstretched arms; he was caught and lifted up as chief. In this evasion there was quite conceivably an element of shyness at being thrust suddenly into the centre of public attention and at the threat of a radical change in his mode of life. But such conduct is also traditionally dictated as an expression of modesty and is adopted in order to avoid suspicion of a desire to grasp power. The Tikopia is peculiarly sensitive to the reproach of being "a person wishing to exalt himself" *(tenea fia pasaki);* this simulated refusal of honour is thus in line with the behaviour of his kinsfolk.

Sensitiveness to such a public reproach provides an overt explanation of the anomalous custom of the election of a chief by members of another clan. But while it allows the chief's own followers to preserve a reputation for modesty and reticence, the custom has certain other functions, perhaps equally important, though they are not stressed by the Tikopia themselves. A reference to the persistent conditions of succession will reveal them. It is clear from what has been said already that there is no right of succession to the office of the chief. However, certain probabilities are recognized informally in everyday life. Where a chief's eldest son is grown up, married and has shown himself to be a person of mature judgment and ability, then normally it is assumed that he will be elected on his father's death. In 1929 it seemed almost certain that Pa Fenuatara would succeed the Ariki Kafika and Pa Rangifuri would succeed the Ariki Tafua. When the Ariki Tafua was very ill during my stay, I asked the Mission leader who would be chief if the old man died. He replied, "We do not know, but we think it will be Pa Rangifuri." This prediction was in fact borne out. In 1952 I learned that Pa Rangifuri had, in fact, succeeded his father, had died in his turn, and had been succeeded by his own sole remaining son. Similarly, in 1952 it was perfectly clear that all Tikopia expected and indeed desired Pa Fenuatara to succeed his father, the Ariki Kafika.[11] When there is no such obvious heir or when the chief's eldest son is still a child, the system of election by the outside group becomes more than formal. The decision then appears to lie in their hands—literally—as to which of several possible persons shall be chosen. In this case their decision removes from the people of the clan the necessity of making what might be a distinctly invidious choice. Alternatively, it removes the possibility of internal disunion within the clan before arriving at a decision. Disagreement and lack of harmony, if there be any, are transferred outside the clan, where there is probably less tendency for permanent resentment to operate and more scope for salving wounded feelings.

The interest of the clan itself may come to expression in one way, when the wishes of a chief as to the succession may be expressed during his lifetime. The Ariki Tafua Pukenga, who had been chief before the Ariki I knew in 1929, had been selected mainly as a stopgap, since the son of the preceding chief, Fokimainiteni, was still young. Before the death of Pukenga there had been some talk of taking his son, Pa Fenutapu, to succeed him, but to this the old man objected. He urged that his son should be "given a breathing space," that is, that he should be allowed to remain a commoner in order that he might serve as an executive officer *(maru)* to the descendant in the direct line. Later he might be elected if circumstances pointed that way. In fact, the son of Fokimainiteni was elected and Pa Fenutapu and his descendants "fell to the rear." By 1929 they were practically out of the chiefly class and by 1952 they were completely out of the line of succession, though still important people.

It is not possible to decide in all cases what degree of certainty has in fact been present in the apparently free elective choice. The fact that elections did not take place at random is shown by the case of the Ariki Kafika who hid himself, obviously with the idea that he would be called upon. Moreover, the whole history of succession in Tikopia bears with it the presumption that a mature eldest son of a chief is most likely to be chosen. But the issue does not seem to be quite automatic. When the Ariki Taumako whom I knew in 1929 had been elected, the Ariki Tafua was not present. He came later on the scene and it was said became very angry that the issue had been decided. It was held that he had wished that Pae Avakofe, younger brother of the deceased chief, should be taken. It is recorded that he uttered a series of whoops to express his exasperation at having been forestalled. But it was too late. Tikopia custom is definite that once the formal elevation has taken place the succession is irrevocably accomplished. To give effect to any view or to assert any personal interference, it is essential to arrive soon after the death of the former ruler. Yet in the complex workings of Tikopia politics, the action of the Ariki Tafua may not have been a genuine protest. Pae Avakofe was the most respected and influential man in Tikopia. Rather earlier Pa Veterei, the eldest son of Pae Avakofe, had been noted for his physical strength and great influence throughout the land. It was alleged that he had allowed it to be known that he should be taken as the next Ariki Taumako. Actually, so I was told, there was a misconception here. The chiefly family of Kafika, talking together one day privately in their house Mapusanga, had agreed to take the son of the old chief—the man actually chosen later by the Ariki Kafika. But in order to placate Pa Veterei, who it was thought might otherwise have felt aggrieved, it was agreed also by the Kafika people to make some show of gripping him, though not in fact actually to raise him aloft. This was "to make his face good" *(fakamatamata laui).* In typical Tikopia fashion, news of this decision reached the old Ariki Taumako through one of his daughters in a garbled version—that the Kafika folk were planning to make Pa Veterei chief. The old man was angry. He said, "Will they allow my son to sit while they take someone from the rear?" —meaning will they neglect the son in favour of the junior branch. Whereupon, it is said, he appealed to his gods and caused Pa Veterei to be poisoned at sea by eating *sumu*, a species of fish, so that he died. This was one *post hoc* explanation of the death of this man; it was given me in 1929 by Pae Sao, a prominent ritual elder. This incident indicates how the Tikopia recognize the possibility of a powerful man of rank aspiring to the chieftainship, although not the most direct heir. Pa Veterei was probably innocent of political ambition. But whether or not he had designs on the chieftainship, popular opinion credited him with some personal interest in the succession. At the time of the death of the Ariki Taumako Pae Avakofe might have been thought to have had some thoughts of the succession. The need for salving wounded feelings is well recognized by the Tikopia. Some concession is often made by a feint. The action of gripping a person as if to elevate him implies that though he just missed selection he is of such great importance that his claims are very seriously considered. Hence, though he may be disappointed, he need not be affronted. Now it is possible that the action of the Ariki Tafua in whooping when he found that he had been forestalled and that Pae Avakofe had not been elected may have been of this feint type. The *fait accompli* might actually have suited him, but his protest was a formal compliment to Pae Avakofe, perhaps still grudging his son's death and still acknowledged to be the most powerful man in Tikopia apart from the chiefs.

Actual competition for the chieftainship is almost unknown. It seems to be possible for a man to indicate privately that he would like to be considered. But a powerful factor operating against any very active move by a candidate is the fear of incurring public reprobation and of prejudicing the chances of his election thereby. I have on record only one instance of such competition—for the chieftainship of Taumako five generations ago. In 1929 the Ariki Tafua told me how Pu Veterei, the chief of the clan a century before, had been lost at sea. His son Pakimoana was still a child, so young that he had not yet donned a waist-cloth—that would be under about ten years of age. Pu Nukuraro, a strong man of Kafika clan, when the news of the death came, took the child and put round his waist the *riri*, the ceremonial bark-cloth which a chief wears on ritual occasions and with which he is invested on his election. He then called out to the assembled people, "There is your chief." But Pu Kavasa, a man of the chiefly house of Taumako though not in the direct line, had already put a new waist-cloth on himself as a sign that he had nominated himself as chief. When he heard the announcement he replied propitiatingly, "I shall sit like this in a dwelling of chiefs, to eat in advance some food for myself; when I die then your offspring shall be lifted into the dwelling place." In other words, he was rather optimistically offering himself as a stopgap, pleading in effect for a concession, a kind of notional regency. But he was rudely pushed aside by Pu Nukuraro and the child was accepted as chief.

As competition for the chieftainship is almost unknown, so also is effective refusal of the honour. I have only one case recorded. When Fakatonuara, the Ariki Taumako five generations ago, died, his son Vakasaua did not wish to succeed and advised that the ritual necklet, which is the symbol of chieftainship, be offered to his father's brother. "Give it to be hung upon him," he said. It was suggested to me that times were then troublous and that he probably felt that he was not strong enough to assume the burdens of office. It is clear then that as far as personal succession goes, a man can refuse election but not secure it.

The descendants of Vakasaua, though senior in kinship to the Taumako chiefly line, from then on counted as inferior in rank. They formed the lineage of Maneve or Resiake. Such a superseded branch did not retain any ritual primacy. They worshipped their own ancestors, but the chief performed the major lineage and clan rituals.

What are the reasons which influence the people who make the selection? Most general seems to be satisfaction in the exercise of power and of making decisions. In the different generations strong men seem to have taken part in more than one election. For example, Pu Nukuraro, who selected the Taumako chief, was also said to have been responsible for the election of Tereiteata, a chief of Tafua. Linked with this is satisfaction in taking the public credit for being responsible for making a chief. The proprietary words of the Arika Kafika quoted earlier illustrate this. But in addition there may be other factors of personal interest. There is no specifically recognized bond of any formal character between the new chief and the people who have elected him. He does not thank them in any way, acknowledge their service by gifts, nor does there seem to be any permanent tie of sentiment between them of the order of bond friendship. But in particular cases it is possible for some benefits to be secured, taking advantage of the kinship structure. The Ariki Tafua in 1929 made the significant statement to me that people desire to get a maternal nephew made chief. "They strive that the *tama tapu* (sister's son) may be lifted, they pull him up; because the dwelling place becomes powerful." He did not specify exactly in what respect, but from the general pattern of the relationship it is clear that possibilities of increased prestige, of influencing the chief's decisions and even of some economic advantage, may be involved. Apart from this, traditionally there was a gain in the religious sphere in that the name of the chief, after his death, could be invoked in the *kava* of his mother's people. This was not to the Tikopia an illusory advantage.

But this choice of a chief on the basis of the personal advantage of the selectors must be subordinated to other factors. In selecting the Ariki Taumako of 1929, for instance, the Ariki Kafika did not choose a maternal nephew of his own but of Tafua, and the Ariki Tafua, in wishing to elect Pae Avakofe, was sponsoring a nephew of Rarovi lineage, of Kafika. On the basis of personal advantage it would have seemed to be more in the interest of the Ariki Kafika to sponsor Pae Avakofe who was married to a woman of his own lineage, since he would thus secure as chief a brother-in-law as well as a man who was a *tama tapu* of the lineage of his clan. Moreover, the Kafika lineage would have been the "mother's brothers" of the son of Pae Avakofe if he in turn succeeded. The choice of Pa Veterei by the Kafika house would have fulfilled this condition—but as mentioned earlier he was rejected by them.

The other factors of greater weight are the personal qualifications of the candidate and in particular their specific status in terms of seniority in the lineage. As discussed earlier, no member of a commoner lineage, however high be his rank, can become a chief. Again, the Tikopia principle is that if the ancestor from whom a collateral member of the chiefly house traces his descent was never himself a chief, then the eligibility of this collateral member is very greatly decreased. He is "cast to one side" as the Tikopia say. The principle of legitimacy is clearly that of primogeniture or the nearest substitute.

When the issue of succession is so closely defined by princple, why then is it not assumed as automatic rather than taking the nominal form of selection from a body of candidates? Considering the formal character and high degree of integration of the religious structure of the Tikopia community, it would be plausible to think that on the death of one chief another would automatically succeed him by religious rule. The apparent freedom of the system of selection requires for its interpretation some further consideration of the relations between the chief and the people of the clan whom he represents, and of the Tikopia community as a whole.

The Tikopia system of social control is expressed at one level in terms of the individual fiat of the chief, and there is no co-ordinating central authority to resolve possible conflicts between the chief and his followers —or indeed between chiefs themselves. In practice, however, the actions of a chief are in fact restrained by those of other people of rank both within and without his clan; they express by their behaviour a general body of opinion. This practical control of a chief's idiosyncrasies appears to be reflected in the means whereby his power is conferred upon him. He does not succeed automatically by divine right. If he did, it might be more difficult to check any assertion of his individual attitudes. But he is elected, and not even by his own clan. He receives the mandate of a chieftainship, he cannot claim it. There is then some case for the control of the chief by people even outside his clan. I do not mean to say that the situation is viewed by the Tikopia very consciously and in a sophisticated way from this sociological angle. But blunt statements that "a chief is made by the body of the land"—as the Ariki Tafua said to me in 1929—express the essence of this view. Pa Maneve in 1952 said to me, "An expression of opinion from of old, from the gods, is that the chief was taken by the body of the land to watch over the body of the land. If a man is hungry, the chief feeds him. If a man is evil, the chief will speak to him. Whatever may be wrong with the land, the chief will speak of it that the land may be good."

In the Tikopia system, election of the chief is by proclamation and public acclaim, not by any process of choice by voting. The system allows room for a certain amount of power politics, for the operation of factional interests. These assert themselves not so much perhaps in the struggle to raise competing candidates to the chieftainship as in some competitive urgency to reach the scene first and have the credit of elevating the obvious candidate. The occasional incidence of debatable cases when the succession is not clear serves to re-enforce the general principle that election as chief is dependent upon the will of the people and not upon an automatic right.

I conclude by a few observations on the effects of the election upon the man mainly involved. The election of a man as chief means an abrupt change in his social condition. He has been a "common man" until now. At one stroke as an *ariki* he is invested with a new set of privileges and becomes responsible for a complex series of ritual duties. It is not possible for me to describe in detail how such a man behaves upon this lightning assumption of power, since I saw no election, but one may assume that the embarrassment which he must feel is mitigated to some extent by a useful mechanism. This is the conventional practice of the other chiefs of taking him aside and giving him instruction in ritual matters and sometimes also private advice. This coaching in new duties is not automatic and is never extensive. But on his election, other reigning chiefs regard it as part of their responsibility to see that the newcomer to their ranks is versed in the ceremonial of his clan. According to tradition, they gather together and question him about his *kava*—not as an examination to put him to the proof, but in order to assist him if his knowledge is faulty. This is known as *te fuatanga o paito ariki* (the dirge of chiefly lineages), I was told by the Ariki Kafika in 1929. The separation of the new chief from his former associates is helped by certain other mechanisms. The change in his status is symbolized linguistically. He at once assumes a new title, that of the leader of his clan; he drops his former house name and takes that of the clan as a whole. Thus, he who was once Pa Teve became Pa Kafika. He who was Pa Rangifuri became Pa Tafua. He who was Pa Raniniu became Pa Taumako. Such a new name may well help in the creation of a new social personality. In it, too, is implicit the idea that the chief is the head or father of his clan since he bears the collective name as part of his title. In kinship, too, some change occurs. The chief tends to be called "father" more widely than heretofore, and frequently the kinship term is qualified as "chiefly father." For instance, in 1929 I heard the eldest son of the Ariki Taumako, speaking of the Ariki Kafika, say "Chiefly father is right" *(e tonu e pa ariki).* Such an expression conforms to the ordinary usages of kinship and still preserves something of the special dignity of the chief. The series of personal taboos involving a bodily segregation of the chief from commoners and respect behaviour by them towards him must stand also to assist the chief in adapting himself to his changed position.

Moreover, the transition cannot be always unexpected. Granted that no man has absolute certainty of succession, but a chief's eldest son if mature may be reasonably sure of it. When such a man is obviously in the line of succession, then his father and other men usually instruct him in the details of chiefly behaviour and especially in the lore of the gods; ritual, formulae and mythology. Moreover, he will have been trained in the exercise of responsibility and in the recognition that a chief has obligations as well as privileges.

Now that after 1956 all the chiefs of Tikopia have become Christians, they are no longer able or necessary to carry on the performance of the traditional religion and take responsibility actively for the welfare of the land. But the Tikopia chief appears still to be a cultural symbol in general to his people and to have a primary responsibility for social order. The principles of succession to this office will presumably, therefore, remain of significance for a long time to come.

A problem of some delicacy may arise if the chiefs are made instruments of administration by the British Solomon Islands Protectorate Government. In such case the administrative requirements of efficiency might seem to point to the advisability of succession of a man as chief who would not necessarily be chosen by the traditional process of election. It is difficult to predict the outcome of such a situation. But a discreet and private sounding out of local opinion, especially among the other chiefs, would seem prudent at an early stage if the government interest in the succession were strong. In general the respect which the chiefs show to public opinion might well inhibit them from acting as very effective innovators of policy on behalf of the government, if any procedure of "indirect rule" were adopted. On the other hand, deference of the people to chiefly authority might give a council of chiefs an even greater power than at present.[12]

NOTES

1. For initial facilities in the preparation of this paper I am much indebted to use of part of a personal research grant from the Behavioral Sciences Division of the Ford Foundation. In preparation of the final version I have been much helped by the facilities available to me as a Fellow in 1958–59 of the Center for Advanced Study in the Behavioral Sciences, Stanford, and by discussion with my colleagues there.

2. See *We, The Tikopia,* pp. 173–360; *Primitive Polynesian Economy,* p. 219.

3. See *We, The Tikopia,* Genealogy I, p. 347. *History and Traditions in Tikopia.*

4. Raymond Firth, "Some Principles of Social Organization," *Journal Royal Anthropological Institute,* Vol. LXXXV, 1955, pp. 8–10.

5. Cf. *Social Change in Tikopia,* pp. 311–313.

6. The title of *Ariki Fafine* (Female Chief) conferred sometimes upon the senior daughter in the chiefly house of Kafika was a token of ritual status with certain privileges and functions attached, but in no way comparable with the status and functions of the clan Ariki.

7. *Primitive Polynesian Economy,* p. 190, indicates the economic role of such a potential heir.

8. See *Social Change in Tikopia,* pp. 280–283.

9. Lack of any heir designated during the lifetime of a chief is not uncommon in Polynesia (e.g., in succession to *matai* titles in Samoa). But the election of a leader of one group by leaders of *another* group seems uncommon. The closest analogy to the practice of Tikopia appears to be in Rarotonga where traditionally F. J. Moss has reported. "The *ariki* is supreme, but largely controlled by the *Mataiapos* (or nobles). The new *ariki* is named by the *arikis* of the other tribes from the *ariki* family of the deceased's tribe. But the confirmation depends on the *Mataiapos,* as the installation rests with them." (*Journal Polynesian Society,* Vol. III, p. 24). E. Beaglehole cites also from Moss, "the bitter dispute among the five prinicipal chiefs of Rarotonga over the right of one of them personally to appoint before her death an adopted son as her successor. The remaining chiefs refused to have what they called 'a cockroach crawling on their mat.'" (*Social Change in the South Pacific,* 1957, p. 115). He also remarks upon the power of chiefs of *Mataiapo* status to elect and control to a large extent the supreme

chief of the district in which the *Mataiapo* held land (*ibid.*, p. 169). The system of election is thus still not quite clear from the literature.

10. Compare my "Authority and Public Opinion in Tikopia" in *Social Structure*, ed. Meyer Fortes, pp. 185–187.

11. I am not sure if this happened when the Ariki Kafika died in 1955 since Pa Fenuatara appears to have died about the same time. Pa Fenuatara's eldest son, Rakeivave (Pa Farikitonga) succeeded very shortly after.

12. Cf. *Social Change in Tikopia*, p. 297.

12

MAN AND SUPERNATURALS ON BELLONA ISLAND

Torben Monberg

This paper presents a brief analysis of the pre-Christian religious concepts on Bellona Island, a Polynesian outlier in the British Solomon Islands. (The data for this study were collected on Bellona during field work in 1958–1959, 1962, and 1963.) The selection is concerned only with the relation of religious concepts to the social organization of the island and to the interaction of man with his natural environment, but not with the actual religious activities (rites, etc.) of the Bellonese.

On pre-Christian Bellona (conversion took place in 1938), the beliefs concerning a host of supernatural beings were an important part of an ordered and meaningful system, which in its totality formed the individual's conception of the world he lived in, and these beliefs were closely integrated with the system of social activities.

For analytical purposes, however, a distinction between concepts and social activities seems useful. Geertz has advocated the view that anthropologists might "attempt to distinguish analytically between the cultural and social aspects of human life, and to treat them as independently variable yet mutually interdependent factors" (1957:33). He uses the term *cultural aspects* for what we may call the ordered and meaningful conception of the world, and he has in a convincing way shown the advantages of this distinction in attempts to analyze social and cultural processes.

In this paper we shall summarize the Bellonese views of supernaturals, and we shall briefly consider how these beings were integrated in the Bellonese world view and how they were related to the system of social activities.

Data concerning supernaturals are summarized in a chart (Figure 1), which gives the outlines of these beliefs. The formulation and classification

Reproduced by permission of the National Museum of Denmark from Torben Monberg, *The Religion of Bellona Island: A Study of the Place of Beliefs and Rites in the Social Life of Pre-Christian Bellona.* Language and Culture of Rennell and Bellona Islands, Vol. II, Part 1: The Concepts of Supernaturals (Copenhagen, 1966, Chap. 11). Revised by the author for this publication.

FIGURE 1. THE BELLONESE SUPERNATURALS.

	Supernaturals Worshipped			*Supernaturals Not Worshipped*			
	Gods		*Ancestors*	*Ancestors*	*Others*		*Gods*
General Terms	***'atua ngangi*** Sky gods	*ngasuenga* District gods	*sa'amaatu'a* Worshipped ancestors	*pengea maangi* Annihilated ancestors	*kakai* Culture heroes	*hiti* Aborigines of Rennell & Bellona	*'apai* Non-worshipped gods
Genealogical Position	At the apex of gods' genealogy	Descendants of sky gods	Ancestors of present-day Bellonese; not related to other supernaturals	Ancestors of present-day Bellonese; not related to other supernaturals	Not related to men or other supernaturals	Not related to men or other supernaturals	Most of them not related to other supernaturals
Homes	Manukatu'u beyond the eastern horizon	Nukuahea beyond the eastern horizon (Mungingangi beyond the western horizon)	In the abodes of the worshipped gods; in graves at their original homesteads	In the underworld, but only as refuse	Formerly in unknown lands and on Rennell and Bellona, but do not exist now	In the bush and at the coast	In the sky, the underground, the bush, and the ocean south of Bellona
Personal Characteristics	Anthtropomorphic, anthroposocial, and anthropopsychic. Invisible to humans except when embodied in animals, mediums, or sacred objects: Behave contrary to social norms of the Bellonese	Behave according to social norms of the Bellonese		Refuse; non-existing	Anthropomorphic, but not anthroposocial or anthropopsychic; communication with man impossible	Anthropomorphic, anthropopsychic, anthroposocial	Anthropomorphic, anthropopsychic, anthroposocial

Places of Contact with Humans							
Ritually	Mostly in temples and in the ritual grounds of home-steads	Mostly in houses and in the ritual grounds of temples	At graves, in living houses, and in the ritual grounds of temples	None	None		None
Casually	Anywhere	Anywhere	Anywhere	None	None	In the bush and at the coast	Anywhere
Types of Contact with Humans	Rituals; possessing people thus creating madness; fearsome, cannibalistic (eating people's life-princi-ples); donators of fertility of gardens, fish, castaway canoes; embodied in animals and sacred objects	Rituals; possessing mediums; controllers and protectors of cultivated plants; donators of crops and children; protectors of man against evil; embodied in animals and sacred objects	Rituals; possessing mediums; inter-mediaries between gods and people; embodied in animals	None	None	Minor rites when fishing and hunting to avert mischief; often embodied in stones	Malignant; spoiling gardens and houses; creating sickness or death; possessing people thus creating madness
General Characteristics	Controllers of the island and of storms, thunder, and other natural phenomena; closely connected with the nonsocial environment	Controllers of humans and of cultivation of plants; protectors of specific patrilineal descent groups; closely connected with social behavior	Protectors and helpers of man, especially of mem-bers of those patri-lineal descent groups of which they are con-sidered originators	None	Characters in oral traditions only; creators of various aspects of life; models for certain moral values	Creators of various aspects of culture and of sites in landscape; timid; small people with long hair	Evil gods whose acts could only be averted through the assistance of worshipped gods; some *'apai* were considered helpers of the sky gods

are to some extent ours. (Needless to say, the Bellonese themselves did not explain their deities as anthropomorphic, anthroposocial, or anthropopsychic. These terms are our translations of their beliefs.) The chart presents only those characteristics of the supernaturals which were manifestly expressed by the Bellonese themselves.

We have endeavored elsewhere [in *The Religion of Bellona Island*] to show that the beliefs in supernaturals also had latent effects. They were important as a means for the individual to adjust himself to the ecological situation and to the present social order. It was a system which could be operated so as to facilitate the individual's adaptation to his surroundings, and to some extent it also supplied a principle for the organization of the entire society.

Relations to Nature

Let us, with this in mind, briefly consider the world from the point of view of the Bellonese individual and attempt a translation of how he structuralized his world and how these structures were utilized by him.

The Bellonese lived in a fairly static ecological milieu. He did not live in lands with extreme variations in nature and climate. His world was the two islands, Rennell and Bellona. There he did not experience extreme seasonal changes, but lived in a fairly well-balanced world where food was only rarely scarce and where gardens yielded a rich crop to anyone who knew how to cultivate them properly; this was supplemented by a rich harvest from the seas, or less abundant harvesting of wild plants. Yet disaster could strike. Hurricanes, thunderstorms with violent downpours, or insects might suddenly, and at unpredictable times, destroy crops and cause a shortage of food on the island. Also the vast ocean had its dangers. To be caught in a storm at sea usually meant disaster. The Bellonese canoes were frail and could hardly withstand powerful attacks from the huge waves of the Pacific.

The Bellonese world was filled with forces much stronger than those of man. These forces were at the same time a blessing and a danger. They provided fertility but they also caused death. They were the sources of food, but also of the violent storms that might destroy the crops or prevent fishing trips.

The belief in sky gods supplied an organizing principle for those powers of the universe which were beyond man's direct control. Empirically, these powers were in many ways non-human; they appeared to be strong and strange, and strength and strangeness were essential characteristics of their controllers, the sky gods. Unlike that of man, the kinship system of these gods was vague, and their behavior was inverted human behavior. They lived in incestuous marriages and they were inclined towards cannibalism. Forces controlling man's non-human surroundings had qualities different from those of man. Yet in order that man could communicate with them, they must be anthropomorphic, anthroposocial, and anthropopsychic. And communication was essential.

In order to induce these forces to provide food and security, man had to perform transactions with them. Just as social relations were enforced in the social universe by man's transactions with his fellow man, universal relations were secured by transactions with the powers controlling nature's forces. Communication with natural forces was possible only if the natural forces resembled man. The sky gods had this likeness, communication was possible, and took place in the rituals.

Such dealings with the supernaturals might succeed or fail. The sky gods might present their human counterparts with rich crops and fishing luck. They might also make the seas calm and stop storms and heavy rainfall. They might bring success in fights by assisting in killing enemies while the gods' worshippers remained unharmed. All this they would do if they were presented with ample offerings and if taboos were not violated.

But even if man kept the taboos and presented the sky gods with elaborate offerings, he might be caught by disaster. In life there were misfortunes which could not be avoided by offerings to the gods. Even the gardens of a faithful worshipper might be spoiled by attacks by insects, the worshipper might die in fights, and even the priest-chief might become sick and die. Such misfortunes which did not seem to have their roots in a breach of religious or other taboos, or in negligence in performing rituals, might be explained as caused by the non-worshipped deities, the *'apai*. These deities, who lived outside the social order in the bush and at the coast, and with little or no kin, only brought harm to humans. They could not be appeased by direct appeals (prayers and rituals), but at times could be reached by appeals to the sky gods. The beliefs in these *'apai* seem to be the Bellonese channelization and rationalization of inevitable and otherwise inexplicable misfortunes which always threatened man's life.

Social Relations

Supernatural assistance was needed not only in man's confrontation with the powers of nature, but also with his fellow men. Although often fraught with conflicts and strain, social interaction was perhaps considered less dangerous than the relations to the immense forces of nature. Social relations were of an entirely different order, and so were the supernatural powers connected with this aspect of life. The district gods were the social gods of Bellona. Unlike the sky gods they provided man with offspring in order that life might be perpetuated, they protected him against the dangers of nature, disease, accidents, and death, and against his enemies. They acted as intermediaries between man and the sky gods, and they convened messages from the sphere of deities through mediums. Their close relations to the social life of man was apparently accentuated by their alleged similarity to humans. They led a social life, and the great district god, Tehu'aingabenga, was married to a semihuman girl, of whom the remaining district deities were descendants. They were instituted by ancestors of different patrilineal descent groups, whose protectors they were. This seems to indicate that the beliefs concerning these deities to some extent served as a symbolic charter for the social relations of the Bellonese, especially in that they formed a conceptual basis for the performance of transactions with the supernatural powers connected with specific social groups. Offerings were presented to certain deities, who were obliged to present goods and services in return. Once given to the gods, the offerings became penetrated by their sacredness and they thus achieved an extraordinary economic value. When redistributed among the participants in the ritual, one phase of economic exchange was carried out. The web of transactions between god, man, and fellow man initiated and confirmed social relations, and the transactions could be performed so as to meet the demands for initiation and confirmation of a variety of such relations. In smaller household rituals, with only few participants, only a limited number of district deities were invoked and presented with offerings. On more formal occasions such as the important feasts in which a man distributed the entire harvest of the year, a whole range of district gods were assumed to be present and to receive portions of the harvest. These portions were then redistributed among members of a large number of lineages who were thus tied together in a network of ritually sanctioned economic obligations.

According to Bellonese traditions, the beliefs in district deities were of a dynamic nature. The number of gods increased with the furcation of the society into more and more patrilineal descent groups. It would, therefore, seem unjust to claim that the ritual transactions with these deities latently resulted in the preservation of an existing social order.

In this connection it might be worthwhile to consider once again the difference between sky gods and district gods. The sky gods constituted a fairly static group of supernaturals. The Bellonese did not institute new gods of this group after they had been invoked by the first immigrants during their voyage to Rennell and Bellona. The sky gods were the representatives of the ecological milieu of the Bellonese. This milieu was static; no great changes took place in the natural surroundings and the supernaturals controlling these powers were not subject to changes either. Transactions with these forces were uniform no matter which social group one belonged to. Not so the district deities. This group of gods was connected with society and its organization. When this organization changed, the system of transactions between social groups changed too, and the supernatural forces involved in this system necessarily changed in step with it.

Ancestors

Ancestors were divided into two groups, namely, those believed to have been annihiliated by an act of the deities or by the deities through the agency of humans, and those serving as *sa'amaatu'a.* The *sa'amaatu'a* (worshipped ancestors) acted as intermediaries between gods and humans. They had their homes in the graves of the homesteads and traveled to the homes of the gods to convey the wishes for children, health, fertility, and good fortune for their patrilineal descendants. In this way they bridged the gap between the sacred gods and the human world. Their degree of sacredness was believed to be between that of the gods and the profane human being. An analysis of which ancestors were considered important as protractors and messengers shows that the founders of particular patrilineal descent groups or other prominent members *(hakahua)* of these groups were in the focus of attention, while the rest was left to oblivion. We have elsewhere [in *The Religion of Bellona Island*] endeavored to show that the belief in ancestors latently supplied a conceptual principle for the maintenance of the unity of the patrilineal descent group, and also for economic transactions which might initiate or perpetuate relations of unity or disunity with other lineages.

Origins and Explanations

The beliefs in supernaturals not only provided the Bellonese with a conceptual charter for his transactions with the surrounding world, but to some extent also with a set of explanations of how the world came to be as it is.

The culture heroes *(kakai)* were believed to have been the creators of various aspects of life. The creation had long been completed. Death had come into this world, body members of humans were pliant, women had their private parts, food plants grew in the gardens, there were sharks on the reef, and coconuts filled with water in the trees. The Bellonese said that the culture heroes were "merely something in the stories," but the beliefs in the former existence of such beings seem to have provided the Bellonese with an explanation of the origin of important aspects of Bellonese life.

They did not serve as a complete charter, however. Many aspects were left unexplained. This is understandable because the Bellonese had no tradition of completeness. They did not share the Euro-american tradition that everything must be explained in detail. Every plant or star need not be named, not every god needed a father and a mother. Some aspects of life and culture, the circulation of blood, the nature of gravity, or grammar, did not need an explanation at all. Thus there was no complete theory of evolution, and there was only little interest in how this world had come to be as it was.

The *hiti* were believed to constitute the original population on Bellona. Like the culture heroes, the *hiti* were creators and teachers, and like the non-worshipped gods they served as explanation for mysterious and otherwise inexplicable sounds in the bush and of bad luck in fishing and hunting coconut crabs or flying foxes, but they were mainly talked of as characters in the stories about the old days.

It will be obvious that our analysis has been far from exhaustive. We have endeavored to point out some of the correlates between Bellonese social organization and religious beliefs. The fact that particular weight has been placed on this aspect of Bellonese religion does not indicate an intention to deny the extreme significance of other elements such as the emotional and aesthetic values of religious beliefs. An analysis of such aspects, however, lies outside the aim of this study.

Transactions

For an evaluation of religious beliefs and their relations to the social activities on Bellona, it may be of particular importance to consider in more detail the relations of humans to those supernaturals who were worshipped.

During recent years a number of particularly promising models for the study of human behavior have been suggested. Homans (1958) has proposed a refinement of the old theory of social behavior as an exchange of goods, material and non-material. (Later, in 1961, Homans elaborated this view.) As early as 1925, Mauss worked along similar lines. Barth (1966) has drawn attention to the analytical importance of concentrating our interests on the processes of transaction in interpersonal relations, and he has shown that it may thereby be possible to create logically consistent models of observable logical processes according to the rules of strategy. In two remarkable essays, Stanner (1958 and 1959) has applied a similar model to the study of religion. He sees sacrifice as a gainful interaction between men and their divinities. Stanner rightly prefers to talk of transactions rather than of interactions because it "compels one to deal at all times with what I have called the natural triad of person-object-person." Stanner distinguishes transitive (two-sided) and intransitive (one-sided and symbolical) transactions and he places the religious sacrifice in the latter category: "Where activities are made up of transitive operations human intentions are actually transferred, and can be shown to be transferred, to the objects of the activities. The activities we call technical are functional because the operations are transitive. We plant crops to grow food: to eat the yield is the proof and demonstration of transitivity. But there are innumerable objects of life—among them sometimes the most longed-for and highly-prized—of which no proof or demonstration of the outcome of our best efforts is, or seems, possible. If we pursue such objects then we have to proceed in hope, belief, or faith" (1959:124–25). A distinction between transitive and intransitive transactions may have its merits on the analytical level. It is, however, important to bear in mind that the duplicity is anthropological ethnocentrism. The Bellonese of course viewed ritual transactions as distinctly transitive, and it would be surprising if this is not the case in all societies. The Bellonese had had ample proof of what was gained by carrying out sacrificial transactions with the supernaturals: fish were led into nets and onto hooks by them; the deities made yam, taro, and bananas grow in the gardens; children were planted in mothers' wombs by ancestors. To the Bellonese this was definite proof that extraneous powers were at work. All these acts were beyond man's abilities, and they appeared as a result of man's transactions with supernatural forces.

In these transactions there was believed to be a gain on both sides. Even the deities gained from the rituals. In many contexts the gods expressed their extreme gratitude for offerings presented to them. This is revealed not only in rituals in which certain religious officials spoke on behalf of the gods, but also in the stories. An example may be found in the story about Ngiuika, who composes a song (Elbert and Monberg 1965: T219) to Tehainga'atua. The god becomes so grateful that he pays back with a turtle and a canoe bearing travelers from overseas (*op. cit.:* T218).

That the Bellonese themselves visualized the relationship to the deities as one of transactions is seen clearly in the general term for offerings and rituals. To make an offer to the deities is called *ngiu,* a word which means to return and to reciprocate. The term for rituals is *hengiu'akinga; he . . . 'aki* being a marker of plurality and reciprocity and *-nga* being a nominalizing suffix, the word literally means a plurality of reciprocities.

In the present paper we have not concerned ourselves with the actual operations carried on within the system of transactions, but only with two of the "corners" in Stanner's triad, namely, person-person—that is, man and supernaturals.

For an understanding of the Bellonese views of supernaturals it seems expedient to see them in the light of a model which considers human behavior processes of transactions.

For these processes to work there must be two or more poles between which the transactions can take place. The mechanisms operating at each pole must somehow be in rapport with those at the other to make communication and transactions possible. This must also be the case where the transactions take place between humans and the powers outside their society. Interaction between man and his fellow men may present fewer problems in connection with the question of personnel as such, but these problems become pertinent in an analysis of how man deals with his non-human surroundings.

The Bellonese supernaturals had so much similarity to humans that man could communicate with them and exchange with them both material and non-material goods. Yet they were different from man in that they had powers to do things which man could not do himself. The worshipped deities and the worshipped ancestors of the Bellonese were considered an *alter* being in possession of goods that could be obtained by humans through a process of exchange. These goods were life, fertility and security, and the goods given in exchange were various kinds of foods and objects which were ceremoniously presented to the supernaturals in rituals. Once presented to the deities or ancestors, and claimed their possession, they were distributed among the human participants in the ritual. Having been owned by the deities, the offerings had become sacred *(tapu);* they had been transformed by being penetrated by the supernatural powers. In Stanner's words: "The sacrifice having been received, or being supposed to have been received is returned to the offerers with its nature now transformed and as yield or fruit of sacrifice it is then shared between those who sustained the loss of the sacrificial object. That loss has been requited by a gain, but of an unlike kind, the margin of gain being a motive of the total act" (1959:109–10).

This system of reciprocity is also seen clearly in other situations. The gods would punish a man who did not present offerings or they would simply stop protecting him. This reaction had its exact counterpart in the field of daily social activities on Bellona. To forget or purposely neglect to present a guest with a share when food was distributed was a grave offense which called for retaliation. The neglected person would feel humiliated *(pa'a)* and become angry *('ika'ika),* and he would either start a fight or compensate by inviting the offender to a feast in which he purposely neglected to present him with part of the distributed food.

The relation of man to gods also in another way resembled relations between humans. It was not one of complete submission. If a deity was believed to have harmed a worshipper, counteraction might be carried out. One might either swear against the gods by calling them obscene names or in other ways humiliate them, or one might use violence. The goddess Sikingimoemoe stole Sengeika's brother, and Sengeika retaliated by destroying the sacred objects of the goddess. Gods killed P.'s wife, and P. took revenge by neglecting to present them with offerings.

Thus the supernaturals not only constituted the organizing forces for the world which surrounded the individual, but also enabled the individual to perform certain transactions with powers greater than his own and these were patterned after his own relations with his fellows. This system of transactions may in its simplest form be illustrated as [in the figure below.]

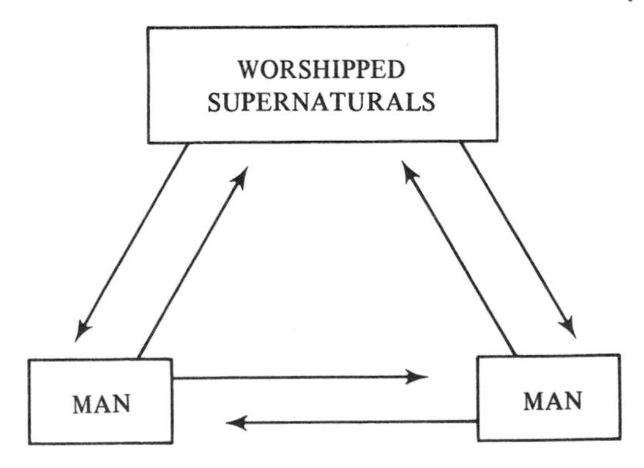

The constant flow of goods and services between these three groups bound together the persons involved in a set of mutual obligations.

At first glance one might perhaps receive the impression that the illustration merely supports the Durkheimian theory that the religion of a tribe helps hold the tribe together; but if we keep in mind that the transactions may be of various kinds, ranging from obligations to kill or harm to lavish exchanges of gifts, it will be obvious that the model does not show that the three groups involved in these mutual obligations are bound together. Moreover, the men and supernaturals symbolized by the three boxes were not constantly the same. The system might be operated according to specific situations. We have shown how the supernaturals invoked differed according to the demands of the performers of the rituals. The illustration thus does not show a fixed, static situation in which an equilibrium exists and in which the reciprocity is balanced, but a system within which transactions take place and which may be operated so as to fulfill existing needs.

In the present study we have not endeavored to analyze the operations which take place within this system. This can only be done through an analysis of the ritual acts. Our aim has been to demonstrate the contents of the boxes in the illustration and to show how the Bellonese beliefs were organized.

Reciprocity between man, gods, and ancestors was, however, only one aspect of the relationship to supernaturals. There were supernaturals with whom no transactions took place, namely the culture heroes and the *'apai.*

The culture heroes had participated in the creation of the world, but they were believed no longer to exist, and communication with them was therefore not possible. This seems to fit neatly into the Bellonese world-view. What the culture heroes had created had been given its final form, once and for all, and there seemed no reason why the Bellonese should enter into transactions with the creators now that the world existed in its final shape. The culture heroes had created things basic to human society, and they were not likely to change with changes in the social order. Man's concern was that these things and these human relations continued to exist, but this was a matter concerning the relationship between man and the deities who controlled them, not the relationship between man and culture heroes.

Nor with the *'apai* were there exchanges. The *'apai* had nothing good to offer, but only acts which tended to disrupt human life. Offerings to them were of no help. From a Bellonese point of view this seems a completely rational way of explaining unavoidable misfortunes. The Bellonese knew from experience that bad luck sometimes fell upon a man in spite of the fact that he had duly presented the gods and ancestors with offerings and avoided any breach of taboos. The world had distress and disaster built into it which could not be avoided by any transactional operations.

In the present analysis we have only sporadically discussed the relations of religious beliefs to social control.

We have seen that beliefs in supernaturals constituted a system which furnished a conceptual basis for transactions which might be carried out so as to enforce social relations.

We have also seen that certain aspects of morale were enforced by reference to the behavior of gods and to religious taboos. But religious beliefs did not furnish the Bellonese with a complete charter of norms for moral behavior, and the breaches of behavioral norms were not believed punished in a post-mortal existence.

Bellonese beliefs, however, supplied norms for a system of transactions within the three boxes shown above. Analyses of how social control was enforced on Bellona, and of how conflicts were solved, might be carried out in the light of the actual transactional operations taking place within the society, but they cannot be made on the basis of the present discussion which has only been concerned with a presentation of the supernaturals acting in this transactional play.

REFERENCES

BARTH, FREDRIK, 1966, *Models of Social Organization.* Royal Anthropological Institute Occasional Paper No. 23.

ELBERT, SAMUEL H., AND TORBEN MONBERG, 1965, *From the Two Canoes: Oral Traditions of Rennell and Bellona Islands.* Language and Culture of Rennell and Bellona Islands: Vol. I. Honolulu and Copenhagen.

GEERTZ, CLIFFORD, 1957, "Ritual and Social Change: A Javanese Example." *American Anthropologist,* 59:32–54.

GOODE, W. J., 1951, *Religion among the Primitives.* Glencoe.

HOMANS, GEORGE C., 1958, "Social Behavior as Exchange." *American Journal of Sociology,* 62:597–606.

1961, *Social Behavior: Its Elementary Forms.* London.

STANNER, W. E. H., 1958, "On the Interpretation of Cargo Cults." *Oceania,* 29:1–25.

1959, "On Aboriginal Religion." Part I. *Oceania,* 30:108–127.

13

LIFE STYLE, EDUCATION, AND ROTUMAN CHARACTER

Alan Howard

The Rotuman World View

[In this chapter we will] consider the relationships among the style of life on the island, the educational practices that nurture it, and the psychological character of the people. Let us begin with the basic premise that underlies Rotuman culture: *social life should be harmonious and free of conflict.* Achieving economic success, being able to support a family comfortably, having friends, and being free from inner conflict are also valued, but they are subordinate to this more central theme. To fail to understand this is to fail to understand Rotuman culture, for almost everything important about the islanders' style of life follows from this premise. It is toward this goal that Rotuman socialization practices are aimed and it is within this framework that they must be understood.

That does not mean, of course, that conflict is nonexistent. On such a small island, where people are in face-to-face contact year after year, conflict is inevitable, but for precisely that reason its management is given high priority in the Rotuman hierarchy of values. Covert conflict is considered less threatening than open confrontation, for the latter forces individuals to take sides, creating social schisms between groups of people and endangering the harmony of the entire community. Many Rotuman cultural practices can best be understood as a means of reducing the possibility of interpersonal conflict to a minimum, and keeping it socially contained when it does occur. Perhaps the most far-reaching example is the body of custom that governs interpersonal relations.

Interpersonal Relations

By providing clear-cut guidelines for behavior, the rules governing interpersonal relations are an aid to avoiding embarrassment and insult. With individuals of higher rank, including senior kinsmen, one is expected to be restrained and compliant. If the person is of especially high rank, a Rotuman

Reprinted with the permission of the publisher from Alan Howard, *Learning to Be Rotuman* (New York: Teachers College Press, Columbia University, 1970), Chap. 6.

is likely to restrain himself to the point of complete silence until asked for an opinion, in which case compliance is expressed by agreeing with the other's view. This has led some European officials to label the Rotumans as "yes men" who offer no ideas of their own. They fail to realize that agreement is a mark of respect rather than an expression of concurring belief. Especially when a European official expresses a strong opinion, as many are prone to do, Rotumans are reluctant to contradict him publicly; to respond with argumentation would be viewed as an attempt at humiliation. Reservations can be expressed, but they are subtle enough to be missed by persons unfamiliar with the expressive code within which they are embedded. Thus, whereas another Rotuman is able to *sense* the difference between "ritual" and personally motivated agreement, an outsider may not be able to make the necessary discrimination.

With persons of lesser rank one can be less restrained and more freely expressive. Nevertheless, Rotuman ethics require that authority be tempered by consideration. It is nearly as bad for a person of senior rank to be publicly disrespectful of someone of lesser rank as the other way around, unless the latter has committed such a blatant offense that the entire community has been offended.

The rules governing relations between persons of equivalent rank are less explicit, but there are guiding principles that are understood by everyone. Most important of these is reciprocity. In Rotuma this requires that individuals exchange goods and favors as an expression of mutual concern. The balance of exchange should never fall too heavily on one side or the other, but it should also never be equalized, for to pay off all obligations would be to eliminate the social fabric that binds a relationship together. Here again is a point of frequent misunderstanding between Westerners and people from cultures not thoroughly dominated by a market economy. For us, reciprocity implies equal payment for a gift or service. Thus we are apt to respond to a gift by quickly giving one of equivalent value; to give one of lesser value is to risk being accused of stinginess, to give one of greater value is to risk embarrassing the recipient. I believe the reason we feel most comfortable when our balance of obligations is equal is because this allows us to disengage at will. For us, reciprocity is a means to non-commitment; for Rotumans, in contrast, it is the very essence of commitment. That is why Rotumans are actually *offended* at times by Europeans who insist on responding to a gift by giving one immediately in return. It is perceived as a sign that the relationship is being rejected; the return gift changes what might have been a commitment to friendship into a contractual bargain. If one waits a while, however, tries to determine the other's needs and desires, and gives a gift or provides a service without reference to the initial overture, he is perceived as affirming the relationship.

There is a difference in the link between goods and people here that is subtle but quite profound. I would maintain that for middle-class Westerners human relationships outside the immediate family are subordinated to a concern for obtaining and accumulating goods (including money), whereas for Rotumans goods are primarily in the service of maintaining relationships between people. This difference is reflected in attitudes toward wedding gifts . . . . We evaluate wedding gifts in terms of their utility for the betrothed couple; the Rotumans give presents in order to affirm relationships. An even more subtle example is embedded in contrasting forms of hospitality. In America it is regarded as appropriate for a host to ask his guest if he would like something to drink or eat, and we expect an "honest" reply. If the person refuses, we assume that he is neither thirsty nor hungry. In Rotuma, however, such an overture by a host would almost certainly be refused, no matter how hungry or thirsty the person might be. If the host really wants to supply his guests he simply gives food and drink without asking. This contrast in custom is consistent with the difference in values. Our asking a guest implies that if we were to provide food and drink and he did not want it, then something valuable would be wasted. The Rotuman host is communicating, "Let us not worry about the food and drink, it is my relationship to you that is important. I give to you freely; if you want it, fine, if you do not, it doesn't make any difference." This, then, is the essence of Rotuman generosity. It is not giving for the sake of living up to an inner belief or to nurture a particular self-image; rather, it is a social phenomenon that is intended to establish and affirm interpersonal relationships.

More generally, the cultural approach Rotumans take toward interpersonal relations can be characterized as one of pragmatic immediacy. This contrasts with the approach of Westerners, particularly middle-class Americans, who tend to give a great deal of weight to an individual's intentions. It is as if to middle-class Americans the primary question at issue when behaving toward others is, "How do I have to act in order to be true to myself (i.e., my beliefs, my conception of correct behavior, etc.)?" The concern is one of living up to a self-imposed standard. It is true that we act contrary to our beliefs and feelings from time to time, particularly if there is a high payoff, but we have been trained to feel guilty about doing so and admire men who refuse to deviate from their ideals regardless of the social cost. The behavior of an honorable person should be consistent through time, in different places and with different people. The term "integrity," which denotes what is perhaps the most highly valued personal attribute for Americans and Europeans, implies just such consistency. Rotumans, however, tend to focus upon overt behavior, particularly upon the immediate social consequences of an act. For them the primary question might be phrased "How do I have to act in order to get along harmoniously with others?" When this is a focus of concern, an individual is best guided by being sensitive to others rather than by following internal dicta.

I should like to make it clear that I regard this distinction between middle-class American and Rotuman culture as one of emphasis rather than kind. To be sure, Americans are concerned with maintaining social harmony, just as Rotumans cannot easily be persuaded to do things they really believe to be wrong. Still, the contrast in emphasis is sufficiently pronounced to give a noticeably different flavor to human relations.

For Europeans, encounters with such people as the Rotumans are often disconcerting. They find an individual expressing one opinion at one time and the opposite opinion a short while afterward. They are offended when a Rotuman agrees to do something in what appears to be perfectly good faith, then does not do it. From our cultural viewpoint such behavior is easily interpreted as willful deceit or dishonesty, but such judgments are almost always unjustified. They merely highlight our preoccupation with internal consistency at the expense of external harmony. The apparent contradictions in Rotuman behavior dissolve as soon as one understands the situational ethic that provides the guidelines. The things it is suitable to do and say in one social circumstance may not be suitable in another, and a promise or commitment is always contingent upon subsequent events. For example, a man may agree to lend someone a horse on a certain day, but the district chief might subsequently ask for the use of the animal in order to carry foodstuff from the bush in preparation for an upcoming feast. The prospective borrower arrives only to find the horse gone. The explanation that a district chief enjoys priority, and that his request was unforeseen, is sufficient to justify the broken agreement. Furthermore, the requirement of avoiding overt conflict also makes it difficult for Rotumans to deny a request, even when they have no intention of complying with it. If one understands that it is a lesser offense to fail to abide by a promise than to reject the validity of a request, this kind of behavior makes sense. After all, to reject an overture for assistance is to deny flatly the significance of a relationship, whereas the failure to comply can generally be attributed to external conditions.

The Concept of Time

This lack of emphasis on keeping appointments and compulsiveness in adhering to verbal commitments has led some observers to suggest that Rotumans "have no sense of time," that they are only concerned with the present. Here again are the roots of a misunderstanding. We are so used to thinking of time as being divided up into units of hours, minutes, and seconds that we think of it as natural, and we organize our lives accordingly. Since these units are as applicable to the future as they are to the past, we have come to think of time blocks as precise periods that can be reserved. When we make an appointment to meet someone on Friday at ten o'clock for an hour, we are promising to set aside a particular segment. Other commitments are then allocated to the remaining segments. We also treat time as a commodity—"Time is money"—and workers are paid more by the time they put in than by any other consideration. To fail to appear busy during "work time" is to risk being accused of laziness, even if it means making work when there is none.

Rotumans think of time somewhat differently. For them time is the interval between events—for the most part, human events. The past is marked by a sequence of weddings, funerals, births, visits from relatives, etc., and the future anticipated in terms of similar events. But future events can be delayed, moved up, or even cancelled. Whereas for us future time is rigidly segmented, for Rotumans it is quite flexible. Future time can only be reserved provisionally, since unanticipated intervening events may infringe on the time period that had been set. Inherent in any Rotuman's promise to do something tomorrow is the qualification that what happens between now and then may negate the agreement. When everyone understands this there are likely to be few difficulties; only when a European administrator or businessman takes someone's word to be sacred do serious conflicts arise. The idea that time can be sold or purchased is foreign to the Rotuman viewpoint. When there is a job to do one works. That work should be scheduled by anything other than pragmatic considerations, such as the heat of the day, the tide, availability of labor, etc., makes no sense to them. From a European viewpoint Rotumans sometimes appear lazy because they do not "keep busy" when there is no compelling work to be done; to the Rotumans, Europeans appear irrational because they set aside time to work quite irrespective of the amount of work or the suitability of conditions.

One should not construe from this that Rotumans do not plan for the future. They do look ahead and lay plans. They encourage their children to get a good education so that someday they will have good jobs, and they are willing to make sacrifices toward that end. They also save money in order to make future purchases and effectively plan such events as marriage ceremonies well ahead of time. The difference is that they see the future as fluid and beyond individual control; it is therefore somewhat foolish to plan things too precisely, and wiser to wait until events unfold before committing one's energy and efforts.

Man and his Environment. Related to this orientation toward time is a view of man's relationship to his environment. We tend to see ourselves separately from our environment. For us nature presents a challenge, its forces to be controlled and harnessed to our advantage. Man's goal is to conquer nature, even if it means climbing mountains just "because they are there." Rotumans, on the other hand, see themselves as being part of their island environment. Man's goal is not to conquer nature, but to live in harmony with it. We prefer that nature react to us in accordance with our whims. The Rotumans are quite willing to be the reactors and to grant to nature her vicissitudes.

Social Behavior. Another aspect of the Rotuman world view related to their orientation toward time is the priority they give to an individual's *current* social behavior in judging him. In part this follows from the emphasis on interpersonal behavior and the situational ethic that accompanies it, just as our holding a person responsible for his cumulative behavior follows from our focus on individual motivational and belief systems. For us any offense, even if it is against another person, is basically an ethical or moral offense. A person who has committed a serious misdeed is forever suspect, for his very nature as a social being is called into question. Everything a person has done in the past is seen as useful for diagnosing his "true" motives; hence the more we know about his past the better we are able to judge him and the safer we feel about anticipating his future behavior. A "bad" person is one whose accumulated unacceptable behavior is not sufficiently balanced by proper behavior.

For the Rotumans, an act of behavior is reprehensible only if it violates the terms of a relationship. All offenses, even those that are conceived as being against God or other supernatural beings, are ultimately interpersonal offenses. Even the Rotumans' commitment to Christianity, and it is very strong, is much less an adherence to a code of morality than a personal commitment to God and his church representatives. But God, too, is bound by the Rotuman ethic of reciprocity. If he fails to live up to his part of the relationship by not tangibly rewarding individuals for their ritual investments and adherence to church rules, then deviation is justified. When the relationship is working properly, God rewards "moral" behavior with good fortune, just as Rotuman parents reward compliance with material indulgence. When a relationship has soured, for whatever reason, steps ought to be taken to restore harmony, with the burden of initiative placed on the shoulders of the offender. The restoration of harmony is served by the custom of *faksoro,* which is a form of ritual apology. No matter how egregious an offense a person may have committed against another, it is always possible to balance the slate by offering recompense and going *faksoro.* Thus the "bad" person in Rotuma is one who is too proud to apologize and make up for his offenses; when he does so the stigma is removed.

CHILD REARING—A SECOND LOOK

Let us now [examine] Rotuman child-rearing practices in the light of this world view. There are two points to keep in mind. One is that the behavior of Rotuman parents toward their children is affected by the dominant concern for minimizing social conflict; it is therefore regulated by the situational ethic that accompanies that concern. The other is that parents want their children to be good citizens of Rotuman society and educate them accordingly. The extensive indulgence, for example, with its physical displays of affection and emphasis on material giving, can now be understood as the culturally-approved strategy for establishing and affirming a relationship. One of the consequences of parental indulgence is that a child incurs an enormous social debt that his parents can use for control and influence purposes. A constant theme in Rotuman life history accounts is the report of parents who were so kind and generous that the person felt a profound obligation to comply with their wishes, even to the extent of marrying someone he did not want because his parents desired it. The power of this parental tactic was dramatized to me recently when I asked a Rotuman girl attending the University of Hawaii about the forms of punishment her parents used with her. After thinking for a few moments she declared that she could not remember being punished at all. When I inquired how her parents got her to comply with their wishes, she replied: "They were always so wonderful to me—they never denied me anything they could give. How can I do anything *but* comply with their wishes!"

One reason she could not remember being punished is probably because the main control technique, shaming by ridicule, is a somewhat disguised form of punishment. When a child does something of which his parents disapprove, they are likely to make very pointed remarks, but usually under a cloak of humor. They are therefore able to communicate to the child that his behavior is offensive without disrupting the relationship. It is significant, too, that parents are not the only ones who use shaming to control a child's actions; virtually everyone does. The child's behavior is thus shaped by an expanded social universe as contrasted with the far more focused parental shaping that is characteristic of the American middle class.

Another important characteristic of the Rotuman socialization pattern is that children are punished for the consequences of their actions rather than for committing the acts themselves. This follows from the interpersonal emphasis described above; it is not what the child *intends* that counts, but how his behavior affects others. One never hears a Rotuman parent ask a child, "Why did you do that?" The question is irrelevant, and the answer would not alter the situation. Accidental offenses are just as likely to be punished as intentional ones. Likewise, an attempt to cause harm that fails is likely to be ignored or laughed at rather than punished.

Related to this emphasis on social consequences is the timing of punishment. Rotuman children are usually punished only after the interpersonal effects of their misdeeds become apparent. They are rarely punished for an act at the point of initiation, the pattern favored by American parents. Thus we communicate to a child that certain acts, such as sexual play and the destruction of property, are inherently wrong, and punish them whenever they occur, in public or private, at their very inception. In contrast, by waiting until the social consequences of an act are realized before inaugurating punishment, the Rotuman parent communicates to his child that right and wrong are a matter of how one's behavior affects others. Since the child's behavior may be offensive only to particular categories of people and in particular circumstances, the same behavior may be punished on one occasion and ignored on the next. The net effect of these contrastive patterns is that American children, when properly socialized, learn generally to inhibit certain classes of behavior, whereas Rotuman children learn that certain acts must be inhibited in certain situations and with certain people, but that it is quite all right to exhibit the same behavior with other people in other situations.

The entire socialization pattern in Rotuma is geared toward producing a child who is sensitive to models; it should therefore not be surprising that personal demonstration is the preferred educational technique. Since children are so frequently in the company of adults while the latter are working, they have a great many opportunities to observe how essential tasks are performed. Children's efforts at imitation are encouraged with subtle praise or non-verbal expressions of approval, unless, of course, they start to "show off." If a child experiences difficulty in performing an action, an adult might physically manipulate the child's body in order to correct an error or refine a movement, but explicit verbal instruction is rarely offered and children rarely ask for it. If they do, they are likely to be told to watch a skillful adult in action.

We might reflect for a moment on the way in which this approach to education contrasts with ours. For most middle-class Americans, education is virtually synonymous with verbal instruction. This is true not only with regard to formal education, but within the confines of the household as well. As soon as a child learns to speak and understand, by far the predominant technique for teaching him is through the use of language. I have heard middle-class parents frequently express the viewpoint that you really cannot teach a child anything important until after he learns to speak. Furthermore, our emphasis is heavily upon the denotative aspects of language, i.e., the literal meaning of the words used. Thus we urge a child who relies upon expressive cues to verbalize his message, even if it is otherwise perfectly clear. As soon as the child is able, reading becomes a major source of knowledge. Reading permits the child to educate himself, and this perhaps is the ultimate educational goal in our society. At the same time, reading depersonalizes the educational process, and places an even more pronounced emphasis on the denotative aspects of language.

This difference in educational strategies is clearly related to the different functional requirements of Rotuman and American society. In Rotuma, the essential tasks a person must learn are not technically complicated, and once learned need not be continually altered. They are tasks that can be learned *in situ*, directly from a competent performer, and the skills involved can be practiced and perfected long before they are needed. For this kind of learning, demonstration by a competent model is an optimal tactic. In our technologically complex society, on the other hand, learning occupational tasks often requires a great deal of foreknowledge. Job functions frequently involve a series of operations disconnected in time and place, and efficient planning and record-keeping are required to run the large-scale organizations involved. Change rather than continuity is the rule, requiring individuals skilled in the manipulation of verbal and other symbols, so that innovative plans can be formed and evaluated without resorting to costly trial-and-error procedures. For transmitting this kind of knowledge, teaching by personal demonstration is less adequate; reliance on a highly elaborated denotative code is a virtual necessity.

A Psychological View of Rotuman Character

The socialization practices that prevail in Rotuma produce individuals who share a number of psychological traits, which can be considered the basic attributes of Rotuman "character." The premise underlying this statement is that individuals who share similar social learning histories are likely to be predisposed to respond similarly to the same social stimuli. Other social scientists have employed such constructs as "basic personality structure" and "modal personality" to summarize such commonalities, with each concept embedded in a well-defined theoretical and methodological framework. Even under the best conditions, however, descriptions of the psychological attributes of a group of people can come perilously close to the stereotypes and glib generalizations carried home by the casual traveler. To do a truly adequate job, an investigator would have to conduct extensive observation of many individuals, carefully select for examination a wide array of variables, both individual and situational, and devise reliable operational measurements. It was outside the scope of my interests to do this in Rotuma. The best I can do, therefore, is to present my subjective interpretation of what Rotumans are like as people. The strongest defense I am able to make is that by the time I left the island, the way in which they did things seemed logical and orderly to me, and I was able to anticipate with a high degree of certainty how they would respond in various situations. In short, I felt as though I understood them. Undoubtedly other observers would arrive at somewhat different characterizations. If I am biased, it is in the direction of evaluating the Rotumans favorably, for I derived so much pleasure from being with them that I have been unable to shed my devotion to the island and its inhabitants in favor of scientific objectivity.

Perhaps the trait that is most central to Rotuman character might be called "acute social sensitivity." On the one hand this sensitivity is expressed in a careful reading of other people's feelings and a constant adjustment of one's own behavior to promote interpersonal harmony; on the other hand it is reflected in personal touchiness and susceptibility to being hurt. As a consequence, Rotumans are motivated to be cautious in any interpersonal encounter with persons they do not know well. Unlike some other South Sea islanders, the Rotumans do not greet strangers with broad smiles and overwhelming cordiality. Quite the contrary—they have been described by many visitors as having a sullen disposition. I think a more correct interpretation would be that they are highly restrained until they get to know something about a person and his attitudes. By quietly observing someone for a while it is possible to get a feeling for what he is like; also by restricting one's own actions it is possible to avoid saying or doing something that might prove offensive. A sensitive person is vulnerable, hence he is unwise to lower his guard before he is sure that a person with whom he interacts is kindly disposed.

In encounters with strangers or persons of unknown disposition, Rotumans focus much more upon the expressive aspects of communication than do Europeans. Being primarily interested in whether a person is safe or not, they have learned that the best information upon which to make such a judgment is not the denotative content of messages, but upon such cues as tone of voice, facial expressions, subtle body movements, and the like. This is often confusing to the European administrator, who is focused upon what is being said rather than how it is said. He thinks a message has been understood for what he intended and is distraught when the response appears inconsistent or bizarre. He often fails to recognize the cues by which Rotumans communicate their dismay, anger, or hurt because he is only "tuned in" to the manifest content of their speech, which is limited to respectful prescriptions when one is talking to a person of higher rank. The European teachers on the island are confronted with the same problem when trying to communicate to Rotuman children within the classroom, unless they have learned to identify the system of expressive cues.

This is not to suggest that Rotumans are motivated to avoid interpersonal involvements; whereas we generally rely on internalized defense mechanisms to cope with interpersonal conflict, however, the Rotumans learn to rely on avoidance. For them the establishment of an enduring relationship depends upon continual assurances that each party will respect the other's integrity. When assurances are continually given, a relationship may develop into a profound commitment, but it still may be brittle; a single breach by one of the parties may void the previous assurances and shatter the relationship. Even marriages that have endured for many years without conflict often buckle under the weight of a single, apparently trivial, incident. My initial temptation when confronted with this evidence was to interpret it as an indication of repressed or suppressed hostility, bursting to the surface when an opportunity to express it occurs, but as I came to know the culture better I changed my mind. It is just that the cultural significance of a hostile confrontation, even a single one, is so great that it can alter the entire substance of a relationship. Once hurt, a person is reluctant to expose himself again, although if the offender formally apologizes, admitting his error and humbly asking forgiveness, the relationship may be re-established.

Given this background, it should not be surprising that the most powerfully expressed emotion is jealousy. It has its roots in the continual reassurance that is required to maintain a relationship; when a person who has been trusted appears to be favoring a commitment to someone else, not clearly entitled to preferential treatment, Rotumans feel highly threatened. Violent outbursts are quite rare among these people, but when they do occur it is usually the result of jealousy.

One effect of this acute sensitivity is to limit explorations into new behaviors. Take, for example, learning a new language. If a person makes a mistake of pronunciation while speaking English or Fijian in front of others who can speak the language, they may latch onto the error and turn it into a riproaring joke. To illustrate: If a person mispronounces a word like "calendar," by saying something like "culundah," the group may begin to call him "culundah" in mockery. Even this form of ridicule is sufficiently painful to cause most Rotumans to say things in the new language only if they are sure of themselves. The use of mockery is sufficiently institutionalized to constitute a custom, called *sapa.* A mistake or absurdity may even become classical and be transmitted through generations, being applied to the descendants of the person who made the spectacular error. The people of one district are still called "biscuit planters" in reference to a woman who, shortly after the island was discovered by the Europeans, planted some biscuits obtained in trade in order to grow her own supply.

Paradoxically, the strong sense of social awareness that characterizes Rotumans also lies behind the almost unbelievable capacity of the islanders to adapt to new social environments. I can still recall the utter amazement I experienced in seeing people I had known on Rotuma behaving in urban contexts in Fiji. They seemed like social chameleons. Within a very short period of time they had learned a whole new code of conduct and appeared to be entirely different kinds of persons. This was not only true of Rotumans coming to Fiji, but also of the majority of educated Rotumans, who were equally adept at switching when they returned to their home island.

Thus the general sensitivity of the people acts on the one hand as a force for conservatism, and on the other as a force for culture change. Any effort by a person to act in a Europeanized fashion in the company of other Rotumans is apt to be interpreted as a form of showing off and becomes the object of ridicule. I was told by some informants that there was quite a bit of resistance to the introduction of tooth brushes into Rotuma because it was felt that people using such instruments were doing so in imitation of the Europeans. The same attribute, however, leads Rotumans to be very concerned with the way in which outsiders, including Europeans, view them. They do not want to be looked upon as primitive or backward and are therefore motivated as a group to make changes that will tangibly enhance their status in the eyes of others. The vigor with which they have engaged in the Government-sponsored co-operative movement is an outstanding example of such group change. Conservatism therefore is most closely exercised over individualized changes, or changes that might affect differential status between persons, whereas cultural change is encouraged in areas that affect all of Rotuma or a substantial group within it.

The resistance to status differentiation does not mean that Rotumans are not competitive with each other. . . . [C]hildren and adolescents are highly competitive, and this motive carries on into maturity. Men strive to produce larger taro, yams, and other foodstuffs than their fellows, and women strive to make finer and more beautiful mats. What they do not do is brag about their achievements or demand recognition. Instead, to the extent that a person *is* outstanding, he is required to belittle his achievements. The excellent farmer suggests that his large crops are the result of unusually fertile soil and the excellent mat-maker asserts that her skill is no more than a gift from her teachers. Indeed, the consequence of conspicuously drawing attention to one's accomplishments would be to lose all the prestige gained by the achievement. In most areas of behavior the goal is to present oneself as competent but not outstanding. At social affairs, for instance, Rotuman women try to dress prettily, but scrupulously avoid gaudiness; a family may furnish their home comfortably, but never lavishly.

Rotuman character can therefore be characterized as being essentially "other-directed." They look for guidance from the people around them rather than from an internalized code or belief system. In the words of some theorists, they are shame-oriented rather than guilt-oriented. Indeed, the Rotumans appear to suffer very little from the pangs of conscience that make Westerners psychologically uncomfortable after having performed a socially disapproved act. This was most tangibly demonstrated to me on those Sundays when I attended the Catholic Church at Upu. On every occasion nearly the entire congregation took Communion, which presumably requires a clear conscience. This contrasts markedly with my observations in the United States, where only a small proportion of the congregation goes to the rail. In further confirmation, one of the priests, whose former parish was in New Zealand, remarked that Rotumans confessed less often than his New Zealand parishioners. They also confess to very few "trivial" sins. "When they do confess they're generally dealing with pretty big things," he remarked.

This is not to say that Rotumans exhibit no anxiety after having done something wrong. They sometimes do, but it appears that a fear of discovery lies behind it. The practical consequence of this kind of anxiety is to motivate violators to avoid blame, whereas the guilt-oriented person may feel compelled to "turn himself in" in order to alleviate the pangs of conscience. Also consistent with this distinction is a lack of motivation to inflict self-punishment to ease one's conscience, whereas guilt-oriented persons are frequently driven to do so. If a Rotuman does confess to a misdeed it is likely to be because he feels that discovery is imminent, or because he is having such bad "luck" that he feels the consequences have already been realized. Under either circumstance confession is a prelude to a request for forgiveness, which is the major technique for mitigating undesirable pragmatic consequences of an act.

The roots of this external control orientation can be traced to the way in which Rotuman parents respond to the social transgressions of their children. Since the parents themselves are not primarily concerned with "good" or "bad" acts in an abstract moral sense, but with the consequences of their children's behavior, punishment, as previously noted, is ordinarily inflicted well after the offense has been committed. The children therefore learn to associate punishment more with the punishing agent than with the act itself, and come to feel more anxiety about avoiding potentially punishing agents than about prohibited acts. Consistent with this is the lack of anxiety Rotumans express with regard to impulse control. For them the practical problem is seeking an appropriate situation in which to express their impulses rather than striving to suppress them.

For the sake of contrast, let us reflect on the treatment of auto-erotic stimulation among middle-class Americans and Rotumans. Unless I am mistaken, the American pattern is for parents to scold or punish a child as soon as they discover a child masturbating. They make such comments as, "Don't do that, it's bad (or disgusting, or sinful)," and demand of the child explicit expressions of regret. As a result the child is conditioned to be anxious and feel guilty in response to his own sexual arousals. The socialization goal implicit in this pattern is the establishment of an internally cued, generalized inhibition. The problems that arise from this type of training have to do with over-bearing guilt over unexpressed impulses, the difficulty of un-learning inhibitions at the proper time (i.e., when one marries), and the socially indiscriminate expression of impulses when controls fail. Rotuman parents, true to the situational ethic, are permissive of their children's auto-erotic activity as long as it remains out of public view. If a child should continue in the presence of visitors, however, he is likely to be reprimanded with such comments as, "Shame on you, doing that in front of everyone." With this training the child does not come to feel anxious about sexual arousal *per se*, but only about the potential consequences of sexual behavior. Thus unmarried adolescent girls fear pregnancy for its social consequences, and are reluctant to become engaged in affairs they feel may become public knowledge, but they do not appear to experience guilt over sexual involvement once these matters are settled. The main problem inherent in this socialization approach is that when external sources of control are removed (e.g., as when a girl is left alone with a seductive male), internal restraints are insufficient to suppress an act that one or both parties would rationally prefer to avoid.

The Rotumans also rely upon shame controls to restrain physical aggression within the community. The large majority of Rotumans will do almost anything to avoid a fight, although a few of the young men are known to be "hot headed" and are easily provoked. Jealousy and frustration during competitive events were the chief motivations behind the few incidents that occurred during my stay on the island, but most of them were quickly stopped by mediators. On a few occasions liquor was involved, but even under the influence of alcohol most Rotumans are strikingly unaggressive. The low tone of physical aggressiveness can be traced to the social cohesiveness of the community on the one hand and to the child-rearing pattern on the other. Parents use very little corporal punishment and are rarely severe when using it. Children are encouraged to avoid physical confrontations and are punished for fighting, particularly with neighbors, as this would create strain on inter-familial relations. From a social learning point of view, therefore, Rotuman children are presented with very few aggressive models and are not reinforced when they act aggressively.

In contrast, verbal aggression, particularly in the form of gossip, is prevalent. The acid tongues of the old women are legendary, and it is said (usually by men) that most of the trouble on Rotuma "starts over the weaving of mats," when the women get together. That people in such a community are quick to criticize one another's shortcomings should not be very surprising. Since an individual cannot enhance his own status by the display of achievement, it is tempting to find fault with others as a way of improving one's own status relative to theirs. Gossip is nevertheless an important form of social control, and because Rotumans are so sensitive it is indeed very effective in limiting deviation.

Although many Rotumans revealed what I felt to be a remarkable insight into their own individual personalities, they did not appear to be preoccupied with the processes of self-analysis and thoughtful contemplation. Until I returned to America I was unaware of just how much time and energy we devote to the analysis of our own and other people's psyche, and more generally, to a consideration of ideological concerns. It is as if we each walk around with a highly developed computer program in our heads to process the incredibly complex messages we are continually being bombarded with; in order to keep the machine running efficiently the "program" must be under constant scrutiny and continual readjustment. Our great reliance on verbalization during the socialization process provides the technical means for developing the elaborate programs we build into our children. In Rotuma there is less need for such elaborate programming. The mastery that most of the islanders come to exercise over their somewhat limited and benign environment does not require a great deal of analytical thought, or complicated and innovative planning. Life in Rotuma is not without hardship, but the customary techniques of problem solving are both universally available and efficient. This is not to imply that every act is a matter of habit or dictated by custom, or that behavior is mechanical. Rather, I am suggesting that since the complexity of problems faced by the people in Rotuma is less great, and their solvability more assured than the problems faced by urbanized peoples, complex analytical thinking is only rarely strategically required. I also do not mean to imply that Rotumans are incapable of abstract or contemplative thought—only that it is not a requirement for success within their cultural system nor is it selectively reinforced for any other reason.

The Rotuman attitude toward religion is indicative of this difference in style. Although many islanders have learned the dogma of their respective churches, they rarely become embroiled in genuine ideological discussions or arguments. Their commitment to a particular church, which may indeed be very strong in the sense that ritual is scrupulously followed, is not primarily a matter of ideological conviction. It is in the nature of an interpersonal commitment to the leaders of the church, particularly to the priests and ministers, and is subject to the same principles as any other human relationship. If church leaders are overly harsh or otherwise do things that members of the congregation construe as a breach, they may cease to practice their religion. Likewise, if other interpersonal commitments taking priority require a person to change his religion, he will readily do so. It is common practice for one partner in a mixed marriage to change to the religion of the other, with the change dependent upon whose home or village they decide to reside in. I was startled at first to find that a person who had been a model Catholic throughout his youth, upon marriage converted and became a model Wesleyan within a remarkably short time.

One of the interesting ramifications of the Rotuman socialization process is that many of the psychological conflicts engendered by our middle-class pattern are eliminated. Thus we are continually confronted with the problem of reconciling our motives and beliefs with the demands of social life. We value honesty, but how honest can one be and still get along adequately? Many young children insist that it is wrong even to tell a "white lie"—one calculated to avoid an insult or injury—but they soon learn that absolute honesty is incongruent with viable social relations. A sense of guilt, however, tends to persist. The Rotumans do not have this problem. The question of "lying" is irrelevant; it is right and proper to say appropriate things irrespective of the "truth" of the statement. Since we focus on intent, we hold a person responsible for his words as well as his deeds, and if as children we learn our cultural lesson well, we come to hold ourselves responsible for our thoughts, too. At the ultimate extreme, we even assume responsibility for our emotions! We experience guilt and anxiety when we *feel* hostile or sexually aroused, or when we fail to *feel* love for our children, grief for a deceased relative, or compassion for someone who is suffering. We surely stretch the logical extremes of rationality with such dicta as, "A mother *should* love her child." Even within our own cultural framework this is an absurdity *par excellence.* Emotions are responses; they cannot be turned on and off like a water tap. They cannot be controlled by intent. One does not always feel love for anyone. In any interpersonal relationship emotions constantly shift. Sometimes we may feel love, at other times anger or disgust, jealousy or resentment, and much of the time, no emotion at all. The notion that feelings can be made subservient to intent is as irrational as the most bizarre primitive customs recorded in the anthropological literature. It is logical only from the standpoint that it is consistent with our cultural focus. We endeavor to control our emotions as we try to control everything else. If one wants to confirm for oneself the problems this creates, all one has to do is reflect upon the response of Americans to funerals. Even if the deceased meant nothing to us we do our best to act sad because that's the way we're *supposed* to feel. For Rotumans this quandary is nonexistent. Feelings belong to the private world of the individual. A person is held no more responsible for his emotions than he is for his biochemical processes (which, of course, lie behind emotion). It is how one *acts* that counts. When a Rotuman mother acknowledges that she should love (*hanisi*) her child she is referring to affectionate, indulgent *behavior.* You can dislike someone and still have *hanisi* for him.

The behavior of Rotumans at funerals fascinated me at first. I saw people on their way to a house where the body was lying in state, and they appeared as casual and unconcerned as if going to a wedding. They were joking and engaging in light banter. Then, upon entering the house and being confronted with the corpse surrounded by his immediate bereaving family, they would burst into a fit of unrestrained crying, or even wailing, that seemed to come from the depths of their inner beings. After engaging in this display of emotional behavior for a half an hour or so, they would emerge and within a few minutes be back with their friends, again joking and otherwise showing no evidence of sadness. My first response was like that of many other Occidentals—the emotion can't be real; they have got to be putting it on. People aren't happy one moment and agonizingly sad the next, then just as happy a few moments later. But the more I thought about it the more I came to see our emotional style as strange. There is no reason why emotions should persist when the stimuli that trigger them are removed. Again, our great concern for internal consistency leads us to think it natural that such emotions as grief should persist for some time. Upon reflection, however, the Rotuman response began to appear more "natural." Their emotions were congruent with the social circumstances in which they were behaving; ours often are not. I think what happens is that these people do not feel compelled to assume an emotional state, but that they genuinely respond to the sight of the deceased and the bereaved with grief, which they freely express. When removed from this stimulus, they begin to feel such other emotions as the pleasure of being with friends, which they also freely express. When finally I was able to shed the compulsion to feel things, I experienced an enormous sense of relief and freedom—freedom from "the tyranny of the should."

Thus Rotumans did not appear to experience all those inner conflicts we associate with neurosis, but this does not mean they are free from emotional pain. It is just that the locus of torment is different. For a people as sensitive as they are, to be shamed is agonizing, and even the threat of shame can make an individual feel extremely uncomfortable. Furthermore, the Rotuman cultural option provides little insulation from external hurt, for shaming depends on what others do, whereas we are skilled at developing defenses against the outside world; instead, we are our own most ardent tormentors.

The sense of mastery that most Rotumans display within their familiar environment is reflected in an absence of a sense of impending danger . . . . For me, at least, watching a three-year-old child playing with a razor-sharp machete is an anxiety-producing experience. Yet it is a common sight in Rotuman villages and adults usually do not interfere if the child appears to be handling the instrument satisfactorily. Eight- and nine-year-old children are permitted to climb forty-foot coconut trees, which they do with ease; they also scale precipitous cliffs like mountain goats and swim in the deep sea like fishes, all without parental disapproval. Accidents do occur, of course, but they are far less frequent than one would suspect. It seems that lack of punishment for experimental behavior leads to the development of a sense of mastery and self-confidence. I came to the conclusion that American children would probably injure themselves more frequently doing these same things precisely because we communicate our own anxiety to the child and weaken his confidence in his own physical dexterity. Whereas the Rotuman parent is apt to respond to a near accident with a joke, an American parent is likely to call the child's attention to the terrible consequences that would have resulted had an accident actually occurred, thereby increasing his anxiety the next time he attempts to perform the same or a similar feat.

In marked contrast to the self-confidence displayed by Rotumans in familiar circumstances, however, is the apprehension they show when confronted with an unfamiliar challenge. In school . . . each new task tends to provoke anxiety, and if it is not readily mastered, children quickly stop trying. This reaction to frustration is indicative of a strong passivity streak, a characteristic that some European administrators have interpreted as either laziness or willful stubbornness. Such criticisms have usually followed attempts to pressure the people to do things in an unaccustomed way, but both interpretations are misleading. Rotumans are neither lazy nor stubborn when confronting problems in a familiar context, or in new circumstances in which they have a reasonable expectation of success. Indeed, they delight in displaying their competence in tasks they can perform well. When preparing a feast they work extremely diligently, and at a pace most Europeans would find exhausting. Under such circumstances they may put in extremely long hours, working around the clock. On the other hand, Rotumans do not feel *compelled* to work in order to validate their feelings of self-worth.

I think this contrast with American middle-class character can be neatly related to the difference in socialization techniques. Thus, middle-class

American parents tend to offer rewards to their children on a contingent basis—the more a child performs to his parents' satisfaction the more likely he is to be rewarded. If he fails to perform, or is inactive, rewards are diminished. He may even be punished. This tends to produce individuals who are unhappy unless they are active. Not only do we come to feel it important to work to reassure ourselves of our worth, we also feel compelled to fill our leisure time with activity in order to avoid depression. Rotuman parents, in contrast, reward children on a non-contingent basis. A child does not have to perform to be indulged, and the amount of increased reward for an outstanding performance is usually not very much. Furthermore, by being passive he reduces the possibility of offending others. Rotuman parents therefore often directly encourage their children to be passive, just as middle-class American parents do what they can to stimulate their children to action—almost any kind of action.

This contrast is clearly reflected in our respective theories of illness. Rotuman parents blame over-activity as the cause of many childhood diseases and have strongly opposed their children's participation in such vigorous sports as rugby and soccer, claiming it increases their chances of contracting tuberculosis. They also try to keep children from engaging in hard physical work for the same reason. When an individual becomes ill, he is encouraged to rest as long as possible. We reverse this prescription. Vigorous exercise is seen as the path to health, and we encourage a sick person to resume his normal activities as soon as possible.

For Rotumans, therefore, work and achievement are valued, but not because of the satisfactions provided by living up to a self-imposed standard of excellence (as is inherent in the concept of *achievement motive*). They are valued as paths to public approval. The payoff is praise or recognition, rather than a feeling of self-satisfaction. In other words, it would seem that Rotumans are motivated to optimal performance by a need for approval rather than a need for achievement. As a motivating force, the need for approval is somewhat offset, however, by a fear of disapproval, which acts as an inhibiting force in uncertain situations. This would appear to explain why Rotuman children stop trying when they encounter problems in schoolwork that they cannot readily master. From their point of view it is better not to try, and hence not to become vulnerable, than it is to try and fail. It also explains why adults prefer a passive strategy when confronted with a new situation. Rather than try out random forms of behavior by trial-and-error to discover which are acceptable and which are not, thereby risking disapproval, they prefer to wait and watch until they feel they have caught on to the game. They then proceed cautiously, encouraged by signs of acceptance and approval, discouraged and motivated to disengage by criticism or disapproval. Thus, although industriousness has its rewards, work is regarded as a necessary evil to the Rotumans—something one must do to survive. It is also a source of approval, but not a good in and of itself.

As far as values are concerned, inactivity is considered a more desirable condition than activity. A favorite way of spending leisure time is to "rest," a pastime very much in evidence on ceremonial occasions. (And remember, this is a pre-television society!) The majority of people at a wedding, for example, spend the entire day sitting in one place. They eat, talk with friends, eat some more, talk some more, and so on throughout the day. There is no felt need to organize activities or to find ways to keep the guests busy. To feed one's guests to satiation without their having to work is a satisfactory formula for a successful party.

The ability to remain inactive and unagitated is an important ingredient of a related attribute—patience. This is best illustrated by an example. One of my first encounters with Rotumans was in a back yard in Suva. The family I was visiting lived in a duplex apartment, and their neighbors owned a large dog. Several young men and women had gathered together and were playing guitars and singing Rotuman songs that I was recording, much to their pleasure. In the middle of a tune the dog began to bark. The musicians stopped playing and I was asked to shut off the recorder. The dog continued to bark for nearly ten minutes without anyone getting angry or even showing much annoyance. A few jokes were made, but that was all. No one made any effort either to pacify the animal or to threaten him. When he finally stopped of his own accord, the musicians began playing again and the recording session resumed.

To the educated Occidental, life on Rotuma might seem monotonous and dull, and there is no question that it lacks variety in comparison with an American or European city. Nevertheless, when one is involved in such a culture as this, life can be rich and fulfilling. People have time to enjoy fully the pleasures that are available; they come to care, often quite ardently, about the events that do take place—the feasts, the marriages, a visit from a relative in Fiji, or even a sojourn to the other side of the island. Leisure time is plentiful and is spent in the company of comrades and relatives. The payoff for a successful life is the sense of contentment that comes from being a member of a community in which one enjoys full acceptance.

Summary

Rotumans are a pragmatic people whose major concern is the maintenance of harmonious social relations. They are extremely sensitive to social approval and disapproval, and their behavior can best be understood as an attempt to maximize the former and minimize the latter. In those circumstances in which mastery is within reach and approval is expected, they display a remarkable competence; in other circumstances, in which success is doubtful and disapproval expected, they tend to disengage themselves.

14

THE MAKING OF A MAORI

James E. Ritchie

INTRODUCTION

Fifteen years have elapsed since research began in the Maori community on which this study focuses. The sole previous work on this group of New Zealand Maori speaks only in sketchy fashion of their social condition:

> They have also been much harassed during their residence of 250 years or so in their present location. They have camped between the devil and the deep sea. On the east they had for neighbours the fierce bushmen of the Urewera and on the other side the tribes of Taupo and Te Arawa. The Ngati Awa and Ngati Kahungungu tribes also paid them a visit occasionally and trouble was their lot (Best, 1924:118–119).

Modern times brought the Pakeha (Europeans) and have served them little better as first the militia, then traders, later foresters, and finally industry forced change deep in the heart of their social organization and culture. Yet the people of Rakau remain Maori, both in culture and in personal identity.

To explain this fact, seven students working in this community for five summers under the general direction of Ernest Beaglehole accumulated a vast collection of psychological test data and other material (Beaglehole and Ritchie, 1958). We can look back now, over a ten-year perspective, and still endorse in large measure the account of personality development which was the earliest report from the field (Ritchie, 1956). In this restatement, the earlier record has been integrated into the relevant parts of the major research report (Ritchie, 1963).

Subsequent work during the past decade has not greatly altered the facts, or sequence, of the earlier work, just as that first sketch built on and confirmed earlier work in another Maori community (Beaglehole and Beaglehole, 1946). The basic pattern of growing up in Maori communities has

Reproduced by permission of A. H. and A. W. Reed from *The Making of a Maori* (Wellington, New Zealand, 1963, Chap. 11) and of the Victoria University of Wellington Publications in Psychology from Ritchie's *Basic Personality in Rakau* (Monographs on Maori Social Life and Personality No. 1, 1962, Chap. 2). Revised by the author for this publication.

proved toughly resistant to many changes in recent New Zealand history. We now have reason to believe that the pattern is quite ancient and generally diffused through the several migrations of Polynesian culture. Just how vigorously the pattern survives, the reader must judge for himself from this account or from a published photographic survey (Westra and Ritchie, 1967), in which childhood is a dominant theme.

The Early Years

> The Maori infant and young child is petted, "spoilt", indulged and affectionately treated, its whims gratified, its needs for love and security fairly adequately fulfilled. It receives no severe toilet training. It is made to feel a welcome member of the group. Both parents and old ladies see eye to eye in this sort of treatment. Punishments and frustrations, either of a physical sort or through deprivation of love, attention, and affection are rare and exceptional. (Beaglehole and Beaglehole, 1946: 125.)

This is childhood as seen by the Beagleholes in Kowhai, and in this broad summary outline it is true almost to the word in Rakau. But there are slight differences, and it is therefore necessary to consider the earliest years, up to the age of two or thereabouts in a little more detail.

Jane Ritchie (1957) rightly began her survey of the earliest years in the life of the Maori child in Rakau with some opinions expressed by mothers which signify their prevailing attitude towards children. Mothers feel that children complete a home and a marriage. They prefer the size of family that they have, but, since they reject any form of contraception, they are forced to accept the naturalness of annual or near-annual births. It is true that the older children tire and worry them, but this is accepted as part of motherhood. They look forward to having girls to help with the housework, but males have the higher status in the community and about half the mothers said that they wanted male children. Whatever the sex, the new arrival will be cared for, coddled, and comforted by many hands, and there will be much visiting of the mother and child, much admiration and interest around the community.

A birth in Rakau is an event of some local importance. In a community where there are many children and where births occur in each family at intervals of approximately one year it is not of such special importance as a wedding or a death, but nevertheless the event is noted and discussed and efforts are made to call on the parents within the fortnight or so following the birth to admire the new baby, congratulate its parents and give a little assistance to the nursing mother. Such incidents are only of passing interest however and visiting of this sort does not go on over a long period nor is there any pattern of repeating visits except by the close relatives and grandparents.

During the first few weeks it will be decided whether the child will remain with his parents, or, as in a minority of cases, adopted by some other household (Jane Ritchie, 1957:61–64), and a name will be chosen for the new child:

> There is no special ceremony for naming the child. Often, the baby is named after a relative, perhaps one who has just died, frequently after the father or mother of either parent. If the name is long or difficult the child will frequently have a nick-name. In some cases the other children of the family give the baby a name before his official name is given to him, and this name persists among the family, but at school he will probably be called by his proper name. Thus the ragged children playing in the dusty backyard during the school holidays under the names of Boy, Laddie, Jumbo, were transformed at school with clean clothes into Charles, Laurence, and Arthur. The oldest boy is nearly always called Boy—but his official name is used at school. (Jane Ritchie, 1957:60.)

Most mothers establish breast-feeding and continue it for four months. It is discontinued and the child weaned to a bottle, or occasionally directly to a cup either because the flow of milk ceases or because it is thought to be too watery to provide adequate sustenance for the child. Though it is possible that dietary limitation might in some cases limit the period of breast-feeding, it seems more likely that failure to maintain milk supply is due to the necessity for the mother to return to her normal round of household duties, or to a belief that the quality of the milk is falling off, rather than purely physical reasons. Weaning is occasionally drastic, indeed there seemed to be a belief that sharp weaning by separating the child from the mother for a short period of time or using bitter substances on the breast, were acceptable practices should they prove necessary when other methods fail. In the majority of cases, of course, they were not.

Toilet training is handled with even less fuss than weaning. While the child is still unable to move around the house it is kept in napkins which are changed as often as the child marks its discomfort by crying. When the child is able to crawl it may continue in napkins but more usually it is allowed to move about without any restraint and such messes as result are easily and quickly removed since few of the homes have any floor covering apart from congoleum or flax mats, or clean sacks which can be frequently replaced when soiled. As in Kowhai the toddler quickly learns to attend to basic functions outside the house, with a minimum of restraint. Often, indeed generally, clearing up after younger children, both inside and outside the house, taking the children out for toilet purposes, and changing the napkins of younger ones, fall to the lot of an older sister, or if there is none, brother, who thus begins a long and close association with a particular child.

This particular community has a rather good record in infant health, better indeed than most Maori villages. However, parents generally felt that most childhood ailments were minor and often left treatment by the district nurse, or nearby doctor or hospital far longer than was desirable. Serious respiratory diseases might be dismissed as an asthma attack, a common cold, or a childhood cough and were particularly difficult for parents to recognise. They were common because the children spend a great deal of time out-of-doors from the time they can crawl. Crawling is actually a quite significant stage in the development of the child. He can come for what he wants. He is taken out of diapers. He can begin to spend time out-of-doors in the yard with the other children. But the real change in his pattern of life arrives when he begins to walk, for it is then that he is expected to take his first steps towards independence. All except first children learn to walk under the tutelage and encouragement of an older child. The change is not sharp. Jane Ritchie reports that:

> When the baby becomes a toddler he starts gradually to wean himself from the mother's continuing care. As long as he is still the baby of the family he is still the undisputed focus of her attention, but he will venture out into the yard with his siblings. If visitors come, the older children are nearly always sent outside to play. The toddler will be treated with leniency. He is allowed to play on the floor of the kitchen with a stick, or his father will hold him on his knee while he talks. If he wants a cake from the table, it will be given to him, while the other children have to wait until after the visitors have eaten. On one occasion a two-year-old baby girl had been playing with the egg beater. No reproach was made, but when her brother picked it up the mother reprimanded him. If the baby reaches out for the visitor's tobacco, the mother will give him her packet to play with. The little girl mentioned above was even allowed to smoke cigarettes by her indulgent parents. They thought she looked so cute with her cigarette, but none of her siblings was indulged in this way. (Jane Ritchie, 1957:79.)

The earliest years are marked with an almost unbroken permissiveness, and lavish, close affection expressed in frequent fondling. A bad-tempered baby is regarded as sick rather than "testy" and the only serious interference with the smooth course of its life is the possibility of frustration through the lack of formal routine. The common Pakeha doctrine of sparing the mother the stress of constant attention is quite foreign to the mothers of Rakau. Mothers exist for the care and breeding of children who remain the centre of activity and interest right up to the time they are able to move around themselves. This is not to say that they cannot from time to time break away from the exigencies of child-rearing by paying social calls, visiting the local shops or receiving visitors. But in general the first two years are continuously bathed in constant attention and affection.

THE BREAK WITH INFANCY

When the next child comes, in most cases within two years of the birth of the last, he then moves to the centre of the family stage, into the close relationship with the mother, and the displaced child's behaviour shows quite a marked change.

Again observations at this age level largely confirm the picture presented by the Beagleholes, though probably because of the extremely rapid rate of population increase in this locality the age of the change from indulgence towards greater independence seems to be earlier by about a year than in

Kowhai. In addition, possibly because of the earlier age, the change is less harsh, though not therefore less severe from the child's point of view. Since we visited homes, and were received as visitors, it may be that the picture is slightly distorted by formal social relations, but in general the break with parental affection is marked rather more by indifference on the part of adults than by 'loud shouting, capriciousness, lack of attention, lack of respect, physical punishment . . .' as was found at Kowhai. It is also necessary to be quite clear that the rejection is not objectively severe. Its personal severity is only apparent when it is contrasted with the liberal love of the pre-rejection period. It is the suddenness and the contrast which make the process so significant.

Infancy is over. The child is on its own but it is difficult to see any consistent pattern of behaviour held out as acceptable to the child. It is almost as though the parents were saying, "Well, the sooner the child is left to mature like old wine the better, and the less interference with it the quicker the process will be". Adult action is a world apart; a world which permits no interference from active children except as adults bid. The helplessness and novelty of new babies is interesting to adults but the activities of toddlers merely immature and best ignored. Actual remonstrations of very young children are decidedly rare in records of observation. Usually very young children would be placed on the floor and left to their own devices. If they interfered with the adults they might be picked up and dandled for a short time and then put back. If they still cried or objected then an older child would be called to take them away. On occasions a child might be cuffed for continued attempts at attracting attention. The rejection is firm and final and where the faint hope of reprieve might appear to be offered from time to time it is equally often withdrawn. Indulgence is not immediately withdrawn for all time as soon as the child can toddle. But after this time it is dependent upon the whim of adults and the reactions of the adult world become unpredictable.

Now this rejection is not of course a thing which characterises Maori society and no other. Extensive cross-cultural comparisons such as those made by Whiting and Child show that the pattern of psychological weaning occurs as part of the process of growing up—is in itself the first step to maturity. The independence thrown on to the young Maori child has no parallel in European society till late adolescence when the child is considerably better equipped to withstand it. But in all these cases of the breaking of an initial major parent-child tie it is not the event so much as the solution to the anxiety, isolation, the aloneness of the situation in which the child is left, which is of such great significance. During the actual rejection period itself the familiar smiling child of the first two years changes into a weeping, ailing child who is first and foremost a nuisance inside the house.

Parents are not, however, harsh or punitive in the way in which they separate themselves from their young children. The infant no longer receives the same attention or care as before. Though he may suffer from an occasional off-handed slap, nothing is comparable to the deep resentment which characterises the rejecting parent in the literature of clinical psychology. Furthermore, the child is not bound by a close, emotionally ambivalent relationship within the constant company of busy parents. He is simply placed outside the door where his siblings must act as surrogate parents to the best of their ability and patience. The following case will serve to illustrate this Rakau attitude:

> David is entertaining his wife's father and his sister's husband in the living room-kitchen of their house. His six sons are playing "bulldozers" in the dusty part of the backyard and from time to time you can hear sounds of their play through the open window. David is discussing an offer made by a local logging contractor for part of his wife's family's bush and has got deeply into the complexities of royalties and lawyers. His wife is preparing afternoon tea and cooking the evening meal at the same time as she carries the youngest baby on the crook of her left arm. David's next eldest enters the kitchen and goes to his mother who goes on with her work and ignores the child. Comes over to his father and tries to climb on his knee. Father pushes him off. Goes over to the open space in front of the fire and begins circling around, quite rapidly on the one spot. Mother crossing to tend cooking brushes him into corner. After mother leaves fire child goes to fire and takes out burning stick. Mother goes and removes stick. Child urinates. Mother calls second eldest child and assigns the other to his care. Both children go outside. Later same child enters with the next eldest. At this point there was a break in the conversation as the story of the negotiations had been completed and both children climbed on to the sofa next to their father and grandfather and begin a hand slapping game. Afternoon tea interrupts and both children are sent off outside without further ado.

The capricious nature of the behaviour of the adults in this very typical example is matched by a semblance of role structure—the beginnings of a systematic world of relationships between child and child, and further examples could be quoted which bring out the patterning of these relationships more strongly. The easiest way for the busy mother to deal with the miserable children of the post-rejection period is to use, not her own labour but the labour of the older children. There is an assignment, quite definite and deliberate, of the younger children to the care of older children. In the example above the mother's actual words were, as she called through the door to the second eldest, "Here, John. Come and take *yours* outside". On another occasion, to the two oldest boys, the term "*yours*" referring to a specific responsibility for a specific child was used in instructing the older children to bring the younger ones inside for their meal. In the case of this family (and at least three others) the pattern was quite definite. In other cases where the older children had been at school for some time it was noticed that the middle children not yet old enough for school yet old enough to know that they must keep out of the way, collected and cared for the younger members of the family. On another occasion, a bus trip to a tennis meeting, the child was cared for on the trip out by an elder late adolescent boy of eighteen or more, handed on to a younger girl of about ten, fed by the mother, left in the care of the research worker, and finally taken into the care of a small seven-year-old boy. With greater or less specificity depending on the family and its composition, the number of children at school and the sex of the children, there is this allocation of care to other siblings. For a while the post-rejection child will go to any and everyone seeking attention and affection, but as the capriciousness of adult behaviour bears in on the child it withdraws and avoids social contact with adults and becomes characteristically shy when alone with a stranger.

Time and again a child sitting silent in the corner or just outside the door or in some other inconspicuous part of the room would come out and show off some quite novel piece of behaviour. In the example above it was whirling like a ballet dancer and doing quite brave things with fire. On other occasions it was the carrying into the house of things the child had found outside and bringing them, significantly, straight to the adults who were talking. Dancing, yelling, throwing objects and all other phenomena associated with direct sibling rivalry were observed but without the other sibling being present. This would be so usual as to be of little interest were it not for the fact that some children "get away" with it, and do so consistently. On the basis of specific mechanical skills, skills of motor control or more generally on the basis of inventiveness in finding new, ever new, situations to attract adult attention some few toddlers and even older children are able to keep their parents and parents' visitors continually amused, willing to reward the extroverted child (so long as it can vary its behaviour often enough) with more attention and affection than it would otherwise receive. Behaviour which in Pakeha suburbia would be regarded as 'skiting' and undesirable exhibitionism, receives open acknowledgment and encouragement when the adults are really amused. But this is not often and the criteria are adult, not merely sentimental. It is only a very few children who are possessed of the abilities necessary to maintain the standards set.

Security can be found amongst their age peers, a security which is limited and harsh but far more predictable than the adult world which is preoccupied with its own concerns. The gangs of middle-year children, tight, close-knit while they last, yet never interfering with personal liberties, roam the fields and roads of Rakau, play along the river banks and in the drainage ditches, and create a world of mutual support in which security can be found: a children's world of children's experience.

Groups and Gangs

The environment, both social and physical, in Rakau, permits the child to find a solution to the problem of whom he shall relate to during his childhood and this solution patterns his later development and, indeed, the whole of later relatedness right through his life. At first it is the band of pre-school children in his own home and in the neighbourhood who provide him with activities, company, comfort, and support throughout the day.

When school is over, an older child, usually a brother or sister, will act as parent surrogate, and when he himself reaches school age he will also have to share in this task of caring for the younger children. But in most families there are more children at school than pre-school children so that the peer-group provides an extension of the sibling group when the child "graduates" to school. Margaret Earle summarises these years in this passage:

Most of the middle-years children are both younger and older siblings. Their relationships with brothers and sisters may be regarded from these two points of view. As younger siblings they frequently are or have been in the care of an older sister or less often an older brother. To a large extent the older children in the family take over the charge of the younger ones and provide substitutes for parents who are now busy with new babies. The older children thus play an important role in the training of the younger members of the family. In some cases they assume almost complete responsibility for one young brother or sister but more often their role as guardian extends to all younger siblings and they become responsible for general care when parents are not available. Many middle-years children therefore have a kind of parent substitute who may not be very many years older but who has quite extensive powers. In some cases there appears to be a strong attachment between the guardian and the ward but often there is an equally strong resentment felt by the younger child who is "bossed round" by older members of the family.

As older siblings the children in their turn assume responsibility for younger brothers and sisters and in their turn are able to "boss" them round. Sometimes the guardian feels resentful of having to bother with younger siblings when she (or he) would rather be playing. In general, however, the children do not appear to mind their task and many of them take it quite lightly. They do not worry unduly over their duties, and a small brother provides an excellent target for aggression when this is required. It is very common for children to abuse their authority and to take advantage of the fact that their mother is unlikely to interfere.

Aggression among siblings is very frequent and appears to follow a "pecking order" in many families. The fact that children are to a large extent cared for by other children and that parents seldom interfere, means that few limitations are placed on aggression down the "pecking order". Sometimes the line is broken for some reason. In cases where an older girl has cared for a small sister or brother, she may protect her charge from the assault of intermediate members of the family. In other cases there may be a strong bond between two children who are close together in age and who team up for mutual protection. However, in general there is a pattern of aggression down the sibling line and when Billy has given Tom a "hiding" it is not surprising to see Tom giving small brother Joe a knock soon after.

The sibling group is also a strong group to which a child really belongs and in which he can shelter from outsiders. Members of the same family tend to play together and to provide support for each other. When the children are at home they usually play with one or more members of their own family together with members of another family. When trouble arises in this situation, the children appear to take the view that it is all right for them to give little sister a "hiding" but no outsider had better try.

The part played by siblings in the training of middle-years children is very important. Because the children are to a large extent cut off from close contact with adults, they look to their older siblings to provide guidance, and they, too, provide guidance for younger siblings. The behaviour of older siblings is as capricious as that of parents, perhaps more so, but at least the children have access to siblings where they cannot reach parents. Thus the children are guided by other children who may know and understand only very little more than they do themselves and who certainly have no clear cut conception of where they are going and why. Goals are hazy except for those of the immediate future, and the goals of the immediate future for the Rakau child centre round getting the work done so that Mum won't give them a "hiding" or a "growling", and then getting out to play with the "other kids". (Margaret Earle, 1958: 23–26.)

Both siblings and peer groups have a similar quality of experience. They are remarkably free from parental supervision—the environment in Rakau allows them to escape to places where there are no adults around—the river banks, forest edges, windbreak plantations, pools along the rivers, and the scrubby foothills which are never very far from any part of the settlements. The play groups are really loosely-knit bands of individuals playing together in a way which is binding on none of the members; the groups split and divide, unite and recombine with great flexibility. There are no gangs in the sense of a permanently structured group with leadership, status, and specialised ranks, or of membership criteria, exclusiveness, or the maintenance of a special code.

Within these groups the children of Rakau learn to enjoy a particular kind of social experience. They neither want, nor are required, to enter into deep or lasting relationships with other children. They learn to be generous in giving: otherwise what they have will be taken away. They learn that others are not interested in their grievances or problems. Though they may get sympathy when in trouble, it is better not to get into trouble. They learn to think of home as a place for work which they do not welcome, of potential punishment that they do not enjoy. They learn to see their social world in simple and definite terms, to resolve conflicts by attack, avoidance, or denial, to move flexibly from group to group. They relate to each group in terms of what it demands, they enjoy the conformity of group membership and the relief it offers from the alien achievement standards of the school. Of these years Earle again writes in these words:

The children spend as much time as possible with their friends and it is with their friends that they have their happiest experiences. Most of them have time to play when they have finished their work at home and when school is over. Because girls have more home ties with household work they have less time to play than boys. Girls also have greater limitations placed on their freedom to wander away from home both because they are needed to prepare the evening meal or some similar task, and because it is an accepted fact that boys may wander where ever they wish whereas girls should not do so.

In general the play groups of the children tend to be as large as possible. There are few close friendships between two children. Occasionally two girls become close friends for a short time but even in this case they most often play with their good friend and with other children as well. Usually groups of children seen playing at home or at school are about six in number or larger. Only when there are few children available do the groups become smaller than this. There is a fairly rigid division between the sexes throughout the middle-years although mixed groups may be seen about the homes where brothers and sisters play together and with boys and girls of another family. At school boys and girls are never seen playing together except in an occasional game of chasing.

The most popular game of the children is one known as "tiggings" which is a simple chasing game. On most occasions when the question is asked "What shall we play?" the answer is sure to be "tiggings". This is a simple game with a minimum of rules and requiring a minimum of imagination. One of the most obvious characteristics of the play of Rakau children is the absence of imagination in most games. For the most part the children simply roam about the paddocks, swim in the rivers, fish, climb trees, and make forts in the long grass. Forts are very common but games involving forts do not often include fantasy. These games usually involve throwing grass at each other or simply chasing each other—a variation on "tiggings". Group games are not highly organised unless the children are playing some game learned at school. Even then the game usually breaks down quite soon. Older children's games are more organised than those of the younger children but in general Rakau play involves a great deal of activity but little organisation. Groups tend to fluctuate in membership and in size and consequently they frequently become disorganised.

Behaviour in the play group is subject to a minimum of adult interference and thus the patterns of behaviour are determined almost entirely by the standards of the children. Aggression, bossiness, and "cheek" are the most disliked forms of behaviour, and also occur rather frequently. There is a good deal of teasing and other forms of verbal aggression as well as direct physical aggression, particularly among the boys. The children show little sympathy for their fellows and enjoy seeing another child in difficulties. However they are sympathetic if a friend is in difficulties and will defend members of their own group against outsiders. There is a good deal of inter-sex aggression and this is permissible. The child who is excessively aggressive towards members of his group will not be well liked but the child who is very good at attacking members of another group will probably be very popular.

Children who aspire too high are cut down to size by their friends, and a child who gets himself into difficulties by showing off or attempting something beyond his capacity will be laughed at and teased. Participation and acceptance in the play group require considerable sacrifice of personal rights and some children do not manage to achieve this. However there are very few Rakau children who do not have some friends some of the time. (Margaret Earle, 1958: 26–28.)

Mulligan's account of adolescent development, which is based mainly on test records collected from forty boys and girls between the ages of thirteen and eighteen years, improves my own picture of Rakau adolescent development made earlier, though for the most part Mulligan's account supports the basic theme as I had described it.

In general both boys and girls must cope with increasing parental interest in their activities. Boys can adjust to this situation more rapidly than girls, partly because parental supervision of them is less vigilant, but also because in general in Rakau men may roam but women stay at home. The growing boy can still find satisfaction in activities that stimulate, entertain, and amuse. He can even change his job should he feel like it.

Girls, however, must prepare for the drudgery, the anxiety over money, the comparative loneliness, of the housewife and the mother. However, both boys and girls become increasingly conscious of, and influenced by, the needs created by advertising which portrays a world outside of Rakau, filled with excitements and pleasures deliberately designed to appeal to them.

Rakau life palls. Its easy-going remoteness is limiting, its security is boring, its authority structure is anachronistic. Many people yearn for the modern, the spectacular, the stylish world of luxury and ease, for titillation and sensation. Although Polynesian by origin, they are young people now becoming for the first time consumers in a modern Western economy. Many of them face the world outside Rakau; many leave the community. They do so, not because there is no work for them in Rakau, but because they purposefully seek a future elsewhere. Acting as they have learned to act, they seek like-minded groups wherever they go. They expect that their peers will still be around them (and so they are), that they will understand them (and so they do), and that non-Maoris will not.

But most stay in Rakau. For them, adolescence brings only transitory problems before they make the minimal adjustment to the adult roles they have observed in others throughout their lives. For example, in my field notes I find this record:

> It is startling to notice the changes in the boy Tahi since I last met him twelve months ago. At that time Tahi was gangling and clumsy, shy, and inclined to sullenness. He would answer when addressed as briefly as possible and in low deep tones; his head bowed and shoulders drooping. Most of the time he would set himself in one place or engage in a rather solitary game of bouncing a basketball against the floor to a wall and then catching it—an activity in which he had mastered the somewhat limited span of variations and which was conducted with a bored, even indifferent air . . .
>
> This year Tahi, brilliantined and suave, displays an adult sophistication throughout the school grounds. He totes a guitar and assembles a group of admirers, exclusively drawn from students older than himself or at least his contemporaries in the limited sense. He does not fringe on activities nor press to their centre but casually allows attention to come to him, expects it of right, and gets it. In conversation he is assured and knowing and immediately adopts a man-to-man basis. Topics —drawn from ex-school environment.

These notes cover the change in one boy from the active, intensely vigorous life of the middle years, roaming free, admitting of little external control, and rarely confronted with adult authority outside of school. The changes from this are twofold: firstly to the morose and sullen withdrawal of last year then to the confident adult-oriented behaviour of this year. The case is not an isolated one. Here is an additional note on another boy:

> Rua over last year's period was still allied with the group of forestry-village boys. After school he would be seen with them down at the deep hole under the bridge swimming and playing the boys' games with flax stems, stones, and so on. After the evening meal he would sit with a few of his age-group and play the guitar or go down to the river to set the *hinaki* (eel trap). He was still part of the groups which engage in games of territorial defence, and on movie evenings would sit in front of the picture theatre with his classmates. He had not yet graduated to the rear of the hall . . . This year Rua is a problem to his teachers who know him to be able but who have noticed his work progressively slipping all year. In appearance he has not

changed much; a little taller perhaps and curbed somewhat in the spontaneous movements typical of the younger children. He has retained his neatness of appearance. But whereas last year he impressed the observer as probably the most intelligent boy in the upper classes he now adopts an almost surly air and pretends an insolent direct stare throughout the interview. In an isolated two-person relationship this mask can be broken down fairly easily and behaviour more nearly that of last year is exhibited, but as soon as another person enters the room the behaviour changes dramatically to the dominant pattern of sullen withdrawal.

One's immediate reaction to this record is to classify it as a fairly typical example of *Sturm und Drang.* Indeed both in character and in genesis such behaviour seems to be very similar to much adolescent phenomena among Pakehas. And yet it does not seem to last quite as long. Rua is entering it now at the age of fourteen. Tahi is beyond it now at the age of sixteen, and it seems to continue in general for more than one year but rarely more than two.

Tahi's behaviour is virtually indistinguishable from that of the unmarried males in general—indeed of all the males, irrespective of marital status, under the age of twenty-five. Tahi is now for all practical purposes a child made into a man in the space of a year; he has made a transition from one sort of role to another one, quite different in form though not actively discontinuous with the major trends of childhood. The departure is from the age scales of the middle years to the role structure associated with unmarried status. His group of associates, his behaviour reference models are now greater in number because they are no longer decided on the basis of strict age association.

But climbing out of the age scale ladder into the larger group means in effect a further limitation on behaviour. This seems to be a paradox. A larger group should offer more models to the truncated 'tradition-directed' person and should encourage a greater richness and variability in personality operation. Yet the phenomena indicate increased stereotyping of response patterns.

Partly this increased stereotyping comes from the renewed interest on the part of the larger community in the person. The child who from the age of about 4 has been subjected to few direct socializing mechanisms, who has been only rarely required to observe behavioural patterns on adult typing is quite suddenly subjected to stern discipline and considerable pressure to conform to adult typings. The wider social group clamps down, increases the pressures towards conformity as though to make up for time lost. The community talks, discusses the individual's behaviour, particularly his sexual activities, allocates tasks at community gatherings and insists on their proper completion and permits competition on adult standards in adult sports. He attends drinking parties and is expected to keep pace with the drinking and join in the activities. He can expect that this behaviour will be closely watched and openly discussed.

But more direct still is the individual's own conception of the role requirements demanded for membership in the older age-category of the unmarried men. He sees a pattern, which is also a desirable status, quite different from that to which he has been accustomed. Before he can change he must 'conceptualize' that pattern and consciously adopt its behaviours, dress, speech and self-image. And the transition must not be delayed. The striving to maintain psychological security in the group cannot be relaxed once it has been embedded early and firmly in the character structure. As soon as childhood is recognized as something past, the process of imitating the next models of social group and gaining their distinctive marks cannot be long postponed. So long as the process is delayed, that is, while the individual is learning the new certainties of role and role expectation, anxiety dominates the individual. So too, of course, in Pakeha society. But there the role patterns are diverse and the group structure more diffuse, the sanctions less rigid and the vigilance less severe. In Rakau a lad can gain the emblems of membership within a short time, within a year, in fact, and from this time on, provided he accepts the limitations resulting from so rapid a transition, he is psychologically secure. He may be limited to a pattern of reaction which makes variety of intellectual and imaginative experience almost impossible, he may be tied to an egocentric superficiality in social relations, and deprived of deep affective experiences; he may be caught up on a continual coping with a round of fads and fashions, a succession of frenzied adaptions; but, so long as the group is there and so long as he limits his demands on it and meets its demands on him, he need not be anxious.

Rakau presents no special occupational role for males. All will work in the forests, presumably, since there is little else to absorb the male working population, and yet few of them say they expect to work there. If they do the work will not be very different from farm labouring, road maintenance or scrub cutting, dull monotonous labour all of it, demanding no special qualities. Most of the immature males can see around them a male population moving from job to job, even from place to place. Socially only the males above forty have any well-defined and well-integrated tasks within the community. There are of course obligations placed on the fathers of families who must assume roles as heads of households which they must provide for and maintain. But the father's role in Rakau is nowhere onerous and indeed it is borne lightly by all but a few. Males seek the company of males and often appear quite at a loss for activities within the house. With the wife to do the housework and older children, particularly the girls, to assist with work and child-care, the father's role is so poorly defined that it usually comprises nothing more than a symbolic authoritarian presence to command and control at certain times of short duration. Frequently the father is occupied with the late adolescent boys but more often he seeks out the association of his male companions for the free periods of the long summer evenings, at weekends, and during his holiday times. Many of the men spend their week days right out of the area, working in bushcamps, and seem to prefer things that way, and return only at weekends, if at all, to their wives and families.

But for the girls, home, motherhood and a family are definite events which will follow logically from their very existence and sex. There is no imprecision of role and the progress from childhood to adulthood is less intense and disruptive. The narrowing of reaction patterns is still seen; the anxiety phenomena, a loss of poise, sullenness, intractibility, withdrawal, as the time comes to leave the close group of the middle years, but it rapidly gives way at about 15 to full psychological maturity—to the adoption of patterns of behaviour, within a well-defined round of role prescriptions which are indistinguishable from those of older females. The male can make of his roles what he will; the female is tied in to a more rigid order permitting little variation. Since few persons are achievers and therefore able to make for variety in role taking, the male pattern sets into a voluntary conformity. Females however are obliged to conform to a definite pattern.

There is for the girls no long period corresponding to the unmarried role-pattern in males. When a girl leaves school she goes home and is immediately absorbed into home duties and these will be her lot from then on. Marriage will make little behavioural difference except in respect of her status among the older women. She will run the home, rear the children, manage the finances and garden and keep the round of social intercourse with other women and their families. There is always present for the girl the certainty of a constricted sort of role effectiveness. Within the limitations of the home and its role structures the frustration of constant adaption in which young males must maintain stability can be avoided. This does not mean that the females are able to achieve more spontaneous or diversified behaviour than the males. It is curious to see working out here a similar limitation in personal development, but one that comes in fact from quite different influences: on the male side the limitation comes through the pressure to keep within the group in a poorly defined role structure, while in female experience the same sort of limitation (based on the same sort of prior experiences) comes about simply because the role structure *is* definite. The difference in process is important because the male act of achieving adult patterning is self-imposed to a greater degree than the female pattern. The family is almost the only institution which retains an interlocking set of roles in this community. Whereas the forces of culture contact have made inroads on economic, religious, political and legal, and educational institutions, the central core of family relations has not become confused and disrupted. There is no marginality in Rakau family structure, but the effect of contact, working through patterns which are undoubtedly indigenous, has been to remove the male from the role structure of the family group. Thus to achieve social effectiveness males must group themselves into a new structure based on their wider roles in the more acculturated aspects of the community life.

In adulthood the young man is on his own, yet never alone. He defends his right to make his own decisions, yet never feels happy making them with others. He enjoys social life but fears social action. His security rests on the peculiar social order that Rakau offers and on its remaining the same.

LEARNING TO BE A MAORI

There are specific cultural contents and customs which children in Rakau learn. There are patterns of speech in Maori and in English. There are "languages" and "idioms" of symbols other than language. There are postural and gestural characteristics. But psychologically these are integrated by the process of identification with successive groups and by a consequent patterning of identity development.

When Maoris in the middle years move away in emotional distance from their parents, they relate to significant others as models and learn through this how to act to lessen hurt, to reduce anxiety, and to feel independent.

As has already been seen the chief characteristics of the adult roles which the child sees being acted out around him are remoteness and capriciousness, a world that from time to time offers again the previously known surfeit of affection and yet later, in apparently identical circumstances, capriciously denies access to these satisfactions. Punishments are firm and immediate but not consistent, and rewards are equally chaotic, the same action receiving now the one, now the other. The adult world is a world apart. And yet in a community in which kinship is still reckoned as a status determinant children in the abstract are valued. This valuing is of the child *qua* child, not of the child as an individual; the child is not so much regarded as a miniature adult as strange and unknown, a creature in a world apart. From this central core of relationships the chief lessons are that adults can provide gratification but that efforts by the child to obtain such gratifications are of no predictable certainty. The self, as a tool in interpersonal processes with adults, is of uncertain value. Self doubt, an excessive vigilance and profound distrust of the adult world may well be the result.

This remoteness of the child from direct identification with adults is not merely a function of the psychological barriers to affection, but is also a function of the lack of direct contact with the parents during the middle years. Children are simply not included in an adult social group during the greater part of the child's time. This is reflected in the use of relationship terms, such as Mum and Dad, which occupy a very low frequency in the conversation of Maori children.

The pattern of allocating children to the care of other children is one which is familiar in the literature of Polynesia, and it is important to stress that the Maori allocation is a tendency, not a rigorous stipulation. The effect of this tendency is to set up a hierarchy within the family; a hierarchy of identification models which gives the Maori family greater linearity than its

Pakeha counterpart. Schematically identification patterns might be constructed as [shown in the figure below.]

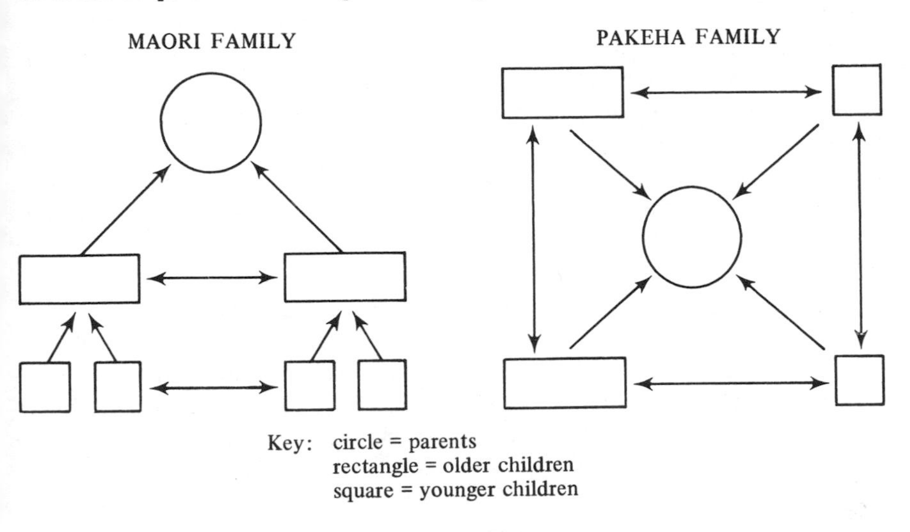

The Pakeha child is able to check his behaviour continually both against sibling conceptions of adult standards and against the adult standards themselves; both are continually available as models. But the Maori child is typing himself against an older sibling's concept of the adult world. His perceptions of adult behaviour and adult roles are being strained through the perceptions of his older sib. The latter will only be approximately varying in their degree of conformity according to the age, sex, intelligence and experience variables of the older child. In this transmission of percepts from a child's view of the world, the value structure is thrown into sharp relief. The limited comprehension of the older child requires that the values he sees around him be used in modifying the behaviour of younger children; he cannot therefore make do with a tentative approximation but must resolve his percepts into a formal structure from which he is able to direct and instruct younger children.

Originality departs. The value-structure sets hard, prematurely, and the child enters onto a plateau in value-learning. The organized model with which he has been presented will do for all situations right up to the time he assumes direct adult behaviour and even then a rigid conformity based on the simplicity and absolutism of the middle years will be a ready source of certainty in conflicting or incipiently dangerous social situations.

To some extent at this stage he will have adopted patterns of absolutism from the family and these he will cling to and make every effort to retain, but at such an early age the content of these family 'absolutisms' will be rather amorphous. If the patterns are generalized then they will stereotype response since a wide variety of experience has not been encountered within the relatively limited family environment. But since the standards of sibling and peer groups are rapidly adopted, it is they and not the family who provide the basis for absolutism. Reciprocity will develop more rapidly within these fluid groups where absolutism is more difficult to achieve. Since these groups replace the family as the child's 'absolute' we will need to consider their role in greater detail.

It is easy to over-estimate the significance of the security group simply because it is all-pervadingly available. It has been noted that children enter and leave the age-peer groups at will; that the structure of such groups is amorphous and volatile. The influence of them on introjection and the self-determined regulation of behaviour is not as significant as that of the sibling group. But they act as surrogates and soften the harshness of the absolutism of the other older children in the family and remove the need to introject. The Maori child is looking sideways at models very like those his older siblings offer and yet different; and he is being looked at in the same way by others. The parallel with Riesman's 'other-directedness' is clear.

One element of the traditional pattern persists very strongly. Status is still ascribed rather than achieved. There are no clear evidences of criteria of achieved status. One man in the area has worked hard over many years and built up a fine farm. For some years he ran a herd of pedigree jersey cows. Later to provide variety of training for his sons he changed to sheep and currently manages his farm as a sheep stud. But the community at Rakau have excluded him from social participation and he remains relatively indifferent to the isolation. Another male has attempted to rise through the hierarchy of occupations in the State Forest but he too is moving towards the fringe of the community. Achievement is negatively sanctioned. Presumably therefore an ascription pattern still prevails. It is difficult to determine the qualities which are ascribed. If a person is a member of one of the historically high ranking families this is recognized and in a vague way the rank of families is acknowledged even though few people are able to state the criteria upon which status of families rests. Personal qualities make up the main features of the ascription pattern. A person is valued as a person and the community is overwhelmingly permissive of all behaviour which is not achieving behaviour.

The sort of concept which is needed to describe the situation is one which seems to have only a tenuous reality. For the society has retained the attitudes and values of tradition-direction without having retained the traditions themselves. Politically the community expects the old pattern of gerontocratic direction to operate but since there is no one capable of operation in the greater complexity of current matters of land deals and social expression, there is simply no organized political control. That the community has remained tradition directed is evidenced by the rapidity with which the traditional patterns can be re-established when the occasion demands—church celebrations and tangis notably. But for most of the time the orientation is backwards, though the past offers few clues to the future. For this reason a pattern of other direction is already beginning to develop. Since people cannot look back for direction the only alternative is to look to the constancy of the group and to take direction from the activities of the others. But the others in turn must be finding some anchorage for their own behaviour and here the effects of the mass media and Pakeha schooling are blocking in rough standards. Sometimes the pattern of action of individuals and groups is in terms of this and sometimes it is bounced off this; that is, the patterns are a deliberate attempt to impose a pattern which is different from the Pakeha pattern and which can be made a 'Maori' pattern by being quickly diffused so that it is universal amongst the Maori group. The truncated tradition directed must construct their own traditions where the old methods and manners have been lost or have ceased to be effective and satisfying. The only requirement for acceptance as a pattern is that enough people can learn to perform the pattern of actions rapidly and effectively. Song crazes sweep through the area, clothing fads, tricks of jargon and catch phrases; even stances and characteristics of gait are widely adopted within a short time because of the constant watch by person of person.

This social vigilance is present and develops rapidly in the middle years where the actions of other children, of parents, teachers, pakehas, are noted in detail and retold in gatherings of age-peer groups often in fun but with great disregard for respect. But these details are noted just as the behaviour of the peer group is noted. These too serve as signposts for future behaviour.

Here again the role distinction between achievers and non-achievers can be seen to be of importance. Other-direction levels behaviour and for most children attempting the novel is to attempt the impossible. (Throughout, "role" is used here to refer to social patterns of individual action which are positively sanctioned, and "role structure" to the interaction of role with role within a social group.)

Maori Identity in Rakau

The transformations of identity (Erikson, 1959) in Maori development in Rakau can now be abstracted from the preceding account.

In Rakau the basic foundations of trust and hope would at first glance appear to be well laid in Maori development. The very young child lives in a warm, devoted, and supporting environment. It is not a mature environment in fact since we now know that he cannot expect these characteristics to continue. But warm supportive trust, the basis of hope, is certainly there for long enough, and often enough, to develop the unconcerned optimism which is one consequence of initial trust. But before the child is out of this stage of identity development, the change in the environment occurs, and the child's identity reaches its first great challenge. The response is simple;

the child continues to *hope* that he will be surrounded by trustworthy others, but he does not *expect* that this will be so. To trust is to make demands and to recognise that reciprocal demands will be made of one. But the Maori child recognises only the first part of this proposition. Since no one meets all demands, no one is completely trustworthy. The later facility which the Maori adult displays in playing the game of local politics is an extension of this essentially realistic (though egocentric) attitude.

He will later learn that while his kin and friendship groups expect that reciprocity of sharing, support, hospitality, and generosity will be maintained, the old order is broken and this basic expectation is often not fulfilled. He will learn that some Maoris in his village who most often err in these matters are said to be "Pakehafied". Their acculturation may therefore be held up to him as a negative model even though he for other reasons may admire their control of Pakeha culture, their material comforts and possessions.

At the relatively early age of two or even younger the child goes out from the family to spend the next three stages in the development of identity not in the family, but in the sibling and peer groups. Here he must fashion, or be fashioned by, experience, to develop will, purpose, and skill. He soon learns that his will and purposes are limited by his ability to manipulate others; his sense of power develops faster and further than his sense of mastery; he becomes skilled at sensing the attitudes and purposes of others; and he learns to express himself in action rather than speech. He becomes a master of understatement. He learns not to make or share plans, or at least not to expect any guarantee of co-operation. He also learns not to compete. He learns that being Maori means many things: having distinctive skin colour and speech; being expected to know esoteric knowledge and lore (though in Rakau few in fact do); accepting minority status in the wider society; expecting unfair treatment from Pakehas (whether they are fair or not); he learns both to value his Maori identity and to be ashamed of it.

Two reference groups are important in building up this sense of shame. The Pakeha group in Rakau contributes to it. But since, most often, the Maori child relates himself to this group in matters which have no particular Maori connotation, this is the more minor of the two groups. More intense than this is the sense of shame which comes when he perceives that he is failing to fulfil the expectations of his elders; that, by not succeeding in the Pakeha world, he is letting his "race" down; that, by not becoming more Maori, he is letting his elders down. While the Pakeha must bear some of the blame for the failure in confidence which stems from this identity crisis in adolescence, the failure of the Maori parent and the Maori community to identify with the aspirations of the young person is the larger factor. The young person is caught in an insoluble conflict. If he aspires to success in the Pakeha world he isolates himself from his family and community background. If he remains at home to be caught up in the non-involved purposelessness of Rakau activities, he is judged comfortable and ordinary but a failure. And the expectation that he should become more Maori, in terms of the historical culture, is at complete odds with his education and experience in Rakau.

Young people in Rakau rarely speak of these conflicts but when they do, they pour out the feeling that there is no justice for them in their world, even from their own folk. They express their longing to be wanderers, to be rootless, to move out into a search for a world compliant with their terms. They take the chip off their shoulder and examine it. But they are not thereby made comfortable, for their world is now so different from that of their fathers that young people are a race of new men, hewing the shape of identity from their own experience without models or sure patterns.

What patterns there might be, become confused or unacceptable because they belong to Rakau and Rakau is the "old" world, the antithesis (for them) of modernity. They are pulled by their perception of the supposed delights of the city, pushed by the belief that the dullness and frustration of life in Rakau will not change fast enough ever to be satisfying. They fear the anonymity of the city while chafing at the surveillance of the Rakau community. Many young people move haphazardly backwards and forwards from town to country. They are caught between two alternative patterns of life each of which contains (as every life-style does for everyone) both positive and negative qualities. But unlike most people, these young Rakau individuals are unable to trust themselves and others to the point where they strike a bargain with their world and settle down to balance the profit and loss in their experience.

As they move into the marriage relationship and become parents the restlessness of their accommodation to the division within themselves moves to a temporary peace. The cultural sanctions and attitudes towards sex permit them free and uncomplicated enjoyment of the physical relationship of marriage. The first years of parenthood are a chance to create a little social group of idyllic satisfaction. But as the children grow, as they become less entertaining and more worrying, the social disassociative solution to conflicts is more and more commonly utilised. The husband moves off into the men's world of Rakau with its drinking and talking sessions and its round of minor political wrangles, never resolved, never disposed of, never providing achievement, but always the satisfaction of expression. The mother is left to care as best she can for too many scratched knees, torn or worn clothes, puddles, messes, and meals. She too, will seek the comfort of non-aspiring expressive groups but she will be able less often to enjoy this pleasure.

The brittleness of relationships, the source of the contemporary granular nature of Maori social organisation, is to be found right here in the Rakau family, loose-knit, providing autonomy, but lacking is sustained maintenance of family co-operation, efforts, or aims. Permissiveness towards children, alternating with harshness, further limits the growth of warm regard between children and parents. An older relative, a grandmother or grandfather often becomes a source of comfort for the child. The wisdom which the old have acquired they can share with their grandchildren, but not with their sons and daughters. Old people have a mourning and a grieving quality which rests on their approaching closeness to death, their role in maintaining highly expressive cultural death customs, their sense of loss of the old culture, and their perceived sense of missed opportunity. They feel ignored, derelict, abandoned, and uncared for. They feel offended when they are not consulted but are frequently obstructive when they are. They are wise in the sense that they see what things might have been in Rakau, but they are wise after the event and in a way which is frequently irritating to their families and to the community at large.

As the old folk drift off into death, the people of Rakau mourn. But it seems to me that they also shrug, for each old person represents both a part of life that a younger person does not comprehend and a future fate that he would rather not comprehend.

Some people expressed to me the feeling that the undoubted distress of the feeling of whakama was simply a stage that will pass. But it is not just a stage in personal development since it is seen in the behaviour of children, youths, adults, and the aged. My informants meant that it was a concomitant of a stage in development of changing Maori adaption to the new world. This is undoubtedly so for Maoris as for any group who stand marginally between some lost past and unachieved future. But whakama is not a constructive response to the challenges of the present. It breaks, rather than makes contact. It inhibits cultural expression rather than affirms it. It damages the integration of the person rather than promotes a confident confrontation of his undoubted problems in understanding and coping with new ways.

Some romantics would say that the effective way to counteract the divisions within would be to reconstruct pride in the ethnic past. This solution is psychologically thin and unsatisfying. In any case the people of Rakau have passed a point of no return in the recovery of a satisfying Maori cultural vitality. There are some old people who could teach the young but they fail to do so. There are some young people willing to learn but too few to change the character of the community. The least whakama of the folk of Rakau are those who have ceased to be concerned with being Maori in any outwardly detectable sense in everyday behaviour. Some Rakau people scorn them as "cultural deserters". But in fact they are not so. These "deserters" fulfil their obligations to the marae and all that it means. Their aroha, their openness to the emotional demands of their kin and the warmth of their hospitality are limited but not entirely denied. But they find little purpose and no satisfaction in the petty wrangling of so much of the Maori activities of Rakau. Some have solved their identity problem by becoming as Pakeha as they can. But still they remain Maori in more subtle matters: they place decided emphasis on those things, emotional and non-material, which make up the core of Maori values.

When a Maori grows up in Rakau he cannot avoid the experience of feeling whakama because his parents and many others use shame sanctions to control his behaviour. Parents play so small a role in shaping the behaviour of children that these sanctions are often applied suddenly and seem extreme. Frustrated, often physically beaten, the child says, in effect, I am bad; I am Maori; Maori is bad; and the Pakeha world confirms his judgment later on. He cannot say why he feels this way. He cannot say why being Maori sometimes makes him feel bad. He blames the situation and withdraws from it. He may find his way out of this identity conflict by saying, I am not Maori (but he will still be brown-skinned and be judged Maori by others); or he may solve it by asserting that it is good to be a Maori (but this he may not be able to prove adequately either to himself or to others in the face of culture loss and critical Pakeha attitudes). This situation would be less damaging if Maori parents were less harsh in their use of shaming, used gentle moulding rather than raw forcing of the development of control, less ready to allow an early independence which they cannot later accept in their children, and more comfortably confident that what is of lasting value in being Maori will persist long after observable signs of outwardly Maori behaviour have departed.

BIBLIOGRAPHY

BEAGLEHOLE, E., AND P. BEAGLEHOLE, 1946, *Some Modern Maoris.* Wellington, N.Z.: N.Z.C.E.R.

BEAGLEHOLE, E., AND JAMES E. RITCHIE, 1958, "The Rakau Studies." *Journal of the Polynesian Society,* 67:132–154. Reprinted in Bert Kaplan, *Studying Personality Cross Culturally.* Evanston, Ill.: Row, Peterson.

BEST, ELSDON, 1924, *Tuhoe: The Children of the Mist.* New Plymouth, N.Z.: Avery.

EARLE, MARGARET J., 1958, *Rakau Children from Six to Thirteen Years.* Wellington, N.Z.: Victoria University of Wellington Publications in Psychology No. 11.

ERIKSON, ERIK H., 1959, "Identity and the Life Cycle." *Psychological Issues,* I, No. 1.

RITCHIE, JAMES E., 1956, *Basic Personality in Rakau.* Wellington, N.Z.: Victoria University of Wellington Publications in Psychology No. 8.

1963, *The Making of a Maori.* Victoria University of Wellington Publications in Psychology No. 15. Wellington, N.Z.: A. H. and A. W. Reed.

RITCHIE, JANE, 1957, *Childhood in Rakau.* Wellington, N.Z.: Victoria University of Wellington Publications in Psychology No. 10.

RITCHIE, JANE, AND JAMES E. RITCHIE, 1970, *Child Rearing Patterns in New Zealand.* Wellington, N.Z.: A. H. and A. W. Reed.

WESTRA, ANS, AND JAMES E. RITCHIE, 1967, *Maori.* Wellington, N.Z.: A. H. and A. W. Reed.

FURTHER READINGS

Almost every piece of social anthropological writing has some bearing on social process, so it is difficult to circumscribe the literature in this area. Two general strategies are recommended in approaching the material. One is to take an island group and explore the literature on it, including reports by explorers, missionaries, and other writers as well as anthropologists. The resources on Samoa, Tahiti, Fiji, and New Zealand's Maori are especially rich in this regard, while Firth's cumulative writings on Tikopia make it one of the best-documented societies in the world. For general bibliographic reviews, see Keesing's *Social Anthropology in Polynesia* and Taylor's *A Pacific Bibliography.*

The second strategy is to focus on particular topics. The bibliographies mentioned above will also provide some guidance for this approach. Those wishing to follow up on the topic of political behavior should read the Keesings' *Elite Communication in Samoa,* which gives a good account of political process Polynesian-style. A review of the older literature, relevant to traditional societies, is provided by Williamson's three-volume work *The Social and Political Systems of Central Polynesia.* Williamson has also reviewed the traditional material on religion in *The Religious and Cosmic Beliefs of Central Polynesia* and in *Religion and Social Organization in Central Polynesia.* Another early approach to religion, emphasizing content of belief and ritual rather than sociological analysis, is Handy's *Polynesian Religion.* For more socially oriented analyses of particular religious systems, Firth's *The Work of the Gods in Tikopia,* Emory's *Kapingamarangi,* and Monberg's *The Religion of Bellona Island* (from which the selection in this part has been adapted) are recommended. Two of Firth's more general interpretive papers, "Totemism in Polynesia" and "The Analysis of Mana," should also be consulted by anyone concerned with Polynesian religious behavior.

On the subject of Polynesian "personality" or social character, three useful bibliographies have been compiled: Langness and Gladwin's "Oceania" in Hsu's *Psychological Anthropology;* Howard, Vinacke, and Maretzki's *Culture and Personality in the Pacific Islands;* and Levy's *Personality Studies in Polynesia and Micronesia.* Langness and Gladwin provide an excellent interpretive essay along with their bibliography, as does Levy. Among the more intensive psychosocial studies of particular cultural groups is Mead's *Coming of Age in Samoa* and the section "Marquesan Culture" by Linton in Kardiner's *The Individual and His Society.* An extensive re-analysis of Samoan character, critically reviewing Mead's interpretation, is being readied for publication by Freeman and should be read in conjunction with *Coming of Age in Samoa.* Freeman's tentative title is *Culture and Human Nature in the Samoan Islands.* For those interested in Ritchie's work on the New Zealand Maori, his summary volume, *The Making of a Maori* (from which the article in this part has been adapted), is recommended. The selection by Howard has been adapted from *Learning to Be Rotuman,* a book dealing with socialization and education in Rotuma.

In addition to the topics treated here, the student could outline several others, depending on his special interests. It is anticipated that within the next few years the newly formed Association for Anthropology in Eastern Oceania will sponsor symposia on specific topics, thereby providing the basis for a comparative sociology not only within Polynesia, but between Polynesia, Micronesia, and eastern Melanesia as well. The first volume is *Adoption in Eastern Oceania,* edited by Carroll.

PART IV SOCIAL CHANGE

Although the serious study of social change in Polynesia was initiated as early as 1928 with the publication of Felix Keesing's *The Changing Maori,* until the end of World War II such studies were few and far between. However, the war drew attention to the Pacific, and the changes wrought by it were too dramatic to be ignored. For the United States, administrative responsibilities came into focus not only on conquered, or "liberated," islands but also on those like Samoa which had been under American control for years before. Administrators needed to understand the islands' inhabitants in order to govern effectively; and to gain necessary insights, they frequently elicited aid from anthropologists. With the focus shifted from traditional to contemporary sociocultural systems, postwar anthropologists began to delve more deeply into processes of social change. The key concept was "acculturation"; the leading question, "What has been the effect of agents of Western culture, such as missionaries, traders, and colonial administrators, on indigenous societies?" Historians and other scholars, working with documents and doing their own brand of field work, joined anthropologists in approaching the task.

In the late 1950's, attention was drawn to the development of sizable towns such as Suva (Fiji), Pape'ete (Tahiti), Pago Pago (American Samoa), and Apia (Western Samoa), and a new concept—"urbanization"—came into vogue. The focal question became "What is the impact of urban centers on the lives of indigenous people?" The shift was from an interest in changes that had already occurred to contemporary processes of change.

The first paper in this part, by Malcolm C. Webb, presents an interpretation of the dramatic abolition by decree of the elaborate Hawaiian taboo system in 1819. Webb relates the sudden abandonment of traditional religious practices to alterations in the chiefly power base which occurred as a result of accommodation to early contact with Europeans. His analysis not only furthers a theoretical understanding of the process of social change, but also provides some insight into the relationship between religious and political systems in the more highly stratified Polynesian societies.

In the next selection, Jeremy Beckett describes changes that have occurred in a society at the opposite end of the spectrum. Whereas Hawaii was one of the larger Polynesian societies, encompassing a population of hundreds of thousands ordered by an elaborate system of rank and hierarchy, Pukapuka is a tiny atoll inhabited by only a few hundred persons. Furthermore, although Hawaii was subjected to intensive contact almost from the time of its discovery by Europeans and is now one of the United States, Pukapuka is still relatively isolated from the Western world. Nevertheless, acculturative changes have taken place even in the remotest of Polynesian islands, and those which have occurred on Pukapuka are characteristic.

The last two articles deal with change in the Society Islands. Robert Levy assesses the response of Society Islanders to the introduction of alcohol and finds evidence that demoralization during the nineteenth century was accompanied by extensive drunkenness. This was no longer apparent during the 1960's, when the pattern he observed was one of controlled drinking. Levy concludes that the current controlling factors are to be found in shared group evaluations about drinking and in aspects of prevalent psychological structure.

Finally, Paul Kay presents a description of Tahitian households as "disorganized" and "woman-centered," a pattern which is familiar among relatively impoverished peoples in the modern urban milieu.

15

THE ABOLITION OF THE TABOO SYSTEM IN HAWAII[1]

Malcolm C. Webb

The abolition of the taboo system and many associated religious practices in Hawaii in the year 1819 was used as the chief illustration of his principle of Cultural Fatigue by the undoubted dean of American anthropologists of the last half century, A. L. Kroeber,[2] and was regarded by Redfield as one of the very few examples of planned, self-conscious reform on the part of a primitive culture.[3] As recently as last winter a summary of these events referred to the taboo abolition and its aftermath, justifiably, I believe, as "this extraordinary state of affairs."[4] There would probably be general agreement that a people's abandonment of their traditional religious practices—not in favour of a new cult, but in exchange for nothing—is a highly unusual event, and one well worth the attention not only of Polynesianists but of all students of society.

There does not appear to be any serious dispute concerning what happened. All three of the accounts consulted by the author—the traditional history of David Kalakaua,[5] Kuykendall's *The Hawaiian Kingdom,*[6] which, while a secondary source, relies heavily upon the first-hand accounts of European residents, and William Ellis's[7] summary made on the spot a few years after the event—appear to be in essential agreement.

Early in May of the year 1819 Kamehameha I, the great king who had united by conquest the entire island group, died. Despite a certain amount of continuing opposition from various of the high chiefs, often men who would formerly have been politically independent, the former king's son, Liholiho, became king under the title of Kamehameha II. Among the powerful chiefs who surrounded Liholiho and composed his court four individuals stood out in the events which followed. The first was Kaahumanu, the favourite wife of the former king, who assumed the newly-created office of *kuhina-nui,* approximately "chancellor," in response to the dying wishes of Kamehameha I (she claimed). Next may be mentioned Keopuoloui, the

Reproduced by permission of M. C. Webb from the *Journal of the Polynesian Society,* 74: 21–39 (1965).

queen mother and also a female chief of the highest rank. Kalanimoku was "prime minister" or "vizier" *(kalaimoku)* and Hewahewa was "high priest" or *kahuna-nui.* Over the course of the following months these individuals seem to have decided to abolish the taboo system, which consisted of elaborate ceremonial safeguards against a person or thing possessed of higher supernatural power coming into contact with a person or thing of lesser power to their mutual detriment and in its extreme development necessitated the carrying of high chiefs across private land so that their personal contact would not render it untouchable to its user. The chief object of attack was the prohibition against women eating with men and against their eating various foods reserved to men, these prohibitions being the most obvious part of the total system and symbolic of the whole. The common fate of the person of lesser rank who violated the eating or other taboos was death; the reign of Kamehameha I was marked by a number of instances of this punishment being meted out to those who did so.[8] As might be expected, the two royal women were the strongest advocates of the taboo abolition. Even before the final public act of abolition these women seem to have violated privately both the food taboo and that upon heterosexual dining. Liholiho himself, who does not seem to have been a very forceful individual, occupied the role of a follower rather than a leader in the entire matter.

The final overthrow of the system took place at a great feast held with this end secretly in view at the capital of Kailua early in November—six months after the death of Kamehameha I, almost to the day. After the women had eaten forbidden foods, the king came over, sat with them and ate with them, although in some agitation.[9] Following this, nation-wide orders were given to destroy the principal idols, to profane the temples, and to ignore the taboos generally. The high priest took a leading part in the iconoclasm. The change was not without opposition, however. This was led by the chief Kekuaokalani, who, as the close cousin of Liholiho, had an approximately equal rank and following, and was the next in line to the high priesthood. Kekuaokalani is said to have been one of the more outspoken opponents of the accession of Liholiho.[10] Moreover, as the man to whom the recently deceased king had at his death entrusted his god, Kukailimoku, he occupied the same role relative to the heir as Kamehameha I himself had done before he came to power by displacing his cousin Kiwalao.[11] The following of Kekuaokalani, which seems to have consisted largely of the traditional territorial chiefs of the middle rank (an important point), was apparently nearly as large as that of the iconoclasts and was defeated—after about six weeks of negotiating, manoeuvring, and skirmishing—at least in large measure because of the central government's superiority in fire-arms.[12] There is rather clear testimony that while some of the commoners may have been genuinely glad of the abolition, and while others were seriously disturbed by, or actively opposed to, the change, a great many simply followed the example of their immediate superior chiefs.[13] Therefore, with the defeat of the one centre of opposition, the changes were being at least passively accepted when the first missionaries arrived in 1820.

An examination of the explanations for these events which can be found even without an extensive historical review reveals a laudably wide range since it includes both a solution in terms of ongoing, extrapersonal cultural process and one in terms of the personal, individual motives of the participants, as well as some which fall somewhere in between these two. However—and confining our attention for the sake of brevity to the ones which are now current[14]—a careful examination reveals that while all are useful, convincing, and true as far as they go, none completely satisfies. That is, none completely fulfils Lowie's requirement of an explanation, that to be adequate it explain the distribution and the occurrence or lack of occurrence of the phenomenon in question.[15]

In taking up the first and perhaps best known explanation, Kroeber's description in terms of Cultural Fatigue, there is, as it happens, a preliminary problem—that of being precisely certain of what was meant by the term.[16] To avoid the imputation of mysticism or improper reification, I at first regarded this phrase as merely referring to the spread of a kind of mass *ennui* which made the population unwilling to support the traditional elaborate system—perhaps a kind of boredom. However, it has been recently pointed out to me that, in view of Kroeber's propensity for explaining cultural dynamics in terms of the previous state of the system itself rather than of the environmental situation, he may very well have meant to imply that cultures, or at least some types of cultures, do indeed have an innate tendency toward an over-elaboration of a basically unvarying pattern which would become so burdensome in time as to actually cause the abandonment of the behaviour.[17] The culture would, in other words, operate *as if* it were "tired." Kroeber's use of this kind of explanation was of course a reflection of his basically excellent theoretical approach which always stressed explanation of cultural phenomena in cultural terms rather than by some reductionist formula or a disguised variant of free will; it would seem, however, that upon occasion—as in the case under discussion—it could go so far as to imply that the future state of a culture is so completely determined by the past patterning of the culture that the environmental setting of the culture is of no effect (the term "environment" is used here to include not only the physical but also the social environment—the new social situation with which the culture's institutions must deal). As in linguistic change—an area frequently used by Kroeber himself as an exemplification—the growing and changing patterns apparently are seen as following the inherent logic of their own best functioning and interaction, regardless of what "external" changes happen to the culture.[18]

Despite the great attractiveness of a position which so greatly stresses the functional reality of cultural phenomena—and also the regularity of their operation—Kroeber's explanation must, nevertheless, be regarded as inadequate. While it is surely the case that in cultural as in biological evolution the previous condition of the organism limits the kinds of adjustments which will take place in a given environmental situation, it clearly is going too far to ignore the environmental effect in any change. Logically, one would expect both the previous state and the impinging circumstances to both cause and condition change. It is, then, not surprising that in fact Kroeber was extremely hard put to find one other example of this Cultural Fatigue. Therefore if it did occur one must either look for further, *local* causes or one must in fact assume some nearly unique kind of inevitable tendency within the particular culture. But if the latter is the case one must then ask why it did not appear to some extent in the other, closely related societies of Polynesia, and also be prepared to accept so independent, self-determining, supra-environmental an existence for this culture type as to approach a belief in cultural orthogenesis.[19] As a matter of fact, since the cause suggested is known only in its effect and actually is coterminous with the effect, we end with the explanation that the culture inevitably abolished its taboos because it was an inevitably taboo-abolishing culture.

Other suggested explanations do not attempt so basic an analysis as that of Kroeber.

The historian R. S. Kuykendall, for example, suggests that the abolition of the taboos was largely at the instigation of the two royal women, who would have found the system especially irksome and humiliating and who would have been successful because unpunished breaking of the taboos by foreigners had weakened faith in the system. The solution is, in other words, simply and directly in terms of *cui bono.*[20] Since this authority does not work in terms of cultural analysis, one can hardly blame him for not seeking cross-cultural regularities. In addition, the solution follows the traditional history of David Kalakaua.[21] Yet, one is loath to see so great a change as being caused essentially by the whim of a pair of even very powerful women. More importantly, not only does this explanation not explain the adherence of the tribal high priest (as Kroeber notes[22]) or of Liholiho himself, who, however pliable he may have been, could (according to Kuykendall himself) hardly fail to realise that the change would remove his traditional chiefly prerogatives, it does not really provide a sufficient motive for the royal women themselves. That is, despite the ritual disabilities of their sex, the status and prerogatives of high female chiefs in Hawaii were very great, as is proven by their very participation in the government.[23] Indeed, this chiefly high status considerably lessened the burden of the taboos upon them in comparison with the women of lower rank.[24] This was also true in Tahiti[25] and probably generally in Polynesia. Yet this great status and power were intimately bound up with the rank-mana-taboo system. Therefore, if to gain the privileges of the male meant the loss of those of the chief, this would have been nearly as costly to them as to the king and the high priest

—if no other factors were operating. For whose advantage indeed?

In the same way, even though recent explanations by anthropologists other than Kroeber do deal with social causes—that is, with observable, definable social causes—something still seems to be lacking. Robert Redfield saw the change as due to the unsettling impact of Western civilisation upon Hawaiian culture. He argued that the prestige and novelty of the new ways stimulated the change on the part of a people who were in fact accustomed to abandon old gods in favour of more successful ones; the willingness of the Hawaiians to abandon their old ways was no doubt increased by the large element of ideological incongruity and social strain which the introduction of European goods and ways had caused in the ruling circles.[26] Douglas Oliver, in his general introductory study of the Pacific peoples, offers essentially the same explanation as does Redfield, with the difference of placing his emphasis on the latter, unsettling factors in the change.[27] Buck was also in general agreement, stressing the reform aspects of the change in the quite brief account of the affair contained in his general survey of Polynesian culture.[28] Now this explanation in terms of Western impact is all true enough, and one may doubt that change would have been so drastic among so isolated a people in the absence of foreign examples showing that other systems could exist and that taboos could be violated with impunity.

It also was the case, however, that the taboo system, as Linton noted,[29] included the idea that foreigners could violate various of the local taboos since they were not part of the same genealogical-ceremonial system, hence the widespread use of natives of other islands as chiefly barbers, etc. Because of this the natives seem to have been surprisingly undisturbed by European violation of the taboos.[30] But one would indeed hesitate to argue that the taboos could be so *completely* ignored as was done by the Europeans without some doubt being cast upon the attendant beliefs.

Yet if one grants that anthropology has the task of making cross-cultural generalisations, one must ask why this effect—the nearly complete rejection of the old religion—has not taken place among many other primitive peoples faced with European contact. Why have some groups on about the same cultural level hung on to their religion so tenaciously? It took strong governmental pressure to stop the Sun Dance of the Plains Indians of the United States and required twenty years of intense missionary activity to cause a similar effect even among such closely related peoples as the Tahitians and Maori.

It is true, to be sure, that Linton avoids the above difficulties somewhat by characterising Hawaii as an extreme development (for Polynesia) toward an absolute monarchy in which an expectable sort of church-state quarrel arose and was followed by an idol-destroying revolt of the commoners.[31] But this falls on the following difficulties. As will be seen, traditional Hawaii was a tribal society, so that one may doubt that the secular and religious spheres had become sufficiently differentiated and organised as to come into conflict; secondly, in a tribal society, or one only recently emerging from a tribal condition, class divisions are unlikely to be sharp enough to allow revolution; finally, as already noted, the chiefs do not seem to have lost control of the commoners. It is perhaps only fair to add that Linton tossed off this explanation in an aside in a semi-popular work; he is supported, however, by the closely similar opinion of William Ellis, who was almost a first-hand observer of the events in question.[32] And, as will be seen, it does indeed contain a large underlying element of truth. What clearly appears to be called for, then, is a somewhat more penetrating investigation of the problem so that we may see in what sense and to what extent his explanation (and that of Redfield to a somewhat lesser extent) may be regarded as correct, granted the nature and level of advancement of Hawaiian culture.

What the underlying element of truth is, what additional factors were present that made the action of the taboo abolitionists not only feasible but inevitable, can only be seen by an examination, however rapid, of the developmental condition of Hawaiian society at the time in question.

Briefly, I would argue that the important and relevant transformation which was then taking place not only in Hawaii but throughout Polynesia was a European-induced shift from tribal and toward state organisation of society, this shift being carried through to as great a degree of completion as local conditions—such things as the size and wealth of the society or the degree of direct European interference—permitted.

Since the term "kingdom" is, however, sometimes applied to the traditional polity of Hawaii, which would suggest that this shift had already been essentially completed in some portions of Polynesia *before* European contact, it may be well to recall that neither in Hawaii nor in the Society Islands nor in Tonga were the following features of a fully evolved state society present: centralised control of an entire island chain;[33] ability to control the foreign relations of subordinate leaders—as is proven by the alliances formed among these subordinates and their freely trading with foreign visitors such as Captain Cook;[34] ability to collect and disburse wealth in other than traditional amounts and ways;[35] and monopoly control of force and capacity to punish the disobedient if such individuals were backed up by strong local sentiment.[36] The fact that the commoners as a whole appear as a rule to have been rather oppressed by the chiefs co-operating for this end does not matter, since these chiefs were not in turn fully obedient to a single authority.[37] Even a most superficial examination of the situation at the initiation of European contact suggests that unification and control were no more advanced under aboriginal conditions.[38] Some, at least, of the early visitors to the islands, for example John Ledyard, seem in fact to have made a tolerably accurate estimate of the degree of advancement toward effective centralised control which had occurred in the various Polynesian island groups.[39] If public works undertaken are any indication of social control, it would appear that these societies reached so advanced a social state by the early part of the second millennium A.D. and remained on essentially this plateau until contact.[40] The societies mentioned are those selected by Sahlins and Goldman[41] as being the most highly stratified in Polynesia, excluding Samoa, which displayed certain notable tendencies toward tribal equalitarianism such as what Sahlins called the "descent line" system of government.[42] The above-mentioned limitations to permanent and orderly centralised power apparently apply even more to Mangareva,[43] Mangaia[44] and Easter Island,[45] the only other conceivable candidates to supra-tribal status.

It is equally clear that the early nineteenth century transformation of these rather hierarchical and at times autocratic but nonetheless tribal societies was due to the introduction of European goods. In an as yet unpublished Ph.D. dissertation I have elaborated upon the idea—by no means original—that the surplus wealth represented by these goods, goods which had to pass through the hands of the senior tribal chieftain since he was the centre of the local redistributive network, would inevitably give the tribal leadership a source of power independent of tribal dues.[46] That is, the novel, rare, superior and therefore precious goods could provide the pay needed to hire and support a band of retainers over and above tribal levies. Since the new goods included fire-arms and metal-edged weapons these retainers also would be better armed than their competitors. Thus chiefs so advantageously situated for trade could with luck extend their power and compel obedience to their will. In other words, they could become kings. The well-armed band supported by a source of wealth independent of tribal gifts is of course the nucleus of a government, since it can now safely compel the surrender of the wealth which it needs for support. This is tax collection.

It is then surely no coincidence that the successive visits of Cook to New Zealand and the Society Islands show an increasing centring of native attention at the harbours, along with, apparently, some build-up of power on the part of the local chiefs.[47] In the wars of conquest which began at this time bands of retainers armed with fire-arms played a vital role in the victory of the winning side in Hawaii,[48] in Tahiti[49] and, less clearly, in Tonga.[50] At times European forces more or less actively aided the winners.[51] Those chiefs so situated in regard to location or rank as to receive the greatest benefit of the new products were the most completely transformed into kings. Moreover, in both the Society Islands[52] and Tonga[53] and, with considerably more success, in Hawaii itself[54] the emerging kings were much concerned to monopolise European trade.

But—and here at last we come to the heart of the matter—once these societies had been considerably transformed toward statehood, the whole basis of the power, and therefore of the social needs, of the leadership would also be transformed. In the tribal condition their authority and power depended upon their prestige and seniority, that is, upon their rank-status in the system of interconnected kinship, ceremonial role, and general sanctity. Therefore these individuals had to remain in the system; not only would its destruction hurt them, the absence of any other source of power probably rendered inconceivable any other kind of social ordering. Under these circumstances, then, the various ritual obligations or prohibitions, even if somewhat onerous physically or emotionally, would not be an insupportable liability precisely because they were the signs of, in a sense the proximate causes of, the desirable high status with which they were associated. They were the natural means by which one certified one's high place within the only significant scale of rank—and power hierarchy—within the society. On the other hand, the leadership of even an archaic state not only possesses another source of power—a military force supported by the tribute which may be predictably extorted by the force itself—which can enable the leadership to free itself from ritual requirements, this leadership absolutely must have the freedom of action which can only be gained by extracting itself from such obstructions and demands. If they were not to do so they could not maintain control of the larger and more fluid state social system.

More specifically, a king and his court cannot maintain the necessary superiority of rank if a sanctified ramage leads, as it must, to continuous gradations in status, with some persons outside the governing circles (no matter how widely drawn) almost equal in rank to those within them; in the same way a government cannot appoint and replace subsidiary governors —needed over a wider area than ever before—on the basis of competence and loyalty if ramage position apportions social power by the whims of birth. Yet this situation was present not only in Hawaii[55] but in other societies that developed significantly toward statehood, Tonga[56] and the Society Islands.[57] Indeed, even the most cursory review of the political situation in Hawaii before and during the rise of Kamehameha I to power shows that precisely this kind of inescapable, legitimate rivalry and "disloyalty" among the various closely related members of the ruling senior kin groups or ramage "core"—generally cousins, and often brothers or even father and son—was not only a leading cause, or at least mechanism, of the aboriginal failure to achieve the consolidation of state power and thus full civilisation, but was also the chief hindrance to state formation after the advent of the Europeans.[58]

In addition, when one has to devote a large part of one's wealth to ritual ends, such as immensely expensive dedicatory temple services, as in Tahiti[59] and Tonga,[60] or great harvest feasts, as in Hawaii[61] and Tonga[62] and to a lesser extent in Tahiti,[63] one does not have it available for foreign trade or as bonuses for one's warriors. It is important to remember, of course, that in the case just mentioned, even though the goods were largely used eventually, there was no control of, nor maximisation of utility in, the expenditure. These were very important considerations at a time when native desire for foreign goods and for foreign ways—and so willingness to follow a leadership who could reward them with these things—was intense, and when the foreigners themselves were most anxious to open up a new market; later, when the leadership of an emerging state had gone heavily into debt to the powerful foreign traders, who could at times be quite threatening, the need, and desire, to divert local wealth from traditional ends must have become quite desperate. Undoubtedly present in all of the Pacific kingdoms, these tendencies were notably well advanced in Hawaii by the end of the second decade of the nineteenth century.[64]

Finally, if—as was the case in aboriginal Hawaii—the ruler cannot travel about unobstructedly except at night, must devote four months of each year largely to ritual (the Makahiki season—but it should be noted that warfare does appear to have been carried on in this period, at least on occasion), and cannot even wage war without the chancy finding of a scarce sea plant,[65] his ability to exercise power freely and in a novel way is seriously crippled. In the same fashion, if a chief must resign his position to his son on the latter's majority as in Tahiti,[66] or if he must share it with a sacred (or secular) high chief as in Tonga,[67] his authority would be directly threatened. However, the secularisation of the office of high chief, that is, the elimination of the sacred nature of the kinship system, is one obvious way to avoid these problems as well as all of those mentioned just above (one should note that no mention has been made of the inhibition resulting from chiefs' being too sacred even to walk, since in fact they seem to have moved around well enough on their own in emergencies).[68] An even better way is to centralise a streamlined, non-obstructive form of the cult under the charge of the government, to make it the prisoner of the political order rather than the reverse.

It would therefore seem that religious change of this kind actually is not at all unexpectable during the transition from tribe to state. This type of change would of course be especially likely to occur if the tribal society undergoing transformation were a chieftainship, since as Service[69] has noted, the "chiefdom level" is necessarily marked by extension of power through kin and ritual ties due to the absence of true governmental institutions; the very strength of those ties which made the "chiefdom" possible is a hindrance when a new freedom of action is required. But because chieftainships are by their size and centralisation those tribal societies most suited to become states, the downgrading of the traditional religious institutions should in fact be a very common or even typical occurrence during state formation and consolidation. In addition to the religious changes—of one kind or another—which accompanied state development in the Polynesian chieftainships, one recalls that among the Zulu Shaka, who was the first founder of a stable state, not only broke the power of the traditional witch hunters but also expelled all of the rainmakers except for his own appointees.[70] In the same way in the area of the so-called "civilised tribes" of the south-eastern United States, that is, in a region of moderately well developed chieftainships,[71] the growth of pan-tribal government, as for example among the Cherokee[72] and the Creek,[73] was marked by the ascendancy of war chiefs and then military dictators over the traditional priest-chiefs even in non-military affairs (other factors were operating here, to be sure). And these are of course merely examples selected from areas with which the author happens to be familiar; they should be sufficient, however, to suggest that wherever chieftainships evolve into states a decline of traditional religious controls is likely to be involved.

The failure adequately to stress this consideration for Polynesia is due, I think, simply to the fact that in most of the area the principal mediators of European goods were, or were accompanied by, the missionaries of a less immediately governmentally troublesome ideology—Christianity, of course. In both Tahiti[74] and Tonga,[75] and also in Mangareva[76] and Mangaia[77] where the small size of the respective social universes inhibited state formation, Christianity was adopted first by the "ins," or at least by the single most nearly dominant group, and provided ready-made a substitute system in which rulers could rise above the ruled and could govern in a less inhibited fashion. It also served, of course, as a route to domination in that Christian adherence assured a source of European goods via the missionaries,[78] but indications are not wanting that, apart from Christianity's role as a source of aid to its adherents, the politico-religious situation in the other islands mentioned was not so different from that in Hawaii.[79] In Tahiti the native ruler clearly meant to keep control over the new religion if he could,[80] and in Tonga Christianity became a state church, opposed by anti-government dissenters in typical European fashion.[81] In both areas, moreover, the missionaries themselves seem to have been worriedly aware of the non-ideological motives of the newly converted rulers.[82] Another indication that Christianity was only a very convenient means to an end may be found in Tonga since, although the sacred high chieftainship (the Tui Tonga) was not finally abolished until the introduction of Christianity, the first steps in that direction were taken two generations before in the early period of European contact. Moreover, the office was empty during much of the intervening period.[83] During much of this period Christianity was a very minor or even negligible factor.

It seems reasonable to suppose also that the relatively much longer period of uninterrupted intensive missionary activity required, first, to achieve any significant number of conversions and, then, to win over a large part of the population in New Zealand and Tahiti in comparison with Hawaii and Tonga, and even to Mangareva and Mangaia, is related to the local utilisation of Christianity as a mechanism of social control. In Hawaii and Tonga centralisation was fairly considerable even under aboriginal conditions and a greater or lesser degree of development toward state society had taken place before the missionaries were on the scene (to a significant degree), while in Mangareva and Mangaia, even though tribal conditions were essentially operative, a senior group was in power when the missionaries arrived. Therefore there was in every case one or more groups which could find use for a centralised state cult, in contrast to Tahiti and New Zealand where when the missionaries landed no person or group had been yet able to consolidate control with the result that there was as yet no need to remove the problems and inhibitions of the native cult system. The consideration that at times (e.g. in Tonga, Mangaia) the missionaries rather than the local rulers became the real masters of the situation[84] need not negate this since their ascendancy could not, of course, have been foreseen by the natives.

I would therefore argue that the way in which Hawaii differed from the rest of Polynesia consisted primarily in not having effective missionary influence present as a major factor until rather late in the process of state formation. It was this which necessitated the reshaping of the *native* religious system. Along this line it is worth noting that even after the taboo abolition, Pele, the volcano goddess, continued to receive widespread worship and that the royal tombs were venerated, which suggests that what was in the offing—and would have emerged had missionaries never arrived—would have been some sort of royally controlled variation of the traditional cult.[85] No extraordinary degree of intelligence would be required to realise that such a change would greatly increase the power and efficiency of the government. The traditional place of the leading ramage member—that is, of the high chief—at the centre of the system of sacred rank, the ability of the higher chiefs to remove or resist taboos upon occasion, and the practice of a new regime's assuming the sacred power and paraphernalia of defeated chieftains taken together would provide models for such action.[86]

Stimulation also was not lacking. Not only had Kamehameha I gained his supremacy through an European-armed following, but also throughout his reign his power was clearly supported in very large measure by his possession of large amounts of foreign weapons and other supplies.[87] Potential centres of opposition to the dynasty were abundantly present. The selection of Liholiho as successor to the throne left disappointed contenders of nearly equal sanctity,[88] and it seems to have been necessary for the old king to turn over to his heir a considerable amount of the royal armament well before his death in order to assure a peaceful accession.[89] Moreover, Davenport[90] —whose conclusions as to the nature and causes of the taboo abolition parallel those of this paper in all major aspects—has, on the basis of a detailed examination of aboriginal history, pointed out that not only did the leader of the opposition, Kekuaolani, have ample examples for his rebellion from Hawaiian history, but the division of power upon the death of a supreme chief into "secular" and "sacred" aspects, leaving the two heirs either to fight it out between themselves or to accept a reversion to a rather more decentralised condition, may well have been a basic pattern of Hawaiian society.[91] There was, then, ample need to bring about a consolidation of power that would be "legitimate." And of course, as has always been known, at the time of the change Liholiho had recently heard of the taboo abolition which had just taken place in favour of Christianity in Tahiti.[92] That the opposition to the destruction of the old system should so largely consist of lesser, local chiefs reflects the fact that any person outside the government would have no real power or place at all once the sacredness of the kin system was ended; a fact of which the court circles also could hardly have been entirely unaware.

The lesser place of missionary contact in the early stages of consolidation was of course due to a perfectly understandable set of causes: the good location of Hawaii relative to the north-west American coast and to China, the chain's capacity for the production of large amounts of foodstuffs useful as ship's stores, and the presence of an important resource, sandalwood, factors which all served to stimulate an early and very rapid introduction of trade.[93] Therefore, the missionary societies with their limited resources simply were not able to participate until the changes introduced by contact were already far advanced. With the arrival of the missionaries, however, the situation rapidly began to resemble that in other areas of Polynesia. That is, the lesser chiefs tended to be opposed to the new religion, the leading chiefs about the throne were favourably disposed, and Kaahumanu, who as regent during the absence and then after the death of Liholiho became, after 1823, the strongest figure in the government, was strongly in favour of it.[94] This exactly matched the division in both Tahiti[95] and Tonga,[96] except, of course, that in these latter areas the split was involved in the fighting required for state consolidation. A final indication that in the early contact period Hawaii religion functioned chiefly to serve political ends is that Boki, the younger brother of Kalanimoku, who as one of the leading chiefs and a member of the government had been strongly in favour of Protestant Christianity, turned toward Roman Catholicism as soon as he went into opposition to the regency of Kaahumanu;[97] this also closely resembles events in Tonga after Christianity was well-established.[98]

Another, most interesting, similarity among all of the principal island chains mentioned—Hawaii, Tahiti, and Tonga—and also among the Zulu is that the time of the religious changes was in the generation *following* the first significant attempts at state formation (although only in Hawaii was the process one of uninterrupted consolidation). It would appear, then, that the limitations of the older ideological systems only became seriously inhibiting, or perhaps that power adequate to replace them only became sufficiently great, or both, at a point well along toward the final establishment of state controls. It rather seems that these little statelets provide a microcosm—immensely speeded up in development because of the influences from regions so much more civilised—of events in the great primary centres of civilisation. One thinks, for example, of the difference in social style between Gerzian Period and Middle Kingdom Egypt, between Late Uruk Period and Early Dynastic Mesopotamia, possibly between terminal Lungshan and Chou China, and of course very definitely between Early Classic and Post-Classic Mesoamerica (compare Steward's characterisation of these periods in their respective regions).[99] So although Linton and Ellis's explanations in terms of a church-state clash is obviously reading into the events an organisational formalisation and separation which did not yet exist, it is correct in that it sees Hawaii in 1819 as simply one more example of the shift from ritual to secular controls which inevitably characterises the development of state societies. Turning to the explanation favoured by Redfield, we can say that a "reform" of older patterns was indeed involved, but that rather than being due to the example of a fortunately-introduced foreign ideology it represents an obvious necessity for any society which has reached the state level.

We may therefore infer that the events of 1819 are in fact an example of a rule of cultural development, of an evolutionary "law," if you will. It is not, perhaps, especially profound, but it has enabled us to explicate a particular puzzling situation as an individual instance of a cross-cultural regularity. Of a regularity, however, which does not refer to a set of supra-environmental, autonomous, self-determining culture patterns but instead to the functionally necessary adjustments which any culture at a specific stage of development must, as a coherent action system, make to characteristic problems.[100] While all honour is due to Kroeber for his stressing of the reality of processes on the cultural ("superorganic") level of interaction—and at a time when this was all too often neglected—it is surely a considerable gain to view these whenever possible as satisfying reasonable, functional ends. This seems in fact to be a necessity if culture indeed is, as it is frequently characterised, man's distinctive survival technique.

Finally, I would stress also that this need not conflict with individualistic explanations; rather, it parallels and justifies them. It is, after all, expectable that the persons who would initiate the kinds of changes dealt with in this paper would be those who suffered status conflict or deprivation under the traditional system, perhaps to the point of abnormality. Thus not only did the Hawaiian royal women have this problem, so to some extent did Pomare I of Tahiti (because of his partly foreign descent),[101] the sceptic Finau, who ruled much of Tonga in Mariner's time (because he was an usurper),[102] Shaka (because of illegitimacy and youthful physical inadequacy)[103] and various of the dictatorial chiefs of the south-eastern United States (because of a half-caste parentage). The point, of course, is that while status-deprived or deviant individuals might be expected to occur randomly, they could only have (successfully) acted as the individuals in question did if the realities of the cultural situation demanded it; that is, the needs of the evolving culture have the same directing and regulating effect upon the chance individuals that natural selection has upon random viable mutations. It is true, to be sure, that the situations mentioned were all unusual in that persons eccentric enough to embrace the cultural changes needed (even if they could not analyse them sociologically), instead of well-enculturated persons, rather unexpectedly had attained or maintained high rank. But here we may note that the very atypical nature of these individuals might give them an advantage over more traditionally oriented persons in a situation in which traditional behaviour was no longer adaptive; this would suggest, then, that the cultural situation even played a part in determining the effective existence of the individual innovators—by enabling them to move into or maintain a position in which they could innovate.

If this view could indeed be maintained it suggests some interesting possibilities for an investigation of the way in which a society creates its leaders as they are needed. An even more intriguing question which follows in turn is that of the manner in which cultural systems maintain themselves without subjecting their members to overt, "external" pressures, a problem which obviously has yet to be handled to the satisfaction of the total anthropological community. However, although the temptation to indulge in a review of these matters is obviously very great, it is equally clearly necessary to defer comment; if nothing else, considerations of space—and prudence—strongly urge that such basic questions of psychology and philosophy receive their own treatment. Therefore, this discussion will be concluded with a simple reminder of a consideration germane to the man-culture relationship which our review has perhaps illustrated especially clearly. This is that for an individual to engage in acts (or innovations) which serve the survival needs of his society, it is not really necessary that he have a completely clear view of the means-end relationship, or even be fully conscious that it exists. This kind of deficiency is perhaps more often the case than not, even in such anthropologically sophisticated groups as modern nations (supposedly) are. But provided that the socially useful acts did not seriously impede individual minimum needs—and it is difficult to imagine a society long continuing to exist in which such an incongruence existed in very many cases—their survival value would insure that they would be performed, even though the motives of the individual concerned might not show any special awareness of the ultimate utility which an objective observer might find in the behaviour. That is, the actions would tend to be carried out because the better functioning of the social system would of itself reinforce them; in other words, they would be performed because when they were done things—for some reason—simply *worked* better. It follows that when examining the social ends served by a custom —or innovation—one can apparently safely factor out personal motivations, at least to a considerable degree. In our example, the novelty-prone Hawaiian rulers certainly did not realise that they were part of "the process of inevitable political consolidation within a newly formed secondary state," but they must have had enough perspicacity to see that the old religious system, in supporting a social structure which worked against the new social reality, was somehow "wrong" and had to be changed to one which was more congruent with the new order. The motives of the innovators themselves may, of course, have been either cynical *or* pious (toward a new, reformed—and centralised—cult), and the end product would surely have been the same. They were no doubt a mixture of both. But the interesting result is that in our new explanation for the changes involved, it has not actually been necessary to worry overmuch about the motives of the individual innovators, surely a great gain in efficiency, if nothing more.

NOTES

1. This paper is a slightly revised form of one read at the November, 1964 meeting of the American Anthropological Association held in Detroit, Michigan.
2. Kroeber 1948:403–405.
3. Redfield 1953:128–130.
4. Davenport 1964a:27.
5. Kalakaua 1888:431–446.
6. Kuykendall 1938:61–70.
7. Ellis 1917:91–96.
8. Davenport 1964a; Malo 1951:56–58; Ii 1963:19, 22–23, 35, 58–61.
9. Kuykendall 1938:68.
10. Kuykendall 1938:62–65; Ellis 1917:94; Kalakaua 1888:439, 444.
11. Kuykendall 1938:62–65; Ii 1963:9–15, 139–140.
12. Kalakaua 1888:439–445; Ellis 1917:38, 93–94, 336–344.
13. Kalakaua 1888:437–438; Ellis 1917:38, 65, 150, 152, 214.
14. I have also excluded, for example, the non-naturalistic explanation offered by some of the early missionaries—that God motivated the destruction of the old religion by miraculous intervention in the minds of the actors (e.g. Dibble 1839:57–74).
15. Lowie 1954:27–29. 354–355.
16. Kroeber 1948:404.
17. The point was very convincingly made by Dr. Elman Service of the University of Michigan in conversation, and after re-reading various of Kroeber's essays on the nature of culture, I find myself in complete agreement.
18. Examples of Kroeber's thinking in terms of patterns and pre-conditioned change are common in Chapters VII-X of his *Anthropology* (1948)—one may note such examples as cultural hybridity, cultural death, parasitic cultures, the content-form dichotomy, and the great interest in matters of style. His essays on "Structure, Function, and Patterns in Biology and Anthropology," "White's View of Culture," and "The Concept of Culture in Science"—all reprinted in *The Nature of Culture* (Kroeber 1952:85–94, 10–117, 118–135)—provide still more insights into Kroeber's basic approach. David Aberle's well-known study, "The Influence of Linguistics in Early Culture and Personality Theory" (1960) may also be consulted. The reader may indeed feel that the issue is a minor one upon which to criticise Kroeber, especially since, as noted, the fault is due to an excess or misapplication of a great virtue—even Homer nods: nevertheless, the present problem is representative of an overemphasis which apparently is quite basic to Kroeber's thinking, and while the theoretical fault is a slight one, it is capable of causing fairly serious errors in the analysis of actual situations, as this study suggests.
19. Simpson 1949:130–159.
20. Kuykendall 1938:67–68.
21. Kalakaua 1888:433–434.
22. Kroeber 1948:404.
23. Malo 1951:30; Kuykendall 1938:63–64; Kalakaua 1888:431–434.
24. Dibble 1839:57ff.
25. Ellis 1829:passim.
26. Redfield 1953:128–130.
27. Oliver 1961:115, 256–257, 259–264.
28. Buck 1959:264–265.
29. Linton 1956:185–186.

30. See, for example, Cook 1906:passim.
31. Linton 1956:190.
32. Ellis 1917:95ff.
33. In order to avoid the lengthy interruptions of the text which references to support these summary characterisations would require, these data have been placed in this and the succeeding four notes. Therefore, for Hawaii see Ellis 1917:110; Kuykendall 1938:9–10. For the Society Islands, Ellis 1829, I:123, 266–268, II:468–469; Handy 1930:75–77. For Tonga see Martin 1827:passim.
34. See for example Cook 1906:21–22, 30–31, 136–137, 261ff., 309, 385–400; Martin 1827:passim.
35. Again, for Hawaii see Malo 1951:53, 140ff., 190–195. For Tahiti, Ellis 1829. II:288–290, 361, 368–378; Handy 1930:49ff. For Tonga, Martin 1827, I:88, 201–205; Gifford 1929:104, 124–127.
36. For Hawaii see Malo 1951:58, 193–195, 198; Ellis 1917:243, 318. For Tahiti, Ellis 1829, II:344, 361–370; Handy 1930: 41, 43, 47–48, 75–76. For Tonga, Martin 1827:passim; Gifford 1929:117, 183ff.
37. The situation seems to have been that the commoners were not able to resist severe and even arbitrary demands from any superior persons of whatever level, while the lesser chiefs could do precisely that; on the other hand, the middle level chiefs would tend to co-operate with each other and to comply with reasonable demands of their superiors simply out of traditional respect and mutual self interest (see Malo 1951:53, 55–58, 64, 68–69 and Ellis 1917:311, 316–317, for Hawaii; Ellis 1829, II:340, 367, 373–375, for Tahiti; Martin 1827, I:201, II:90ff., and Gifford 1929:104, 117, 127, for Tonga). While this does in fact suggest an European feudal kingdom, one should remember that much of the characteristic polity of feudal Europe was a result, ultimately, of the breakdown of governmental controls and the influx of peoples who were on a tribal level or nearly so.
38. Beaglehole 1947:160–161, 184, 242–245, 259, 284ff., et passim.
39. Ledyard 1963:13ff., 26ff., 57–58, 111, 129–131.
40. Suggs 1960:94–101, 119–128, 142ff., 160–163.
41. Sahlins 1958:11–48; Goldman 1960.
42. Sahlins 1958:29–37.
43. Buck 1938:140–161.
44. Buck 1934:passim.
45. Metraux 1940:129–149; Beaglehole 1947:218.
46. Webb 1964.
47. Cook 1906:passim.
48. Martin 1827, I:68; Kalakaua 1888:394–403, 439–445.
49. Ellis 1829, I:84, 123, 240–260.
50. Martin 1827, I:96–98, 138–164; Thomson 1894:316, 333, 338; Gifford 1929:220ff.
51. Kuykendall 1938:40–50; Ellis 1829, I:112ff., 240ff.; Thomson 1894:353–355.
52. Ellis 1829, I:87, 187, 438, II:391–401.
53. Ledyard 1963:26–30; Thomson 1894:312ff.
54. Kuykendall 1938:82–94, Ii 1963:128–129, 146; Ellis 1917:273–277, 290, 300, 316–317.
55. Malo 1951:52–55, 191–193.
56. Gifford 1929:15–17, 29–34, 112–114.
57. Handy 1930:11–12, 23–24. The ramage is, of course, common in Polynesia (Sahlins 1958:passim). As has been suggested, in those areas which became states it was replaced as a source of power by a non-kin following and officialdom paid for, surely, by the proceeds of trade and the profits of plunder (see Ellis 1917:110, and Malo 1951:58–59, for Hawaii; Ellis 1829, I:214–215, and Handy 1930:46, for Tahiti; and Gifford 1929:204, and Thomson 1894:195ff., for Tonga).
58. Ledyard 1963:130–131; Ii 1963:49–54.
59. Ellis 1829, I:528–529; Handy 1930:24–35.
60. Martin 1827, I:passim; Gifford 1929:185–203.
61. Malo 1951:142ff.
62. Martin 1827:passim.
63. Ellis 1829, II:207ff.
64. Ii 1963:86–88, et passim; Kuykendall 1938:82–95; Davenport 1964b.

65. Malo 1951:57, 141, 148–152, 163, 188; Ii 1963:51–52; Ledyard 1963:111–114.
66. Ellis 1829, I:64–65, 93, 108ff., II:346–354.
67. Martin 1827, II:126–127; Ledyard 1963:28ff.; Gifford 1929:48, 205.
68. For example, see Ellis 1829, I:passim.
69. Service 1962:164–174.
70. Ritter 1957:90ff., 241–254, 274–275; Gluckman 1940. The case of the Zulu, incidentally, provides an especially good example of secondary state formation; in addition to the operation of the process suggested for Polynesia, a land shortage which generated increasing inter-tribal war (in addition to the works cited in the text, see Gluckman 1960) also played a part.
71. Swanton 1928a:passim.
72. Gearing 1962:99ff.
73. Swanton 1928b:310–315, 320–327, 357, 453.
74. Ellis 1829, I:87, 187–220.
75. Thomson 1894:194–220, 344–350.
76. Buck 1938:96ff.
77. Buck 1939:75–79.
78. For example, see Ellis 1829, I:66, 90, 136, et passim.
79. Two other important benefits which Christianity provided for the royal leaders may be noted. One was that adherence to Christianity provided a party tie which, by cutting across local loyalties, enabled an easier build-up of a more fervent body of followers (Ellis 1829, I:192ff., 216–260; Thomson 1894:347ff.; Gifford 1929:218). The second was that after Christianity had been generally accepted, its (theoretically) pacifistic orientation would set opinion against the possibility of rebellion, in contrast to the older religion, which laid no onus on fighting (Ellis 1829, II:123; Buck 1939:76–77; Ellis 1917:121). Probably no more need be said, since both features are really more positive aspects of the same qualities of Christianity which made it more convenient to state government than the old tribal cults—rejection of kin loyalty, lack of interference with governmental needs, and support of a stable social system.
80. Ellis 1829, I:207–208, 243, 394–395, 438, II: 102–107, 254.
81. Thomson 1894:195–203, 350–360.
82. Ellis 1829, I:188, 243, II:250–255; Gifford 1929:215.
83. Gifford 1929:passim; Martin 1827, I:289ff., II:27ff.
84. Thomson 1894:190, 203ff.; Buck 1939:87–91.
85. Ellis 1917:124–126, 198–199, 210, 230ff., 262, 270.
86. Davenport 1964a: Ii 1963:51–53; cf. Ellis 1829, I, II:passim.
87. Ii 1963:54, 66, 120–121; Martin 1827:68; Kuykendall 1938:22–23, 35, 40–50.
88. Ii 1963:37–38.
89. Ii 1963:139–141.
90. Davenport 1964b.
91. The author owes a considerable debt of gratitude to Dr. Davenport, not only for commenting upon his paper during the recent meetings of the American Anthropological Association, but also for suggesting further bibliography relating to early Hawaii. Despite the remarkable similarity between this paper and his own, Dr. Davenport gave the author every encouragement to revise and publish this paper. His courtesy towards a junior colleague is greatly appreciated.
92. Ellis 1917:95.
93. Ellis 1917:34–35, 299, 310–311; Kuykendall 1938:passim.
94. Ellis 1917:38, 336–344; Dibble 1839:87–92; Kuykendall 1938:117–118, 123–125, 133, 173.
95. Ellis 1829, I:143ff., 207–208, 217, 267–268, II:468–471.
96. Gifford 1929:347; Thomson 1894:200–203.
97. Ii 1963:153–157; Kuykendall 1938:140–142.
98. Thomson 1894:263ff., 355–360.
99. Steward 1955:178–222.
100. Strictly speaking, the changes discussed in this paper are, like anthropological "laws" generally, an example of what may be called a scientific "rule." That is, although the changes occur as expected with considerable frequency, our lack of ability to measure and correlate at all adequately the various factors operating results in variations and apparent exceptions that

can not be explained at this time. These problems, however, do not nullify the regularities which do exist.

101. Handy 1930:51.

102. Martin 1827:passim.

103. Ritter 1957:11–20.

REFERENCES

Aberle, David F., 1960. "The Influence of Linguistics in Early Culture and Personality Theory." In Gertrude E. Dole and Robert L. Carneiro, eds., *Essays in the Science of Culture in Honor of Leslie A. White.* New York, Crowell.

Beaglehole, J. C., 1947. *The Exploration of the Pacific.* 2nd ed. London, Black.

Buck, Peter H., 1934. *Mangaian Society.* Honolulu, Bernice P. Bishop Museum, Bulletin 122.

——— 1938. *Ethnology of Mangareva.* Honolulu, Bernice P. Bishop Museum, Bulletin 157.

——— 1939. *Anthropology and Religion.* New Haven, Yale University Press.

——— 1959. *Vikings of the Pacific.* Chicago, University of Chicago Press.

Cook, James, 1906. *Voyages of Discovery,* Edited and abridged by John Barrow. London, Dent.

Davenport, William, 1964a. "Hawaiian Feudalism." *Expedition,* 6, 2:14–27.

——— 1964b, "Political Consequences of the Hawaiian Cultural Revolution" (Paper delivered at the Sixty-third Annual Meeting of the American Anthropological Association, Detroit, Michigan, November 19–22, 1964).

Dibble, Sheldon, 1839. *History and General Views of the Sandwich Islands Mission.* New York, Taylor & Dodd.

Ellis, William, 1829. *Polynesian Researches During a Residence of Nearly Six Years in the South Sea Islands . . .* 2 vols. London, Fisher.

——— 1917. *A Narrative of a Four Years' Journey Through Hawaii or Owhybee; with remarks on the history, traditions, manners, customs, and language of the inhabitants of the Sandwich Isles,* with an introduction by Lorrin A. Thurston. Honolulu, Hawaiian Gazette Co.

Gearing, Fred, 1962. *Priests and Warriors: Social Structures for Cherokee Politics in the 18th Century.* American Anthropological Association, Memoirs No. 93.

Gifford, Edward Winslow, 1929. *Tongan Society.* Honolulu, Bernice P. Bishop Museum, Bulletin 61.

Gluckman, Max, 1940. "The Kingdom of the Zulu of South Africa." In M. Fortes and E. E. Evans-Pritchard, eds., *African Political Systems.* London, Oxford University Press, for the International African Institute.

——— 1960. "The Rise of a Zulu Empire." *Scientific American,* 202, 4:157–168.

Goldman, Irving, 1960. "The Evolution of Polynesian Societies." In Stanley Daimond, ed., *Culture and History: Essays in Honor of Paul Radin.* New York, Columbia University Press, for Brandeis University.

Handy, E. S. Craighill, 1930. *History and Culture in the Society Islands.* Honolulu, Bernice P. Bishop Museum, Bulletin 79.

Ii, John Papa, 1963. *Fragments of Hawaiian History.* Honolulu, Bishop Museum Press.

Kalakaua, David, 1888. *The Legends and Myths of Hawaii, the Fables and Folklore of a Strange People.* Edited, with an introduction, by R. M. Doggett. New York, Webster.

Kroeber, A. L., 1948. *Anthropology.* New York, Harcourt, Brace.

——— 1952. *The Nature of Culture.* Chicago, University of Chicago Press.

Kuykendall, Ralph S., 1938. *The Hawaiian Kingdom 1778–1854, Foundation and Transformation.* Honolulu, University of Hawaii Press.

Ledyard, John, 1963. *A Journal of Captain Cook's Last Voyage . . .* Chicago, Quadrangle Books [First pub. 1783].

Linton, Ralph, 1956. *The Tree of Culture.* New York, Knopf.

Lowie, Robert H., 1954. *Toward Understanding the Germans.* Chicago, University of Chicago Press.

Malo, David, 1951. *Hawaiian Antiquities (Moolalo Hawaii).* Translated from the Hawaiian by Dr. Nathaniel B. Emerson, 1898. Honolulu, Bernice P. Bishop Museum, Special Publication 2.

Martin, John, 1827. *An Account of the Natives of the Tonga Islands, in the South Paci-*

fic . . . , arr. from The Extensive Communications of Mr. William Mariner. 3rd ed., 2 vols. Edinburgh, Constable.

METRAUX, ALFRED, 1940. *Ethnology of Easter Island.* Honolulu, Bernice P. Bishop Museum, Bulletin 160.

OLIVER, DOUGLAS L., 1961. *The Pacific Islands.* New York, Doubleday.

REDFIELD, ROBERT, 1953. *The Primitive World and Its Transformations.* Ithaca, Cornell University Press.

RITTER, E. A., 1957. *Shaka Zulu: The Rise of the Zulu Empire.* New York, Putnam.

SAHLINS, MARSHALL D., 1958. *Social Stratification in Polynesia.* Seattle, University of Washington Press.

SERVICE, ELMAN R., 1962. *Primitive Social Organization, an Evolutionary Perspective.* New York, Random House.

SIMPSON, GEORGE GAYLORD, 1949. *The Meaning of Evolution.* New Haven, Yale University Press.

STEWARD, JULIAN, 1955. *Theory of Culture Change.* Urbana, University of Illinois Press.

SUGGS, ROBERT C., 1960. *The Island Civilizations of Polynesia.* New York, Mentor Books.

SWANTON, JOHN R., 1928a. "Aboriginal Culture of the Southeast." *Forty-second Annual Report of the Bureau of American Ethnology to the Secretary of the Smithsonian Institution, 1924–1925* : 673–726. Washington, United States Government Printing Office.

——— 1928b. "Social Organization and Social Usages of the Indians of the Creek Confederacy." *Forty-second Annual Report of the Bureau of American Ethnology to the Secretary of the Smithsonian Insitution, 1924–1925* : 23–472. Washington, United States Government Printing Office.

THOMPSON, BASIL, 1894. *The Diversions of a Prime Minister.* Edinburgh and London, Blackwood.

WEBB, MALCOLM C., 1964. "The Post-Classic Decline of the Peten Maya, An Interpretation in the Light of a General Theory of State Society." Unpublished Ph.D. Dissertation in Anthropology. Ann Arbor, University of Michigan.

16

SOCIAL CHANGE IN PUKAPUKA

Jeremy Beckett

The celebrated "winds of change" have blown less keenly in Polynesia than in most other parts of the colonial world, but there can be few spots which have not been subject to some recent political and social development. However, a number of the more remote islands have still barely emerged from the state of stagnation which was so general in the years between the wars. Nowhere in Polynesia can one find an indigenous culture intact, but there are communities which, having made an initial adaptation to European dominance—often as many as four generations ago—continue in what might be called a secondary growth of tradition. Typically, this involves participation in a cash economy, though insufficiently to permit total abandonment of the old subsistence economy; submission to a European government, generally with no more than diffuse opposition; and a strict adherence to mission Christianity.

Pukapuka, one of the Northern Group of the Cook Islands, retains this character and has changed little over the last 35 years. It has been shielded from outside influences by its isolation and its lack of exploitable economic resources, but there has generally been internal resistance to such influences as have penetrated. A communal system of land tenure, a profound suspicion of the New Zealand Administration, and a feeling of being different from other Cook Islanders, have all militated against change. The Pukapukans evince a deep attachment to the institutions of their society, whether stemming from the first or second growth of tradition, yet they should not be dubbed conservative too hastily. Their approach to European culture has been selective, but they are by no means blind to the virtues of its material products. Rather should it be said that their opportunities for change have been few, and that these few have not often proved acceptable.

The data on which this article is based come from a number of written sources and a short period of field work. Ernest and Pearl Beaglehole spent

Reproduced by permission of Jeremy Beckett from the *Journal of the Polynesian Society*, 73:411–430 (1964).

seven and a half months on the island in 1934–35, presenting their findings in their *Ethnology of Pukapuka*, several articles, and a popular book.[1] An anthropologist, Peter Vayda, spent a few weeks there in 1957, but apart from two brief articles[2] his findings have yet to be published. My own visit lasted a mere six weeks, running over the months of July-September, 1964, though further information was gathered in the Pukapukan settlement on Rarotonga.[3] Inevitably, there were severe limitations on the amount and quality of new data that could be gathered in so short a time; however, the reader may find it useful to have previously recorded data re-examined from the point of view of social change and in the light of the present-day situation.

Communications

Pukapuka is 390 miles east-north-east of Samoa and 715 miles north-west of Rarotonga. Though not completely isolated, it seems to have had no regular contact with other islands before the modern era began, and though known to European seamen from the 18th century it was very rarely visited, having few attractions and a dangerous anchorage. The London Missionary Society did not commence work there until 1857 (34 years after its arrival in Rarotonga and Aitutaki), and the New Zealand Administration was only nominally represented there before 1914. The island has produced copra since the last decades of the 19th century, but in insufficient quantities to merit the visit of a cargo boat more than a few times a year. Now that communications with Samoa have been severed, since all traffic must pass through Rarotonga (the administrative centre of the Cook Islands) isolation has, if anything, been increased. Over the last decade the annual number of visits has averaged a little over four.

The Pukapukans have had limited contact with other Polynesians but almost none with Europeans. Church pastors and Administration representatives have almost invariably been Cook Islanders; a Dutch priest has cared for the Roman Catholic congregation over the last seven years, but before him the only long-term resident was the writer, Robert Frisbie.[4] Poor communications have also limited the Pukapukan's opportunities to visit other places, as can be seen from Table 1. Opportunities have not greatly improved since the war except for adolescents, a number of whom are now sent to school on Rarotonga by the Government. As described later, Pukapukans on Rarotonga tend to avoid close contact with other groups, by whom their dialect cannot be understood. In recent years a number have emigrated to New Zealand, though, so far, few have returned home to retail their experiences.

The Economy

Pukapuka is a low atoll, consisting of three islets within a lagoon which have a total area of 1,250 acres. The 800 inhabitants[5] have their permanent

Table 1. Mobility among 287 Pukapukans, Resident on Pukapuka, Aged 20–70+

	Age Groups						
	20–9	*30–9*	*40–9*	*50–9*	*60–9*	*70+*	*Total*
Total number	73	68	48	52	30	16	287
Number never leaving Pukapuka	35	27	15	16	6	7	106
Number visiting New Zealand	0	2	1	1	1	0	5
Average years of stay	—	(5.2)	(5.0)	(5.0)	(5.0)	—	(4.0)
Number ever visiting Rarotonga	25	37	31	33	21	8	155
Average years of stay	(6.4)	(3.7)	(2.5)	(4.7)	(4.5)	(11.9)	(3.3)
Number visiting other Cook Islands	14	14	8	3	9	1	49
Number visiting Samoa, Society Islands, New Guinea	1	1	2	5	4	1	14

Notes:

1 This sample includes the greater part of the Pukapukan adult population; the only ones omitted were those for whom adequate information had not been collected.

2 Pukapukans occasionally went to work in Samoa, in the days when regular contact was maintained. Those visiting New Guinea went as missionaries.

3 Visits to Nassau have not been taken into account.

settlement on one islet, Wale, keeping the other two as reserves, to be visited only at certain times. The soil of the atoll, mostly coral sand and rubble, permits a relatively dense vegetation, but few food-bearing plants other than coconut palms. Taro, which together with a few *puraka* (atoll taro) and banana provides the people with their carbohydrate, can be grown only in excavated pits filled with plant material. Twice in the last 60 years Pukapuka has fallen prey to hurricanes which have ravaged the coconut palms and carried salt water into the taro pits, causing acute food shortages which eased only gradually over several years. Shortage of these food staples, then, is by no means unknown. Fish is normally plentiful, though fishing outside the reef is hazardous during part of each year.

Pukapuka offers little scope for economic development. Unlike the other atolls of the Northern Group its lagoon seems to be inhospitable to pearl shell, leaving copra as the only marketable product. The small island of Nassau, 40 miles to the south, which the Pukapukans purchased in 1950, likewise lacks any economic potential other than copra. According to one estimate,[6] earnings from this source have ranged from £ 640 in 1948–49 to almost £ 9,000 in 1954–55. The market price of copra is notoriously variable, but the tonnage produced has also ranged from a mere 20 tons in 1948–49 to 213 tons in 1956–57. It is not altogether clear what determines these fluctuations: the size of yield obviously sets a ceiling and the frequency of shipping may also have some effect, but there is no apparent correlation between production and price. It is difficult to assess the potential for increased earnings. Copra making is at present only a part-time occupation, but it is uncertain how much more time could be devoted to it without neglect of subsistence economy on which the people are and will remain dependent. Again, more copra could be made if the people would eat fewer nuts, but these play an extremely important part in their diet which could only be replaced by store foods. The increasing population will provide more hands to work but also more mouths to feed. There is little prospect of extending plantations for almost the entire area of Pukapuka and Nassau is already covered with trees. A change from sun- to kiln-drying, which was unsuccessfully attempted some years ago, might effect a slight increase in the price commanded; but even assuming that cash income could be doubled, the Pukapukans would not be able to escape their dependence on the subsistence economy, nor do they envisage any such possibility. The infrequency of cargo boats, the value attached to traditional foods and economic skills, and a strong desire to save money, induce even the few Government employees (teachers, radio operators, and police) to go fishing regularly and their wives to work in the taro pits.

The Pukapukans nevertheless appreciate money and are indeed notorious among other Cook Islanders for their canny ways. Even allowing for the generally low household incomes, spending is extremely modest and the living standards of those few who are better off are not strikingly different from the rest. Everyone needs clothes, and though workaday wear is ragged enough, no one likes to appear badly dressed in church. Many adults smoke habitually. Flour, rice and occasional tinned foods are bought to vary the normal diet or to tide over shortages. Many women have sewing machines for dress-making and most men own carpentering tools. Housing materials are the only major item of expenditure, but even here there are no sharp differences: one sees some old houses built of coral lime, a number of pandanus leaf and wood; others combining local materials with a cement floor or perhaps iron roofing. Only a few are made entirely of imported materials and even these are modest.

Conspicuous consumption and elaborate presentations were not a marked feature of the indigenous culture. The lineage of the principal *ariki* did feast the island on rare occasions, but the exchanges between villages of foodstuffs to which they had exclusive access were more important from an economic and social point of view.[7] The villages still exchange food from time to time, though rarely cash or store goods, but exchanges between individuals are generally unimportant. Distributions of as much as £ 40 to church leaders at funeral *apari*[8] seem to provide an exception to this rule, though my informants regarded them as abnormal. Church dues, particularly to the majority who adhere to the London Missionary Society (now called the Cook Islands Christian Church—C.I.C.C.), are substantial, but members pay a fixed sum and special funds—for example, the £ 500 to mark the centenary of the Gospel's arrival[9]—are raised on a *pro rata* basis.

The only major item of investment, the purchase of Nassau, was organized on a community-wide basis. The only individuals to have invested their money are the island's six store-keepers, the most prosperous of whom may have as much as £ 1,000 in goods on the arrival of a ship, and whose annual income may exceed £ 300. None of them, however, enjoys any particular standing or influence in the community as a result of his economic position; nor are their living-standards strikingly above the average. Perhaps they, like other Pukapukans, simply hoard their wealth. Although it is impossible to assess the amount of money held on the island, the tales of Chilean silver dollars and gold sovereigns, and the faded worm-eaten notes which periodically appear, leave little doubt that such hoards exist.

But whatever abstract value it holds for Pukapukans, money remains somewhat marginal to their everyday life. A substantial part of their time is taken up with subsistence activities carried on in the traditional manner. Steel fishing hooks and carpentering tools are in general use (though adze-blades are hafted in the old way), but the techniques of fishing and canoe-making, even to the use of sinnet lines and lashings, have scarcely changed.

The Pukapukan system of land tenure has largely escaped the strains to which that of the Southern Cook Islands has been subject. This has been partly due to the lesser importance of cash cropping, but also to the communal control of much of the land. As the Beagleholes have shown,[10] the two uninhabited islets, Motu Ko and Motu Kotawa, together with a section of Wale called Uta, are owned as reserves by three "companies". Each company is identified with one of the villages, Yato, Ngake or Roto, but while membership and residence normally coincide they need not do so; it is up to the company to decide who shall be admitted, and while multiple membership is inadmissible, occasional transfers are not.

The village leaders are the executives of the company, decreeing when its reserves shall be opened and how much of its resources—coconuts, taro, crabs, seabirds, or fish—shall be taken. Each year the *ariki* receive a number of nuts in recognition of their status; otherwise each adult receives an equal share and each child a part-share of whatever there is. The executives are empowered to reduce an adult's share to that of a child as a punitive sanction, though it is but rarely done. It is the duty of adult male members to take turns at guarding the reserves and they have the traditional right to inflict some kind of punishment on trespassers—nowadays a trifling fine.

This system has been adapted to copra production without suffering any significant modification. Some months before a cargo boat is expected, the village leaders take their people to the reserves for a number of weeks. Having inspected the plantations, they decide how many nuts are to be prepared, assigning an equal number to each member, though if he is old or infirm he may get someone else to do the actual work. The dried copra is brought to the store-house and in due course sold to a trader. The trader usually owns the cargo boat and in the absence of competition is in a position to dictate the price; although each corporation is nominally autonomous and negotiates its own price, the buyer usually gives the same to each. On receipt, the money is then shared out among the members.

Copra production has been organized along these lines as long as anyone can remember. The only modification occurred in the late 1940s when a section of Ngake company decided to sell its copra to the Cook Islands Progressive Association (a political-cum-cooperative movement, based in the Southern Cook Islands), and put up a separate store-house in Yato, which also favoured the C.I.P.A. The movement came to nothing and everyone now sells to the same buyer, but the two sections still retain separate copra houses; however, the Ngake reserve has always remained under unified control.

Copra making does not involve a radical departure from traditional work patterns. People seem to enjoy staying on the reserves for the change and the opportunities to get fish and other food novelties. Each can work at his own pace and there is ample time for other activities and amusements. The number of nuts to be worked is not usually very great, though the more energetic Yato company sets itself a higher target than the other two.

The villages have generally been more important in economic organization than the community as a whole. According to tradition, the few families who survived the great seismic wave, approximately 300 years ago, placed the atoll's resources under unified control but restored the old village divisions once the population began to increase.[11] The near-famine conditions which followed the hurricane of 1914 similarly resulted in the placing of certain taro pits under unified control and their division equally among the people.[12] This arrangement has persisted and the divisions are revised from time to time to maintain the equality of holdings, just as are those under village control. A more important venture involving the whole community has been the purchase and exploitation of Nassau which has been organized according to the same principles as apply to the village reserves.[13] Indeed, one might almost regard Nassau as a fourth reserve, inasmuch as anyone going there becomes entitled to an equal share of its products but loses, for the duration of his stay, any share from the company to which he normally belongs. However, there is the important difference that no one is allowed to stay there permanently. In 1964, a number who had remained for several years, establishing taro beds and banana plants, asked to be allowed to stay on indefinitely. A public meeting (held soon after my arrival) almost unanimously insisted on their recall, not because others were waiting to take their place—in fact there were few—but for fear that they would come to regard Nassau as their own.

The village companies, between them, control the greater part of Pukapuka's land, including coconut plantations and taro pits. The remainder of the land is owned according to other, more familiar principles. A system of *double descent*[14] originally operated in this sector, whereby certain taro beds were inherited through females, but residential sections and land growing coconuts and other trees (including the trees themselves) were normally inherited through males.[15] Matrilineal descent was relatively unimportant, except that Ngake company had no taro pits on Wale so that its members would have been obliged to go to Motu Ko for taro had they not individually had access to pits inherited in this way.

The sub-patrilineages and matrilineages seem to have had some residual right over the holdings of their members. Informants claimed that, to inherit, an heir had to become a member of the testator's sub-lineage if he were not one already and that this was subject to approval by the other members; however, I discovered at least one instance in which heirs had never joined the sub-lineage of the original owner. But whatever the original system may have been, both patrilineal and matrilineal sub-lineages are now virtually defunct and inheritance is decided by the immediate owner.[16]

My stay was too brief to permit anything like a thorough investigation of land inheritance, but there appeared to be considerable confusion over what the rules should be. It was said that a pre-war Government Agent attempted to "reform" the traditional system, requiring wills to be put in writing and deposited at his office, and insisting that daughters should receive a share of land which traditionally went only to sons and vice versa. Later Agents have allowed the people to make up their own minds, but there is now considerable uncertainty as to who is and who is not entitled to inherit. Even when a female line has been excluded in a written will, its members may claim to be entitled to a share. Disputes over land often arouse great bitterness and they are said to bring Pukapukans closer to violence than any other disputes, but there is no way of settling them. The Resident Agent can sometimes settle petty boundary disputes and cases where one party is patently in the wrong, but more difficult cases have accumulated over forty years, waiting for the Cook Islands Land Court, which has never come.[17]

It is hard to tell whether such uncertainties have adversely affected the production of copra from individually-owned trees. At the time of my visit, forty men sold copra on their own account, but the quantities were always small and their total earnings were a mere £ 300 as against the £ 1,800 of the three village companies.

Other types of economic activity require little comment, for there has been little change.[18] Fishing, taro cultivation, canoe and house-building are normally performed either individually or in small *ad hoc* groups, generally recruited from among the principal's kin; however, the villages form fishing teams and work bees on special occasions.

The economic change which Pukapuka has undergone since contact has been limited and its social consequences have not been very great. Although isolation and poverty of resources have been partly responsible for this, the communal system of control over a large part of the land must also be taken into account. It has proved adaptable to cash cropping and has even been extended to new holdings. It may be argued that the communal system restricts copra production by holding back the more energetic; however, many if not most may make additional quantities from their own trees if they so wish.

Isolation and lack of commercial importance, together with a thoroughly anomalous tenure system, have also saved Pukapuka from the land "reforms" of the early New Zealand Administration.[19] The traditional modes of inheritance have suffered some disruption, but the communal system has remained intact and attempts to modify it have met with bitter resistance, as will be described in the next section.

The stress upon equality in effort and reward is also apparent in living standards. Thus, although there are differences in income, hoarding tends to conceal them.

POLITICS AND ADMINISTRATION

The incorporation of Pukapuka, first in a mission-dominated theocracy, later in a secular, colonial-type administrative system, has clearly wrought important changes in the mode of island government, though our knowledge of the indigenous system is very incomplete. The little that can be learned has been reported by the Beagleholes:[20] the chiefs were honoured with relatively elaborate demonstrations of respect, but they did not exercise arbitrary authority, and probably an egalitarian council of elders was the most powerful political group.

Rarotongan missionaries reached Pukapuka in 1857 and seem to have displaced the old religion within a few years.[21] Little else is known of the early Christian period, but by the end of the century they had established a theocracy on the Rarotongan model,[22] though probably less rigorous. The mission extended its recognition to the chiefs, who in return became its secular arm, trying the thieves, brawlers, fornicators, adulterers and Sabbath breakers brought before them by their constables, and imposing fines, periods of confinement, and other more humiliating punishments such as head shaving and the stocks.

The New Zealand Government left Pukapuka to its own devices during the early years of its administration.[23] Between 1914 and 1925, European Agents were in residence for short periods, but immediately prior to this date,[24] and during the later interregna, local government was left in the charge of a Pukapukan 'Acting' Resident Agent. This man, named Ura, had been a constable under the old regime and a deacon of the church; probably these evidences of his standing and vigour, together with his literacy in Rarotongan, recommended him to the Administration. Pukapukans say that the period of his office was marked by a succession of disturbances, as he came into conflict, first with the principal chief *(te ariki wolo)*, and later with the L.M.S. pastor, that is, the two authorities dominant up to 1914.

In 1917 a religious schism appeared, originating, so it is said, with the decision of the L.M.S. to change from Saturday to Sunday worship. This innovation encountered the opposition of a small minority who presently embraced Seventh Day Adventism. Ura, as principal deacon, was the spearhead of L.M.S. resentment, which took on further point through the power of his secular office. For example, it had been the practice for village leaders to subtract church contributions from the copra earnings before distribution; when the Adventists claimed the right to exemption from this levy he refused them. Among the minority was the *ariki wolo* (together with the brother who followed him during the years 1933–38), who, whether or not he had taken up this position as a challenge to the usurping Ura, now came into open conflict with him. Although Ura's application to the Administration to have the *ariki* removed from office failed, he was on one occasion fined for trespassing on land he claimed to be his, and on another had his *raui* (tapu) torn down.

The intervention of a visiting European official eventually established some sort of *modus vivendi*, but a few years later the L.M.S. split yet again. This time it was Ura who broke away, after a quarrel with the Pukapukan pastor. Disagreements over the design of the new church buildings and over land seem to have been the immediate issues. Beaglehole, visiting the community only a few years after, heard tales of "threats and flashing knives, fist fights and mild brawling, before another official came from Rarotonga and relieved Ura of his civil power and the island of a possible bloody conflict."[25] The old man then withdrew from the church with his numerous family, all of them being presently received into the Roman Catholic Church. It is worth noting that neither schism was the work of outside missions; each was initially spontaneous, though subsequently stabilized by affiliation with a recognized denomination. Once established, the churches ceased to function as political units, due, perhaps, to the death of Ura and the advanced age of the *ariki* and his successor.

Since 1925 the Resident Agent has always been an outsider, though generally Polynesian, and it would appear that the dominant political cleavage has run between him and the people, rather than between sections of the people. The functions of the office are numerous: magistrate, chief of police, director of public works and, in earlier years, school teacher and medical practitioner. Because of isolation, incumbents have been subject to little surveillance from their superiors and thus left to carry out their duties according to their own lights. A subsidiary organ of local government has been the Island Council, consisting of the *ariki wolo*, who, once his succession has been approved by the Administration sits *ex officio*, and two councillors for each of the three villages, nominated by the Resident Agent until 1947 and thereafter elected. The precise functions of the Island Council are not very clearly defined. It is apparently intended to deal with the Administration on behalf of the people, but also to co-operate with the Administration in the implementation of some of its policies—for example, those relating to health and hygiene. The Council has been empowered to pass local ordinances, subject to the approval of the Resident Agent, but one suspects that, at least in earlier years, the main initiative in such legislation has rested with the Resident Agent. Discussing the Aitutaki Island Council, Beaglehole questions whether it serves any useful political function;[26] in Pukapuka, however, the councillors play an important role which is not directly connected with the Administration, having become the principal leaders of their respective villages.

The actual enforcement of Cook Island laws and local ordinances is the responsibility of the Agent and his policemen. The Court Books suggest that the Pukapukans are a peaceable folk: there is no mention of homicide or even serious assault, nor of rape; "wandering stock" and "keeping untidy premises" are the most common offences. Young lovers have sometimes found themselves in conflict with authority, for, particularly in earlier years, Resident Agents have sometimes felt it their duty to punish those indulging in extra-marital love affairs.[27] Young men, found in their sweethearts' houses when everyone is asleep, have been punished for trespassing, while the nine o'clock curfew, an ordinance dating from the period of L.M.S. theocracy, has at certain times been enforced to keep young people at home.

The people have no particular objection to the Resident Agent dealing with these matters (though they may not like the way in which he deals with them), and if young people find his occasional interference with their love-making disagreeable, church leaders are bound to support him—at least in principle. However, he encounters stiffer resistance in other spheres of his work, particularly when innovation is proposed. Attempts to get the people to build latrines were fended off by delaying tactics for years, and even now the people revert to using the beach when living on the reserves. A recent attempt to bring order to the unloading of cargo encountered bitter resistance and entailed interminable debate before it could be effected. The Pukapukans have never failed to charge the Administration a good price for whatever it needed from them, and they have consistently refused to work without pay even in projects which the Administration believed to be for their own benefit—for example, building a house for a medical practitioner. Although the Administration initially succeeded in obtaining land for its building—albeit, on the mosquito-ridden side of the island—there is strong resistance to its holding being extended by even a few feet; there were many months of fruitless negotiation before anyone could be persuaded to provide land for the accommodation of public water tanks. Relations between the Resident Agent and the people are frequently strained by such differences, and one senses exasperation on both sides; however, they have only become critical once, when the reserves were threatened.

Most Resident Agents have left control of the reserves to the villages and their leaders, confining themselves to encouraging copra production, making periodic tours of inspection and giving official sanction to the raising and lowering of the *raui.* However, Pukapukans tell of one Resident Agent in the mid-1940s who not only presumed to enter the reserves at will but challenged the authority of the guards to levy fines on other trespassers. When a constable was sent to impose nine o'clock curfew on Motu Kotawa (at seven o'clock, according to the story), the well of indignation overflowed. Under most Residents the curfew has been applied flexibly where it has not been ignored; the then incumbent, however, had resolved to enforce it strictly, causing inconvenience not only to young lovers but to everyone habituated to late night fishing, gossiping and card playing.[28] Its enforcement on the reserves was evidently intolerable, and the authority of both constable and Resident was openly defied. Further fuel was added to the flames when the Resident opposed the decision of several villages to sell their copra to the C.I.P.A. In the ensuing clash a number of Pukapukans were gaoled, while the people reduced the police to the status of children in village distributions and, in a rare outburst of violence, burned down the house of one and the canoe of another. Soon after, the Resident was replaced by another less severe, and conditions returned to normal.

The position of the police in such situations is a difficult one, and it seems that they have generally aligned themselves with the Government in such a way as to retain their jobs. The councillors, however, even in the days when they were the Resident's nominees, have tended to align themselves with the people, rarely, indeed, taking up any stand without lengthy consultations with their people. The *ariki wolo* and lesser chiefs, insofar as they have taken up a position at all, have likewise stood with the people, and the same has been true of the C.I.C.C. pastor.

It seems Pukapuka has been largely free of factions since the days of Ura. The introduction of Council and, later, Legislative Assembly elections, has created the occasion for periodic political competition, but (see Table 2) the number of contestants for office has always been small and in several instances there has been no opposition. There has been a strong tendency to return the sitting member, while unsuccessful candidates do not stand again. One of the present councillors ("A") has served for 17 years and three ("B", "G" and "P") for more than 14 years; another ("Q") had served for 33 years (i.e. he had first been nominated by the Resident Agent) before being ousted in 1961—probably because of his advanced age. Only one other councillor ("H") has lost his seat since the 1953 elections: I could elicit no explanation for this.

Pukapuka's leaders are scarcely differentiated from one another except in terms of personality. Five of the councillors are aged between 47 and 56; the sixth is 37, which is about the age at which the others were first ap-

TABLE 2. PUKAPUKAN VOTING BEHAVIOUR IN THREE ISLAND COUNCIL ELECTIONS

Village	Candidate	Elections 1953	1956	1961
YATO	"A"	30*	unanimous*	44*
	"B"	* 24*	,,*	18*
	"C"	* 16	—	—
	"D"	22	—	—
	"E"	—	—	16
	"F"	—	—	11
ROTO	"G"	* 47*	32*	38*
	"H"	28*	27*	22
	"I"	26	—	—
	"J"	6	—	—
	"K"	—	11	—
	"L"	—	6	—
	"M"	—	—	24*
	"N"	—	—	18
	"O"	—	—	14
NGAKE	"P"	* 23*	unanimous*	67*
	"Q"	* 21*	,,*	19
	"R"	8	—	—
	"S"	6	—	—
	"T"	—	—	28*
	"U"	—	—	21

An asterisk indicates that the candidate was successful; an asterisk to the left of the first column of figures indicates that the candidate held office immediately prior to 1953.

pointed. Most candidates have belonged to the C.I.C.C. majority (four of the councillors are deacons), but "H" of Roto, who was twice elected, is a Roman Catholic. None has had any educational distinction—no school teacher has ever stood for office. Two councillors have never left the island, while only one has spent more than a few months on Rarotonga and none has been to New Zealand.

The first election to the Cook Islands Legislative Assembly, in 1958, attracted a different kind of candidate. The successful one had spent 19 years in Rarotonga and five in New Zealand, but had little formal education and no English. The two runners-up had lived most of their lives on Rarotonga, where they were trained as school teachers and gained a fair grasp of English. Both the teachers are Adventists, but the size of their vote indicated substantial support outside their own denomination. Neither they nor anyone else opposed the sitting member in the 1961 elections.

While there is some concern over who should represent Pukapuka in the Legislative Assembly, there is little over what he does when he is there. At each session he has transmitted certain requests from his people to the Government—for example, for more regular shipping—but has contributed little or nothing to the general deliberations.[29] His apparent lack of interest, and sometimes of comprehension, is a reflection of his people's usual attitude to matters not immediately affecting themselves. The poor attendance at meetings at which the Assembly member "reports back" is in striking contrast to meetings of village or island to discuss local matters. Although these matters are generally routine—the time for departure to the reserves, the number of nuts to be made into copra, the organization of a feast or entertainment—the discussions are often long drawn-out, allowing everyone who wishes to express an opinion. This process, though tedious to the outsider, allows the councillors to gauge public opinion.

The councillors vary in the extent to which they attempt to form public opinion, but they all try to avoid taking decisions before they have sounded it out, and rarely, if ever, act in defiance of it. In one recent instance where Ngake village was divided over the Resident Agent's new arrangement for unloading cargo, its councillors declined to take any decision at all. Being governed by public opinion, councillors rarely find themselves on different sides; in any case, since each village elects its councillors and generally reaches decisions independently of the others, no more than two councillors can be in direct competition at any one time. It is in keeping with the traditional rivalry between villages that there should be more political disagreement between them than between sections of any one village; however, the means for direct political competition between villages seem to be lacking. For example, when Yato agreed to build a house for the visiting medical practitioner it earned enmity of Ngake and Roto who had refused to do so, but suffered no retaliation. It might be argued that political rivalry becomes merged with the more general, institutionalized rivalry between villages, and finds expression in non-political forms of competition, such as cricket, dancing, wrestling and derisory chants, which, according to Beaglehole, reduce the level of aggression in the community "to a socially safe pressure".[30]

The majority C.I.C.C. congregation is also organized along village lines; however, although village rivalry comes through in such things as hymn singing, there seems to be little sign of political conflict, perhaps because the church has changed so little over the last generation and more that its activities have become routine. The pastor and deacons no longer exercise their old dominance over the community, but they have had 40 years in which to work out a *modus vivendi* with the secular government and they can rest in the assurance that they are well represented on the Council.

The *ariki wolo* has not played an independent political role since the time of Ura. During the '20s and '30s, and again over the last decade, the incumbent has been so old and infirm as to be almost inactive, though, being a member of the Council he has been associated with its decisions, even when unable to attend its meetings. The present line of *ariki,* which succeeded in 1938,[31] has belonged to the C.I.C.C., but it has not been able to recover the *mana* lost in the days of Ura. The lesser chiefs are of little consequence, being overshadowed by the councillors in their villages, while the patri-lines which they once headed are now functionless.

Like the other islands of the Cook Group, the governmental structure of Pukapuka has undergone important changes as a result of its incorporation, first in the L.M.S. theocracy and later in New Zealand's colonial administration. As on the other islands, the establishment of secular government meant the political eclipse of both pastor and *ariki,* though the fact that it was a Pukapukan, Ura, who was the spearhead of the new order may have added a dimension of personal animus and ambition to the conflict. Incorporation within a wider governmental system meant that Pukapukans could draw upon outside sources of power in their political dealings with one another: thus, in the early days the authority of the *ariki* was reinforced by the church and later Ura could pursue his ambitions as representative of the Administration. However, subsequent Resident Agents, who have all been outsiders, seem to have been politically isolated. Some councillors may have been more ready to co-operate with the Administration than others, but there has been no emergence of pro- and anti-Administration parties, nor any manipulation of the Administration for political advantage. Councillors have generally given first consideration to their representative functions, sometimes at the expense of their duties as members of the Administration.

The villages have endured as key-groupings in the governmental structure. They have retained certain traditional functions and taken on new ones, notably in the fields of copra production, church organization and local government. The sound economic base of the village group and the availability of economic sanctions which can be turned against any who break discipline, have done much to ensure its continued success as an organizational and political unit. Attempts to prune village rights and functions have encountered stiff resistance.

Beaglehole notes that, while "there was no institutionalized warfare nor any socially approved method of resorting to physical violence to settle disputes between groups", Pukapukan tradition does record rare instances in which "blood lusts" for a time ruled the community.[32] There has been nothing so extreme within living memory, yet we have seen that there have been three serious disturbances in the last 50 years, each following innovations or attempted innovations of an unprecedented and radical nature. Short of these crises, however, Pukapuka appears to be lacking in any techniques of political competition stronger than obstruction in its dealings with the Administration, and debate in its internal affairs. This normally low level of political activity may be partly attributed to a deeply ingrained disapproval of any form of quarrelling (even school children do not fight), but partly also to the normal absence of issues which radically threaten the *status quo.*

THE CHURCHES AND SOCIAL CONTROL

Every Pukapukan is attached to one of the three churches and attends its gatherings regularly. The Cook Islands Christian Church holds approximately three-quarters of the population, while the Roman Catholic and Seventh Day Adventists hold the remainder in a ratio of about 2:1. This distribution has not changed appreciably since 1945. Beaglehole claims that the Catholics were never interested in recruiting new followers[33] and today none of the churches attempts to do so; nor have Pukapukans shown any interest in other sects. Children normally take the religion of their parents, transfers occurring only through marriage and adoption. Where parents are of different denominations, the children are divided between the two, according to the same traditional rule whereby parents name the children by turns. However, it is usual for one spouse to embrace the religion of the other, a decision which may encounter some opposition from his or her parents, and which will certainly be opposed by their church, especially if it is the Roman Catholic. In 26 "mixed marriages", 10 men and 16 women transferred to the church of their spouse, 6 joining the C.I.C.C., 9 the Adventists, and 11 the Catholics; 20 of the "converts" came from the C.I.C.C., 5 from the Catholic and 1 from the Adventists. The greater number of women changing their religion probably reflects the male bias in Pukapukan culture; however, it is apparent that the minority churches lose fewer and gain more through "mixed marriages" than the C.I.C.C.

The strict sabbatarian Christianity which the L.M.S. introduced to the Cook Islands is still preached by the C.I.C.C., but Pukapuka is probably the last place where it is to any degree practised. The sabbath is strictly observed, even to food being cooked before sunrise, and church attendances are near the maximum possible. Total abstinence from alcohol is the rule at all times and if anyone returns from other places with a taste of it, he will soon find himself before the deacons, threatened with loss of church membership. Adventists maintain a similar sabbatarianism (albeit on a different day) and extend the rule of abstinence to tobacco and certain foods. Roman Catholic conduct has not differed significantly from that of the others, except that over the last seven years their priest has organized Sunday evening games.

The attitude of all three churches to sexual relations outside marriage is totally at variance with the permissiveness traditional among Pukapukans, as among most Polynesians; and on Pukapuka, as elsewhere, it is employed in judging the behaviour of pastors and deacons, rather than of ordinary mortals. Generations of pastors and Resident Agents have failed to stop unlawful love-making or even the singing of traditional chants which treat of sexual matters with un-Christian frankness.

According to the Pukapukan Birth Register, 16.5% of all births were illegitimate over the years 1919-1924; the figures were 21.2% for 1939-44, and 16.0% for 1959-64. The rate must be judged in the light of what is probably a fairly late maturing amongst females[34] and the general prevalence of marriage, usually entered into at a fairly early age. According to the Marriage Register, over the three periods given above the average age of women at first marriage has ranged between 21.3 and 22.6 (that of men has remained at around 24).

All three churches condemn divorce, though only the Roman Catholic is absolute in its refusal to re-marry divorcees, but divorces are granted by the secular authorities, who can also perform civil marriages. Divorce seems to have been fairly common in pre-Christian times[35] and it is not uncommon now. Some idea of the frequency can be gained from the following sample of 50 males and 50 females, all of whom were alive at the time of my visit and had at some time been married, and none of whom were first degree kin to one another. Eleven of the women had been divorced, and fifteen of the men (one twice, another three times). The divorce rate amongst C.I.C.C. members of both sexes was 28% (22/78), slightly above the average for the total sample, 26%. Only two of the twelve Roman Catholics had been divorced.

TABLE 3. A COMPARISON OF MARRIAGE STABILITY, BASED ON TWO SAMPLES: 1933 AND 1964

Sample	*Total Marriages in Sample*	*Dissolved by Divorce*	*Dissolved by Death*	*Extant*
1933 (Beagleholes)	128	18	42	68
1964 (Beckett)	200	35	26	139

It is not easy to establish whether divorce is less or more prevalent than in earlier years. The Beagleholes break down 128 marriages in the manner set out in Table 3,[36] and I have broken down 200 for the purpose of comparison. The proportion dissolved by the death of one partner is much higher in the earlier sample; however, this may be due to the way in which it was selected, though we are not told the method employed. My own sample was drawn from my genealogies at random, save that at least one of the couple must be alive. The ratio of marriages dissolved by divorce to marriages still extant is very nearly the same in the two samples. Of marriages ending in divorce, 61% (11/18) in the earlier group, and 66% (23/35) in the later were childless. Now, as formerly, adultery is the most commonly offered ground for divorce, but in many instances it has been committed after the couple have separated.

The Pukapukans conform strictly to certain tenets of the Christian code, but deviate from others. Deviation, however, is in the direction of traditional values and practices, not towards those of secularized Rarotonga. As far as the figures can be interpreted, its character and incidence have not changed significantly in 40 years. The three churches may differ slightly in the degree of social pressure brought to bear on their respective members, but none has sought to extend its influence outside the spheres traditionally considered proper to it.

MIGRATION

Since the war, and more particularly over the vast decade, there has been an increasing movement of Cook Island population, mostly from the Outer Islands to Rarotonga, and from Rarotonga to New Zealand. The social consequences of this have not been studied, but it is generally supposed that they have been considerable, not only for the migrants themselves but for those left at home. At the time of writing there are about 60 Pukapukan adults living in Rarotonga and about 100 in New Zealand, both groups being accompanied by a considerable number of children. But even if one subtracts the 50 or so living on Nassau, the population of Pukapuka is still larger than it has ever been in this century.

Migration to Nassau requires little discussion. It is always temporary, rarely lasting more than one or two years; it involves no contact with non-Pukapukans, and life there is very much like a prolonged stay on one of the reserves.

In Rarotonga, the Pukapukan is confronted with a very different way of life, though his participation in it is generally limited. After the hurricane of 1914 at Pukapuka, the Administration evacuated a number of families to Rarotonga, placing them on a small plot of land in Pue, Avarua, which Vakatini Ariki made available. Most of the refugees returned in due course, but others came to take their place, and though there are few who can be regarded as permanent residents Pue has become known as the Pukapukan settlement on Rarotonga. Career interests and attractive jobs have kept a few Pukapukans in Rarotonga for most of their adult lives, and their children have grown up as Pukapukans by parentage and identification rather than by upbringing. A few others have married into the local population, moving in with their affines. The transient element has come for secondary education, for medical attention or, in some cases, simply to have a look around. Some seem to come in the hope of obtaining more money, but in this they are generally disappointed. Regular employment is not easily obtained and even in casual work the Pukapukan is at a disadvantage, having a reputation for laziness and awkwardness which may be attributed to his inexperience in plantation work and, indeed, any work routine. Few Pukapukans earn much more than £3 a week, and while this may be a welcome supplement to the income of a Rarotongan who has taro swamps and orange groves, it is meagre to an Outer Islander who has none. Pukapukans in Pue have little opportunity to fish and they would not know how to plant taro under Rarotongan conditions, even if they had the land. Wage earners may have to support sickly and unemployed relatives, and those planning to return home often hide their money so as to be able to buy a few things to take back. Everyone in Pue complains about the lack of food and this is obviously a source of tension among the overlarge domestic units; as several residents said, "whenever you hear an argument it's always about food". Small wonder, then, that almost all Pue residents regarded their stay on Rarotonga as temporary.

Although Pukapukans are inevitably impressed by their first sight of mountains, motor-cars, aeroplanes, films and well-stocked shops, they are not overly impressed by the Rarotongan way of life. The cinema, much patronized by the younger set on Rarotonga, soon loses its appeal for Pukapukans. Drinking, which is widespread amongst men on Rarotonga, runs counter both to their religious principles and their desire to save money. As at home, they are punctilious in their religious observances, and through the mediation of two long-term residents who also act as village leaders, they are articulated with a number of Rarotongan institutions, but their personal dealings with non-Pukapukans are limited.

More than other Islanders, the Pukapukans are regarded as distinct. This derives in part from their residential concentration, their incomprehensible dialect, their apparent exclusiveness, and what many insist to be a physical distinctiveness. The Pukapukan stereotype is slothful, clumsy and stingy, but pious, peaceable and law-abiding.

Except among the professionals and elite, the Rarotongan social network is defined in terms of kinship, and so excludes all but a very few Pukapukans from casual visiting and entertainments. The failure of all but a few schoolboys to participate in sports, due to lack of experience of football and standard cricket, and the rejection of drinking, bar two other possible points of entry into the wider community. In any case Pukapukans do not appear to crave the company of others. Several young people complained that they were criticized if they attempted to associate with outsiders, and it was noticeable that the few outsiders living in Pue were somewhat isolated. Enquiring of a middle-aged women whether she had made any Rarotongan friends during her stay, I was told that one woman had proposed herself as a friend, but that she did not regard her as such. A young girl who had married a Rarotongan in the vicinity spent most of her time in Pue and often spent the night there, excusing her conduct with complaints about her in-laws and unpalatable Rarotongan cooking. Other "mixed marriages" fared better, but it is remarkable that they total only 26, including those domiciled on other islands.

The first Pukapukan to settle in New Zealand was a veteran of the 1914-18 war who married a Maori wife there and never returned home. It was not until 1948 that he sponsored the emigration of a relative, but thereafter the usual pattern of chain migration became established, most of the arrivals settling in two districts of Auckland. Only three have so far returned home, but many send back money to their families. Many young Pukapukans express discontent with the lack of economic opportunities at home and a desire to visit New Zealand at least for a few years. Lack of money or transport, or parental obstruction keep back some, but there can be little doubt that many will go in the coming years.

Most Pukapukans manage to get to Rarotonga at some time in their lives (see Table 1), and the experience no doubt increases their sophistication and raises their economic aspirations, though rarely providing them with the means to achieve them. In other respects, however, the impact of Rarotonga is superficial and those returning home, even after a prolonged absence, seem to find no difficulty in fitting in to the quieter and more limited atoll life. The prospect of emigration to New Zealand is more attractive, primarily in material terms, though more disturbing in that ties with home must become more attenuated and the likelihood of return less; so far, however, neither form of migration has had any discernible effect on the Pukapukan social structure.

PUKAPUKANS AND PROGRESS

Pukapukan society has changed under the impact of modern industrial civilization, but most of the major changes were effected long ago and it cannot now be said to be developing in any way. Accustomed to a life that involves few uncertainties and demands little in the way of personal adaptation beyond what is required of everyone in the course of the normal life cycle, Pukapukans probably retain a prejudice against innovation; but they must not be represented as wholly opposed to it because they have opposed particular instances of it. They finally bought the island of Nassau, overcoming their suspicion of the Administration and despite their conviction that it was already theirs by right. They recently allowed the Administration to take over reserve land for a new school, albeit—turning the tables, perhaps —at a price of £200. In Rarotonga, the Pukapukans formed their own youth club, though having little to do with other clubs and refusing to affiliate with the Government's Department of Social Development; and they have almost all joined the new Cook Islands Party, which is currently being canvassed round the home community.

None of these innovations, however, threatens the key institutions of Pukapukan society. If sections of reserve land are reluctantly surrendered (at a price), village control of the reserves remains intact. New land may be acquired, but it is administered in the old way. A new political party may be accepted, since it displaces nothing else, but a new church is not. Individuals may emigrate to New Zealand, but at home life continues as before.

NOTES

1. Beaglehole and Beaglehole 1938; Beaglehole 1937, 1944.
2. Vayda 1958, 1959.
3. The visit was undertaken as anthropological adviser to the Wellington Hospital Research Unit, which was supported by the Medical Research Council of New Zealand and the World Health Organization. My thanks are due to the Resident Agent of Pukapuka, Mr. Tipuia Tiro, and to Messrs. John Tariau, Pareura Katoa and Rakuraku Eliu for their help, though they are in no way responsible for any opinions expressed in this article.
4. See Frisbie 1930.
5. An informal census taken by the Resident Agent in 1963 estimated that the population of Pukapuka and Nassau was 847. In the official census of 1961 the total was 718 (362 males and 356 females); in that of 1945, 660 (330:330). The population has risen steadily since the first census in 1902, when it numbered 505 (House of Representatives: 1906).
6. These tonnages are taken from the Annual Reports of the Department of Island Territories for the appropriate years. No figures are available for the price paid for copra on Pukapuka; the estimate, based on the Rarotonga price, has been made by Mr. John Kolff, research student of the Department of Economics, Victoria University, in a personal communication to the writer.
7. Beaglehole and Beaglehole 1938:90-95.
8. The *apari* is a longstanding practice among members of the Cook Islands Christian Church, whereby deacons and other church elders visit the bereaved and comfort them with hymns and pious meditations throughout an evening. It is usual to make a small gift of money to the church section of each of the villages represented.
9. Thorogood 1960:74.
10. Beaglehole and Beaglehole 1938:32-40.
11. Beaglehole and Beaglehole 1938:21, 386-387.
12. Beaglehole and Beaglehole 1938:32.
13. Vayda 1958.
14. Goody 1961:12.
15. Beaglehole and Beaglehole 1938:41-44.
16. Firth notes in other parts of Polynesia "the tendency for corporate groups of the larger unilineal type to lose coherence and jurisdiction" under the impact of European contact. (Firth 1959:350.)
17. Crocombe 1964:161.
18. cf. Beaglehole and Beaglehole 1938:48-51.
19. cf. Crocombe 1964.
20. Beaglehole and Beaglehole 1938:233-237.
21. Gill 1876:180-181.
22. Beaglehole 1957.
23. House of Representatives 1903.
24. House of Representatives 1915.
25. Beaglehole 1944:112-113.
26. Beaglehole 1957:207.
27. Davis and Davis 1955:142.
28. Some impression of the tension existing at that time can be gained from Davis and Davis 1955:142.
29. Legislative Assembly 1958-1964.
30. Beaglehole 1937:320.
31. Till 1938 the succession hung in the balance: the reigning line had no male issue, but it remained undecided whether a son of the *ariki*'s sister had prior claim over a more distant patrilineal kinsman (see Beaglehole and Beaglehole 1938:243). In the event it was the former who succeeded and when he died in 1963 his brother, aged about 79, was preferred to his son, aged about 19.
32. Beaglehole 1937:325.
33. Beaglehole 1944:113.
34. According to the 1961 census only 3.5% (5) of Pukapukan women having their first child were under 16 years of age; 43% (61) were under 20.

35. Beaglehole and Beaglehole 1938:297.
36. Beaglehole and Beaglehole 1938:297.

REFERENCES

Appendices to the Journal of the New Zealand House of Representatives. "Pacific Islands", 1903; "Cook and Other Islands", 1906; 1915. Wellington.

BEAGLEHOLE, E., 1937. "Emotional Release in a Polynesian Community." *Journal of Abnormal and Social Psychology,* 32:319-28.

——— 1944. *Islands of Danger.* Wellington, Progressive Publishing Society.

——— 1957. *Social Change in the South Pacific.* London, Allen and Unwin.

BEAGLEHOLE, E. AND P. BEAGLEHOLE, 1938. *The Ethnology of Pukapuka.* Honolulu, Bernice P. Bishop Museum Bulletin No. 150.

CROCOMBE, R., 1964. *Land Tenure in the Cook Islands.* Melbourne, Oxford University Press.

DAVIS, T. AND L. DAVIS, 1955. *Doctor to the Islands.* London, Michael Joseph.

FIRTH, R., 1959. *Social Change in Tikopia.* London, Allen and Unwin.

FRISBIE, R., 1930. *The Book of Pukapuka.* London, John Murray.

GILL, W. W., 1876. *Life in the Southern Isles.* London, The Religious Tract Society.

GOODY, J., 1961. "The Classification of Double Descent Systems." *Current Anthropology,* 2:3-12.

Proceedings of the Legislative Assembly of the Cook Islands, 1958-64. Rarotonga, Government Printer.

THOROGOOD, B., 1960. *Not Quite Paradise.* London, London Missionary Society.

VAYDA, P., 1958. "The Pukapukans on Nassau Island." *Journal of the Polynesian Society,* 67:256-65.

——— 1959. "Native Traders in Two Polynesian Atolls." *Cahiers de l'Institut de Science Economique Appliquée,* Ser. V, No. 1, pp. 119-137.

17

MA'OHI DRINKING PATTERNS IN THE SOCIETY ISLANDS

Robert I. Levy

Introduction

This paper considers drinking behaviour in the Society Islands in French Polynesia with particular reference to the form and extent of drunkenness associated with drinking. The presentation concerns the *ma'ohi*, or traditionally oriented people, and not the rather distinct *demi*, or culturally mixed group. Although the historical and some of the contemporary material which follows refers to the Society Islands in general, or at least to the areas which were first in Western contact, most of the generalities on contemporary forms are based on field work in a rural village (with a population of 284 in 1962), which will be called "Piri," on the island of Huahine in the Leeward group, supplemented by observations in a section of the major Tahitian port town of Papeete.[1] Piri has been somewhat more isolated than many other Society Island communities from the main stream of influences towards social change, and had, at the time of the study, relatively high community stability. I believe that the drinking patterns observed there are, however, generally true for the Society Islands. My purpose here is to portray some general forms, and not to consider in any detail differentiated ones in the village or between villages.

1. Historical Background

The Society Islanders, discovered by Samuel Wallis in 1767, like other Polynesian peoples did not have alcoholic beverages at the time of first Western contact. They used the mildly narcotic *kava*, or *'ava* as it was called in Tahitian, prepared from the root of the *Piper methysticum* plant. As James Morrison, who was at Tahiti between 1788 and 1791, wrote:

"Yava, or intoxicating pepper, is cultivated here with much care and pains; with the root of this, they intoxicate themselves. They always drink it before they eat and it is prepared thus—several hands have each a proportion of the root given them to

Reproduced by permission of Robert I. Levy from the *Journal of the Polynesian Society,* 75:304-320 (1966).

chew, which, when they have done sufficiently, they spit into a large platter. Some of the leaves are then infused and squeezed to pieces in it. And in the meantime another prepares a strainer from the stems of coarse grass called *mo'oo*, something like hemp, and the whole being well mixed is wrung through the strainer, and the leaves and chewings thrown away. The juice is then divided according to the number who are to drink it by dipping the strainer into the platter and wringing into each man's cup his share. They now drink their dose which as it is of a tolerable thick consistency and smells something like a mixture of rhubarb and jalap can be little better to take. [This] almost immediately deprives them of the use of their limbs and speech, but does not touch the mental faculty, and they appear in a thoughtful mood and frequently fall backwards before they have finished eating. Some of their attendants then attend to chafe their limbs all over till they fall asleep, and the rest retire and no noise is suffered to be made near them. After a few hours they are as fresh as if nothing had happened, and are ready for another dose. A jill of this juice is a sufficient dose, but if they eat anything immediately before it, it has no effect . . . It is common to all but is more used by the chiefs and their families, servants, etc., than by the common people . . . It is in much request among the people of rank, but even some of them never taste it."[2] [3]

If some people did not use *'ava,* others may have overused it by Tahitian standards. According to Lieutenant William Bligh's journal for November 5, 1788, "Tynah's[4] youngest brother, Whydooah, came on board today with his wife, a very pretty woman. I have before described this man as a person much addicted to the use of the *'ava,* and he was at this time so drunk with it, that he could scarce stand or speak. Tynah saw him and said he was a drunkard and would not speak to him."[5]

'Ava drinking was not apparently used in any ritual contexts as it was in other parts of Polynesia such as Samoa and Tonga, and the more closely related Tuamotu Islands.

Alcoholic drinks were offered to their guests by the first explorers. Joseph Banks, who was on Cook's first voyage to Tahiti in 1769, wrote:

"Some there were who drank pretty freely of our liquors and in a few instances became very drunk but seemed far from pleased with their intoxication, the individuals afterwards shunning a repetition of it instead of greedily desiring it as most Indians are said to do."[6]

Visitors to Tahiti after Cook noted occasional episodes of drunkenness among men and women in the "chiefly class," both on *'ava,* and on alcoholic beverages given by the Europeans. Alcoholic spirits were named *'ava no peritane,* or "British *'ava,*" and *'ava* has persisted as the name for strong liquor. (The English language later provided the words for beer, *pia,* and wine, *uaina.*)

In 1797 the first missionaries came to Tahiti. By 1815, due to a variety of factors, Tahitian society was disorganized. A missionary, William Ellis, who worked in the Society Islands between 1817 and 1824, summarized his predecessors' reports for the year around 1815:

"Intemperance at this time prevailed to an awful and unprecedented degree. By the Sandwich Islanders, who had arrived some years before, the natives had been taught to distill ardent spirits from the saccharine *ti* root, which they now practised to a great extent, and exhibited, in a proportionate degree, all the demoralizing and debasing influence of drunkenness . . . Whole districts frequently united to erect what might be called a public still. When the materials were prepared, the men and boys of the district assembled in a kind of temporary house, erected over the still, in order to drink the *'ava,* as they called the spirit. The first that issued from the still being the strongest they called the *ao;* it was carefully received, and given to the chief; that subsequently procured was drunk by the people in general. In this employment they were sometimes engaged for several days together, drinking the spirit as it issued from the still, sinking into a state of indescribable wretchedness, and often practising the most ferocious barbarities . . . Under the unrestrained influence of their intoxicating draught, in their appearance and actions they resembled demons more than human beings. Sometimes in a deserted still-house might be seen the fragments of the rude boiler and the other appendages of the still scattered in confusion on the ground, and among them the dead and mangled bodies of those who had been murdered with axes or billets of wood in the quarrels that terminated their dissipation."[7]

Drinking in Tahiti, the central commercial and administrative centre for the Society Islands and thus the area of maximum western impact, continued throughout the years. The Belgian trader Moerenhout noted for about 1830 that when there were a number of ships in port at Papeete, "the excesses of these foreigners had a bad effect on the Indians, who, like all the nations in their state, are only too easily given to drunkenness; thus one soon saw, everywhere, only drunks, at any time, on all sides, day and night, women and men."[8] Moerenhout believed "that such an order of things, constantly getting worse, would have finished by ruining the islands, if a remedy had not been brought . . ."[9] The remedy was an attempt by the missionary-influenced native government to control the distribution of alcohol.

In 1843 Tahiti officially became a French protectorate. In 1849 a French observer, who had lived in Tahiti from 1846 to 1848, noted:

["The Tahitian] likes strong liquors, in excess, not for themselves, but for the drunkenness that they produce. Therefore, he prefers brandy to the best wine. His goal is to lose instantly his reason, he wishes to drown it at once."[10]

Henry Adams, writing from Tahiti in 1891, noted,

"To me the atmosphere is more than tinged by a South Sea melancholy, a little sense of hopelessness and premature decay. The natives are not the gay, big, animal creatures of Samoa who sang and danced because their whole natures were overstocked with life; they are still, silent, rather sad in expression, like the Hawaiians, and they are fearfully few in number . . . Except in the remote places, the poor natives are all more or less diseased. They are allowed all the rum they want, and they drink wildly. They are forbidden to dance or to keep any of their old warlike habits."[11]

In spite of these references to continued drinking there is no further reference to violent, destructive behaviour when drinking, of the type reported by Ellis. Most reports stressed the gentleness and peaceableness of the Tahitians, both drunk and sober.[12]

There is little information on the nature and extent of drinking in the past on the outer islands. The missionary, John Williams, returning from the Cook Islands to Ra'iatea in 1832, noted:

> "On arriving at Raiatea, I was perfectly astounded at beholding the scenes of drunkenness which prevailed in my formerly flourishing station. There were scarcely a hundred people who had not disgraced themselves; and persons who had made a consistent profession of religion for years had been drawn into the vortex. The son and successor of old Tamatoa was a very dissipated young man, and when he succeeded to the government, instead of following his father's good example, he sanctioned the introduction of ardent spirits. Encouraged by him, and taking advantage of my absence, a trading captain brought a small cask on shore, and sold it to the natives. This revived their dormant appetite, and, like pent-up waters, the disposition burst forth, and with the impetuosity of a resistless torrent carried the people before it, so that they appeared maddened with infatuation. I could scarcely image that they were the same persons among whom I had lived so long, and of whom I had thought so highly.
>
> As the small cask which had been imported was sufficient only to awaken the desire for more, they had actually prepared nearly twenty stills, which were in active operation when I arrived."

Williams quickly restored order and soon had reports from his supporters that, "every still was demolished, and every still-house burnt to the ground." Finally, "having accomplished at Raiatea the destruction of the stills, and the re-establishment of law and order, we prepared to depart for Rarotonga . . ."[13]

Other dim glimpses are available of outer island drinking, such as E. H. Lamont's mention of a trip to Huahine in the 1860's that he "resided in the house of the old native teacher . . . [whose] sons were wild scamps, addicted to the bottle."[14]

The drinking suggested by these brief descriptions differs from the more restrained and integrated contemporary drinking practices. It is tempting to interpret it as the sort of socially and personally destructive drinking thought to be related to conditions of stressful culture change in which most non-pathological paths of adaptation have been psychologically or socially blocked. This is the explanation often given for the destructive drinking practices of some American Indians:

> "Among all those who drink to excess, whether Indian or non-Indian, there is a background of emotional troubles, frustrations and dispppointments. Alcohol under these circumstances temporarily gives a sense of superiority and confidence, while dulling the senses so that the unpleasantness of life may be forgotten. Since drinking and criminality seem highest among Indians of all groups in the United States, it is pertinent to ask whether conditions of deprivation are, or have been, more severe among these people . . . An examination of Indian-White relations through time gives some support to such a hypothesis."[15]

Contemporary experience, however, suggests that the historical reports as to the severity of native drinking should be taken with a certain caution.

French officials in French Polynesia, visitors, and "demis" commenting on "natives" tend to present a distorted picture of *ma'ohi* drinking behaviour. They state that "natives drink to excess, they don't know how to control their drinking, they should be protected." This is so out of line with the actual behaviour that it suggests stereotype formation related to the paternalism and anxieties of the colonial stratified situation. It is probable that these and similar psychological sets—missionary puritanism, nostalgia for the undisturbed "noble savages" of the romantics, fears of primitivism ready to resurge—affected, as they still affect, evaluations of the severity of drinking.

But even with the grain of salt added there seems to have been throughout the nineteenth century evidence of demoralization and extensive drunkenness which were not evident during the early 1960's, when the observations presented in this paper were made. Most Society Island communities had, apparently, developed a new balance—an integrated, "neo-polynesian" culture, built around the village branches of the Tahitianized Protestant Church.

The Society Islands are now, at the time of writing, beginning to undergo major economic, demographic, and political changes due to the development of tourism, the building of an international airport, and the development of a nuclear weapons testing site in the territory. It seems most likely that these changes will be associated with a disruption of the interactional and psychological patterns conducive to restrained drinking, and that a significant increase in socially and personally disruptive drinking may once more be expected.

2. Contemporary Drinking Behaviour

In an article, *Drinking in Three Polynesian Societies,* Lemert[16] contrasted Society Island, Cook Island and Samoan drinking patterns. He considered Tahitian drinking to be predominantly "festive," rather than "ritual" (i.e. under the control of fairly strict rules and supervision) as in the Cook Islands, or "secular" as in Samoa, where "drinking lacks all but the basic elements of patterning, is without ritual, and seldom if ever has been the basis of village or district wide festive behaviour." He believed that Tahitian drinking was integrated with Tahitian values, in contrast to Samoa where, "drinking practices are unintegrated culturally and disruptive in extreme." Lemert felt that Tahitian drinking was "contrary to the demands of a wage-work economy, and, as they are more drawn into such economy, the form of the drinking can be expected to change, presumably in a more secular direction." He also noted for Tahiti the pattern of plateau drinking, the "long slow drunk." He noted that Tahitian males "when sober, are quiet, shy and almost timid [which] also suggests one of the main motivations for male drinking—to overcome shyness sufficiently to make sexual approaches to their women." For Polynesia in general he stated that, "Alcoholism in the sense of addictive drinking, with complex personality changes and serious organic pathology, such as cirrhosis of the liver, is nowhere found among full-blooded Polynesians." He also noted "the large number of heavy drinkers who have successfully stopped their drinking," and that "guilt over drinking or drunkenness does not seem to develop in Polynesian society."

Lemert's generalizations about Society Islands drinking behaviour are in agreement with my observations. In covering again several of Lemert's points I intend, besides indicating consensus of different observers, to add some further details and analysis.

The *ma'ohi* population of the Society Islands (there are also *Demi*, European, and Chinese populations) drink mostly beer, made by a local brewery,[17] red Algerian wine, and, in the more rural areas, illegal, home brewed orange "beer," which was the standard drink of twenty or thirty years ago in the outer islands. The beer, Hinano, is 5% alcohol by volume, and the wine varies between 10% and 12%. According to brewery officials[18] beer has become more popular than wine in recent years. Village observations indicate that orange beer is now a much more rarely used drink than either wine or beer. Its illegality and "traditional" history give it some special meanings and uses reminiscent of Prohibition drinking in the United States. Brewery officials believe that beer has become popular because it is less expensive than wine, and because "the Tahitians say that it makes them feel less heavy and tired than wine drinking does."

The amount of beer and wine consumed varies closely with local economic conditions, which in most parts of the Society Islands in the recent past have been dependent on fluctuations in the world vanilla market. The island of Huahine, for example (with a population of 3,214 people in 1962), used about 5,000 cases of beer (each case containing fifteen 65 centiliter bottles) in 1961, and an average of about 3,000 cases a year for 1962 and 1963 when the vanilla price had fallen.

Beer and wine are sold at bars and restaurants and licensed retail outlets in the small port towns in the outer islands. Before 1930 the sale of alcohol in the territory was controlled by "racial origin." These laws have been successively modified. The present laws regulating the distribution of alcoholic beverages date largely from 1959.[19] Distribution is controlled by a system of licenses. Those licenses which permit the sale of all kinds of alcoholic beverages are more expensive and more difficult to get. The classes of licenses permitting only beer and wine sales ("liquids of less than 14% alcohol") are those which are applied for and granted for the rural areas. There is also some control over the shipment of hard spirits in any quantity from Tahiti to the outer islands. There is no indication that this control is a hardship on Society Island drinkers. Those who drink seem to prefer mild alcoholic beverages.[20] Those who live in or visit Papeete, where hard liquor is available, still drink beer or wine.

Drinking in Piri

Drinking is socially integrated in Piri in that it is an accepted part of community life, and in that there are community patterns of use, and shared attitudes and norms concerning it.

The relation of drinking to social structure is of a "de-differentiating" kind. The historical pattern of intoxication as primarily a behaviour of higher status people does not exist now. Drinking tends often to be connected with those occasions when people who would not ordinarily be associating associate. That is, most activities are performed by small relatively stable groups of people (household, kin group segments, small work groups) who are, as they put it, "accustomed, *mātau,* to each other, and therefore not embarrassed, *ha'ama,*" within the range of the conventional tasks of the group. There are a series of discreet, and more or less isolated groups, a cellular pattern, in the village. There are out of group, pan-village, or intervillage activities, but when they do occur, drinking tends to be associated with them. It helps, it is generally said, overcome people's embarrassment.

Drinking represents part of a complex of behaviours which villagers identify as traditional, *ma'ohi,* behaviour and about which they are ambivalent. These are behaviours which are often opposed to the modern values which are beginning to be felt in the village, such as saving, self improvement, and striving. Too much *ma'ohi* behaviour is felt to be a little simple and regressive, reminiscent of the dimly conceived old "heathen" days. Yet *ma'ohi* behaviour is the kind of behaviour people feel most comfortable with. Those who deviate too strongly from *ma'ohi* values are distrusted, and treated with relative restraint and coolness.

For example, the chief of Piri (and reportedly this is true of many of the elected village chiefs throughout the Society Islands) had been a "heavy drinker" by local standards before and during the first years of his office. This increased his acceptability as chief. Consensus politics are practised in the village, and there is fear of a striving, ambitious, domineering man in the chief's role. Drinking indicates that a man is not "superior" to anyone else.

Adults in the village of Piri were classified roughly in four groups in village discussions of drinking behaviour. There were "heavy drinkers," "those who used to be heavy drinkers, but gave it up" (or more rarely cut down to occasional, moderate drinking), "normal drinkers," and a vague residue of people who "don't drink" and who were never heavy drinkers. This last group includes some who didn't drink at all (the Protestant pastor; a small group of adults recently converted to Mormonism, of whom only one had previously been a "heavy drinker"; several women who were strongly opposed to drinking), and many who only took an occasional glass of beer or wine during special occasions. When people were described by villagers to strangers the first two categories, "heavy drinker" or "ex-heavy drinker" figure prominently in the descriptions.

There were probably no adults in Piri who had never tasted beer or wine, many had had their first sample as children. But most women had not gone beyond occasional tasting. There were two women in Piri who drank and got drunk occasionally during the year, and several others who drank moderately during festivals and special occasions, but for Piri drinking was mostly a man's affair.

Most men drank "normally." This meant that they would drink during the big festivals, but that they would drink only rarely during the occasions on which the "heavy drinkers" drank regularly, on trips into the port town, or on minor special events in the village such as the finishing of some group work project, the birthday party of a small child, or a marriage. When they did drink at these latter occasions they would limit themselves to two or three glasses.

There were at least five men in the village who had been "heavy drinkers" and who had given it up. Four of them had stopped entirely, one had cut down to two or three moderate one-day episodes a year. Four of these had stopped by signing the "Blue Cross," a pledge encouraged by the Protestant Church, which is felt to carry supernatural sanctions. The fifth stopped on joining the Mormons. There are "ex-heavy drinkers" in other villages in Huahine who reportedly stopped drinking without any religious reinforcement.[21] There are some men in other villages who had signed the Blue Cross for a limited period of time, and then began to drink again. Four of the five "ex-heavy drinkers" at Piri seemed to have permanently stopped drinking; a fifth left the village to work in Papeete, and reportedly started drinkiing again.

There were six men in Piri who were "heavy drinkers." The youngest was in his thirties, the oldest in his early sixties. Five of them were considered, in spite of their ages, to be still in some ways "adolescents," or *taure'are'a*, the life stage of which pleasure seeking and irresponsibility were characteristic. Three of these had established families, and although the men were perhaps the least active in working their fields, they did provide for their families in at least minimally adequate ways. The other two "old adolescent" drinkers were bachelors. One lived alone, and the other with relatives. To be a bachelor after one's early twenties was a quite deviant pattern in the village. These five men usually drank together, and had done so for many years. They would gather every week or two in the evening in a house belonging to one of them. Sometimes they would make and drink orange beer. They would drink through the night, joking and singing and occasionally fighting. The fights were not at all violent and it was rare for anyone to be bruised. The next morning after a drinking bout they would often sleep. Occasionally if they felt sick they would take a medicinal drink, but by the afternoon they would be fishing, or at work in the gardens, and it would be a week or two before they drank again.

The sixth "heavy drinker" did not drink with the other drinking group. He was a very energetic cultivator, who had carefully accumulated and developed his lands. He had a large family, and a comfortable "European style" house. He alternated dry periods of several days, periods when he would drink a water glass or two of beer or wine with his meals, and rare occasions when by himself or with friends he would drink several bottles of wine or beer. During trips to the port town, and during any gathering at his house, he would also drink. What made him different from others who drank during such occasions was that he looked drunk after he had been drinking; he would stagger, his head would roll around, he would fall off his chair onto the floor. He would then lie down and sleep. Later the same night he might be up working on some task around his house, and the next morning he would be at work. On several occasions after having looked dramatically and unco-ordinatedly drunk he would, in response to some development of interest "pull himself together," and act in a relatively co-ordinated way. For the few drinkers who showed unco-ordinated drunken behaviour there seemed to be a dramatic, exaggerated quality to it, which was beyond the actual neurological dysfunction as indicated by the amount of alcohol which they had apparently taken, and by their frequent ability to recover quickly.[22]

In Huahine twenty or thirty years ago, drinking during the later *taure'are'a* period, between perhaps eighteen and twenty-three or four, was very much more common than it is now. At that period orange beer was brewed in a barrel in the bush outside the village, and some young men and women, joined by village "heavy drinkers," would drink around the barrel, dance, sing, fight, and initiate sexual affairs. The details of this kind of drinking are obscured by sentiment or retrospective moral indignation on the part of villagers today. The drinking was festive and occasional, and did not involve most of the adult villagers. Older *taure'are'a* now do not have any special drinking patterns, and are among the village's "normal drinkers." (On the island of Tahiti, particularly in Papeete, and in districts close to Papeete, there are special patterns of *taure'are'a* drinking. These are related to problems of urban adjustment and will be treated elsewhere).

"Heavy drinkers" drink more frequently and more than "normal drinkers." But the difference between them is much less than in groups where pathological drinking exists in contrast to normal drinking. There are certain behaviours and interpretations which are generally characteristic of drinking, including most "heavy drinking." These are outlined in the following sections.

Drinking Behaviour

1. Drinking is usually kept at controlled levels or plateaus. Levels are reached, maintained, and not overshot. The heavier drinkers reach a some-

what higher level, but they can usually maintain this without getting very drunk. There are two questions involved—first, the desire and ability to maintain a level; and second, the *particular* level, the depth of drunkenness, that is sought.

The minor celebrations which were one type of reward to a work group upon the completion of a joint task provided good examples of plateau drinking. A large quantity of wine or beer was provided by the host for whom the work had been done. The participants would keep drinking until the wine or beer was gone, which might take an afternoon, a night and most of the following day. The drinkers ate from time to time, and occasionally took a short nap. Occasionally a participant would leave for a brief period to do some task at his house, and would then return. Most of the drinkers looked dulled and bleary in the later stages of this sort of drinking, but kept their drunkenness below a staggering level; others showed some unsteadiness. But greatly unco-ordinated drunkenness, with marked physical and verbal incoherence, was extraordinarily rare. In observing hundreds of examples of rural Society Islands drinking behaviour, sometimes in festivals which went on for ten days, I saw such behaviour only five or six times. (This, as noted, was complicated by dramatic exaggeration.)

There are other types of Tahitian behaviour in which the ability to maintain a controlled level of expression, or discharge, is noteworthy, in contrast to other cultural groups in which "overshooting" frequently occurs. Hostile behaviour, for example, is expressed at low levels and does not, except in extremely rare cases, rise to violent levels.[23] Romantic affectionate behaviour and dependent behaviour are also expressed at relatively controlled, low levels of intensity.

2. There are, in addition to control of levels of intoxication, temporal controls. Even "heavy drinkers" stop in time to keep up with their tasks, and well before they become seriously ill. During the two major yearly festivals people declare that they will drink until they are *fiu*, "fed up," until the desire has disappeared. The desire is sure to disappear, sometimes within a day, sometimes after three or four days. Many will drink, and stop, and then start again three or four times during the festival, but the festival is no bacchanal. After several days of festivals people in Huahine seemed ready to stop "enjoying themselves," and ready to get back to their usual routines.

3. At festivals and special occasions in which drinking does occur there was formal urging by the host or by a village official for people to drink. For those who are not "heavy drinkers" there is a hesitancy which must be overcome.

4. The major visible effect of drinking was that drinkers seemed more relaxed and at ease. There was more talking, joking, and laughing.

At drinking at home gatherings older men would occasionally sing the old courting and humorous sexual songs, and dance the erotic *tamure.* There was often a good deal of male homoerotic play. Two men would dance the *tamure* together, men would affectionately embrace each other, in ways characteristic of young male adolescents but never of sober adults.

Affectionate or sexual behaviour cross-sexually was very rarely displayed in public drinking behaviour. In general such expressions were much more controlled than homoerotic behavior. In festival settings, where there is Western ballroom type dancing for young couples, this is, even for those who have been drinking, restrained. This heterosexual restraint is a response to the public setting.[24] For some of the young men, drinking gave them more courage, after they left the public amusement area, to approach a girl in the hopes of arranging sexual intercourse. Reportedly some types of foreplay such as kissing and cunnilinctus were more common after drinking.

Public aggressive behaviour is very rare, even in crowds of people who had been drinking for two or three days. There was more aggression in drinking in the household, but this was of limited violence. Some young men would, after drinking, engage in the thrill-motivated semi-sport of sneaking into someone else's house in the dark to steal some food.

5. Non-drinkers, or light drinkers, would interact with relatively drunken people in a normal fashion. Even in the few episodes of uncoordinated drunkenness, people would continue in close discussion and interaction with the drinker. However, if the drinker began to act in a hostile fashion, and if joking with him did not stop him, people would disengage from him, and try not to provoke or react to him.

Ma'ohi Interpretations of Drinking

Villagers' informal discussions of drinking and statements during recorded life-history interviews, supplemented behavioural observations.

Some extracts from an interview with a 17 year old boy, "Toro," are illustrative:

"I started drinking at fourteen. I did not drink all the time. Perhaps every two months I would feel like drinking, and then I would go and drink orange beer or wine . . . When I was a child I tried beer or wine sometimes at our house, but not very much. [This was with his elders' approval.] After I got older I drank more, but not very often. The times I felt bored, that is when I wanted to drink. When one feels weary, one wants some fresh thoughts, then one drinks to chase away the boredom. I drank maybe once a week if there was something around to drink, if not, I just let it go . . . I would drink until my head started to feel strange, then I'd want to drink more to increase the feeling, to get drunk [*ta'ero,* which also means poison, or poisoned]. Then I feel happy, and want to go and have a good time. You don't feel embarrassed or worried any more; you don't feel fear any more—you just want to go and enjoy yourself. It is nice, but the next morning it isn't nice any more. You still have a strange feeling in your head. All you want is some cold water to drink."

He goes on to talk about other effects of drinking:

"If you have been feeling angry, you drink and the anger goes away. You just want to enjoy yourself, you don't pay any attention any more . . . If you want a woman, if you are drunk it is easy. You aren't timid. You go and talk to her. Even if she teases you or insults you, you don't pay any attention . . . When I'm sober I'm sort of timid about talking. When you are drunk you can respond to her. If you are not drunk, it is very difficult." [The shifting from I, *vau,* to the more impersonal "you" or "one," *'oe,* is general.]

"Sometimes you remember [the next morning]. You are ashamed at the things you did when you were drunk. Those people who saw you, you are ashamed because of them. They mock, 'That young man, he is not worth anything'."

Asked if he thought he would keep on drinking in the same way all his life, he said, "No. When you get older, you don't have the desire to do that sort of thing any more. You want to sometimes, but not frequently. When you are a *taure'are'a* you don't trouble yourself. If you want to drink, you drink. But when you settle down with a woman, when you are mature, and when you have children, if you keep drinking, that is shameful. The children don't eat, they don't have clothes to wear."

He tried to stop once at his adoptive mother's urging, and did stop for several months.

"until there came a time when the *taure'are'a* were drinking. They came and pulled at me to go. If you don't go and drink, it is a very embarrassing thing, so you go. And so you start again."

Statements by Toro and others about drinking agreed in several aspects:

1. Drinking, within clear limits, is natural. It is not unusual, forbidden, or rebellious behaviour. It does not set one off from others.

2. It is not only natural but, again with set limits, it is a good thing. It is good for the body, good for the enjoyment of life. The chief of the village of Piri put it, "Drinking is good, if you don't get very drunk. It is good for the body, especially orange beer . . . It makes people energetic and well nourished."

The major evaluation of moderate drinking as a good thing was not shared by everyone. Many women felt that drinking beyond a glass or two was always bad and could lead to dangerous consequences. As one woman said, "Some people say that drinking is a good thing, that it brings good ways of thinking. I don't think it is a good thing. It causes people to steal, to have bad thoughts. They want to commit adultery, to beat up their own parents, to beat up their own children."[25]

3. Describing the effects of drinking on them, people stated that it increased their sense of energy and liveliness, decreased feelings of boredom, decreased embarrassment and social and interpersonal timidity. One of Piri's heavier drinkers felt that he would become weak and ill if he stopped his once a week drinking. He felt that when he drank his food did him more good.

Toro stated that his feelings of anger disappeared when he drank. Others, and Toro at other times, said that when they drank they were able to express verbally anger (or disappointment or other negative feelings) towards someone, which they could not do otherwise.

4. The limits within which drinking is natural and good are clear. It is

wrong if it makes you sick, or if it makes you feel badly—if you drink too much and lose your sense of well being. The hangover is often stressed in discussions of drinking. Thus the chief of the village said, "People are changed when they drink, the body is changed. It is as if it gets more powerful . . . It is an agreeable feeling, of course, but a little while afterwards it isn't anymore, because it goes back to its old state. There isn't any place without pain after one has been very drunk. The body is full of pain the next morning."

Drinking is wrong if one's behaviour gets "out of control." Some informants found their first experiences of relatively heavy drinking unpleasant because they did things, such as steal food, which they remembered with anxiety the next morning. Some drank tentatively and lightly for years before they began to drink more heavily.

Drinking was also wrong, as Toro noted, if it caused adults to neglect their responsibilities.

5. There are two sorts of explanation given by an individual for the regulation (starting, stopping, amount drunk, etc.) of his drinking behaviour. One is the externally directed sense of shame, *ha'ama,* which, depending on the situation, can influence either towards more or towards less drinking. The other is one's inner state of desire, *hina'aro.* This desire may be gratified, *maha,* and no longer operative; or it may be negated by a feeling of irritation or discomfort or lack of gratification, the complex concept best glossed, perhaps, as being "fed up," *fiu.* Explanation of one's behaviour in terms of *hina'aro* or *fiu* refer to perceived inner conditions which have more reference to one's own self than does *ha'ama.*

When "heavy drinkers" stop after many years of drinking, the explanation for the decision was usually that they were *fiu,* that they didn't want to drink any more. Illness or a family crisis might have influenced the timing of the decision and the Blue Cross might have reinforced and strengthened it, but the major explanation was a change in one's inner state. It is this change that young "heavy drinkers" expect will happen to them to cause them to become lighter drinkers as they mature. Though shamefulness may be mentioned, they do not expect that the community through shaming will have to struggle against their own recalcitrant inner desires. They expect the desire to change in the proper direction. In general, desire rather than shame is presented in explanations as the strongest determinant in drinking regulation.

3. Psychodynamics of Ma'ohi Drinking

If, from a cross-cultural viewpoint, the higher degrees of *heavy* drinking include drinking to unconsciousness, or to marked degrees of unco-ordination, and the higher degrees of *maladaptive* drinking include significant rates of physical pathology related to drinking (gastritis, delirium tremens, neuritis, hepatitis), addictive drinking, and seriously disruptive interpersonal acts, then drinking in Piri, and from all indications throughout the Society Islands in general, is neither very heavy nor maladaptive.

The form and severity of drinking behaviour in a community is related to both the community regulation and integration of drinking behaviour, and the culturally (and perhaps genetically and physical-environmentally) influenced prevalent internalized psychological structure of socialized individuals. Various balances of control between public community forces and private internalized ones are conceivable. For Piri, I believe that the most effective aspects of drinking regulation are the internalized ones.

These include the following:

1. The prevalent personal motives for drinking are gratified by low level intoxication.[26] People in many situations feel constricted, embarrassed, self-conscious, timid and bored. When they drink these feelings are quickly altered, and they feel stronger, more lively and comfortable. (The psychological and neuro-physiological reasons for these shifts and the reasons for the feelings of constriction are not at issue here.) They are able to do things which they felt timid about before. Most of these things are socially useful, and approved. For these shifts moderate drinking is sufficient. Heavy drinking obliterates the social effectiveness and sense of well being produced by the moderate drinking.

2. Conversely, motives for drinking for which high and prolonged levels of intoxication would be necessary are not prevalent: a desire for forgetfulness related to identity confusion, low self esteem, stress and frustration which may have entered into Nineteenth Century Tahitian drinking patterns; a guilt ridden desire for alcohol-induced illness and purification, or for simple annihilation.

There is no indication that the people of Piri, or Tahitians in general, are struggling to control the expression of strong, socially dangerous drives. Crime rates are low, violent crime is exceedingly rare, people in conditions of social or personal breakdown act mildly. There is no indication that people avoid drinking for fear of an uncontrolled explosion,[27] or drink deeply to permit the explosion, or drink more deeply still to reach some narcotic safety.

3. If people drink to relieve feelings of constriction and social anxiety, why don't they overshoot? Why don't they get involved with the formula supposedly associated with much addictive drinking, "If a little drinking makes me happy, why shouldn't more drinking make me happier?" To some degree they do sometimes overshoot moderately and lose their sense of well being, lose control to a degree of which they later feel ashamed, and suffer from mild hangovers. But this mild overshooting acts as corrective "negative feedback," as a reinforcement towards the maintenance of moderate levels in subsequent drinking.

I believe that there are positive factors operating against overshooting, which are related to the effects of certain pervasive socialization practices. There is gross discouragement in the socialization of children about four or five years of age of close attachment to their parents, of overt dependency behaviour, and of regressive behaviour. The young child now learns that he must suddenly become emotionally "self sufficient,"[28] and that helpless babyish behavior will only be ignored or punished. Self-sufficiency, the early, abrupt transition from baby to independent child is the major crisis that he has to surmount in growing up. Lessons in the dangers of becoming deeply involved emotionally in dependent relations, or any other relationships in which one does not maintain some ability to escape, are reinforced throughout life. Dependent behaviour which is evidenced is on a controlled, reconstructed level. The group life in Piri is in peculiar balance with this essential atomism.[29]

If dependency, helplessness, regression, are perceived as disturbing, dangerous, and valueless (i.e. they do not pay off in the response of others), then in the absence of any other pervasive motives for drinking severe enough to produce such states, helplessness-producing drinking should be avoided.

This is related to the findings of Peter Field, in a cross-cultural survey of some variables associated with drunkenness that *indulgent* behaviour of parents towards children between five and twelve years old was positively and significantly correlated with severe drunkenness. Field notes in a footnote that, "It is probably relevant in this connection that Parker has found fifteen articles reporting a close mother-son attachment in alcoholics, and several authors have reported that youngest children in a family are both relatively indulged and over-represented among alcoholics."[30]

Anxiety about becoming regressively dependent and helpless is compensated by the learned orientation that the world is not dangerous, and that one will not become helpless if one stays in balance with the physical and social world. This balance means low key, accepting, easygoingness. Departing from this by being too ambitious, too covetous, too violent, will produce imminent retaliation from the universe . . . sickness, crop failure, bad luck. Drunkenness as imbalance, like drunkenness as helpless dependency, threatens a central aspect of personal adjustment.[31]

4. If there is little need to seek high levels or prolonged periods of intoxication, and, in fact, needs not to do so, it must be assumed that individuals have enough understanding of the effects and tempo of intoxication to prevent the undesired levels. Villagers have the opportunity to learn to drink, and to come to understand the meaning of the clues as to levels of intoxication.

Summary

Drinking in Piri has been described with the belief that it is representative of rural Society Islands drinking. It has been presented as a common and important activity, which, contrary to popular suppositions about Tahitian "native drinking," has associated controlling factors which tend to prevent it from becoming disruptive to the drinker or his group. These controlling factors are partially found in shared group evaluations about drinking, but most importantly in aspects of prevalent psychological structure.

Disruptive drinking was more severe in the nineteenth century during a period of major cultural readaptation, and may soon become a problem again as a consequence of new social changes. But, for the present, a complex, integrated balance has been achieved.

NOTES

1. The field work on which this paper is based was a general study of psychological behaviour made during June and July 1961, and from July 1962 to June 1964 in two Society Islands communities. It was supported by Research Grant M-5567-A from the National Institute of Mental Health, United States Public Health Service, and by Research Grant NSF-G23476 from the National Science Foundation. The study was in collaboration with a general study on social change in the Society Islands, under the direction of Douglas Oliver.

In this paper the adjective "Tahitian" refers to the Society Islands in general, unless the context indicates that it refers to the island of Tahiti in contrast to the outer islands.

2. Morrison 1935: 151.
3. In this and the following quotations from late Eighteenth and early Nineteenth Century sources, spelling and punctuation are modernized.
4. "Tynah" was the chief of a district in Tahiti.
5. Bligh n.d.: Vol. 1, 388.
6. Banks 1962: Vol. I, 345.
7. Ellis 1829: Vol. I, 229-231.
8. Moerenhout 1837: Vol. 1, 312.
9. Moerenhout 1837: Vol. 1, 234.
10. Lecucq 1849: 66.
11. Adams 1930: 467.
12. Tahitian aggressiveness and hostility are treated in Levy, in press.
13. Williams 1837:403-407.
14. Lamont 1867:64.
15. Dozier 1966:74-75.
16. Lemert 1964a.
17. There is now a second brewery at Papeete.
18. For information on the consumption of beer I am indebted to M. F. Fourcade, and M. Albert Montaron of Papeete.
19. The 1959 law, and a listing of previous related legislation are published in the *Journal officiel de la Polynésie Française* for October 31, 1959, pp. 711-717.
20. In a study of the comparative drinking practices of Hawaiians and other ethnic groups in a Hawaiian plantation setting, Lemert notes that Hawaiians in answering questions about the type of beverage usually consumed "indicate an ethnic preference for beverages of moderate rather than high alcoholic content."—Lemert 1964b:697.
21. In an ongoing study of a Hawaiian Homestead community, under the direction of Alan Howard of the Bishop Museum, a relatively large number of men who were "heavy drinkers" and who then discontinued abruptly and presumably permanently has been noted. Lemert, in his plantation study, notes, "It is of interest to note that the high percentage of nondrinkers in the Hawaiian group is largely due to the relatively large number, 28%, who had drunk at one time but later gave up. . . . Caucasians are unique among the groups in having no persons who had given up drinking."—Lemert 1964b:692.
22. Examples of this kind of behaviour are given in t'Serstevens 1950:301. "They often put a childlike imagination into their drunkenness. They walk straight before entering the village, but begin to stagger when they reach the first houses," etc.
23. Levy, in press.
24. Those who have observed Tahitian public mores at Papeete bars are witnessing a special

sub-cultural setting. Tahitian sex behaviour will be treated in other publications.

25. There are a number of indications that anxiety about the possible dangerous effects of drinking, anxiety which is not justified by actual behaviour observed in the village, is shared even by those drinkers who stress the beneficial effect of drinking. This anxiousness about the effects of loss of control is responsible for some of the stress on balance (see below) and on the control of level. This kind of anxiety has many special features which are considered in Levy (in press). As is touched on below (compare footnote 28 for example) this anxiety is not related to a struggle with tenuously controlled strong impulses, pressing for discharge. It seems to be more a matter of special interpretations of reality.

The complementary roles of men and women in their drinking behaviour, and in their expression of attitudes about drinking, will be discussed elsewhere.

26. This and the following discussion is based on the concept of the use of alcohol fulfilling a variety of diverse psychological and social functions. See, for example, Levy 1958, Chafetz and Demone 1962, Washburne 1961, and many of the articles in Pittman and Snyder 1962.

27. For example, for the Alorese "the whole system of organized aggression or self-assertion becomes blocked, and the individual has a life-long struggle to contain these impulses within limits. He thus lives in constant fear that they will spill over and then get completely out of hand. Hence he must avoid all intoxicants which diminish the powers of control. . . ."—Kardiner 1945:166.

28. This "self-sufficiency" has many different qualities from the Western ideal.

29. Ritchie has described similar qualities of atomism, or "granularity," for the New Zealand Maori.—Ritchie 1963.

30. In Pittman and Snyder, editors 1962:48-74, especially 65f.

31. It is noteworthy that until a generation ago the use of opium was not uncommon among Chinese in Tahiti, and it is still used by some older Chinese, and a few Europeans. According to police authorities at Tahiti there were no known cases of its use among "pure" Tahitians. One may cautiously raise the question whether the effect of opium, producing passivity rather than the release of inhibition, might have been in conflict with aspects of Tahitian self-regulation.

REFERENCES

ADAMS, HENRY, 1930. *Letters of Henry Adams* (W. C. Ford, editor) Boston and New York, Houghton Mifflin.

BANKS, JOSEPH, 1962. *The Endeavour Journal of Joseph Banks* [1768-1771] (J. C. Beaglehole, editor) Sydney, Angus and Robertson. Two volumes.

BLIGH, WILLIAM, n.d. *The Log of the Bounty* (Owen Rutter, editor) London, Golden Cockerel Press. Two volumes.

CHAFETZ, M. E. AND H. W. DEMONE, JR., 1962. *Alcoholism and Society.* New York, Oxford University Press.

DOZIER, E. P., 1966. "Problem Drinking Among American Indians." *Quarterly Journal of Studies on Alcohol,* 27:72-87.

ELLIS, WILLIAM, 1828. *Polynesian Researches.* London, Fisher, Son and Jackson. Two volumes.

KARDINER, A., 1945. *The Psychological Frontiers of Society.* New York, Columbia University Press.

LAMONT, E. H., 1867. *Wild Life Among the Pacific Islanders.* London, Hurst and Blackett.

LECUCQ, L., 1849. *Question de Tahiti.* Paris, Librairie Militaire de Blot.

LEMERT, E., 1964a. "Forms and Pathology of Drinking in Three Polynesian Societies." *American Anthropologist,* 66:361-374.

——— 1964b. "Drinking in Hawaiian Plantation Society." *Quarterly Journal of Studies on Alcohol,* 25:689-713.

LEVY, R. I., 1958. "The Psychodynamic Functions of Alcohol." *Quarterly Journal of Studies on Alcohol,* 19:649-659.

——— in press. "On Getting Angry in the Society Islands," in W. Caudill and T. Lin, editors, *Mental Health Research in Asia and the Pacific.*

MOERENHOUT, J. A., 1837. *Voyage aux îles du Grand Ocean.* Paris, Bertrand.

MORRISON, JAMES, 1935. *The Journal of James Morrison.* London, Golden Cockerel Press.

PITTMAN, D. J. AND C. R. SNYDER, 1962. *Society Culture and Drinking Patterns.* New York, John Wiley and Sons.
RITCHIE, J., 1963. *The Making of a Maori.* Wellington, Reed.
T'SERSTEVENS, A., 1950. *Tahiti et sa couronne.* Paris, Albin Michel.
WASHBURN, C., 1961. *Primitive Drinking.* New York, College and University Press.
WILLIAMS, JOHN, 1837. *A Narrative of Missionary Enterprises in the South Sea Islands.* London, J. Snow.

18

URBANIZATION IN THE TAHITIAN HOUSEHOLD

Paul Kay

The effects of urbanization on family life in Tahiti will be examined in this paper. I shall consider certain aspects of household structure in one Papeete[1] neighborhood, Manuhoe, and, when occasion calls for it, contrast these with the corresponding patterns and measures in a rural district of Tahiti Island, Mahaena.

The Area Studied

Manuhoe is the name of a largely residential *quartier* of Papeete. It does, however, contain six businesses, ranging in size and importance from a large and prosperous vehicle repair and body rebuilding garage to an enterprise in which a single, elderly Tahitian prepares, in discarded wine bottles, a medicinal mixture of sugar, water, and herbs, which he sells for 10 francs a bottle. There is only one house in the neighborhood made from native materials, the others being of wood or cement with galvanized iron roofs. Indoor toilets and cooking facilities are the exception rather than the rule, but are, nonetheless, much more in evidence here than in Mahaena, where they are virtually nonexistent. The area covered in the study is all in the interior of the city block and the majority of the houses are inaccessible by automobile when a rain has turned the ground to mud. In terms of the income levels, standards of living, racial composition, length and permanence of residence, types of housing, and so forth, Manuhoe is probably as "typical" a Papeete neighborhood as can be found. By this I mean that the distributions for Manuhoe on each of these variables cover all or most of the corresponding ranges for Papeete as a whole. One important exception to this statement should be mentioned: There are no pure Caucasoids in Manuhoe.

Mahaena is a district located approximately 35 kilometers from Papeete. As in most of the Society Islands, the two most important economic activi-

Reproduced by permission of the Bernice P. Bishop Museum and Paul Kay from *Pacific Port Towns and Cities* (Honolulu, Hawaii, 1963, pp. 63–73).

ties are: (1) subsistence agriculture and fishing; and (2) cash crop agriculture, the two important cash crops being copra and vanilla. However, Mahaena and certain other Tahiti districts differ from other rural areas of French Polynesia in two important economic respects. First, instead of making copra, the majority of individuals cut their coconuts at an earlier stage and sell them daily to truckers, who transport them to Papeete and sell them as drinking nuts *(pape ha'ari).* Second, there is some commercial fishing and shrimping for the Papeete market and considerable commuting to Papeete for wage work. Two trucks daily, carrying passengers and produce at very reasonable rates, connect Mahaena with the town. In the most general terms, Mahaena is still a rural district, but one that is increasingly becoming economically, and consequently culturally and socially, influenced by Papeete. Since it is already a partially urbanized, or suburbanized district, we may assume that differences observed between Mahaena and Papeete will be reflected to an equal or greater degree by most other nonurban areas of the Society Islands.

The Household

In considering the effects of urbanization on family life, our primary focus is on transformations in the structure of the household. By "household" I mean a group of persons who habitually eat together. Commonly this group is coterminus with a number of other groups; those who sleep under the same roof, those who keep their personal property (particularly clothes) under the same roof, and those who bear certain close consanguineal or affinal relationships to each other. However, since in a small, but not a negligible, number of cases these groups do not precisely coincide, it has been decided to use the criterion of common eating as the diagnostic sign of the household. This usage is theoretically convenient, since in defining households in this way, we come very close to the usual meaning of the term as a minimal kinship grouping sharing common residence and engaging in common consumption and socialization activities. It is also in accord with the native practice, since whenever there is doubt concerning where an individual lives, Tahitians always appear to attach more importance to where he eats than to any other aspect of the situation.

The Urban Household

Manuhoe households may be typified, and contrasted to those of Mahaena and other rural areas, in three respects. I shall list these dimensions of contrast, discuss each in turn, and conclude with an attempt to draw these various considerations together into a pattern which furnishes some explanation of the phenomena observed. Manuhoe households are in general: (1) larger, tending away from the nuclear family in the direction of a more extended family; (2) more matrilocal and woman-centered, residential continuity being, to a much greater degree than elsewhere in the Society Islands, assured through relations between women; and (3) more disorganized, having a more rapid rate of turnover of personnel, less stability in place of residence.

The Housing Shortage

The primary normative pattern of household composition is, in Papeete, as elsewhere in the Society Islands, that a household should consist of a single nuclear family. This statement must be qualified to the extent that older people, particularly in the least Westernized areas, tend strongly to deplore the passing of the "good old days" of extended family residence. In any case, if Manuhoe people differ from other rural Society islanders on this normative variable, it is in the direction of valuing strictly nuclear family residence more, rather than less, highly. Nevertheless, the actual pattern of residence conforms poorly to the norm, and most subjects are both conscious of this discrepancy and willing to talk about it. Informants commonly, and correctly, observe that they don't like living in extended families, and that they would not do so if it were not for the limited supply of low-rent housing. The facts bear out this contention.

According to our census definitions, discussed below, Manuhoe contains 186 persons and Mahaena 223. These persons are distributed among 41 households in Manuhoe and 50 households in Mahaena. Hence households are of about the same average size in the two areas. In both places, the median number of persons per household is four. The means are 4.54 persons per household for Manuhoe and 4.46 persons per household for Mahaena. However, for a number of reasons, these figures fail adequately to represent the degree of residential crowding in the urban area.

First, both censuses represent *de jure* populations. That is, they count only permanent residents. In Mahaena, the *de jure* and *de facto* populations differ little, since the population is quite stable in the short run compared to Papeete. On the other hand, the *de jure* population of Manuhoe seriously underestimates the *de facto* population because of the large number of temporary visitors. It is the *de facto* population, the number of bodies physically present, which affects the degree of crowding.

Second, the date chosen for our "official" census, January 1, 1960, happens to coincide with a lower than average *de jure* population in Manuhoe. For example, corresponding to the January 1 population of 186 were October and March populations of 198 and 200.

Third, the average amount of living space per household and per person is considerably smaller in Manuhoe. Detailed data on this variable were not collected, but the general direction of difference is clear to anyone viewing the two areas. The majority of people in Manuhoe occupy multihousehold dwellings, where the number of people sleeping in a single small room may run as high as fourteen. There are no multihousehold dwellings in Mahaena.

Fourth, the proportion of children—persons who are under sixteen years of age or who are still attending school—in the total population is higher in Mahaena than Manuhoe, 49.8 percent compared to 42.4 percent. This effect aggravates the crowding problem in Manuhoe to the extent that adults require more living space than children. The lower proportion of children in the urban area also implies that, since households contain the same average number of persons in the two areas, the urban ones will probably contain more extended families. Addition of minor children to a nuclear family does not create an extended family, whereas addition of related adults does.

Finally, the figures exclude from consideration Chinese households. Were these included, the contrast between the two areas with respect to crowding would be magnified.[2]

The words "residential crowding" are used here to refer to two related but distinct concepts: (1) number of persons per household; and (2) amount of living space per person. By either criterion, Manuhoe exhibits considerably more residential crowding than Mahaena. The housing shortage appears to be the chief cause of the shift to extended family living in the urban area, a shift which runs counter to the explicit desires of the people.

More direct evidence of the increased importance of extended family residence in Manuhoe can be adduced. The structure of each household in both communities was transcribed symbolically to show the deviation from perfect nuclearity, if any, in terms of the number of extra, and missing, persons, and the exact relationship of these persons to the central nuclear family. It was found that in Manuhoe, out of the 41 households, 16 or 39 percent must be classed as extended families either on the basis of containing consanguineals who were not members of the central nuclear family, or on the presence of three or more interlocking nuclear families. The corresponding proportion for Mahaena was 20 percent, or 10 extended families out of 50 households. In Manuhoe 58.1 percent of the people live in extended families, whereas this is true of only 25.6 percent in Mahaena. In Manuhoe 37 individuals, or 19.9 percent of the total population, are not members of the central nuclear family of their households; the corresponding figures for Mahaena are 14 individuals, or 6.3 percent of the total population. The reader will note that for each of these three measures of family extension in residence, the Manuhoe measure is about two or three times that for Mahaena.

Nuclear family living remains the ideal pattern in Manuhoe, and may also be considered the primary pattern of household structure in terms of the actual situation. It has, however, been considerably modified in the direction of the extended family, due to economic pressures. These pressures are, of course, not unique to Manuhoe but apply to Papeete as a whole. Indeed, it would be profitless to speak of the housing market of Manuhoe, as it is in no sense isolated from the rest of Papeete. The trend appears to be accelerating as a positive function of the growth of the economically most depressed element of a town with very limited natural possibilities of expansion (see Jullien, 1961, 1963). It is also directly related to the fact that the amount of available low-cost housing is actually declining as many of the poorest houses are being replaced by new construction whose rental vastly exceeds the ability of a common laborer to pay. It seems unlikely that this trend will abate or reverse itself until there is some change in one or both of the major causal factors.

THE WOMAN-CENTERED HOUSEHOLD

Of the 186 individuals in Manuhoe, 85 were males and 101 females, yielding a male-to-female ratio of .842. The divergence of this index from 1.000 is considerable, especially in view of the general tendency in the territory for men to outnumber women (Jullien, 1961). Mahaena, on the other hand, shows a surplus of men over women in keeping with the general trend. However, it would be a serious mistake to attribute much significance to the difference of the Manuhoe sex ratio from that of the territory. In the first place, the population of Manuhoe is not a probability sample of the territorial population (or of any other known population), and it is therefore not possible to draw valid inferences concerning the significance of observed differences from population parameters. Second, even if we could consider Manuhoe as a random sample of some population, a sex ratio this small might arise as often as 12 times in 100 on the basis of chance alone, when the true population value was about one.

Nevertheless, there are certain factors which render the observed differences in sex ratio worthy of further discussion. The excessively low sex ratio in Manuhoe, in the light of the generally high ratio for the territory as a whole, is rendered a bit more comprehensible by the fact that, whereas in 1956 the ratio for the entire territory was 1.06, the ratio for Papeete was only .98. One is inclined, therefore, to suggest that Manuhoe exhibits an extreme value on a characteristic in which Papeete, or certain sections of it, differs from the rest of the territory. In Manuhoe there are a number of households in which the only adults are females, and none whose adults are all males, except for a few solitary bachelors. Also, family histories reveal in a number of instances a continuity over time of adult females in residence, with a considerably greater turnover among adult males.

Thus a second modification of the primary pattern of nuclear residence is suggested. It would appear that the basis of household organization and of continuity of household tenure has shifted somewhat from pure nuclearity and nonunilinear transmission to a situation in which basic organization and residential continuity tend to be assured through a collection of lineally or collaterally related females. That is, we find that in addition to being more extended than elsewhere, the Manuhoe household tends to achieve this extension primarily by the intermediacy of consanguineal relationships among females. Furthermore, this continuity through females shows up over time, as well as in the synchronic analysis of household composition, an important aspect of the situation in an area of such high residential mobility and household fragility.

A part of this phenomenon is the considerably greater residential mobility of adult males than females. The population of Papeete is certainly the most mobile segment of a highly mobile population. This is, of course, true of Manuhoe as well and, as mentioned above, in speaking of that population, I have taken as a base line a point of time about midway through the study, January 1, 1960. Compared to the 105 adults of the base-line population, 47 adults either took up permanent residence in Manuhoe or left the area permanently during a 12-month period. By "permanently" is meant that the individuals in question either arrived in Manuhoe more than one month before the end of the period of study and did not leave, or were present at the start of the study and left more than one month later, without returning. Also these figures do not include the very large number of individuals who made visits of a few days or weeks. The ratio of the number of adults who permanently changed residence to the number in the total adult population (47/105 = 44.8 percent) furnishes a rather conservative index of the degree of mobility of the population. Considering males and females separately, the corresponding proportions are 55.6 percent for males and 36.7 percent for females.

There is further evidence of the female-centered nature of the household in Manuhoe. All individuals in Mahaena and Manuhoe were scored as to whether they were either: (1) part of the central nuclear family of their household or members of multinuclear households; or (2) members neither of the central nuclear family nor of a multinuclear family. There were only two multinuclear families, both in Manuhoe. All individuals of Type 2 are referred to as "extensions" of the nuclear family. Extensions were scored as being related to the nuclear family through the wife (uxori-extensions), through the husband (viri-extensions), or through neither one more than the other (including cases of nonrelatives and lower generation lineal relatives). The ratio of uxori-extensions to total extensions gives an index of the importance of kinship links through females in the creation of the extended family. The ratios are, for Manuhoe and Mahaena respectively, 18/21, or 85.7 percent, and 4/14, or 28.6 percent.

Disorganization in the Urban Household

The concept of disorganization is, like many of the more interesting concepts of social science, difficult to operationalize. I shall try, nevertheless, to show what I mean by the word in the context of urban Tahitian household structure.

One aspect of household disorganization is illustrated by the high degree of over-all adult mobility and the concomitant impermanence of household personnel. This phenomenon is very early borne in upon the researcher when he discovers that the maintenance of an accurate census is an affair demanding virtually daily attention. The fact, cited above, that the number of adults permanently establishing or relinquishing residence in Manuhoe during one year amounted to 38.5 percent of the base-line adult population is, in itself, suggestive evidence of disorganization in the urban household. Unfortunately, the time spent in Mahaena did not permit gathering comparable data for that district. However, judging from detailed census and some family history data in Mahaena, I should be surprised if the index of mobility exceeded 10 to 15 percent and my best guess would be something under 5 percent. In any case, the vast majority of residence changes recorded in Mahaena family histories involved going to or coming from Papeete. Most of the relatively recent immigrants to the district came from Papeete, having gone there from other districts and islands. This pattern, of Papeete serving as a clearing house for rural-rural migration, as well as being the recipient of a great deal of rural-urban migration, appears to be a quite general and firmly established one. The result is that Papeete has a very fluid population. And because of the factors discussed in connection with the housing shortage, the tendency exists for immigration and emigration to affect the composition of already existing households rather than, as in Euro-American society, for example, merely to increase or reduce the total number of households. This situation contributes materially to impermanence and consequent disorganization in the urban household.

Considering the normatively valued nuclear family as a standard, and allowing for the secondary patterns of forced extension and female-centeredness which have been grafted onto this pattern, we can construct a fairly accurate index of the degree of household organization or disorganization in our subject communities. In the previous discussion I have not everywhere made explicit that "central nuclear families" are not necessarily complete nuclear families, but may lack one spouse, or children. The rules for determining which is the central nuclear family in such cases are unequivocal but complicated. If we compare, then, the number of households which contain no complete nuclear families—bearing in mind that these households may simultaneously be classed as extended families according to our procedures—with the total number of households in a community, we have a measure of the degree of household disorganization in that community. This measure can be justified on two grounds; first, the norm of nuclear-family living in the Society Islands, and, second, the voluminous sociological and anthropological literature asserting the virtual ubiquity and structural necessity of the nuclear family in viable societies. In Manuhoe, 19 out of 41, or 46.5 percent, of the households contained no complete nuclear family, while for Mahaena the comparable figures are 12 out of 50, or 24.0 percent. This disorganization of the urban household from the strictly structural point of view has definite correlates in the economic and affective aspects of family life, but consideration of these aspects would take us outside the scope of the present paper.

INTERPRETATION

In the preceding discussion, I have attempted to demonstrate that Manuhoe households, which are taken to be as typical of Papeete as those of any single neighborhood, excluding pure Chinese and European enclaves, may be characterized as: (1) crowded and tending toward extended family organization; (2) woman-centered; and (3) disorganized. These three aspects are related and may be explained as a coherent pattern in terms of certain social, and particularly economic, parameters of the general society of Papeete and its island hinterland. Moreover, this pattern appears to have been manifested elsewhere under circumstances, which, although totally different historically, bear formal economic analogies to that obtaining currently in Papeete.

I refer specifically to the situation described by Frazier (1939, 1949), Myrdal (1944), and others, concerning the structure of the Negro household among the lower classes in American cities. Briefly, this form of "family" is characterized as extended, containing more nonnuclear relatives than in white families; "matriarchial," in the sense of the impermanence of husbands and fathers and the consequent importance of women in all aspects of family affairs, including furnishing the basis for family extension and the transmission of residential continuity; and disorganized, in the twin senses of deviation from the norm of nuclearity and temporal impermanence with rapid turnover of personnel. There are, of course, many aspects of the American Negro urban family described in the voluminous literature on the subject which bear no particular relation to the Papeete household. These in particular refer to specific American caste pressures, relations to particular American social and economic institutions, and the psychodynamic aspects of family life. Nevertheless, within the scope of the present essay—the structural aspects of household composition—the formal similarities of these two household types, so widely separated in historical and cultural terms, are striking.

What are the formal socioeconomic conditions which have operated in different historical and cultural contexts to produce such similar household structures? First, both cases involve the migration of a rural population into an urban mileu, where it finds that it is an economically subordinate group. Second, the group finds that, for various reasons, it is extremely difficult to rise in the socioeconomic hierarchy in less than two generations. It is worthy of note here that strictly racial prejudice, as contrasted to economic and social class attitudes, is virtually inoperative, if not nonexistent, in Papeete. Finally, in this setting, two important factors contribute to great residential mobility of adult males. First, the limited economic prospects of the individual furnish little economic reward for job responsibility and industriousness. About the greatest economic security which a Polynesian immigrant to Papeete can be certain to obtain by years of conscientious effort is steady work at a semiskilled job which pays the equivalent of about $75 a month, in a town in which food prices, including native produce, are about on a par with those in an American supermarket. Second, such values of thrift, industriousness, and budgetary responsibility as have resulted in the new immigrant from the socialization process are attuned to a rural context, and consequently he is ill prepared to deal successfully with the differences in work rhythm and budgetary exigencies found in the urban setting.

Extension of the normatively nuclear family is, of course, a response to a delicate economic position by the means of cutting per capita rent. Reinforcing this trend is the traditional Polynesian economic practice of reciprocal exchange of economic aid among relatives. The woman-centeredness of the household results from the greater residential mobility of males than females, the major factors restricting female mobility being the demands of caring for children and the limited employment opportunities which could motivate and defray the cost of changing residence. In the lower economic sector of the population, the high costs of moving are more likely to be incurred through the time lag involved in re-establishing mutually satisfactory relationships of goods and services exchange with a new set of neighbors than in the actual money spent on the transport of property. The characteristics of woman-centeredness and extension naturally coalesce in a general pattern of extension through women. The general mobility of the population, the differential economic pressures and attractions exerted on men and women, and the absence of the system of economic and social rewards accruing to a successfully married pair in the rural district all serve to weaken marital ties and thus the nuclear core of household organization.

Perhaps the favorite phrase of Papeete informants, even those speaking relatively little French, when contrasting Papeete life to that of the islands and districts is: "*Chacun pour soi!*"

Suggested Practical Implications

Two possible welfare applications of the above data are offered as hypotheses for further research.

1. Recent research has disclosed an association between the woman-centered, high mobility household and a number of largely unfortunate social conditions. Perhaps the most significant and relevant of these to the Papeete case is the matter of delinquency and adolescent gang behavior. Briefly, the lack of a permanent male role-model during early years is held theoretically to cause confusion in adult male sex identification, and a consequent imperfection in the process of learning responsible adult roles. Whether or not the theoretical explanation is adequate, the empirical evidence of the association, gathered from many societies and cultures, is

impressive. For a summary of both theoretical and empirical aspects of the question and a review of recent literature, the reader is referred to Burton and Whiting (1961). For a summary of data and opinion concerning the increase of delinquent, and particularly juvenile delinquent, behavior in Papeete, see Bouvet and Iorsch (1960).

2. Although the peculiar residence situation in Papeete may well have certain unfortunate consequences within the town itself, it does appear to be performing an important function in the territory as a whole. Life-history data from Mahaena show that a surprising number of nuclear couples contain one individual native to the district, with the spouse coming from another rural area. In almost every case, these couples met in Papeete in their late 'teens or twenties, and moved back to Mahaena, where the individual native to that district stood to inherit land. Similarly, landless youths from Mahaena have, upon moving to Papeete, found spouses with land in other districts, and subsequently moved there to cultivate that land.

I must emphasize that the data on this point are only suggestive. Nevertheless, an interesting research hypothesis would appear to be that Papeete is currently serving as a territorial marriage market, performing the important function of maintaining some sort of equilibrium in the distribution of individuals relative to available agricultural land. It seems possible that, given the excessively irrational and complicated system of effective inheritance currently in operation,[3] and the often-encountered difficulty of finding a mate in one's own district,[4] the "marriage market" function of Papeete may be absolutely necessary to the continued functioning of the society of the territory in its present form.

NOTES

1. For a general description of the society of Papeete and its relation to the society of the Society Islands and French Polynesia generally, see papers by Douglas L. Oliver (pp. 43-45) and Michel Jullien (47-62).
2. In the rest of this paper I shall continue to exclude from consideration the three Chinese households in Manuhoe, but will include two households in which the husband and father is Chinese and the other members of the family are generally classified socially as non-Chinese.
3. As contrasted to the ideal system defined in the law.
4. Due to (1) small populations per district, (2) relatively good memory of genealogical connection, (3) previous generations of intermarriage, and (4) generally great, but highly variable, bilateral extension of the incest taboo.

LITERATURE CITED

BOUVET, CAPITAINE, AND ADJUTANT CHEF IORSCH, 1960. "Etude sommaire sur l'évolution de la criminalité à Tahiti et en Polynésie entre 1810 et 1959. Papeete: Gendarmerie National—Groupement de Polynésie." (Bound, mimeographed.)

BURTON, R., AND J. WHITING, 1961. "The Absent Father and Cross-Sex Identity." *Merrill-Palmer Quart. Behavior Develop.* 7,2.

FRAZIER, E. FRANKLIN, 1939. *The Negro Family in the United States.* Chicago: Univ. of Chicago Press.

1949. *The Negro in the United States.* New York: Macmillan.

JULLIEN, MICHEL, 1961. Situation démographique de la jeunesse à Papeete. O.R.S.T.O.M. Papeete. (Typescript, interoffice report.)

1963. "Aspects de la configuration ethnique et socio-economique de Papeete," *In* Alexander Spoehr (editor), *Pacific Port Towns and Cities: A Symposium*, pp. 47-62. Honolulu: Bernice P. Bishop Museum.

MYRDAL, GUNNAR, 1944. *An American Dilemma.* 2 vols. New York: Harper.

FURTHER READINGS

A general overview of social change in the Pacific can be obtained from Oliver's *The Pacific Islands,* but the interested student might find it profitable to refer also to Keesing's prewar study, *The South Seas in the Modern World.* An important comparative study, describing social change in Fiji and Western Samoa after World War II, is provided by Stanner in *The South Seas in Transition.*

The most thorough study of change from a traditional baseline is Firth's *Social Change in Tikopia.* Another well-documented account is Beaglehole's *Social Change in the South Pacific,* which traces the processes of social change on Rarotonga and Aitutaki, two islands in the Cook group. Whereas Firth's study involved a revisit after nearly twenty-five years, Beaglehole relied mainly on missionary and government records for information, so that the reader is provided with an interesting contrast in method. Beaglehole has also documented social changes among the Hawaiians and the New Zealand Maori in *Some Modern Hawaiians* and (with Pearl Beaglehole) *Some Modern Maoris.* Fiji and Samoa are two of the better-studied island groups with regard to social change. For Samoa, Davidson's *Samoa Mo Samoa* will provide a useful starting point, and Belshaw's *Under the Iwi Tree* will do the same for Fiji.

The overthrow of Hawaii's taboo system has been subjected to further treatment in two papers subsequent to Malcolm Webb's contribution. One is by Davenport, entitled "The 'Hawaiian Cultural Revolution' "; the other, by Levin, is "The Overthrow of the *Kapu* System in Hawaii."

Those interested in urbanization should refer to *Pacific Port Towns and Cities,* edited by Spoehr. "Port Town and Hinterland in the Pacific Islands," by Spoehr, will also be of value. Additional studies of recent change in Tahiti are Finney's "Polynesian Peasants and Proletarians" and Kay's "Aspects of Social Structure in a Tahitian Urban Neighbourhood." An excellent study of urbanization among the New Zealand Maoris is provided by Metge in *A New Maori Migration.* Other valuable sources of social change among the Maori are *The Maoris of New Zealand* by Metge and *The Maori People in the Nineteen-Sixties,* edited by Schwimmer.

BIBLIOGRAPHY

Atoll Research Bulletin. Washington, D.C.: Pacific Science Board, National Research Council.

BARRAU, JACQUES, 1961, *Subsistence Agriculture in Polynesia and Micronesia.* Honolulu: Bernice P. Bishop Museum Bulletin No. 223.

BEAGLEHOLE, ERNEST, 1939, *Some Modern Hawaiians.* Honolulu: University of Hawaii Research Publication No. 19.

1957. *Social Change in the South Pacific: Rarotonga and Aitutaki.* New York: Macmillan.

BEAGLEHOLE, ERNEST, AND PEARL BEAGLEHOLE, 1941, "Personality Development in Pukapukan Children." In Leslie Spier, A. Irving Hallowell, and Stanley S. Newman, eds., *Language, Culture and Personality.* Menasha, Wis.: Sapir Memorial Publication Fund.

1946, *Some Modern Maoris.* New Zealand Council for Educational Research. Wellington, N.Z.: Whitcomb and Tombs.

BELL, F. L. S., 1931–32, "The Place of Food in the Social Life of Central Polynesia." *Oceania,* 2:117–135.

BELSHAW, CYRIL, 1964, *Under the Iwi Tree.* London: Routledge & Kegan Paul.

BEST, ELSDON, 1925, *Maori Agriculture: The Cultivated Food Plants of the Natives of New Zealand with Some Account of Native Methods of Agriculture, Its Ritual and Origin Myths.* Dominion Museum Bulletin No. 9. Wellington, N.Z.: Government Printer.

BOWMAN, ROBERT G., "New Zealand." In Freeman, ed., 1951.

BRYAN, EDWIN H., JR., "Central and Western Polynesia." In Freeman, ed., 1951.

CARROLL, VERN, ED., 1970, *Adoption in Eastern Oceania.* Honolulu: University of Hawaii Press.

DANIELSSON, BENGT, 1955, *Work and Life on Raroia: An Acculturation Study from the Tuamotu Group.* Stockholm: Saxon and Lindstrom.

DAVENPORT, WILLIAM, 1959, "Nonunilinear Descent and Descent Groups." *American Anthropologist,* 61:557–572.

1969, "The 'Hawaiian Cultural Revolution': Some Political and Economic Considerations." *American Anthropologist,* 71:1–20.

DAVIDSON, J. W., 1967, *Samoa Mo Samoa: The Emergence of the Independent State of Western Samoa.* Melbourne: Oxford University Press.

EMORY, KENNETH, 1965, *Kapingamarangi: Social and Religious Life of a Polyne-*

sian Atoll. Honolulu: Bernice P. Bishop Museum Bulletin No. 228.

FINNEY, BEN, 1965, "Polynesian Peasants and Proletarians: Socio-economic Change among the Tahitians of French Polynesia." *Journal of the Polynesian Society,* 74:269–328.

FIRTH, RAYMOND, 1930–31, "Totemism in Polynesia." *Oceania,* 2:291–321, 377–398.

1936, *We, the Tikopia: A Sociological Study of Kinship in Primitive Polynesia.* London: Allen & Unwin.

1939, *Primitive Polynesian Economy.* London: Routledge.

1940a, "The Analysis of Mana: An Empirical Approach." *Journal of the Polynesian Society,* 49:483–510.

1940b, *The Work of the Gods in Tikopia.* 2 vols. London: Percy Lund Humphries.

1957, "A Note on Descent Groups in Polynesia." *Man,* 57:4–8.

1959a, *Primitive Economics of the New Zealand Maori.* Rev. ed. Wellington, N.Z.: Government Printer.

1959b, *Social Change in Tikopia: Re-study of a Polynesian Community after a Generation.* New York: Macmillan.

FOSBERG, F. R., ED., 1963, *Man's Place in the Island Ecosystem: A Symposium.* Honolulu: Bernice P. Bishop Museum Press.

FOX, JAMES W., AND KENNETH B. CUMBERLAND, EDS., 1962, *Western Samoa: Land, Life and Agriculture in Tropical Polynesia.* Christchurch, N.Z.: Whitcomb and Tombs.

FREEMAN, DEREK, in preparation, *Culture and Human Nature in the Samoan Islands.*

FREEMAN, OTIS W., "Eastern Polynesia." In Freeman, ed., 1951.

"Geographic Setting of the Pacific." In Freeman, ed., 1951.

"Hawaii and American Island Outposts." In Freeman, ed., 1951.

FREEMAN, OTIS W., ED., 1951, *Geography of the Pacific.* New York: Wiley.

GOODENOUGH, WARD H., 1955, "A Problem in Malayo-Polynesian Social Organization." *American Anthropologist,* 57:71–83.

GROVES, MURRAY, 1963, "The Nature of Fijian Society: Review of (Sahlins, Marshall D.: *Moala: Culture and Nature on a Fijian Island*)." *Journal of the Polynesian Society,* 72:272–291.

HANDY, E. S. CRAIGHILL, 1927, *Polynesian Religion.* Honolulu: Bernice P. Bishop Museum Bulletin No. 34.

1940, *The Hawaiian Planter.* Honolulu: Bernice P. Bishop Museum Bulletin No. 161.

HOWARD, ALAN, 1963, "Land, Activity Systems and Decision-Making Models in Rotuma." *Ethnology,* 2:407–440.

1970, *Learning to Be Rotuman.* New York: Teachers College Press, Columbia University.

HOWARD, IRWIN, W. EDGAR VINACKE, AND THOMAS MARETZKI, 1963, *Culture and Personality in the Pacific Islands: A Bibliography.* Honolulu: Anthropological Society of Hawaii.

KAY, PAUL, 1963, "Aspects of Social Structure in a Tahitian Urban Neighbourhood." *Journal of the Polynesian Society,* 72:325–371.

KEESING, FELIX M., 1941, *The South Seas in the Modern World.* New York: John Day.

1953, *Social Anthropology in Polynesia: A Review of Research.* Melbourne: Oxford University Press.

KEESING, FELIX M., AND MARIE M. KEESING, 1956, *Elite Communication in Samoa: A Study of Leadership.* Stanford Anthropological Series No. 3. Stanford, Calif.: Stanford University Press.

LANGNESS, L. L., AND THOMAS GLADWIN, in press, "Oceania." In F. L. K. Hsu, ed., *Psychological Anthropology.* Rev. ed. Homewood, Ill.: Dorsey Press.

LEVIN, STEPHENIE SETO, 1968, "The Overthrow of the *Kapu* System in Hawaii." *Journal of the Polynesian Society,* 74:402–430.

LEVY, ROBERT I., 1969, *Personality Studies in Polynesia and Micronesia: Stability and Change.* Working Paper No. 8. Honolulu: Social Science Research Institute, University of Hawaii.

LINTON, RALPH, 1939, "Marquesan Culture." In Abram Kardiner, ed., *The Individual and His Society.* New York: Columbia University Press.

MEAD, MARGARET, 1928, *Coming of Age in Samoa.* New York: Morrow.

1930, *Social Organization of Manua.* Honolulu: Bernice P. Bishop Museum Bulletin No. 76.

METGE, JOAN A., 1964, *A New Maori Migration: Rural and Urban Relations in Northern New Zealand.* London School of Economics Monograph on Social Anthropology No. 27. London: Athlone Press.

1967, *The Maoris of New Zealand.* London: Societies of the World.

MONBERG, TORBEN, 1966, *The Religion of Bellona Island: A Study of the Place of Beliefs and Rites in the Social Life of Pre-Christian Bellona.* Part I. Copenhagen: National Museum of Denmark.

NORDHOFF, CHARLES B., 1930, "Notes on the Off-Shore Fishing of the Society Islands." *Journal of the Polynesian Society,* 39:137–173, 221–262.

OLIVER, DOUGLAS, 1951, *The Pacific Islands.* Cambridge, Mass.: Harvard University Press.

OTTINO, PAUL, 1967, "Early 'Ati of the Western Tuamotus." In Genevieve A. Highland et al., eds., *Polynesian Culture History: Essays in Honor of Kenneth P. Emory.* Honolulu: Bernice P. Bishop Museum Special Publication No. 56.

RITCHIE, JAMES E., 1963, *The Making of a Maori.* Victoria University of Wellington Publications in Psychology No. 15. Wellington, N.Z.: A. H. & A. W. Reed.

SAHLINS, MARSHALL D., 1957, *Social Stratification in Polynesia.* Seattle: American Ethnological Society Monograph.

1962, *Moala: Culture and Nature on a Fijian Island.* Ann Arbor: University of Michigan Press.

SCHEFFLER, HAROLD W., 1966, "Ancestor Worship in Anthropology: or Observations on Descent and Descent Groups." *Current Anthropology,* 7:541–551.

SCHWIMMER, ERIK, ED., 1968, *The Maori People in the Nineteen-Sixties: A Symposium.* London: C. Hurst. New York: Humanities Press.

SPOEHR, ALEXANDER, 1960, "Port Town and Hinterland in the Pacific Islands." *American Anthropologist,* 62:586–592.

SPOEHR, ALEXANDER, ED., 1963, *Pacific Port Towns and Cities: A Symposium.* Honolulu: Bernice P. Bishop Museum Press.

STANNER, W. E. H., 1953, *The South Seas in Transition: A Study of Post-War Rehabilitation and Reconstruction in Three British Pacific Dependencies.* Sydney: Australasian Publishing Company.

TAYLOR, C. R. H., 1965, *A Pacific Bibliography.* 2nd ed. London: Oxford University Press.

WIENS, HAROLD J., 1962, *Atoll Environment and Ecology.* New Haven: Yale University Press.

WILLIAMSON, ROBERT W., 1924, *The Social and Political Systems of Central Polynesia.* 3 vols. Cambridge: Cambridge University Press.

1933, *The Religious and Cosmic Beliefs of Central Polynesia.* 2 vols. Cambridge: Cambridge University Press.

1937, *Religion and Social Organization in Central Polynesia.* Ed. by R. Piddington. Cambridge: Cambridge University Press.

INDEX OF PERSONS CITED